INFORMATION PROCESSING IN ANIMALS:
Memory Mechanisms

Edited by
Norman E. Spear
Ralph R. Miller
State University of New York
at Binghamton

 LAWRENCE ERLBAUM ASSOCIATES, PUBLISHERS
1981   Hillsdale, New Jersey

Lawrence Erlbaum Associates, Inc., Publishers
365 Broadway
Hillsdale, New Jersey 07642

Library of Congress Cataloging in Publication Data
Main entry under title:

Information processing in animals, memory mechanisms.

"Based upon the Binghamton Symposium on Memory
Mechanisms in Animal Behavior which was held at the State
University of New York at Binghamton on June 10–12, 1980"
—Pref.
Includes bibliographies and indexes.
1. Conditioned response—Congresses. 2. Memory—
Congresses. 3. Psychology, Comparative—Congresses.
I. Spear, Norman E. II. Miller, Ralph R., 1940–
III. Binghamton Symposium on Memory Mechanisms in Animal
Behavior (1980: State University of New York at
Binghamton)
BF319.I53   591.51   81-15198
ISBN 0-89859-157-0   AACR2

Printed in the United States of America

Contents

Preface

During the past fifty years, dramatic changes have occurred in the use of laboratory animals to study learning and memory. Yet the basic reasons for this research, diverse as they are, have not changed. At one extreme is the need for relatively direct application of findings with animal models to medical or educational problems of humans; at the other extreme, the quest for understanding animal behavior for its own sake. It is probably fair to say that no chapters in this book represent either of these extremes, although in each case the author's purposes can be said to be like those of some scientists working in this area fifty years ago. In contrast to this continuity of purpose, the approach that scientists now take in this area of study is really quite different from that of most or all scientists in the 1930s.

It is of course frequently possible to find current ideas similar to those expressed long ago. But today the conceptual frameworks that dictate what specific experiments are conducted and exactly how they are performed differ in important ways from those seen fifty or even twenty-five years ago. To an observer unfamiliar with this area for the past twenty years or so, the theoretical concepts that direct study in this area would seem distinctly different and the underlying technology decidedly improved. This is so for the experimental paradigms applied, the responses measured, the tests used to infer learning and retention, and the inferences drawn from the consequences of the experimental treatments. One theme representing these differences is the greater concentration on the consequences of the learning process relative to its dynamics—consequences such as what is learned, the structure of what is learned, and the determinants of what is remembered afterward. These consequences are frequently discussed under the heading "memory processes." We felt that a book describing the state of the art on this topic was needed to help document the changes in this field and perhaps contribute to the direction of future research.

On a more practical level, this book and the symposium from which it was derived were a logical outgrowth of a continuing spontaneous exchange of ideas and information among several of its participants. The need for increased interchange among persons interested primarily in basic conditioning and learning and those more concerned with memory seemed to demand more formal interaction. To accomplish this we gathered together at Binghamton a set of speakers who presented their ideas and data and discussed them together with a number of distinguished visitors. From the benefit of these lectures and subsequent discussions, the speakers prepared the chapters presented in this volume.

The order in which the chapters appear is in accord with a not wholly successful attempt to achieve some sort of conceptual grouping. Each of the chapters will be seen to be a rather complete document in itself, addressing a variety of important issues, any of which could have served as a basis of its categorization. From one rough characterization, the first four chapters can be said to be concerned with the determinants of basic conditioning and learning; the next four, with the structure of memory as a representation of what is learned; and the last four, with the remembering. Another categorization might group the chapters by Wagner, Miller-Balaz, and Rescorla-Durlach as emphasizing classical conditioning; those of D'Amato et al. and Adams-Dickinson, as emphasizing instrumental learning; those of Honig, Maki, and Grant, as focused upon retention after relatively short intervals; and those of Thomas, Riccio-Ebner, Gordon, and Spear as dealing with retention after relatively long intervals. Neither of these classification schemes is very satisfying. Essentially every chapter presents, for analysis and explanation, phenomena of proven generality, derived from a number of different kinds of tests, and often having explicit contact with other issues of importance for learning and memory broadly speaking, including those performed with human subjects. There is, by intent, a great deal of overlap in the subject matter from chapter to chapter although, we believe, little or no redundancy.

The material is written for professional scientists, graduate students, and advanced undergraduate students. Each chapter should prove useful both to persons working directly on these problems and also to those whose interests touch the topics of learning and remembering from other disciplines, such as human cognition or neuroscience. In its focus upon the role of memory mechanisms in the retention and expression of acquired information, the present collection of new chapters has much in common with two previous books of the same kind, *Animal Memory,* edited by Honig and James in 1971, and *Processes of Animal Memory,* edited by Medin, Roberts and Davis in 1976.

This volume is based upon the Binghamton Symposium on Memory Mechanisms in Animal Behavior which was held at the State University of New York at Binghamton on June 10–12, 1980. The Symposium was generously supported by the SUNY Conversations in the Disciplines Program, Lawrence Erlbaum Associates and the SUNY-Binghamton Office of the Provost, Dr. Arthur K. Smith. Additional support was provided by the Center for Neurobehavioral Sciences and the Department of Psychology at SUNY-Binghamton. Gratitude is due to Teri Tanenhaus and Wesley Kasprow for their assistance in preparing the manuscript. Finally, the cheerful and efficient cooperation of Larry Erlbaum, Sandi Guideman and the entire LEA staff is fully appreciated, and we continue to be grateful for their help.

The success of the Symposium stemmed not only from the high quality of the presentations, but from the dialogues that occurred during the discussion periods and throughout the days and nights of the Symposium. Underrepresented on these pages are the important contributions of the numerous distinguished guests who attended the Symposium and provided much of the critical commentary that made the Symposium so stimulating and the social occasions so enjoyable. Among the many observers to whom we are grateful are Harold Babb, Richard Burright, Jaw-Sy Chen, Alexis Collier, Ruth Colwill, Helen Daly, Michael Domjan, Peter Donovick, Bruce Dudek, Vahram Haroutunian, Gary Horowitz, Robert Isaacson, Herb Jenkins, Donald Kendrick, Donald Levis, Robert Malmi, Michael Nagy, William Pavlik, Michael Rashotte, Mark Rilling, William Roberts, Ronald Salafia, Stanley Scobie, Shepard Siegal, Linda Spear, Andrew Strouthes, Delos Wickens, and Ronald Weisman.

N.E.S.
R.R.M.

Prologue

Richard L. Solomon
University of Pennsylvania

REMINISCENCES

Although I was asked for an "overview," this definitely is not. Instead, it is a very personal, partly nostalgic consideration of the ways that my father figures and I would have looked at the contents of this symposium, had it been held many years ago. This stance is quite necessary for me because I've been very much out of touch with developments in animal cognition and memory over the last 15 years. My major focus has, during those years, been emotion and affect in the reinforcement process. The animal's memory has been far from my thoughts.

I can, however, identify some old and persistent problems. Quite often they are problems that interested some of my colleagues and teachers of long ago. Take, for example, the treatment of delays of reinforcement, as elucidated in this symposium by D'Amato, by Grant, and by Honig. Some of the methods look familiar. The delayed reaction experiment was invented by my first professor, Walter S. Hunter, in order to study what he termed "symbolic processes." Hunter was interested in the symbols or traces animals carried around with them and appeared to use at the proper occasion. When the cues were well controlled, different species seemed to have different capacities, as measured by the amount of time they could successfully tolerate between being shown where a reinforcer was hidden and later being given a chance to relocate that reinforcer. The method was thought to be a valid instrument of comparative psychology at the time.

Hunter's work was designed to enhance the measured performances of the various species of subjects used. Species-specific testing techniques were developed, so that children, pigs, crows, rats, raccoons, etc. would, so to speak, be able to perform at their best (Hunter, 1913). This seems to me to be a bit different

1

from many of the techniques used today, because today's techniques often degrade purposely the situational supports for delayed responses in order to highlight the decrements occurring as a function of time. Prettier decremental functions of time passage are thus produced in a subject that may be at a disadvantage in showing off its real capacity. I am one of the romantics who believe that most nonhuman animals are much smarter, much more capable, than they appear to be, either in their natural habitat or at the hands of experimental psychologists. Some notable examples of animal brilliance come from recent work of Olton and Samuelson (1976) with rats, and of Premack and Woodruff (1978) and Menzel (1978) with chimps. We are just beginning to obtain glimpses of the true dimensions of animal cognitive capacity. Thus it may be premature to spell out beautiful, orderly parametric data on the effects of delays, when, with more understanding of the nature of each creature, the functions might be quite different.

One persisting question is "what is learned?" The four candidates from the past were S–S associations, S–R associations, R-reinforcer associations and S-reinforcer associations. Harold Schlosberg, who directed my doctoral thesis in 1947, was deeply concerned with such matters. So was Hobart Mowrer, who was my colleague at Harvard in the late 1940s. Their particular concerns are reflected in one way or another in the presentations by Rescorla, Dickinson, Miller, Honig, and Grant. It appears from these reports that associations of all four kinds can be established with the right procedures. However, Rescorla's findings go beyond the S–S formulation to include within-S associations. I wonder whether Rescorla's principles of within-S associations also apply to within-reinforcer associations and within-R associations? It seems possible.

Edward Tolman was my colleague at Harvard during the California loyalty oath battles in the early 1950s. His insightful grasp of the rat's cognitive processes always startle me. He would agree with me that our experimental procedures often degrade not only the important stimuli but also the rat itself. I tend to be impressed by Howard Hoffman's demonstration of the intact retention of an aversive (conditioned emotional response), CER together with its generalization gradient, for a large segment of the life-span of the pigeon. I am less impressed with techniques that reveal decremental memory effects over time, using items in memory of reduced importance to the rat or pigeon, because I think memory seems to be decremental partly because we don't know too well how to reveal it. Yet, I am willing to accept as a matter of faith that these decremental techniques may help us to discover variables that allow us to "reveal" retention.

The problem of memory for me isn't too different from the Freudian characterization or Hullian formal theory of it. One moment, in one circumstance, the subject can't recall some stimulus attributes or some event. But a moment later, or in another place, the subject can. What does this mean? In one way or another, the participants in this symposium have taught me much about why this might be so. The work of Riccio, D'Amato, Grant, Maki, Thomas, and Gordon reveals several variables of importance in facilitating recall. The cuing effect and context effect appear to be reliable phenomena. Am I to conclude that all processed information creates a permanent structure in the brain, as did Hull $(_sH_r)$ and Freud, but that situational and contextual cues and motivational states often determine accessibility? I am reminded of the experiments of E. E. Anderson in the early 1940s. He was the first to show a facilitation in the accuracy of maze choices in the rat by virtue of giving the rat a tiny taste of the familiar goal box food prior to the test run (Anderson, 1942). Gordon's work indicates that this may be better than an errorless run prior to the retention test. If so, memory must be very much influenced by motivational context as well as by cues and background external to the animal. Indeed, this is what Robbins and Meyer (1970) were trying to tell us through their remarkable work demonstrating that the amnesia effects of electroconvulsive shock depend on motivational states.

Riccio's report of the retrograde effects of ECS tries to put cooling in the role of a state mediator in the way that Robbins and Meyer used fear and food as mediators. But Riccio was trying to understand retention whereas the others were trying to understand selective forgetting. One of Riccio's more telling lessions is that there can be loss of memory for the attributes of stimulus context, yet that context can still elicit conditioned fear. There may be important differences between dispassionate associations and those formed in the heat of emotion. Rescorla's comparison of sensory preconditioning and higher-order conditioning suggests this. So does the work of Riccio and of Robbins and Meyer.

There is no need for comment on Wagner's elegant model of enhancement and habituation effects in memory. It has the great virtue of specifying the conditions under which we can expect one or the other of these two phenomena to be salient. It is a persuasive tour de force. I believe it will stimulate important new lines of research on memory.

I have a quarrel with Miller's attempt to search out the adaptiveness of Pavlovian conditioning as a way of making it more similar conceptually to operant conditioning. Miller believes that Pavlovian CRs have adaptive significance. So he looks for the beneficial consequences of such CRs. Like others before him, namely Schlosberg (1937) and Mowrer (1947), he finds none when the artifactual variables are well controlled. In his very elegant psychophysical experiments on shock intensity judgment in rats, the results were the opposite to what one might have expected on the basis of the assumed preparatory or anticipatory functions of CSs as aversiveness attenuators. I don't believe *any* finding would have made an adaptiveness interpretation scientifically tenable. The concept of adaptiveness explains nothing. Adaptiveness is relative to criteria of adaptiveness: adaptive in what respect, in what circumstance? It might be more adaptive to receive unsignaled shocks if they are more aversive that way, because this might support better avoidance behavior. And so it goes. We can invent criteria of adaptiveness as we go. But they are not part of a coherent theory of behavior. I must admit to a bit of pleasure on hearing about Miller's failure to establish empirically an adaptive role for his conditioned responses.

I was struck by the lack of attention in this symposium to motivation for good performance. Why should a rat reveal its memories if it isn't very important to do so? What about motivation to process information, as contrasted with the orthogonal motivation to retrieve information? Why aren't these being manipulated? In addition, there was relatively little attention paid to lack of forgetting of some learned behaviors. Will I ever forget how to count? Finally, the symposium was calm and very cool. Why were there no heated theoretical controversies?

I appreciate very much the efforts of all the symposium contributors to educate me about recent work on animal memory. It is rather comforting to find that most of the persistent theoretical issues are still with us. On the other hand, the advance of science is marked by the asking of startling, new questions, and so I worry about the concepts and facts of animal memory because they may be misleading us by constantly pointing to old questions. But perhaps I worry because I've been in this business so long. We do know more facts than we did when my teachers were thinking about memory processes. I do, however, wish that those facts would engender novel ideas with higher frequency.

REFERENCES

Anderson, E. E. The externalization of drive, IV. The effect of pre-feeding on the maze performance of hungry non-rewarded rats. *Journal of Comparative Psychology*, 1942, *30*, 326–336.

Hunter, W. S. The delayed reaction in animals and children. *Behavior Monographs*, 1913, *2*, 21–30.

Menzel, E. W. Cognitive mapping in chimpanzees. In S. H. Hulse, H. Fowler, & W. K. Honig (Eds.), *Cognitive processes in animal behavior*. Hillsdale, N.J.: Lawrence Erlbaum Associates, 1978.

Mowrer, O. H. On the dual nature of learning—a reinterpretation of "conditioning" and "problem-solving." *Harvard Educational Review*, 1947, *17*, 102–148.

Olton, D. S., & Samuelson, R. J. Remembrances of places passed: Spatial memory in rats. *Journal of Experimental Psychology: Animal Behavior Processes*, 1976, *2*, 97–116.

Premack, D., & Woodruff, G. Does the chimpanzee have a theory of mind? *The Behavioral and Brain Sciences*, 1978, *4*, 515–526.

Robbins, M. J., & Meyer, D. R. Motivational control of retrograde amnesia. *Journal of Experimental Psychology*, 1970, *84*, 220–225.

Schlosberg, H. The relationship between success and the laws of conditioning. *Psychological Review*, 1937, *44*, 379–394.

1 SOP: A Model of Automatic Memory Processing in Animal Behavior

Allan R. Wagner
Yale University

Current information-processing theories of memory phenomena emphasize an interplay of "automatic" and "controlled" processing. The exact nature of the distinction between the two kinds of processing can be somewhat different in the hands of different theorists (Posner & Snyder, 1975; Shiffrin & Schneider, 1977). But the contrast generally addresses the degree to which processing is assumed to proceed mechanically according to relatively invariant operating characteristics and stable "structural" features of the system (automatic processing), versus the degree to which processing is assumed to call upon flexible routines that may be "volitionally" exercised in a task-specific manner under the attention of an executive monitor (controlled processing).

Given this distinction, it is commonplace to assume that the human subject is unique in the richness, pervasiveness, and plasticity of its controlled processing, limiting the direct generalizability of observed memory phenomena between the human and other species. On the same grounds, however, one could assume that the infrahuman subject may present us with a clearer visualization of examples of automatic processing, unembellished by contributions of controlled processing. Whether or not automatic processing is the same in detail in all species, we may be instructed by comparative investigations as to its likely forms in biological systems (including the human) and perhaps be constrained in what need be attributed to more complex, controlled processing. This is, of course, only a rephrasing, in modern terminology, of one of the major strategic rationalizations concerning the investigation of animal memory (Hobhouse, 1915; Morgan, 1894).

I begin with these remarks as they help to announce the intended scope of the theoretical speculations that follow. A model of a memory system is presented

5

that is meant to be a theory of automatic processing. The acronym, '*SOP*,' seemed fitting to suggest that it is concerned with what may be presumed to be the *standard operating procedures* in memory. Flexible routines of controlled processing could be envisioned to interact with the mechanics of the model. But the model itself carefully ignores such potential complications. This scope is consistent with the data that the model was primarily designed to address, i.e., the learning and retention of infrahuman subjects in circumstances of simple conditioning and habituation.

The model is a formalization and extension of a set of assumptions that my students and I have promoted over the last several years concerning the variability in "rehearsal" and the consequence of "priming of short-term memory" (Pfautz & Wagner, 1976; Terry & Wagner, 1975; Wagner, 1976, 1978, 1979; Wagner, Rudy, & Whitlow, 1973; Wagner & Terry, 1975). The nature of these assumptions is better articulated in due course. But it may help to introduce the present theoretical effort to hint briefly at them here and try to convey some sense of why the development of a more formal model such as SOP was deemed necessary (if not desirable) at this juncture.

Variable-Rehearsal (Priming) Theory

The central thesis has been that the immediate behavior, as well as the learning, occasioned by an external stimulus is dependent on the course of "active" representation of the stimulus in a short-term memory (STM) store. The more active the representation at some moment, or the longer active during some episode, the more vigorous will be the subject's immediate response, the more persistent will be evidence of memory for the stimulus, and the more associative learning may be witnessed between the stimulus and other contemporaneous events (Wagner, 1976, 1978). Added to this thesis was the notion that two states of activation in STM could be distinguished, an especially active state (dubbed "rehearsal," after the terminology of Atkinson & Shiffrin, 1968) and a less active state (given no special label). Then, it was importantly assumed that, whereas the presentation of a stimulus de nova normally would lead to a state of rehearsal of its representation in STM, the presentation of a stimulus that was already represented, or "primed," in STM would not provoke this specially active state (Wagner, 1976, 1978).

Following this reasoning, it was possible to rationalize a considerable number of phenomena, in which a stimulus may be seen to be less effective than it otherwise would be, if it is preceded by a recent instance of the same stimulus or by some associatively related stimulus. The prevention of stimulus "rehearsal" due to the priming of STM could account for such phenomena as the short-term refractorylike effect in studies of habituation (Davis, 1969; Whitlow, 1975), the "conditioned diminution of the UR" in Pavlovian conditioning (Kimble & Ost,

1961; Kimmel, 1966), the less persistent memory of signaled versus unsignaled samples in a short-term memory paradigm (Terry & Wagner, 1975), and the apparent decrease in the associative learning occasioned by a signaled US in studies of "blocking" in Pavlovian conditioning (Kamin, 1969).

Problems of Indeterminancy

By this time there are a considerable number of analytical studies (e.g., Best & Gemberling, 1977; Pfautz & Wagner, 1976; Terry, 1976; Wagner, 1978) that further encourage the basic propositions. Nonetheless, it must be acknowledged that certain of the critical phenomena that have been listed are embraced by the formulation more in the sense of being *allowed* than being necessarily *predicted*.

Consider, for example, the phenomenon of the "conditioned diminution of the UR," which is a reduction in the amplitude of the response following a US, when preceded by an associated CS than when presented alone. It is supposed that responding at the time of a US is determined finally by the degree of activation of the US representation that is provoked in STM. If a CS produces some measure of US representation prior to the US occurrence, it is assumed that the US *itself* will be less likely to produce a "rehearsed" representation and thus be less likely to provoke its usual response. But what is indexed in behavior is presumably *not* just this effect but the combined action of the CS and US. Will the total US representation in STM be less, immediately following a CS–US sequence, than following a US-alone presentation? Only on the possibility that what US representation in STM is instigated by the CS to provoke responding (as witnessed, for example, in some CR) is more than offset by the loss in contribution of US representation in STM by the US. The priming theory allows that this may happen and that a "conditioned diminution of the UR" may then be observed, but it does not necessarily predict it.

The same reasoning can be followed in regard to a phenomenon reported by Terry and Wagner (1975). A US was used as a sample in a short-term memory paradigm. If a US were presented, then one reinforcement contingency was in effect for a vibrotactual cue presented 2, 4, 8, or 16 sec later. If a US were not presented, then an opposite contingency was in effect. With such training, subjects learned to respond differentially to the vibrotactual cue depending on the prior presence versus absence of a US, and performed less accurately the longer the interval between the sample and the vibrotactual cue. The major observation was that if the US were preceded on test trials by a CS with which it had otherwise been paired, there was a reduction in its behavioral control at the time of the vibrotactual cue. An "expected" or "primed" US did not appear to be as memorable several seconds later as an "unexpected" or "unprimed" US. Terry and Wagner (1975), however, also reported an important ancillary observation. The CS that was otherwise paired with the sample US, when presented *alone* as a substitute sample, controlled delayed responding in the same direction, only to a lesser degree than did the US. It appeared that either the CS or the US could provoke a representation of the US in STM. If a CS → US sequence was less memorable than a US alone, it had to be because the positive contribution by the CS was more than offset by the attendant loss in contribution by the US. The priming theory clearly allows that this may happen but does not necessarily predict it.

These two example cases are not unusual.[1] Our theorizing has emphasized a particular presumptive effect of priming of short-term memory, a decreased likelihood of rehearsal that should decrease evidence of stimulus processing. In many circumstances the same manipulations of priming should be expected to have other effects that would appear to complement stimulus processing. Although we can be encouraged that the former effect has been detected (Kimble & Ost, 1961; Terry & Wagner, 1975) in spite of the latter possibilities, a determinate theory must acknowledge both. SOP is an attempt to do this. Because the more comprehensive treatment of the mechanism of priming of short-term memory that is included leads to theoretical effects that are only sometimes in opposition to evidence of stimulus processing, the theory could be called a *sometimes opponent-process* theory. The appropriateness of this additional justification for the acronym "SOP" should be more apparent as I take the opportunity to indicate some formal similarities (and differences) between the theory and the opponent-process formulations of Solomon and Corbit (1974) and Schull (1979).

Organization of the Chapter

The basic workings of SOP are rather simple. Nonetheless, the degree of determinancy that has been sought, over the range of situations to which the background priming notion has previously been applied (Wagner, 1976, 1978, 1979), has begged a considerable number of specific assumptions. And in this regard we have made use of some conceptual twists that initially might seem more novel than, in fact, they are. Thus, it will be helpful in the section that immediately follows to indicate how the general formulation and the more specific assumptions have been shaped by prevailing theoretical viewpoints about the memory system. Then it will be possible in subsequent sections succinctly to summarize the SOP model and display its ability to account for a variety of phenomena.

---

[1]In fact, Miller and Balaz present a related example in this volume (Ch. 2). There are abundant data (Badia, Culbertson, & Harsh, 1973; Lockard, 1963) to indicate that a signaled shock is less aversive than an unsignaled shock. However, Miller and Balaz, using a novel interrogation procedure, report that signaled-shock episodes appeared to be judged more aversive than unsignaled-shock episodes. Priming theory can suppose that shock per se is less aversive when signaled than when unsignaled but not necessarily predict that the *combined* aversiveness of signal-plus-shock is less than the aversiveness of shock alone.

GENERAL ASSUMPTIONS

The design of SOP was not intended to support some novel premise about the structure or functional dynamics of memory. Rather, it was intended to provide a more articulate rendering of certain prevailing conceptualizations by embracing them in a consistent and tractable theoretical framework.

Memory as a Graph Structure

The general manner of conceptualization of the memory system is as a graph structure with representative nodes complexly interconnected via directional associative links. This is in keeping with many current information-processing theories (Anderson & Bower, 1973; Norman, 1968; Shiffrin & Schneider, 1977), in which the nodes may be referred to as "ideas" or "logogens," but is as familiar to theories of conditioning (Anokhin, 1958; Asratyan, 1965; Konorski, 1967; Pavlov, 1927), in which the nodes may be referred to as stimulus "centers" or "gnostic units."

Nodes as Collections of Elements

Each node is, itself, conceived as consisting of a set of informational elements. Our use of this notion is in the spirit of stimulus-sampling theory (Estes, 1955a, 1955b) to allow description of variation in nodal "activation" (see the following section) in terms of the proportion of like elements that are in theoretically discriminable states. It could be assumed that subsets of the elements correspond to separable aspects of represented events (Bower, 1967), and that generalization phenomena may be approached in terms of overlapping nodal elements, as conceived by Estes, or similarly by Konorski (1948). But as Shiffrin and Schneider (1977) have pointed out, to speak of a collection of elements as a node is to assume that the elements are somehow *unitized*. In this regard, we assume that there exists for each experimental stimulus a set of elements such that certain events that would provoke a state change in one element of that set have equal (probabilistic) effects on all elements of the set that are in the same state.

Activity State Distinctions

Different spaces of the memory structure are distinguished in terms of whether or not the nodes involved are currently "active" or currently "inactive." It is common (Anderson & Bower, 1973; Norman, 1968) to say that whereas all the representative nodes are in "long-term store," those that are active are in "short-term store," in "working memory" or some similar manner of distinguishing between dormant and active states. In fact, we wish to discriminate carefully not only between active and inactive nodes, but between two separable states of activity. This notion is again rather commonly acknowledged in some form or another by different theorists. In the language of structuralist psychology (Morgan, 1894), there was a distinction between the active representations that are at the margin versus the focus of consciousness. This has been carried over in more modern theories. Konorski (1967) distinguished between the totality of active gnostic units that are in "transient memory" versus the smaller subset that is the object of "attention." Likewise, Bower (1975) distinguishes between a marginal "working memory" and a focal "short-term store." Somewhat different in overall conception, but also related, is Wicklegren's (1970) notion of an "intermediate-term store" distinct from "short-term store." And, of course, there is Wagner's (1978) previously mentioned distinction, patterned after that of Atkinson and Shiffrin (1968), between the totality of "short-term store" and the especially active representations in "rehearsal." Given the different, and sometimes inconsistent terminologies that have been employed by different theorists to capture relatively similar ideas, we distinguish as neutrally as possible among a state of inactivity (I) and two states of activity, a primary state ($A1$) and a secondary state ($A2$).

State Transitions (Unconditional)

In fact, this labeling of the states of activation is meant to be somewhat suggestive. The memory system is assumed (Atkinson & Shiffrin, 1968) to be interfaced with the sensory environment via a Sensory Register such that presentation of any experimental stimulus will tend to activate the elements of its corresponding memory node that are currently inactive. This unconditioned effect is presumed to involve an initial transition of elements from the I state to the $A1$ state. From the $A1$ state, elements are assumed to "decay" to the $A2$ state and eventually from the $A2$ state back to inactive (I). This description of state transitions is intended to correspond to the commonly voiced notion that stimulus presentation is likely to produce an initial representation in a focal, short-term buffer, from which it will drift to more marginal, working memory, before falling back to rest in long-term store (Bower, 1975).

There are a number of points to be made about this sequence of memory state transitions following an unconditioned stimulus. First, although individual nodal elements are assumed to be momentarily in one of the three states, the set-theoretic, stochastic conception that has been mentioned provides for variation in the degree of initial representation (in the proportion of nodal elements activated to $A1$) due, for example, to differences in stimulus intensity, and for a continuous trace decay (with different proportions of nodal elements variously in $A1$ and $A2$ before being reabsorbed in I).

Second, we can rationalize the decay process in terms of common theoretical assumptions that we will more generally exploit. It is a characteristic of this type of theory to assume that there are differential limitations on the number of nodes that can be concurrently in the several states of activation (Bower, 1975; Konorski, 1967). There is, presumably, no practical limitation on the number of inactive nodes in the memory system. There are, however, generally assumed to be limitations on the number that can be active at any moment, and especially on the number that can be in focal, or primary ($A1$) activity. We will correspondingly assume that there are relatively severe limitations on the $A1$ state, so that only on the order of magnitude of 2 or 3 nodes could be *fully* in this state, whereas there are less severe, but nonetheless real limitations on the $A2$ state, so that, by comparison, perhaps, only 10 or 15 nodes could be fully in this state. The major reason for introducing such assumptions in prior theories has been to accommodate the apparent loss in transient memory due to overload or distractor manipulations (Peterson & Peterson, 1959), and we shall similarly use them. But, as is frequently recognized (e.g., Atkinson & Shiffrin, 1968), the limitation assumptions also could be seen as the basis for the decay process. In this spirit, we will assume that the "spontaneous" decay from the $A1$ to the $A2$ state, and from the $A2$ to the I state, are the result of extraexperimental stimulation that competes for nodal activation. Then it follows that the decay of an element from $A1$ to $A2$ should be assumed to be more probable in any instant (and occur faster over time) than the decay from $A2$ to I, with the ratio of the decay probabilities (and corresponding decay rates) being the inverse of the ratio of the size limitations of $A1$ and $A2$.

Third, it will be assumed that the *only* momentary effect of a specified unconditioned stimulus on its corresponding memory node is to activate a given proportion of the *then inactive* (I state) elements to the $A1$ state. Any elements that are already in the $A1$ state or the $A2$ state are presumably unaffected. This assumption may be recognized as a rephrasing of Wagner's (1976, 1978) priming notion: Elements that are already in a state of activation (i.e., primed) in memory will not be provoked to the primary state of activation ("rehearsal") as they otherwise might be.

Response Generation

Any behavioral product requires some connection between the memory nodes and an action system. We follow the conventional theoretical dodge of assuming that the memory system is interfaced to a "Response Generator" (Atkinson & Shiffrin, 1968) where much of what we wish presently to ignore is accomplished. We do assume, however, that the "Response Generator" is sensitive not only to what nodes are active but to the nature of the activity (i.e., whether $A1$ or $A2$). If the activity of some node tends to provoke some response, R_j, we assume that $R_j = f_j(W_{1,j}p_{A1} + W_{2,j}p_{A2})$, where p_{A1} and p_{A2} are the proportions of nodal elements in the subscripted states, W_1 and W_2 are linear weighting factors, and f_j is a mapping function appropriate to the response measure. This assumption may seem relatively bland: We allow that behavior may be controlled not only by an immediate memorial trace, but, additively, by a more persistent trace. However, it should be apparent, from what has been said, that the temporal course of nodal activity following stimulation involves one immediate "process" ($A1$) that decays while another "process" ($A2$) first increases and then more slowly decays. If W_1 and W_2 were assumed to be of opposite sign, there would be some formal similarity between our formulation and the opponent-process theory of response dynamics proposed by Solomon and Corbit (1974). We do *not* generally assume that W_1 and W_2 are of opposite sign, but do allow that they sometimes may be.

Spread of Activation

Thus far we have dealt only with assumptions concerning unconditional memorial effects. Nothing has been said that necessarily involves the associative network. However, when one node is excited via peripheral stimulation, there is assumed to be a "spread of activation" according to the pathways provided by the associative links (Collins & Loftus, 1975; Konorski, 1967). Thus we must characterize the "spread of activation" in terms of the conditions of the initiating node that provoke it, the nature of the associative links that accomplish it, and the states of the recipient node that are its consequence. I address these three questions in reverse order.

Wagner (1978) has assumed that associatively activated representations do not enjoy the same specially active state of "rehearsal" in STM as do peripherally activated representations. Konorski (1967) likewise assumed that, whereas peripheral activation of a node is likely to cause it to be "attended to" in "transient memory" due to a "targeting reflex," associative activation of a node does not have this benefit. We make a corresponding assumption, that spread of activation does not result in inactive nodal elements being initially provoked to the $A1$ state, but in their being provoked directly to the $A2$ state.

Because this assumption is so central to the derivations from the SOP model, it deserves special scrutiny. We suspect that it would be reasonably agreeable to most theorists in the tradition of the general model type that has been adopted to assume that a stimulus representation that may be provoked by some associated retrieval cue is "weaker," less "vivid," or somehow different from one that may be provoked by the actual presentation of the stimulus itself. The interesting twist in our proposal is that associatively promoted nodal activity differs from unconditionally promoted activity not necessarily in being a "weaker" version, but in being identical to a "decayed" version, *with whatever effective properties the latter may have.* Consider, for example, what has been said about the response dynamics of an unconditioned response (i.e., initially reflecting the $A1$ "process," then some mixture of $A1$ and $A2$, as elements decay from the former to the latter state, and eventually the $A2$ "process" only, before all elements revert to the I state). By comparison, the response dynamics of a conditioned response should correspond to only the latter part of this sequence. If the contribution of $A1$ and $A2$ to some response measure (i.e., W_1 and W_2) are of the same sign, the CR will mimic the initial response to the US. If the contribution of $A1$ and $A2$ to some response measure are of opposing sign, the CR will appear antagonistic or compensatory (Siegel, 1978) to the initial response to the US. In either case, however, the CR should mimic the *later* response to the US, as both reflect the $A2$ state of the US representation.

Our assumptions concerning the nature of the associative connections are most like those of Konorski (1948). We suppose that a pair of nodes may be linked by directional "excitatory" and/or "inhibitory" connections. An excitatory link is one that provides for the activation of a recipient node, depending on the degree of activity in the initiating node and the strength of the link. An inhibitory link is one that provides for a decrease in the sensitivity of the recipient node to the action of excitatory associations, depending on the degree of activity in the initiating node and the strength of the link. This view allows not only for "excitatory" associative effects, but for a variety of "inhibitory" associative effects that have been of major importance in theories of Pavlovian conditioning (Anokhin, 1958; Asratyan, 1965; Konorski, 1948; Pavlov, 1927; Rescorla & Wagner, 1972). It may be noted that the general manner of approaching such inhibitory effects that we have followed has recently been recommended by Rescorla (1974, 1975) as adequate to the available data. We find it further attractive insomuch as it obviates the necessity of assuming that a node take on any states other than I, $A1$, or $A2$. An associatively "inhibited" node is one for which associatively "excitatory" links are rendered less likely to provoke constituent elements from the I state to the $A2$ state.

I deferred addressing the question of what conditions of the initiating node provoke spread of activation until the nature of the theoretical choice could be clear. It has been assumed that an unconditioned stimulus provokes inactive nodal elements into the $A1$ state (from which they decay into the $A2$ state) whereas an associated conditioned stimulus can only provoke the same inactive nodal elements into the $A2$ state. If one assumed that $A1$ activity of an initiating node were necessary to cause activation in a recipient node, the spread of activation would be extremely limited, i.e., would be only one node deep. We take the available literature on sensory preconditioning (e.g., Pfautz, Donegan, & Wagner, 1978; Rizley & Rescorla, 1972) to discourage this assumption: One appears to be able to activate a US representation by presenting a CS that has never been associated directly with that US, but has been associated with a stimulus that has, in turn, been associated with the US. On the other hand, if one assumes that the $A2$ activity of an initiating node is potent in causing activation in a recipient node, there can be troublesome theoretical consequences, e.g., in the likelihood that stimulation would produce nodal activity in infinitely reverberating loops. In order to avoid such implications, without recourse to an ad hoc damping mechanism, such as that proposed by Anderson (1976), we assume that

$A2$ activity is much less effective than $A1$ activity in producing spread of activation. The system is then kept in bounds by assumptions we otherwise make concerning "spontaneous decay" (i.e., limited activity capacities) and the development of associative connections (i.e., effective variation in the strengths of different links).

Genesis of Nodes and Links

The final set of general views that must be announced concerns the genesis of the representative nodes and the associative links that connect them. SOP is expressly noncommital on the issue of how representative nodes come to have the identities that are assumed. It is true that, in supposing that any isolable experimental stimulus has a representative node and in not appealing to any change in nodal character as a result of training, the formulation is more in the spirit of Anderson and Bower's (1973) naive nativism than, for example, of Konorski's (1967) vigorous empiricism. But this is only a default characteristic. Even with some provocative recent work on "natural concepts" (Herrnstein, 1979; Herrnstein, Loveland, & Cable, 1976) and "configural integration" (Rescorla, 1980a; Rescorla & Cunningham, 1978), there is a paucity of critical data that would guide specific theorizing.

Our assumptions concerning the development of associative connections are much more definite. The most basic proposition is that the associative learning that is produced between any pair of stimuli, in any episode of training, is a direct function of the exact course of joint activation of the stimulus nodes that occurs in the episode. Information-processing theories commonly assume that associative changes occur only as the stimulus representations are "in short-term memory" or are subject to "rehearsal" (Atkinson & Shiffrin, 1968; Bower, 1975; Norman, 1968), and Wagner has echoed this theme in a variety of animal learning contexts (Wagner, 1976, 1978; Wagner et al., 1973; Wagner & Terry, 1975). But conditioning theories have emphasized equally that associative changes occur only as stimulus "centers" are in prescribed states of relative activation (Anokhin, 1958; Konorski, 1948; Pavlov, 1927). And the latter theories have addressed, in these terms, the rules for *inhibitory* learning as well as excitatory learning, in a manner that information-processing theories have not. What we have attempted to arrange is a compatible marriage of these viewpoints.

The distinction we exploit is that any nodal element may, when active, be in either the $A1$ state, corresponding to focal STM, or the $A2$ state, corresponding to marginal working memory. What we shall assume is that the joint activation of two nodes in different combinations of these active states is what produces either excitatory or inhibitory associations between the nodes.

Given two representative nodes, identified with stimuli X and Y, we assume that an excitatory connection will be formed from the node of X to the node of Y, and symmetrically from the node of Y to the node of X, depending on the proportion of their combined elements that are jointly in the $A1$ state. Alternatively, we assume that an inhibitory connection will be formed from the node of X to the node of Y, depending on the joint proportion of X elements in the $A1$ state and Y elements in the $A2$ state, whereas a similar connection will be formed from the node of Y to the node of X, depending on the joint proportion of Y elements in the $A1$ state and X elements in the $A2$ state. Finally, we assume that there is no associative product of the overlapping sets of nodal elements of X and Y that are both in the $A2$ state or either in the I state.

It may help to make this somewhat more concrete. Consider the case in which X is a conventional CS and Y is a conventional US in Pavlovian conditioning. The important notion is that when either stimulus is first presented, its nodal elements will be probabilistically activated to the $A1$ state, from which they will decay to the $A2$ state and then back to the inactive state. The consequences for associative learning, in the sense of the CS coming to have excitatory or inhibitory influence on the US node, will depend on the degree to which the $A1$ "process" of the CS overlaps the $A1$ "process" of the US (producing excitatory learning) and the degree to which the same $A1$ "process" of the CS overlaps the $A2$ "process" of the US (producing inhibitory learning). Generally, some of each will occur in a trial, but it may be recognized that with a forward CS–US temporal relationship, excitatory learning will predominate, whereas, with a backward US–CS temporal relationship, inhibitory learning may predominate.

The power of the formulation comes from generalizing these notions, so that the associative changes are perfectly indifferent to how the relevant nodal activity comes about. To the degree that two nodes are both in the $A1$ state at any moment, each will form an excitatory link to the other, regardless of the temporal relationship between the stimuli that produced the representational activity. To the degree that one node is in the $A1$ state and the other in the $A2$ state at any moment, a directional inhibitory link will be formed between that one in the $A1$ state and that one in the $A2$ state, regardless of the stimulation that provoked the two states.

These assumptions seem agreeable enough to current information-processing theories and yet embrace both excitatory and inhibitory associations. However, when they are coupled with the assumptions we have been encouraged to make concerning the products of excitatory and inhibitory connections, they may seem to come out at odds with conventional premises of conditioning theories. "Pairing" the $A1$ process of a CS with the $A1$ process of a US does not imbue the CS with the tendency to activate the $A1$ process of the US. Rather, it strengthens an excitatory link between the CS and US nodes so that $A1$ activity in the CS node has the tendency to produce $A2$ activity in the US node. "Pairing" the $A1$ process of a CS with the $A2$ process of a US does not imbue the CS with the tendency to activate the $A2$ process of the US. Rather, it strengthens an inhibitory link between the CS and US nodes so that $A1$ activity in the CS node has the tendency to *decrease* $A2$ activity in the US node that might otherwise be produced.

Nonetheless, there is a way in which one could view what has been suggested as more "conditioninglike." Schull (1979) has followed Solomon and Corbit (1974) in assuming that a US provokes an initial a process followed by an opposing b process. Taking a lead from the work of Siegel (1978) on conditioned compensatory responses with pharmacological USs, Schull supposes that pairing of a CS with each of these states leads to "conditioned opponents." That is, pairing of a CS with the a process is assumed to imbue the CS with the tendency to activate the b process. Pairing of a CS with the b process is assumed to imbue the CS with the tendency to inhibit the b process. If one likens the $A1$ and $A2$ states to the a and b states of opponent-process theory, the associative rules of SOP can be seen to be quite similar to the conditioned-opponent formulation of Schull (1979). Indeed, certain of our derivations concerning conditioning phenomena are qualitatively similar to those of Schull, because of this likeness. There are, to be sure, major differences between our formulation and that of Schull. For example, Schull (1979) restricts his use of these conditioned-opponent notions to addressing the tendency of a CS to modify the effectiveness of a US (e.g., either to provoke a UR or to serve as a reinforcer); he does not assume, as we do, that the b (or $A2$) process mediates the observed CR, and thus sometimes mimics the a (or $A1$) process. Furthermore, Schull does not acknowledge that any unconditioned a and b processes intrinsic to the CS are important for determining conditioning. But there are enough similarities between our view and that of Schull (1979) to more than justify the "sometimes opponent-process" label.

THE SOP MODEL

The foregoing discussion will be assumed to have made evident the broader intellectual framework in which the assumptions of SOP are rooted. It should also have made evident how various assumptions of the model have been articulated to allow a quantitative formulation that might lead to determinate predictions. In this section we more succinctly summarize the essential features of the model with emphasis on its quantitative implementation. This takes the form of announcing specific assumptions, consistent with the preceding discussion, and exhibiting various basic characteristics of the model as they are evident in either computer simulations or mathematical derivations.

The presentation is intended as an overview. In the space available it is not possible to elaborate the full details of SOP as they may be important for the range of topics that the model is meant to address. Nor will the attempt be made to document fully the various derivations included here or in the subsequent sections of the chapter. More extensive discussions of different features of the model may be found in a series of papers by Donegan and Wagner (note 1), Mazur and Wagner (note 2), and Pfautz (1980).

The Course of Activity in an Individual Node

We can start by considering the expected course of activity in an individual memorial node under different circumstances of stimulation. Figure 1.1 will be helpful in this regard. Panel *a* is intended to depict an individual memorial node, assumed to be made up of a large set of informational elements. The connected circles, labeled *I*, *A*1, and *A*2, indicate the several states of activation in which the individual elements may reside, and can be conceived as each containing

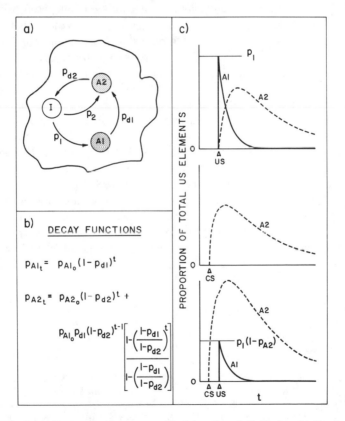

FIG. 1.1.   Concerning the course of activity of an individual node: Panel *a* depicts the three activity states and the transitional probabilities assumed in SOP; panel *b* presents the decay functions for the proportion of elements in *A*1 and *A*2 over successive moments of time, *t*, when p_1 and p_2 are zero; panel *c* exemplifies the course of p_{A1} and p_{A2} following a punctate US (top graph), following a punctate CS with acquired excitatory influence on the same node (middle graph), and following the two stimuli in a CS–US sequence (bottom graph).

some specifiable proportion of the total nodal elements at any moment. The connecting arrows indicate the allowable state transitions: The probability that any individual element in one state will move to some other state in some moment of time is indicated by the p assigned to the particular transitional possibility; the values that the ps take on will depend on the nodal environment at that moment; where no arrows are shown it is simply assumed that $p = 0$ in all circumstances.

By this diagram it may be seen that we allow that elements may be activated to the $A1$ state only if they are in the I state and p_1 has some nonzero value. The latter is assumed to occur only in moments of exposure to the stimulus that the node represents (i.e., its US), with the value of p_1 being assumed to increase monotonically with increasing stimulus intensity. We allow that elements may "decay" from $A1$ to $A2$ in any moment, according to the probability p_{d1}, and subsequently "decay" from $A2$ back to I, according to the probability p_{d2}. The values of p_{d1} and p_{d2} are assumed to reflect cross-nodal capacity limitations on the $A1$ and $A2$ states and thus be increased by experimental distractors. But, in the absence of explicit experimental stimulation, they are treated as situational constants with $p_{d1} > p_{d2}$. We here assume throughout the simulations described that $p_{d1} = 5p_{d2}$ as a first approximation concerning the order of magnitudes.

These assumptions lead to a characteristic course of nodal activity following the presentation of a US. This is shown in the top graph of panel c in Fig. 1.1, which portrays the expected proportions of nodal elements in the $A1$ state and in the $A2$ state at successive times after the presentation of a punctate US. In this example, all elements were in the I state prior to the US. Upon momentary action of a US, p_1 of these elements are activated to $A1$. Thereafter the proportion of elements in $A1$ decays in a simple exponential fashion, dependent on p_{d1}, while the proportion of elements in $A2$ at first increases and then eventually decreases, depending on p_{d1} and p_{d2}. The two decay functions are described by the equations presented in panel b of Fig. 1.1.[2] These functions and variations upon them are basic to many predictions of the model.

---

[2]Although the interpretation of the equation for p_{A1}, should be obvious, that for p_{A2}, will be less so. In the general case, the proportion of elements in $A2$ after t moments of decay will depend on the proportion of elements in $A2$ and the proportion of elements in $A1$ when $t = 0$, i.e., p_{A2_0} and p_{A1_0}, respectively. The first term in the equation describes the fate of the elements initially in $A2$, a simple exponential decay equivalent to the course of p_{A1}, except for the substitution of p_{d2} for p_{d1}. (In the case of the function for p_{A2} in the top panel of Figure 1.1c, $p_{A2_0} = 0$, so that this term can there be ignored.) The second term in the equation describes the proportion of elements that have decayed from $A1$ to $A2$ but have not decayed from $A2$ to I, by moment t. It is equivalent to the value,

$$\sum_{i=1}^{t} [p_{A1_0}(1 - p_{d1})^{i-1} p_{d1}(1 - p_{d2})^{t-i}],$$

which may be appreciated as the proportion of elements that were in the $A1$ state at $t = 0$, remained there for $i - 1$ moments, decayed to $A2$ in the ith moment, and remained in $A2$ for $t - i$ moments, summed over all possible values of i.

By the diagram in panel a of Fig. 1.1, it may be seen that we allow that elements that are in the I state may be directly activated to the $A2$ state when p_2 has some nonzero value. This is assumed to occur only as a result of activity in another node, or set of nodes, that has net excitatory connections with the depicted node, i.e., that represents an excitatory CS. Because p_2 is dependent on the activity dynamics of another node or set of nodes, the temporal course of nodal activity produced by a CS can be complex (as we better explicate later). However, the middle graph in panel c of Fig. 1.1 depicts an expected course of US–nodal activity following presentation of a punctate excitatory CS. In this example, all elements were again in the I state prior to CS application. The important feature of this function, for present purposes, is that there is now simply some recruitment of elements to the $A2$ state, followed by eventual decay back to the I state.

To assure an understanding of these assumptions, as well as to emphasize the important tie with our previous priming theory (Wagner, 1976), consider what should be the expected course of nodal activity if the same US assumed in the top graph of Fig. 1.1c were preceded by the same excitatory CS assumed in the middle graph of Fig. 1.1c. This case is illustrated in the bottom graph of Fig. 1.1c.

An obvious major result is that the US produces a lesser proportion of elements in the $A1$ state, immediately, and thus over the following time period. This is the simple result of the fact that the CS caused some proportion, p_{A2}, of the nodal elements to be in the $A2$ state at the time of US presentation. As a consequence, p_1 occasioned by the US could act only on a reduced population of elements: Whereas, when the US was presented alone, p_1 of the total nodal elements, i.e., p_1, were provoked to $A1$; when the CS preceded the US only p_1 of the $(1 - p_{A2})$ nodal elements, i.e., $(1 - p_{A2})p_1$, could be provoked to $A1$. What we further acknowledge here, that was not explicit in the priming formulation, is how representation in the $A2$ state also has a predictable course, pre- and post-US, that is different from the case of isolated US presentation (compare the functions for $A2$ in the top and bottom graphs of Fig. 1.1c), which may be important to various behavioral outcomes.

Learning Rules

How activity in one node can come to have influence on the activity of another node, via the p_2 of the latter, can be summarized with the aid of Fig. 1.2. Panel a reminds us that we are concerned with the development of associative connection between two nodes, each with a population of elements, specifiable proportions of which may momentarily be in the several states and each with similar state transition rules. One node is labeled as a CS representation, the other as a US representation, to declare in conventional terms the interest in how the former can come to influence the latter. Then, we are interested in the *directional*

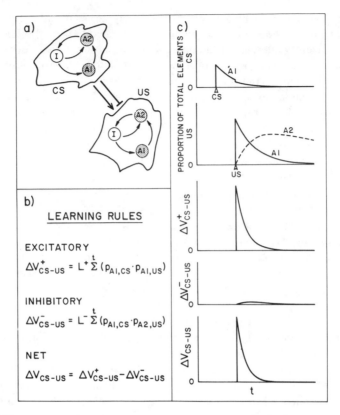

FIG. 1.2. Concerning the learning rules: Panel *a* depicts a CS and US node and two of the directional excitatory (pointed arrow) and inhibitory (stopped line) linkages that may be developed; panel *b* presents the rules describing the increments in the relevant excitatory (V^+_{CS-US}) and inhibitory (V^-_{CS-US}) linkages, as well as the net associative tendency (V_{CS-US}), as a function of the course of specified conjoint activity states in the two nodes; panel *c* exemplifies in the bottom three graphs the consequences of the learning rules, given a single CS-US pairing provoking the temporal course of nodal activity depicted in the top two graphs.

linkages suggested by the pointing and stopped lines from the CS node to the US node. However, it should be understood that what will be said about the development of such linkages is perfectly general so as to imply additional directional linkages from what is here called the US node to that called the CS node.

The assumed learning rules are presented in panel *b* in Fig. 1.2. A strengthening of the excitatory connection between the CS and US nodes is assumed to be produced when elements in both nodes are in the *A*1 state. The increment in strength of the excitatory connection, ΔV^+_{CS-US}, over any episode is thus expressed as the summed momentary conjoint proportions of CS elements in the *A*1 state and US elements in the $A1$ state, times a learning rate parameter, L^+. A strengthening of the inhibitory connection from the CS node to the US node is assumed to be produced when elements in the CS node are in the $A1$ state while elements in the US node are in the $A2$ state. The increment in strength of the inhibitory connection, $\Delta V^-_{\text{CS-US}}$, over any episode is thus expressed as the summed momentary conjoint proportions of CS elements in the $A1$ state and US elements in the $A2$ state, times a learning rate parameter, L^-. The net associative change over any episode, $\Delta V_{\text{CS-US}}$, is simply a subtractive consequence of the amount of excitatory and inhibitory learning. Like other theorists (Bush & Mosteller, 1955; Rescorla & Wagner, 1972), we assume that $L^+ > L^-$. In the simulations described it is consistently the case that $L^+ = 5L^-$. This specific relationship was tied to the assumption that $p_{d1} = 5p_{d2}$, for reasons that can be appreciated later—see Footnote 7.

Panel c in Fig. 1.2 exemplifies the application of these learning rules for a single, *initial* "pairing" of a punctate CS and US, as in a conventional forward, trace-conditioning procedure. For the directional linkages of interest, we must take into account the temporal course of the $A1$ activity in the CS node in conjunction with the $A1$ and $A2$ activity in the US node. The proportions of the respective nodal elements in these states over time are presented in the top two graphs. The only feature of these functions that may not have been anticipated is the discontinuity in the decay of the $A1$ activity of the CS at the point of occurrence of the US. This is a distractor effect that has been mentioned, but the rules for which have not yet been announced. They will be shortly.

The bottom three graphs in panel c describe, in turn, the corresponding momentary increments in the excitatory connection, $\Delta V^+_{\text{CS-US}}$, in the inhibitory connection, $\Delta V^-_{\text{CS-US}}$, and in the net associative consequence, $\Delta V_{\text{CS-US}}$, over time. As may be seen, in this example there is considerable excitatory learning, very small, but, nonetheless, some inhibitory learning, leading to a net excitatory consequence of the training episode. The associative process is assumed generally to operate in this fashion. What will be different in other examples is the relative balance of excitatory and inhibitory learning, as the examples may involve different CS–US arrangements, different stages of training, and different conditions of ancillary (e.g., pretrial and posttrial) stimulation.

Rules for Nodal Interaction and Response Generation

Having characterized the course of activity in individual nodes under the most common circumstances, and the rules for development of associative connections, we can now finally express the rules for nodal interaction and response generation. These are presented in Fig. 1.3.

We have already noted that a CS is assumed to influence a US node via the p_2 value of the latter node. But there may be multiple CS nodes active at any moment, each with its own balance of excitatory and inhibitory connections with the US node, as is suggested in panel *a* of Fig. 1.3, in which the CS_A and CS_B nodes both impinge on the US node. And each CS node may be expected to have its own momentary distribution of elements in the several states. The retrieval rule in panel *b* of Fig. 1.3 embodies the assumption that any CS node influences $p_{2,US}$ in accordance with the product of the momentary proportion of its active elements and the net value of its associative connection with the US node. The rule then states that these products are summed over all CS representations to determine $p_{2,US}$.

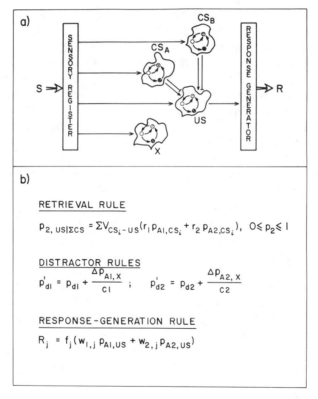

RETRIEVAL RULE

$$p_{2,\,US|\Sigma CS} = \Sigma V_{CS_i-US}(r_1 p_{A1,CS_i} + r_2 p_{A2,CS_i}), \quad 0 \leq p_2 \leq 1$$

DISTRACTOR RULES

$$p'_{d1} = p_{d1} + \frac{\Delta p_{A1,X}}{c_1} \quad ; \quad p'_{d2} = p_{d2} + \frac{\Delta p_{A2,X}}{c_2}$$

RESPONSE-GENERATION RULE

$$R_j = f_j(w_{1,j}\, p_{A1,US} + w_{2,j}\, p_{A2,US})$$

FIG. 1.3.   Concerning the rules for nodal interaction and response generation: Panel *a* depicts some assumed relationships among memorial nodes and input and output mechanisms for which rules are specified in panel *b;* the retrieval rule summarizes how the p_2 value of a US node varies with the product of the net associative strength (V) and weighted activity states $(r_1 p_{A1} + r_2 p_{A1})$ of all impinging CSs. The distractor rules summarize how the p_{d1} and p_{d2} of all nodes are increased to p'_{d1} and p'_{d2}, when there is an increment in the p_{A1} and p_{A2}, respectively, of the node of any experimental stimulus, $X;$ the response generation rule summarizes how certain responses are a weighted function of the p_{A1} and p_{A2} of a US node. (See text for further explanation.)

It can be noted that the rule allows an effect of the proportion of active CS elements in the $A2$ state as well as in the $A1$ state. As indicated earlier, this is necessary to address certain phenomena such as the expression of sensory preconditioning effects. However, we have assumed that $A2$ state elements of the CS are generally much less effective than the $A1$ state elements in promoting US nodal activity, and we accomplish this by differential weightings, r_1 and r_2. For simplification, in all present examples we have set $r_1 = 1$ and $r_2 = .01$: With such a small ratio of r_2/r_1, the reader may assume that the retrieval influence of $A2$ state elements was, in fact, made negligible in any of the simulations reported.

Since p_2 is restricted to the unit interval, it should be clear that an individual CS node that has a net inhibitory association (i.e., $V_{CS\text{-}US} < 0$) with the US node can have no effect in isolation on the latter node. However, when active in concert with another CS node that has a net excitatory association (i.e., $V_{CS\text{-}US} > 0$) with the US node, it will be effective. That is, its contribution will enter into the summed quantity to reduce $p_{2,US}$ below what it otherwise would be. (Analogous statements can be made about an individual CS node, the associative strength and activity product of which might exceed unity. In isolation it could not be distinguished from a less effective node that also caused $p_{2,US}$ to equal 1. But in concert with an inhibitory stimulus it could be.)

The distractor rules presented in panel b of Fig. 1.3 apply to the occasions of any experimental stimulus. We presume that at any moment the summed proportion of elements in the $A1$ state across all memorial nodes is some constant, $C1$. When a proportion of elements of some stimulus node, such as X in panel a, are incremented to the $A1$ state, we assume that the momentary increase, $\Delta p_{A1,X}$, must be compensated for by some decrease in the proportion of $A1$ elements over all nodes so that the summed proportion will still equal $C1$. This is accomplished in SOP by increasing the decay probability, p_{d1}, that is applied to the proportion of $A1$ elements in *each* node in the system, by the value $\Delta p_{A1,X}/C1$, to yield a higher momentary probability, p'_{d1}. (Following this reasoning, one can rationalize p_{d1} as the ratio of the expected momentary increments in proportion of elements in the $A1$ state resulting from *extraexperimental* stimulation over $C1$. Then $\Delta p_{A1,X}$, occasioned by an experimental stimulus, simply adds to the numerator of this ratio.) As may be seen in Fig. 1.3, exactly the same rule is applied, with the same rationale, in regard to p_{d2} when a proportion of elements (e.g., $\Delta p_{A2,X}$) of some experimental stimulus node is incremented to the $A2$ state. The only difference is that the summed proportion of elements in the $A2$ state is assumed to be greater than that in the $A1$ state, so that $C2 > C1$ in the corresponding equations. In the simulations that are reported we have consistently assigned $C1 = 2$ and $C2 = 10$, the ratios of which are consistent with the designation of $p_{d1} = 5p_{d2}$.

The final rule presented in panel b of Fig. 1.3 is the response-generation rule. This was anticipated in an earlier section. It simply says that any response that is the reflection of activity in some memorial node will be a function of the proportion of nodal elements in the $A1$ state and the proportion of nodal elements in the $A2$ state, each with a separate multiplicative weighting. The theory adopts the convention that W_1 is nonnegative, but has no prejudices about the relative values of W_2 in different instances, and leaves the mapping function, f_j, as subject to empirical determination with each response measure.

AN EMPIRICAL APPLICATION

In the introductory remarks it was observed that certain phenomena that were allowed by the priming theory (Wagner, 1976) begged more determinate accounts. It is thus appropriate to ask whether SOP provides more satisfying treatment of these phenomena. One of the cases was the so-called conditioned diminution of the UR in Pavlovian conditioning. I will concentrate on this effect because it is prototypical of a larger class of phenomena, because the application of SOP is relatively simple, and because I can present some new data, consistent with SOP, that appear to clarify an otherwise confusing picture.

Conditioned Diminution of the UR

To be reminded again, the conditioned diminution of the UR is a reduction in amplitude of the response that immediately follows a US, as a specific result of preceding the US by a CS with which it can be presumed to have excitatory association. What has been confusing about the conditioned diminution of the UR is that it does not always occur, indeed, that the opposite, i.e., a *conditioned facilitation* of the UR, is sometimes observed. Thus, although it is conventional to cite the original studies by Kimble and Ost (1961), in human eyelid conditioning, and by Kimmel (1966), in human GSR conditioning, as attesting to conditioned diminution, Hupka, Kwaterski, and Moore (1970), in rabbit nictitating-membrane conditioning, reported a conditioned facilitation, while Wagner, Thomas, and Norton (1967), in limb flexion conditioning in the dog with a cortical US, reported a mixture of facilitation and diminution with different measures: The probability of a detectable UR to a threshold US was increased by a preceding CS^+, while the vigor of the UR to a training-level US was decreased.

Consider how SOP would approach this situation. We assume that the measured response is finally determined by the activity in the US node. Specifically, we assume, as has been noted, that

$$R_j = f_j(W_{1,j}p_{A1} + W_{2,j}p_{A2}). \tag{1}$$

What is presumed to be different on CS–US trials, in comparison to US-alone trials, is the proportion of nodal elements in the $A1$ and $A2$ states immediately following the US. And this difference is what must be responsible for the conditioned facilitation or conditioned diminution that is observed.

Prior to application of a US alone, we can assume that all elements of the US node are in the I state, i.e., that the vector describing the proportion of elements in the three states, (p_I, p_{A1}, p_{A2}), is $(1, 0, 0)$. Immediately upon application of the US, some proportion, p_1, of the elements in the I state should be activated to the $A1$ state so that the resulting post-US vector, (p'_I, p'_{A1}, p'_{A2}), will be $(1 - p_1, p_1, 0)$. Thus, returning to the response-generation rule we can see that on US-alone trials,

$$R_j|\text{US} = f_j(W_{1,j}p_1). \tag{2}$$

On CS^+US trials the case will be different. As a result of the retrieval action of the CS^+, we must assume that some proportion of the nodal elements have been provoked to the $A2$ state and remain there at the time of US application. That is, the pre-US vector, (p_I, p_{A1}, p_{A2}), will be $(1 - p_{A2}, 0, p_{A2})$. Immediately upon application of the US, the US-defined proportion, p_1, of the elements in the I state will be activated to the $A1$ state so that the resulting post-US vector, (p'_I, p'_{A1}, p'_{A2}), will be $[(1 - p_{A2})(1 - p_1), (1 - p_{A2})p_1, p_{A2}]$. Substituting the relevant values from this vector in the response-generation rule, we can see that on CS^+US trials,

$$R_j|\text{CS}^+\text{US} = f_j[W_{1,j}p_1(1 - p_{A2}) + W_{2,j}p_{A2}]. \tag{3}$$

In general, statements about conditioned "diminution," i.e., $R_j|\text{CS}^+\text{US} < R_j|\text{US}$, or conditioned "facilitation," i.e., $R_j|\text{CS}^+\text{CS} > R_j|\text{US}$, are understood to refer to the designated directional effects upon a response measure that is construed to increase with increasing US intensity, i.e., in which f_j in equation 2 (and equation 3) is a monotonically increasing function. According to equations 2 and 3, whether one then sees diminution or facilitation depends on the combined contribution of two effects of signaling: There will be fewer elements in the $A1$ state on CS^+US trials than on US-alone trials, which, because W_1 is positive, will favor diminution; there will be more elements in the $A2$ state on CS^+US trials than on US-alone trials, which, if W_2 is positive, will favor facilitation or, if W_2 is negative, will favor diminution.

A more specific characterization of the conditions that favor conditioned diminution or conditioned facilitation may be seen by rewriting equation 3 for the expected response on CS^+US trials:

$$R_j|\text{CS}^+\text{US} = f_j[W_{1,j}p_1 - p_{A2}(W_{1,j}p_1 - W_{2,j})]. \tag{4}$$

The first term in this equation is identical to the single term in equation 2 for the expected response on US-alone trials. Thus, it may be appreciated that the expected response will be comparatively less on CS^+US trials when the subtractive second term in equation 4 is positive, whereas the expected response will be comparatively greater on CS^+US trials when the term is negative. Furthermore, we can see that the latter term will be positive (predicting a conditioned diminution) when $p_1 > W_{2,j}/W_{1,j}$. Correspondingly, we can see that the latter term will be negative (predicting a conditioned facilitation) when $p_1 < W_{2,j}/W_{1,j}$. The quantity, p_{A2}, determined by the degree of conditioning to CS$^+$, will simply influence the size of these differences.

This leads to some testable predictions. First, because p_1 is assumed to be a function of US intensity, we should be more likely to observe conditioned diminution the more intense the US. Second, because we assume that the ratio W_2/W_1 is a fixed parameter of any response, but can differ across responses, we should be prepared for different pictures of facilitation versus diminution in different concurrent responses (i.e., with exactly the same CS and US). To elaborate, with two different response measures with different fixed values of W_2/W_1, we should consistently expect an interaction of the difference between responding to US alone and to CS$^+$US with variation in US intensity (p_1), but we might well expect that, at some selected US intensity, there would be diminution of one response while there is facilitation of the other.

Before the fact, we can be counseled further by knowledge of the conditioned responding that may be observed to CS$^+$, in relationship to the UR that is observed to the US alone. For example, when the CR mimics the immediate UR, we must assume that W_2 is positive, whereas the larger is the *maximum* CR in relationship to the *maximum* UR, the greater is the ratio W_2/W_1 (assuming the maxima are determined, respectively, by ($W_2 p_{A2}$) and ($W_1 p_{A1}$) when p_{A2} and p_{A1} both equal 1).

Donegan Dissertation

In order to evaluate these notions, Nelson Donegan conducted an appropriate set of studies in his dissertation (1980). Rabbits were trained in a conventional eyelid-conditioning situation, with one visual or auditory stimulus (CS$^+$) consistently followed after 1 sec by a paraorbital shock (US), and the alternative stimulus (CS$^-$) consistently nonreinforced. Two response measures were taken. One was the closure of the subjects' eyelid adjacent to the point of application of the shock. The other was of gross body activity, recorded via a movement transducer attached to the floor of the subjects' restraining box. In the study to be summarized, subjects were conditioned with a 5-mA US and received seven sessions of discrimination training, each with 50 reinforced and 50 nonreinforced trials, prior to collecting the data of interest.

Over the next seven sessions of similar discrimination training, occasional test trials (81 in all) were inserted in which the US was either of 1 mA, 2 mA, or 5 mA in intensity and was preceded by either CS$^+$, CS$^-$, or no stimulus. It was thus possible to ask, in comparing the responses to the US alone and to the US preceded by CS$^+$, whether the tendency for a conditioned diminution generally increased with increasing US intensity (p_1). And it was possible to ask whether the form of this generally expected pattern would differ in the two response measures, according to assumptions that we would be encouraged to make about the relative values of W_2/W_1 in the two cases. In the latter regard, we would assume that W_2/W_1 was greater in the case of the eyeblink response than in the case of the gross movement response: In the preceding discrimination sessions there were sizable and consistent anticipatory, eyelid-closure CRs to CS$^+$ but no *detectable* anticipating movement CRs. The CS$^-$US trials were, of course, included for comparison to offer assurances that any effects of CS$^+$ on the response measures could be attributed to associative processes, as opposed, for example, to some more general pre-pulse modulation of reflex activity (Hoffman & Ison, 1980).

Figure 1.4 summarizes the data from the 1-mA and 5-mA test trials, separately for each of the two response measures. In this figure the 2-mA data have been ignored (as they were simply intermediate to these from the more extreme intensities), and the two measures are presented on comparable scales. One can

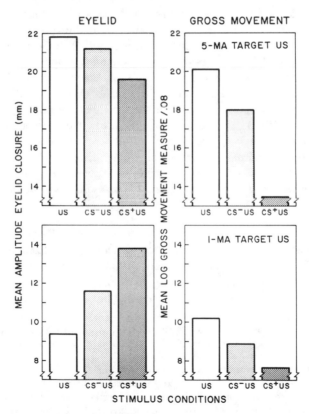

FIG. 1.4. Mean amplitude of eyelid closure and gross body movement to a 5-mA US (top panels) and a 1-mA US (bottom panels) on trials when the designated US was presented alone, was preceded by a CS$^-$, or was preceded by a CS$^+$. The data are drawn from Donegan (1980).

see that *overall* there was prominent conditioned diminution of the URs: Less responding was observed on CS$^+$US occasions than on US-alone occasions in both response measures when the US was 5 mA (see top two panels); such was also observed in the movement response when the US was 1 mA (see bottom right panel). However, what is more important, in relationship to SOP, is the more detailed pattern: In the case of the eyelid measure, there was a *conditioned facilitation* with a 1-mA US, changing to a conditioned diminution with a 5-mA US (compare bottom and top, left panels); in the case of the gross-movement response, there was a conditioned diminution with a 1-mA US, changing to a more sizable conditioned diminution with a 5-mA US (compare bottom and top right panels). These tendencies were reliable when the CS$^+$US responding was contrasted with the US-alone responding, or with the CS$^-$US responding. (That the responding on CS$^-$US trials was consistently in the direction of responding on CS$^+$US trials is presumably indicative of generalization between CS$^+$ and CS$^-$.)

It appears that the p_1 associated with a 1-mA US was less than the W_2/W_1 of the eyelid response but greater than the W_2/W_1 of the movement response, whereas the p_1 associated with a 5-mA US was greater than the W_2/W_1 of either measure. It is beyond the scope of the present summary to indicate how this was done, but Donegan (1980) could estimate these parameter values. He estimated that p_1 had values of .41 at 1 mA and .92 at 5 mA, whereas W_2/W_1 had values of .73 for the eyelid response and .22 for the movement response.[3]

The Donegan (1980) data are, potentially, instructive in relationship to the rather confusing literature on conditioned diminution of the UR that was previously mentioned. And the findings are clearly consistent with the SOP model. We do not yet know how confident we should be in generalizing upon them,[4] but we have some reason to be encouraged in this regard, as will be indicated.

Pfautz Dissertation

Especially consistent are some data reported by Penn Pfautz (1980) as part of his dissertation. Pfautz recorded the same eyelid and movement responses of rabbits, to the same 1-mA and 5-mA US intensities as did Donegan, but under conditions in which the target US was either in relative isolation or was recently preceded by

---

[3]The estimated value of $+.22$ for the W_2/W_1 ratio of the gross movement response has an interesting implication. It suggests that Donegan (1980) should have been able to observe anticipatory movement CRs that mimicked the UR. Although Donegan did not detect such movement CRs, their *predicted* amplitude was less than the resolution of his measuring system.

[4]One province to which we would generalize is worth noting. Wagner (1976) has treated long-term habituation as a special instance of the conditioned diminution of the UR, with contextual cues playing a role like the explicit CSs of Pavlovian conditioning, even though phasic "CRs" may not be observed under these conditions. According to the foregoing theoretical analysis and the Donegan (1980) data, we should then be prepared sometimes to see little or no long-term habituation with iterated stimulation (i.e., when $p_1 \approx W_2/W_1$) or even to see long-term facilitation (when $p_1 < W_2/W_1$).

another, priming *US* rather than a CS. According to the SOP model this case is more complex than preceding the target US by a CS$^+$: We must assume that US nodal elements are initially provoked to the $A1$ state from which they will decay to the $A2$ state (before decaying back to I) rather than being provoked to the $A2$ state directly. Thus, with different US–US time intervals, we would have to calculate the predicted effects of the target US when different proportions of elements are presumably in $A1$ as well as $A2$. However, for comparison with the Donegan data, we can ask what is observed at *intermediate* intervals when it may reasonably be presumed that the majority of any active elements will be in $A2$. Will we then see a pattern of responding to a primed US as compared to an isolated US that parallels that observed by Donegan?

In the experiment to be summarized (Pfautz, 1980, Exp. 3), subjects were run in a single session with pairs of USs separated by 150 sec and within-pair US–US intervals varying irregularly among .5, 2, and 16 sec. With this brief training and irregular presentations of USs, there were no observable anticipatory "CRs." The intensity of the initial US, and of the second US in the pairs was independently either 1 mA or 5 mA.

Figure 1.5 follows the format of Fig. 1.4 to summarize the data separately from each of the two measures following either 1-mA or 5-mA "target" USs. In

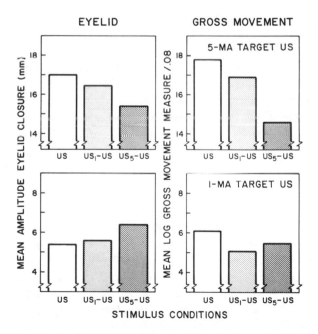

FIG. 1.5. Mean amplitude of eyelid closure and gross body movement to a 5-mA US (top panels) and a 1-mA US (bottom panels) on trials when the designated target US was presented in relative isolation, was preceded by a 1-mA US (US$_1$), or was preceded by a 5-mA US (US$_5$). The data are drawn from Pfautz (1980), involving a 2-sec interstimulus interval.

this case the target USs were either the relatively isolated initial USs in the pairs or had been preceded 2 sec earlier by another US of either 1 mA or 5 mA. What should be apparent is the close correspondence between these data and those reported by Donegan (1980). There was *overall* a clear tendency for responding to the target US to be less when recently preceded by another US than when presented in comparative isolation. But such a short-term refractorylike effect would hardly be newsworthy. What is notable is that, like the Donegan (1980) data with CS priming, the decremental effect was more pronounced the more intense the target (as p_1 was presumably greater), and there was the same differential pattern in the two response measures (presumably having different W_2/W_1 ratios). In the case of the gross-movement response, there was a priming-produced decrement in responding to a 1-mA US and simply a larger such decrement in responding to a 5-mA US. In the case of the eyelid response there was a priming-produced *facilitation* in responding to a 1-mA US, that was replaced by a priming-produced decrement in responding to a 5-mA US. In general, the priming effects were greater with a 5-mA priming stimulus than with a 1-mA prime, although this was not the case in the gross-movement data with a 1-mA target. The latter observation may reflect a variety of complications in this situation, beyond the simplifications that have been offered here (see Pfautz, 1980).

Conclusions

The general conclusion is that SOP appears to offer a reasonably satisfying integration of certain reflex modulations that can result from recent presentation of a CS^+ or another instance of the same US. It anticipates incremental effects as well as decremental effects and points to the manner in which these may be determined by the parameters of stimulation as well as the characteristics of different response systems.

OTHER APPLICATIONS

In indicating the reasons for dwelling on the "conditioned diminution of the UR" and for presenting new data relevant to it, I mentioned that it was prototypical of a larger class of phenomena. I hope that it is possible to envision how SOP would follow analogous reasoning to address a variety of other effects. I parenthetically noted how our approach to the conditioned diminution of the UR might be extended to related phenomena of long-term habituation. Other phenomena as mentioned in introduction would include the differential memorability of "expected" versus "unexpected" samples in a short-term memory task (Terry & Wagner, 1975) and the differential preference for signaled versus unsignaled motivationally significant events (Lockard, 1963; Prokasy, 1956). Stepping outside the animal literature, I would also include the likes of semantic-priming effects in lexical decision tasks (Meyer, Schvaneveldt, & Ruddy, 1975; Neely, 1977), in which, incidentally, the target stimulus can usually be considered to be impoverished, making the *facilitation* typically produced by priming quite understandable via SOP. Indeed, Becker and Killion (1977) found that priming-produced facilitation was greater the lower the target intensity.

Still, these phenomena can be approached via the most skeletal assumptions of SOP. In the space remaining an attempt will be made to give some feeling for its application to a broader range of phenomena involving association formation. Mazur and Wagner (note 2) develop such application in more detail to draw out some novel implications of SOP. In the present overview the emphasis is necessarily on how we have attempted to address certain major, familiar phenomena with the aid of computer simulations. This is not to say that the simulations will, thus, necessarily be uninteresting. Many familiar empirical phenomena of associative learning have not been explained, as we have attempted, they have only been accepted.

CS–US Interval Effects with Punctate Stimuli

In discussion centered around Fig. 1.3, it was indicated how SOP would account for the associative learning that is produced by a single trace-conditioning trial with a punctate CS and US in a "forward" relationship. Figure 1.6 generalizes upon this case to derive the expected net associative learning, $\Delta V_{CS\text{-}US}$, with different temporal relationships between the same CS and US. The left-hand graphs of panel a repeat what was previously assumed in Fig. 1.3. Given the course of proportion of CS elements in the $A1$ state overlapping the course of proportions of US elements in the $A1$ and the $A2$ states, respectively, there is an expected sizable increment in excitatory learning, $\Delta V^{+}_{CS\text{-}US}$, a small increment in inhibitory learning, $\Delta V^{-}_{CS\text{-}US}$, leading to a net positive association, $\Delta V_{CS\text{-}US}$. The right-hand graphs of panel a present, for comparison, what may be assumed with a selected "backward" conditioning arrangement, i.e., when the CS follows the US. What is obviously different is that the course of proportion of CS elements in the $A1$ state overlaps with a small proportion of US elements in the $A1$ state but a large proportion of US elements in the $A2$ state. The result is a smaller increment in excitatory learning, $\Delta V^{+}_{CS\text{-}US}$, than in inhibitory learning, $\Delta V^{-}_{CS\text{-}US}$, leaving a net *negative* associative tendency, $\Delta V_{CS\text{-}US}$.[5]

Panel b of Fig. 1.6 summarizes the expected net associative product from examples as depicted in panel a, but with continuous variation in the CS–US interval. For reference, it is indicated where the two examples of panel a would

---

[5]Effects of the distractor rule can be seen in Fig. 1.6, in the discontinuities in the $A1$ and $A2$ processes of the US when the CS is presented in backward arrangement, as well as in the previously noted discontinuity in the $A1$ process of the CS when the US is presented in the forward conditioning case. Similar effects will be apparent in subsequent figures and will be assumed to be recognizable.

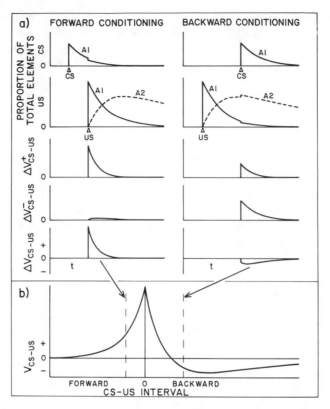

FIG. 1.6. Simulations of the theoretical processes involved in a single conditioning trial with a punctate CS and US at different interstimulus intervals. Panel *a* illustrates for a case of "forward" CS-US pairing and a case of "backward" US-CS pairing how the overlapping of the *A*1 process of the CS and the *A*1 process of the US leads to increments over time in an excitatory connection, $\Delta V^+_{CS\text{-}US}$, whereas the overlapping of the *A*1 process of the CS and the *A*2 process of the US leads to similar increments in an inhibitory connection, $\Delta V^-_{CS\text{-}US}$, to produce a net change in associative tendency, $\Delta V_{CS\text{-}US}$. Panel *b* describes the predicted $V_{CS\text{-}US}$ from trials involving different interstimulus intervals, with the location of the two example cases of panel *a* indicated for reference. Reprinted from Mazur and Wagner (note 2).

fall on this function. Several features are notable. As the forward CS-US interval is increased there is less associative learning predicted. In the backward case, inhibitory learning is *not* the universal product. With close US-CS relationships, substantial excitatory conditioning should result from a *single* pairing as here assumed. This prediction is in sympathy with recent data (Burkhardt & Ayres, 1978; Mahoney & Ayres, 1976). Indeed, at an empirical level, what has not been demonstrated is inhibitory backward conditioning following a single trial, although it is well documented after multiple trials (Siegel & Domjan, 1971).

A provocative prediction is that simultaneous CS–US presentation should produce the maximum net excitatory learning. This does not seem to square with our usual characterization of CS–US interval effects. However, Rescorla (1980b) has recently presented data to suggest that conventional experimental designs may systematically underestimate the degree of simultaneous conditioning, and that, in fact, simultaneity may be optimum, if one controls for the degree of concurrent stimulation during CS presentation and for the degree of stimulus change between training and eventual testing.

Delayed Conditioning

One way in which a forward, as compared to a simultaneous, CS–US relationship can facilitate conditioning on a single trial, according to SOP, is to allow the $A1$ activity of the CS node to become greater at the time of US application than it otherwise would be. This can happen in a so-called delayed-conditioning (Pavlov, 1927) procedure, in which the CS continues for some duration of time prior to the US. Fig. 1.7 will be helpful in making this clear.

Panel a of Fig. 1.7 describes the expected proportion of nodal elements in the $A1$ and $A2$ states, as a result of successive moments of continuous exposure to the stimulus represented by that node. Assuming that all elements were in the I state prior to stimulus presentation, p_1 of the elements will be moved to $A1$ in the first moment. In each of the following moments, p_1 of the residual elements in I will likewise be activated to $A1$, while p_{d1} of the elements in $A1$ decay to $A2$, and p_{d2} of the elements in $A2$ decay back to I. The characteristic effect is as portrayed, a gradual growth in the proportion of elements in $A1$ (if $p_1 < 1$), followed by an eventual decline, to a point of stability in the distribution of elements among the several states.[6]

Panel b of Fig. 1.7 follows this to exemplify two cases of delayed conditioning in which the CS and US overlap and terminate together, but the CS is either of a "long" duration or of an "intermediate" duration. What differs, to influence the associative product, $\Delta V_{CS\text{-}US}$, in the two cases is the resulting $A1$ process of the CS that overlaps with the $A1$ and $A2$ processes of the US. With the intermediate duration CS, there is a greater proportion of CS elements in the $A1$ state over the interval following the US, and hence more conditioning. Panel c describes the degree of net excitatory conditioning that would be expected under conditions equivalent to these examples, but other durations of the CS. As may

---

[6]With continuous stimulation, the relevant state-transition probabilities, p_1, p_{d1}, and p_{d2}, are constants. Thus, the equilibrium point of the Markov process can be calculated. The general result is that p_{A1} will stabilize at

$$p_{d1}^{-1}/(p_1^{-1} + p_{d1}^{-1} + p_{d2}^{-1}).$$

Similarly, p_{A2} and p_I will, respectively, stabilize at p_{d2}^{-1} and p_1^{-1}, over the same denominator.

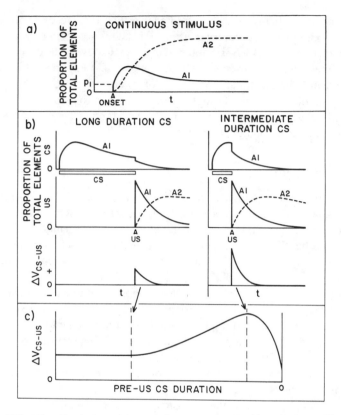

FIG. 1.7. Simulations of theoretical processes involved in a single conditioning trial with an extended CS of different durations terminating with a punctate US. Panel *a* describes the expected course of nodal elements in $A1$ and $A2$ following the onset of a continuous stimulus. Panel *b* illustrates how the net associative strength, $V_{CS\text{-}US}$, is incremented with two selected CS durations that produce in the manner of panel *a* different proportions of CS elements in the $A1$ state at the time of US presentation. Panel *c* summarizes the predicted $\Delta V_{CS\text{-}US}$ from trials involving different CS durations, with the location of the two example cases of panel *b* indicated for reference. Reprinted from Mazur and Wagner (note 2).

be seen, the "intermediate" duration CS of panel *b* is identified with the duration producing the maximum conditioning and was so selected. With shorter CSs there would be less conditioning, as fewer CS elements would have been recruited into $A1$ by the time of the US. With longer CSs there would be less conditioning, as fewer CS elements would have remained in $A1$ but would have been more concentrated in $A2$.[7]

---

[7]It may be noted in Fig. 1.7c that with very long pre-US CS durations there is still predicted to be a positive $\Delta V_{CS\text{-}US}$. It should be pointed out that this is predicted when the CS *terminates with the US*, as was simulated in the cases of Fig. 1.7. When the CS continues for sufficiently long durations after the US as well as before the US, there will be no net associative effect, either excitatory or inhibitory.

In effect, SOP attributes an advantage to intermediate CS–US intervals on rather intuitive grounds. Such intervals serve to make the CS "well noticed" (in its $A1$ state) at the time the US is "well noticed" (in its $A1$ state).

Pretrial CSs

A closely related empirical phenomenon involves the effects of a "pretrial" presentation of a CS, as in the studies of Best and Gemberling (1977), Best, Gemberling, and Johnson (1979), Kalat and Rozin (1973), and Primavera and Wagner (cited in Wagner, 1978). Given some CS–US pairing adequate for excitatory conditioning, what will be the consequences of administering a like CS shortly before the terminal pairing? The theoretical answer is that it will depend finally on the proportion of $A1$ elements of the CS that overlap the nodal activity produced by the US. But this proportion may be either increased or decreased by a pretrial CS.

Figure 1.8 is intended to exemplify this fact in regard to a single, initial conditioning trial. For simplicity, it again assumes the use of punctate CSs and USs. On the left in panel a are depicted the courses of $A1$ and $A2$ activity in the CS node along with the $A1$ and $A2$ activity in the US node, in the case of an isolated CS–US pairing. The result is a net excitatory association. To the far right in panel a are depicted the corresponding quantities in an instance in which a "pretrial" CS has been arranged to precede closely the terminal CS–US pairing. The result in this example, in comparison to the no-pretrial-CS condition, is to *increase* the proportion of CS elements in the $A1$ state contemporaneous with the US nodal activity, and thereby to increase conditioning. This effect is essentially identical to the beneficial effect of increasing CS duration that would be expected with brief CSs as depicted in Fig. 1.7. (One may thus appreciate that it would *not* be anticipated if the trial CS were already of optimum duration, as opposed to the brief CSs assumed in this set of examples.)

In the middle graphs of panel a are depicted the theoretical activity state functions, assuming a more distant pretrial CS. In this instance, in comparison to the no-pretrial-CS condition, the effect is to *decrease* the proportion of CS elements in the $A1$ state contemporaneous with the US nodal activity, and thereby to *decrease* conditioning. The decrease occurs, of course, because at the time of the "trial" CS, the CS elements are largely in the $A2$ state and inaccessible for activation to $A1$. This is the general manner of effect emphasized by Wagner's (1976) priming notion. The more complex dependence of conditioning on the CS-trial interval, as predicted in panel b of Fig. 1.8, is in better accordance with the available data (Best & Gemberling, 1977).

That a *truly static* CS should acquire no associative tendencies with a US that occurs in its presence was arranged by assuming that $L^+/L^- = p_{d1}/p_{d2}$, and, given the values of p_{d1} and p_{d2} that had otherwise been assumed, provided the rationalization for the relative values of L^+ and L^- that have been employed throughout.

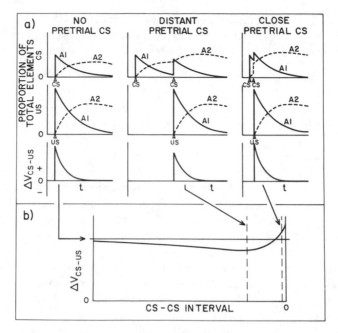

FIG. 1.8. Simulations of theoretical processes involved in a single conditioning episode in which the terminal CS–US pairing is preceded or not by a pretrial CS. Panel *a* describes the course of CS-node elements in the $A1$ and $A2$ states along with the course of US-node elements in corresponding states for three example cases that produce different changes in net associative strength, $\Delta V_{\text{CS-US}}$. Panel *b* summarizes the predicted $\Delta V_{\text{CS-US}}$ from episodes involving different CS-trial intervals, with the location of the example cases of panel *a* indicated for reference. Reprinted from Mazur and Wagner (note 2).

Pretrial USs

Conditioning may be diminished by presenting a "pretrial" US, just as it may be diminished by presenting a pretrial CS (Terry, 1976). Indeed, we know that the decremental effect may occur even when the relationship between the pretrial US and the following, trial CS would itself produce "backward" excitatory learning (Domjan & Best, 1977). Figure 1.9 exemplifies how this may arise, according to SOP, with the same punctate CSs and USs that were seen in Fig. 1.6 to generate substantial one-trial backward conditioning.

Panel *a* describes the courses of the proportion of CS elements in the $A1$ state and of US elements in the $A1$ and $A2$ states in an instance with no pretrial US (see left-hand graphs), and in an instance with a pretrial US (see right-hand graphs). What is clearly different in the latter case is a diminished proportion of $A1$ elements activated by the trial US, and a greater proportion of $A2$ elements continuing from the two USs, over the course of the $A1$ activity of the CS. Panel

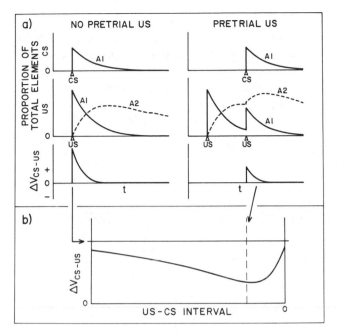

FIG. 1.9.   Simulations of theoretical processes involved in a single conditioning episode in which the terminal CS–US pairing is preceded or not by a pretrial US. Panel *a* describes the course of US-node elements in the $A1$ and $A2$ states, along with the course of CS-node elements in the $A1$ state, that produces change in net associative strength, ΔV_{CS-US}, in a case with no-pretrial US and in a case with a pretrial US. Panel *b* summarizes the predicted ΔV_{CS-US} from episodes involving different US-trial intervals, with the location of the example cases of panel *a* indicated for reference. Reprinted from Mazur and Wagner (note 2).

b summarizes the expected consequences of conditioning with the same stimuli but with variation in the US-trial interval. As may be seen, a decrement in conditioning relative to the no-pretrial-US condition is predicted at *all* intervals, with a maximum decrement at some intermediate interval.

I must add that the parameters in these examples were chosen for their direct comparability to cases presented in Figs. 1.6 and 1.8. The function shown in panel *b* is *not* prefectly general in the important respect of a pretrial US universally producing a decrement. For example, with a *weak* US (i.e., one with a low value of p_1) one may expect an incremental effect of a very closely preceding pretrial US, just as one may expect (see Fig. 1.8) an incremental effect of a closely preceding pretrial CS. But any such incremental tendency *is* universally less in the case of pretrial USs than in the case of pretrial CSs, due to the fact that a pretrial US places elements in the $A2$ state that add to inhibitory learning, V^-_{CS-US}, whereas a pretrial CS does not. (With multiple trials, of course, we would not say this.)

Posttrial Distractors

The other form of ancillary stimulation, in addition to pretrial CSs and USs, that we know to modulate associative learning is a posttrial "distractor" (Wagner et al., 1973). The way in which SOP approaches the effects of distractors is noteworthy, in the simple manner in which it correlates the effects with the usual state transition assumptions in a perfectly general manner. In moments when the nodal elements of some distractor are provoked to $A1$, this has the effect of increasing p_{d1} of all nodes (e.g., of a preceding CS and US). In moments when elements of the distractor node (or of the CS and US) subsequently enter $A2$, this has the effect of increasing p_{d2} of all nodes. Figure 1.10, panel a, illustrates the

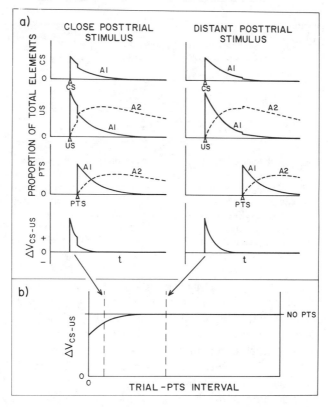

FIG. 1.10. Simulations of theoretical processes involved in a single-conditioning episode in which a CS–US pairing is followed by a posttrial, distractor stimulus. Panel a illustrates the manner in which a close or distant posttrial stimulus may alter the persisting activity in the CS and US nodes to decrease the net associative product, $\Delta V_{\text{CS-US}}$. Panel b summarizes the predicted $\Delta V_{\text{CS-US}}$ following episodes with different intervals between the trial and posttrial stimuli, with the location of the example cases of panel a indicated for reference. Reprinted from Mazur and Wagner (note 2).

consequences of these effects of a posttrial distractor (PTS) either closely following a CS–US trial or more distantly following a trial. The most salient consequences of the distractors are the decrease in $A1$ processes of the trial stimuli and the resultant decrease in net excitatory association produced by the trial. The comparable results for various trial–distractor intervals are summarized in panel b with no surprises—the shorter the interval the more decremental the effect on the CS–US association.

Multiple-Trial Acquisition and Extinction

All the examples of associative learning that have thus far been described have been restricted to cases of a single, initial conditioning trial. These cases are simple, insomuch as we can assume that on such trials the node representing each stimulus is activated only by its "own" stimulus. Over trials, of course, the important change is in the tendency for activity in one node to influence the other, via the acquisition of excitatory and inhibitory connections.

Figure 1.11 shows the important theoretical changes that are assumed to occur in relationship to the directional CS→US association over the course of simple acquisition and extinction with an extended CS. Panel a summarizes the episodic course of $A1$ activity in the CS node along with the similar courses of $A1$ and $A2$ activity in the US node, followed by the expected increments in excitatory connection, ΔV^+_{CS-US}, in inhibitory connection, ΔV_{CS-US}, and net associative connection, ΔV_{CS-US}. And it does this, separately, for the first trial of acquisition, the 50th trial of acquisition (near asymptote), and the first trial of extinction. The happenings on the first acquisition trial are familiar from preceding figures, leading to a substantial net excitatory increment. The happenings on the 50th acquisition trial are appreciably different: The $A2$ process of the US node occurs in anticipation of the US, as a result of the associative action of the CS (and is likely to be witnessed in a CR); the $A1$ process of the US node is correspondingly reduced when the US does occur. As a consequence, there is a smaller excitatory increment, a larger inhibitory increment, and a net associative change that is essentially zero. Especially noteworthy in this case is the net associative change at different points within the episode: There is first a decrement as the $A1$ state of the CS overlaps the CS-initiated $A2$ state of the US, then an increment with application of the US and the $A1$ state it produces, and finally a smaller decrement with the faster decay of $A1$ than $A2$ of the US—all balancing to near zero. The happenings on the extinction trial are simple. The CS associatively provokes US-nodal elements to the $A2$ state, which, in overlapping the $A1$ elements of the CS, produce a singular decrement in the net associative tendency. With continued extinction trials the acquisition of inhibitory tendencies will reduce the retrieval action of the CS, until no US elements are any longer provoked to activity and no learning occurs. Panel b summarizes the course of acquisition and extinction that is thus predicted.

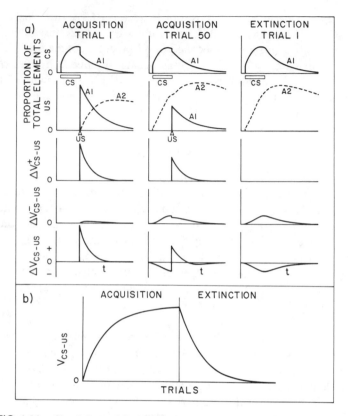

FIG. 1.11.   Simulations of theoretical processes involved in single training trials at different stages of an acquisition and extinction series. Panel *a* contrasts the courses of nodal activity and the consequent associative products on Trial 1 of acquisition, Trial 50 of acquisition, and Trial 1 of extinction. Panel *b* summarizes the predicted form of the resulting acquisition and extinction functions. Reprinted from Mazur and Wagner (note 2).

Rescorla–Wagner Model and Compound Conditioning

A large number of acquisition phenomena have been integrated by the equations of the Rescorla-Wagner model (Rescorla & Wagner, 1972; Wagner & Rescorla, 1972). Basically, the model proposes that on any conditioning trial, involving some constellation of CSs, the change in associative tendency to each of the component CSs is directly proportional to some quantity $(\lambda - \bar{V})$ where λ is the asymptotic associative strength that the US will support, and $\bar{V}$ is the summed associative strength of all the CSs present on that trial. There is no simple isomorphism between these terms and the basic processes of SOP. Yet SOP does lead to most of the same predictions, over the proper domain of the Rescorla-

Wagner model, because it similarly assumes that CSs combine to influence the associative consequences of a trial, and that these consequences involve a varying balance of incremental and decremental tendencies.

To illustrate this, we may see how SOP leads to some similar predictions as the Rescorla–Wagner model, when some CS, *X*, is trained in compound with another CS, *B*, that is either: (1) equally novel; (2) previously trained as an excitatory stimulus; or (3) previously trained as an inhibitory stimulus. Figure 1.12 summarizes, in order, for each of these cases, the expected course of acquisition for each cue in the compound phase (right panels) and in the necessary pretraining phase (left panels).

The top graph depicts the case in which *B* and *X* are equally novel during compound conditioning. The inserts are meant to indicate the course of US-nodal activity that will overlap with the CS-nodal activity at the start and at the end of

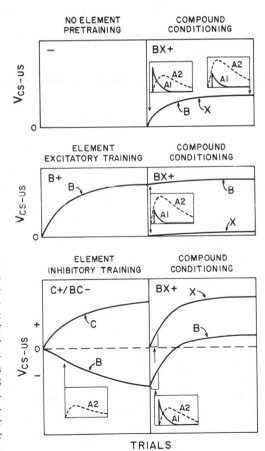

FIG. 1.12. Simulation of the acquisition of associative strength, V_{CS-US}, by the elements *B* and *X* during compound conditioning, following no pretraining of the *X* element (top panel), excitatory pretraining of the *X* element (middle panel), or inhibitory pretraining of the *X* element (bottom panel). The inserts indicate the presumed course of US node activity, important to the predicted effects, at the points in training indicated. (See text for further description.) Reprinted from Mazur and Wagner (note 2).

training. As in the previous figure, the reinforced trials are presumed to become less incremental over training because the $A2$ process of the US node is increased while the $A1$ process is diminished, by the associative effects of the CSs.

The middle graph depicts the case in which B is pretrained as an excitatory cue. The important presumption is that the course of US-nodal activity that will overlap the CS-nodal activity at the start of the compound phase has been brought to its asymptotic form by cue B alone. Thus, little additional learning occurs to either B or X, i.e., "blocking" (Kamin, 1969) occurs.

The bottom graph depicts the case in which B is pretrained as an inhibitory cue, by contrasting the reinforcement of cue C alone versus the nonreinforcement of the BC compound. In this pretraining the B cue acquires net inhibitory association, because its $A1$ process is consistently made to overlap an $A2$, US process produced by the otherwise reinforced C cue, until $V_B + V_C = 0$. What is interesting, in the compound phase, is that the inhibitory contribution from B will not initially alter the US-nodal activity. However, as B and X each acquire excitatory connections over the compound trials, the inhibitory tendencies from B will offset their combined retrieval influence, thus maintaining the total reinforcing character of the compound trials undiminished for some number of trials. That is, there will be a period of "supernormal" conditioning of X (Wagner, 1971).

CONCLUDING COMMENTS

The theoretical model that has been described was formulated with several aims. Whether or not it will satisfy our goals, either in its present form or with further development, remains largely to be determined. My strategy in the immediately preceding sections has been to let SOP speak for itself via the simulation of a variety of phenomena. I conclude with only some further reflections about the general theoretical approach.

On the Complexity of the Model

One reaction that I anticipate is the following: Do we really need to go through all of this complex mathematizing? Consider, for example, the phenomenon of the conditioned diminution of the UR. Why not more casually acknowledge that a CS is likely to produce a conditioned diminution of the UR in all response measures, but also a CR in some response measures that can overlap it. We can anticipate, then, that whether one will see a diminution or facilitation in some response on the occasion of CS$^+$US, as compared to a US alone, will depend on the combination of the two. The answer, of course, is that, casually, one can anticipate anything. Whatever one's theoretical predilections, there is need to develop *some* determinate account. And we now know, in the case of the conditioned diminution of the UR, that such account must embrace the observable variation produced with different US intensities, as well as with different response measures. SOP indicates one systematic way to do this.

One might wish that the model appealed to fewer processes and involved a smaller number of parameters. But one should not confuse the attempt to articulate assumed processes in a careful manner, or to specify the parametric choices that must be made, with their invention. In the absence of a relatively formal model such as SOP, we can more surely "fit" any outcome to our theoretical viewpoint, by undisciplined appeal to the multiple processes and parametric variation abundantly acknowledged in our more casual treatment of memory phenomena.

On the Theoretical Amalgamation

The general assumptions of SOP were guided in basic ways by a conception of the memory system that has some currency in information-processing theories. At the same time, it borrowed freely from related notions in Pavlovian conditioning, made important use of some machinery from stochastic models, and in the end has much in common with the opponent-process formulation of Solomon and Corbit (1974) and Schull (1979). This kind of amalgamation is probably guaranteed to offend devotees of each of these separate approaches. However, my colleagues and I have been encouraged in the development of SOP by the formal compatibilities that we could discern in the various approaches to different problems of learning and memory. They beg integration.

On the Restrictiveness of Assumptions

From the point of view of information-processing theories, SOP has, conscientiously, been very restrictive. It has assumed a fixed set of allowable transitions among the several states of activation under different circumstances of stimulation. For example, it assumes that an associatively activated node will always be initially provoked to the $A2$ state from which it will tend to decay back to the I state. It is certainly at odds with conventional thinking to assume that a node *cannot* be brought from the $A2$ state, corresponding to working memory, to the $A1$ state, corresponding to focal representation. What has been proposed are only what might be taken to be the standard operating procedures of automatic processing. In addition to these characteristics, one might assume (Bower, 1975; Konorski, 1967; Shiffrin & Schneider, 1977) that there are processing routines that can "search" the working memory of nodes in the $A2$ state, and promote selected ones to the $A1$ state by an act of attention. Such routines are not denied by our theorizing, but are simply relegated to the domain of controlled processing that is outside of the purview of SOP, and perhaps outside of a necessary theory of infrahuman memory.

ACKNOWLEDGMENTS

The development of SOP and preparation of the present chapter were supported by National Science Foundation grant BNS 77–16886. The theoretical formulation is the result of a series of collaborations as cited with Nelson H. Donegan, James E. Mazur, and Penn L. Pfautz. The chapter, itself, has drawn freely upon their individual and collective efforts at every juncture. These contributions are respectfully and gratefully acknowledged.

The occasion is taken to pay special thanks to Neal E. Miller. By his example and shared wisdom he has encouraged us all in the investigation of animal learning. By his interest and friendship he has supported the work of my laboratory from its beginnings. This chapter is dedicated to Neal in his 71st year.

REFERENCE NOTES

1. Donegan, N. H., & Wagner, A. R. Conditioned diminution and facilitation of the UCR: A sometimes-opponent-process interpretation. Chapter prepared for publication in I. Gormezano, W. F. Prokasy, & R. F. Thompson (Eds.), *Classical conditioning III: Behavioral, neurophysiological, and neurochemical studies in the rabbit*. Hillsdale, N.J.: Lawrence Erlbaum Associates.
2. Mazur, J. E., & Wagner, A. R. An episodic model of associative learning. Chapter prepared for publication in M. Commons, R. Herrnstein, & A. R. Wagner (Eds.), *Quantitative analyses of behavior: Acquisition* (Vol. 3). Cambridge, Mass.: Ballinger.

REFERENCES

Anderson, J. R. *Language, memory, and thought*. Hillsdale, N.J.: Lawrence Erlbaum Associates, 1976.
Anderson, J. R., & Bower, G. *Human associative memory*. New York: Winston, 1973.
Anokhin, P. K. *Internal inhibition as a problem of physiology*. Moscow: Medgiz, 1958.
Asratyan, E. A. *Compensatory adaptation, reflex activity, and the brain*. Oxford: Pergamon Press, 1965.
Atkinson, R. C., & Shiffrin, R. M. Human memory: A proposed system and its control processes. In K. W. Spence (Ed.), *The psychology of learning and motivation* (Vol. 2). New York: Academic Press, 1968.
Badia, P., Culbertson, S., & Harsh, J. Choice of longer or stronger signalled shock over shorter or weaker unsignalled shock. *Journal of the Experimental Analysis of Behavior*, 1973, *19*, 25–32.
Becker, C. A., & Killion, T. H. Interaction of visual and cognitive effects in word recognition. *Journal of Experimental Psychology: Human Perception and Performance*, 1977, *3*, 389–401.
Best, M. R., & Gemberling, G. A. The role of short-term processes in the CS preexposure effect and the delay of reinforcement gradient in long-delay taste-aversion learning. *Journal of Experimental Psychology: Animal Behavior Processes*, 1977, *3*, 253–263.
Best, M. R., Gemberling, G. A., & Johnson, P. E. Disrupting the conditioned stimulus preexposure effect in flavor-aversion learning: Effects of interoceptive distractor manipulations. *Journal of Experimental Psychology: Animal Behavior Processes*, 1979, *5*, 321–334.
Bower, G. H. A multicomponent theory of the memory trace. In K. W. Spence & J. T. Spence (Eds.), *The psychology of learning and motivation*. New York: Academic Press, 1967.

Bower, G. H. Cognitive psychology: An introduction. In W. K. Estes (Ed.), *Handbook of learning and cognitive processes* (Vol. 1). Hillsdale, N.J.: Lawrence Erlbaum Associates, 1975.

Burkhardt, P. E., & Ayres, J. J. B. CS and US duration effects in one-trial simultaneous fear conditioning as assessed by conditioned suppression of licking in rats. *Animal Learning & Behavior,* 1978, *6,* 225-230.

Bush, R. R., & Mosteller, F. *Stochastic models for learning.* New York: John Wiley & Sons, 1955.

Collins, A. M., & Loftus, E. F. A spreading activation theory of semantic processing. *Psychological Review,* 1975, *82,* 407-428.

Davis, M. Effects of interstimulus interval length and variability on startle response habituation. *Journal of Comparative and Physiological Psychology,* 1979, *72,* 177-192.

Domjan, M., & Best, M. R. Paradoxical effects of proximal unconditioned stimulus preexposure: Interference with and conditioning of a taste aversion. *Journal of Experimental Psychology: Animal Behavior Processes,* 1977, *3,* 310-321.

Donegan, N. H. *Priming produced facilitation or diminution of responding to a Pavlovian unconditioned stimulus.* Unpublished doctoral dissertation, Yale University, 1980.

Estes, W. K. Statistical theory of distributional phenomena in learning. *Psychological Review,* 1955, *62,* 369-377. (a)

Estes, W. K. Statistical theory of spontaneous recovery and regression. *Psychological Review,* 1955, *62,* 145-154. (b)

Herrnstein, R. J. Acquisition, generalization, and discrimination reversal of a natural concept. *Journal of Experimental Psychology: Animal Behavior Processes,* 1979, *5,* 116-129.

Herrnstein, R. J., Loveland, D. H., & Cable, C. Natural concepts in pigeons. *Journal of Experimental Psychology: Animal Behavior Processes,* 1976, *2,* 285-311.

Hobhouse, L. T. *Mind in evolution.* London: Macmillan and Co., 1915.

Hoffman, H. S., & Ison, J. R. Reflex modification in the domain of the startle: I. Some empirical findings and their implications for how the nervous system processes sensory input. *Psychological Review,* 1980, *87,* 175-189.

Hupka, R. B., Kwaterski, S. E., & Moore, J. W. Conditioned diminution of the UCR: Differences between the human eyeblink and the rabbit nictitating membrane response. *Journal of Experimental Psychology,* 1970, *83,* 45-51.

Kalat, J. W., & Rozin, P. "Learned safety" as a mechanism in long delay taste-aversion learning in rats. *Journal of Comparative and Physiological Psychology,* 1973, *83,* 198-207.

Kamin, L. J. Predictability, surprise, attention and conditioning. In B. Campbell & R. Church (Eds.), *Punishment and aversive behavior.* New York: Appleton-Century-Crofts, 1969.

Kimble, G. A., & Ost, J. W. P. A conditioned inhibitory process in eyelid conditioning. *Journal of Experimental Psychology,* 1961, *61,* 150-156.

Kimmel, H. D. Inhibition of the unconditioned response in classical conditioning. *Psychological Review,* 1966, *73,* 232-240.

Konorski, J. *Conditioned reflexes and neuron organization.* Cambridge: Cambridge University Press, 1948.

Konorski, J. *Integrative activity of the brain.* Chicago: University of Chicago Press, 1967.

Lockard, J. S. Choice of a warning signal or no warning signal in an unavoidable shock situation. *Journal of Comparative and Physiological Psychology,* 1963, *56,* 526-530.

Mahoney, W. J., & Ayres, J. J. B. One-trial simultaneous and backward fear conditioning as reflected in conditioned suppression of licking in rats. *Animal Learning & Behavior,* 1976, *4,* 357-362.

Meyer, D. E., Schvaneveldt, R. W., & Ruddy, M. G. Loci of contextual effects in visual word recognition. In P. M. A. Rabbitt & S. Dornic (Eds.), *Attention and performance* (Vol. 5). London: Academic Press, 1975.

Morgan, C. L. *An introduction to comparative psychology.* London: Scott, 1894.

Neely, J. H. Semantic priming and retrieval from lexical memory: The roles of inhibitionless spreading activation and limited-capacity attention. *Journal of Experimental Psychology: General*, 1977, *3*, 226-254.

Norman, D. A. Toward a theory of memory and attention. *Psychological Review*, 1968, *75*, 522-536.

Pavlov, I. P. [*Conditioned Reflexes*] (G. V. Anrep, trans.). London: Oxford University Press, 1927.

Peterson, L. R., & Peterson, M. J. Short-term retention of individual verbal items. *Journal of Experimental Psychology*, 1959, *58*, 193-198.

Pfautz, P. L. *Unconditioned facilitation and diminution of the unconditioned response*. Unpublished doctoral dissertation, Yale University, 1980.

Pfautz, P. L., Donegan, N. H., & Wagner, A. R. Sensory preconditioning versus protection from habituation. *Journal of Experimental Psychology: Animal Behavior Processes*, 1978, *4*, 286-295.

Pfautz, P. L., & Wagner, A. R. Transient variations in responding to Pavlovian conditioned stimuli have implications for mechanisms of "priming." *Animal Learning & Behavior*, 1976, *4*, 107-112.

Posner, M. I., & Snyder, C. R. R. Facilitation and inhibition in the processing of signals. In P. M. A. Rabbitt & S. Dornic (Eds.), *Attention and performance* (Vol. 5). New York: Academic Press, 1975.

Prokasy, W. F. The acquisition of observing responses in the absence of differential external reinforcement. *Journal of Comparative and Physiological Psychology*, 1956, *49*, 131-134.

Rescorla, R. A. A model of Pavlovian conditioning. In V. S. Rusinove (Ed.), *Mechanism of formation and inhibition of conditioned reflex*. Moscow: Academy of Sciences of the U.S.S.R., 1974.

Rescorla, R. A. Pavlovian excitatory and inhibitory conditioning. In W. K. Estes (Ed.), *Handbook of learning and cognitive processes: Conditioning and behavior theory* (Vol. 2). Hillsdale, N.J.: Lawrence Erlbaum Associates, 1975.

Rescorla, R. A. *Pavlovian second-order conditioning: Studies in associative learning*. Hillsdale, N.J.: Lawrence Erlbaum Associates, 1980. (a)

Rescorla, R. A. Simultaneous and successive associations in sensory preconditioning. *Journal of Experimental Psychology: Animal Behavior Processes*, 1980, *6*, 207-216. (b)

Rescorla, R. A., & Cunningham, C. L. Within-compound flavor associations. *Journal of Experimental Psychology: Animal Behavior Processes*, 1978, *4*, 267-275.

Rescorla, R. A., & Wagner, A. R. A theory of Pavlovian conditioning: Variations in the effectiveness of reinforcement and nonreinforcement. In A. H. Black & W. F. Prokasy (Eds.), *Classical conditioning* (Vol. 2). New York: Appleton-Century-Crofts, 1972.

Rizley, R. C., & Rescorla, R. A. Associations in second-order conditioning and sensory preconditioning. *Journal of Comparative and Physiological Psychology*, 1972, *81*, 1-11.

Schull, J. A conditioned opponent theory of Pavlovian conditioning and habituation. In G. H. Bower (Ed.), *The psychology of learning and motivation* (Vol. 13). New York: Academic Press, 1979.

Shiffrin, R. M., & Schneider, W. Controlled and automatic information processing: II. Perceptual learning, automatic attending, and a general theory. *Psychological Review*, 1977, *84*, 127-190.

Siegel, S. A Pavlovian conditioning analysis of morphine tolerance. In N. A. Krasnegor (Ed.), *Behavioral tolerance: Research and treatment implications. National Institute of Drug Abuse Research Monograph Series*, Number 18, 1978.

Siegel, S., & Domjan, M. Backward conditioning as an inhibitory procedure. *Learning and Motivation*, 1971, *2*, 1-11.

Solomon, R. L., & Corbit, J. D. An opponent-process theory of motivation. *Psychological Review*, 1974, *81*, 119-145.

Terry, W. S. The effects of priming US representation in short-term memory on Pavlovian conditioning. *Journal of Experimental Psychology: Animal Behavior Processes*, 1976, *2*, 354-370.

Terry, W. S., & Wagner, A. R. Short-term memory for "surprising" versus "expected" unconditioned stimuli in Pavlovian conditioning. *Journal of Experimental Psychology: Animal Behavior Processes*, 1975, *1*, 122–133.

Wagner, A. R. Elementary associations. In H. H. Kendler & J. T. Spence (Eds.), *Essays in neobehaviorism: A memorial volume to Kenneth W. Spence*. New York: Appleton–Century–Crofts, 1971.

Wagner, A. R. Priming in STM: An information processing mechanism for self-generated or retrieval-generated depression in performance. In T. J. Tighe & R. N. Leaton (Eds.), *Habituation: Perspectives from child development, animal behavior, and neurophysiology*. Hillsdale, N.J.: Lawrence Erlbaum Associates, 1976.

Wagner, A. R. Expectancies and the priming of STM. In S. H. Hulse, H. Fowler, & W. K. Honig (Eds.), *Cognitive processes in animal behavior*. Hillsdale, N.J.: Lawrence Erlbaum Associates, 1978.

Wagner, A. R. Habituation and memory. In A. Dickinson & R. A. Boakes (Eds.), *Mechanisms of learning and motivation: A memorial to Jerzy Konorski*. Hillsdale, N.J.: Lawrence Erlbaum Associates, 1979.

Wagner, A. R., & Rescorla, R. A. Inhibition in Pavlovian conditioning: Application of a theory. In R. A. Boakes & M. S. Halliday (Eds.), *Inhibition and learning*. New York: Academic Press, 1972.

Wagner, A. R., Rudy, J. W., & Whitlow, J. W. Rehearsal in animal conditioning. *Journal of Experimental Psychology*, 1973, *97*, 407–426. (Monograph)

Wagner, A. R., & Terry, W. S. Backward conditioning to a CS following an expected vs. a surprising UCS. *Animal Learning & Behavior*, 1975, *3*, 370–374.

Wagner, A. R., Thomas, E., & Norton, T. Conditioning with electrical stimulation of motor cortex: Evidence of a possible source of motivation. *Journal of Comparative and Physiological Psychology*, 1967, *64*, 191–199.

Whitlow, J. W., Jr. Short-term memory in habituation and dishabituation. *Journal of Experimental Psychology: Animal Behavior Processes*, 1975, *1*, 189–206.

Wicklegren, W. A. Multitrace strength theory. In D. A. Norman (Ed.), *Models of human memory*. New York: Academic Press, 1970.

2

Differences in Adaptiveness Between Classically Conditioned Responses and Instrumentally Acquired Responses

Ralph R. Miller
Mary Ann Balaz
State University of New York, Binghamton

The intent of this chapter is to compare both the acquisition processes and memorial structures underlying classical conditioning with those underlying instrumental learning to ascertain if there is a reasonable basis for differentiating these two types of learning. Most of the recent models of animal memory, our own included (Miller & Marlin, 1979), actually fail to differentiate classically conditioned memorial processes from those of instrumental learning. Yet, many of the currently popular textbooks and contemporary models of response generation speak of the two types of learning as if there were no doubt about their independent bases.

For a number of years, our laboratory used electroconvulsive shock to probe the nature of memory. As an explanation of one of our findings, specifically the reversibility of experimental amnesia (Lewis, Misanin, & Miller, 1968; Miller & Springer, 1972), Schneider, Tyler, and Jinich (1974) suggested that the memorial processes underlying classical conditioning differed from those responsible for instrumental learning. The details of their explanation are not relevant to this discussion; however, the basis for their distinguishing two distinct memory systems arose from an alleged difference between the two kinds of memory in vulnerability to electroconvulsive shock. In response to this hypothesis, over the past few years, we have published several studies indicating that classically conditioned memories are qualitatively equivalent to instrumentally acquired memories in their susceptibility to electroconvulsive shock (Miller & Kraus, 1977; Miller, Ott, Daniel, & Berk, 1976). However, despite the similarity of these two types of memories in respect to the induction and reversal of experimental amnesia, we grew apprehensive about the generality of our data, which had been gathered largely from instrumental preparations, and we resolved to examine critically the bases for distinguishing between classical conditioning and instrumental learning. Parenthetically we acknowledge that the issue of distinguishing Pavlovian conditioning from instrumental learning may sound somewhat archaic given the recent emphasis on the interactions of these two supposedly independent processes as seen in autoshaping and similar phenomena, but archaic questions are not necessarily poor ones.

Our basic approach consisted of making a list of the characteristics that define classical conditioning and an equivalent defining list for instrumental learning. One may conclude that there is a single process underlying these two types of learning if and only if the two lists are found to be identical. These two lists proved far too long to present and examine in detail here. For the present purposes it suffices to point out that both lists include such obvious features as negatively accelerated acquisition curves, extinction, spontaneous recovery from extinction, stimulus generalization, discrimination, overshadowing, and blocking. In fact, not only has an instrumental equivalent to blocking in classical conditioning been reported (Pearce & Hall, 1978; St. Claire-Smith, 1979), but there are reports of blocking effects across these allegedly different processes (i.e., response-stimulus associations appear able to block stimulus–stimulus associations and vice versa [Mackintosh & Dickinson, 1979]). Clearly classical conditioning and instrumental learning have many properties in common; however, there are some characteristics of each that at first glance appear to be unique.

SOME POSSIBLE DISTINCTIONS BETWEEN CLASSICAL CONDITIONING AND INSTRUMENTAL LEARNING

Before examining potential differences in the adaptiveness of the acquired responses resulting from classical conditioning and instrumental learning that constitute our focal issue, it might be useful to review briefly some of the other grounds for differentiating classical conditioning from instrumental learning that have been raised in the past.

1. Operational Definitions

As nearly every college freshman knows, the unconditioned stimulus (US) in classical conditioning is delivered independently of the behavior of the subject, whereas in instrumental learning the presentation of the reinforcer, which is comparable to the US in classical conditioning, depends on the emission of an appropriate response by the subject. Despite the frequency with which this difference is invoked, it obviously is inadequate as a fundamental distinction between the two learning processes. The two operational definitions denote a difference in the behavior of the experimenter, not necessarily any differences in the underlying processes within the subject.

2. Dependence on Memory

Closely related to their operational definitions, operant but not classically conditioned behavior is often said to be controlled by its consequences. On the one hand this suggests differences in adaptiveness, an issue constituting the central focus of this discussion starting with (10), below. (We shall argue that classically conditioned responses (CRs) are controlled by their consequences in the same sense as are operant responses.) On the other hand, to some researchers the statement implies differences in the role of memory. Specifically, if operant responding alone is controlled by its consequences, one might conclude that it is less dependent on memory than is classical conditioning. However, the consequences that control operant behavior are those that have occurred in the past in similar circumstances, a relationship required by the inevitable temporal ordering of cause and effect. Thus, there is no reason to assume that instrumental behavior is any less dependent on memory of past events than is Pavlovian conditioning.

3. Instrumental Control of the Autonomic Nervous System

It has been suggested that striated muscles are not subject to classical conditioning, and smooth muscles and glands are not subject to instrumental control. In truth, examples of classical conditioning of the skeletal system have been available for many years (Twitmyer, 1902, republished in 1974). However, in recent years considerable attention has been given to the issue of whether or not instrumental conditioning can cause an animal to modify the functioning of its autonomic nervous system (Miller, 1969). The literature on this issue is voluminous. However, an examination of this research and a reevaluation of the supporting arguments leads us to believe that this distinction is not capable of carrying much weight today, Neal Miller's (Miller & Dworkin, 1974) recent difficulty in demonstrating instrumental control of heart rate in curarized animals notwithstanding. The fact that a noncurarized animal can modify its heart rate instrumentally merely by changing its activity level leaves open a multitude of questions concerning mediating mechanisms, but to our mind constitutes an adequate example of instrumental control of the autonomic nervous system in an intact animal, albeit indirect. To ask if a less than intact animal can demonstrate comparable instrumental control is a useful question in terms of understanding mediating mechanisms, but the answer to the question in no way mitigates the importance of the phenomenon in the intact animal.

4. Differences in Anatomical Loci

Although not necessarily implying different processes for classical conditioning and instrumental learning, there have been suggestions that different regions of the brain mediate the two processes (DiCara, Braun, & Pappas, 1970). The usual hypothesis is that the neocortex is necessary for the associations underlying operant behavior but not for those underlying classical conditioning. Several of the studies of neodecorticated animals commonly cited to support this position failed to demonstrate adequately that the deficit in instrumental behavior was more than a sensory or motor disability (Bloch & Bello, 1974), a flaw that DiCara, Braun, and Pappas (1970) appear to have avoided. More to the point, Oakley (1980) and Oakley and Russell (1978) report that neodecorticated rats and rabbits are capable of instrumental learning. Furthermore, Oakley (1979) offers a plausible explanation of several of the previously reported failures to see instrumental behavior in neodecorticated animals. Finally, it should be recognized that a reasonably large degree of brain localization is seen for most functions, and future research is apt to find more. Such observations will be of interest to the classical–instrumental distinction only if greater variation in localization is seen between classical and instrumental tasks than is seen between different classical conditioning tasks and between different instrumental learning preparations. And even then, the observation of different anatomical loci would only suggest but hardly prove different underlying processes.

5. Partial Reinforcement Extinction Effect (PREE)

The superior resistance to extinction seen following partial reinforcement frequently has been considered to be a phenomenon unique to instrumental learning; however, it recently has been observed in classical conditioning as well (Gibbs, Latham, & Gormezano, 1978; Hilton, 1969; Holland, 1979). In fact, the many years that it took to obtain a PREE in a classical conditioning preparation bespeaks the recurring problem of appropriate correspondence between the critical variables of classical conditioning and those of instrumental learning.

6. Partial Reinforcement Acquisition Effect (PRAE)

The PRAE, which refers to superior asymptotic acquisition by partially reinforced animals relative to consistently reinforced animals (Weinstock, 1958), has not yet been observed in a classical conditioning paradigm; however, it should be noted that it is a rarely observed phenomenon in instrumental learning (Bacon, 1962). We do not yet know all the parameters that determine when a PRAE will occur in an instrumental setting. Thus, it is not surprising that the PRAE has not yet been produced in a classical conditioning preparation, assuming that it is in principle possible to do so. Nevertheless, at this time the PRAE stands as one possible basis for distinguishing classical conditioning from instrumental learning.

7. Differences between Discriminative Stimuli and Conditioned Stimuli

Attempts to reduce classical conditioning and instrumental learning to a single process frequently have attempted to view discriminative stimuli as conditioned stimuli (CS). Inconsistent with this notion, Mackintosh and Dickinson (1979) have pointed out that a discriminative stimulus will not block subsequent acquisition by a potential conditioned stimulus. In our view this difference may arise not from different underlying processes but rather in an error in identifying the role of various stimuli during instrumental learning. For example, it might be more appropriate to conceive of the discriminative stimulus as the basis for a conditional discrimination and think of the lever and/or the food hopper of the typical operant task as the eliciting CS.

8. S-S or S-R Connections?

Attempts to differentiate classically conditioned memories from instrumentally acquired memories frequently focus on the content of the two allegedly different kinds of associative memories. Traditionally classical conditioning results in stimulus–stimulus (S-S) associations, whereas instrumental learning results in stimulus–response (S-R) associations. Mackintosh (1974) has argued compellingly that S-R associations are better regarded as response-reinforcement ($R-S_{Reinf.}$) associations; however, such a modification still maintains the classical-instrumental distinction. This basic distinction in the knowledge structure (see Dickinson's chapter in this volume) is not an issue that can be lightly dismissed. Nevertheless we shall gloss over the potential distinction in the present discussion by suggesting the universality of an $S-R-S_{Reinf.}$ model. The issue would then reduce itself to the degree of control that the response has over the reinforcer. We are inclined to view classical conditioning and instrumental learning as opposite ends of a continuum along which the response goes from having no control to total control over the effective magnitude of the reinforcer.

9. Arbitrariness of the Response

It has often been pointed out that the response in classical conditioning is innately determined, whereas in instrumental learning the critical response can be defined arbitrarily by the experimenter. The recent research on autoshaping and similar phenomena emphasizing differences in the propensity of an animal to emit one operant response as opposed to another as a function of both discriminative stimulus and reinforcer (Hearst & Jenkins, 1974; Moore, 1973; Shettleworth, 1972) has surely caused psychologists to reappraise their notions concerning the arbitrariness of operant responses. However, the apparent distinction still remains that within restricted bounds CRs are hard wired into the animal, whereas instrumental responses are not so rigidly constrained. We do not deny this distinction, but are inclined to view it as akin to the difference in operational definitions. If one assumes that the function of a CR is to improve the state of the world for the subject, either by reducing the damage inflicted by an aversive stimulus or enhancing the benefit of an appetitive stimulus, then CRs may be thought of as the efforts (largely of innate determination) of the animal to make the best of the anticipated US under conditions in which the impinging US is unmodifiable. Instrumental responses are not really any more arbitrary. They are merely defined by the same variables plus the experimenter-imposed reinforcement contingency. From this viewpoint the seeming arbitrariness of operant responses in contrast to classically conditioned responses can be regarded as arising from the experimenter-imposed reinforcement contingencies of instrumental learning rather than in any difference in processes within the subject.

10. Adaptive Value of the Response

The foregoing remarks concerning the arbitrariness of operant responses as opposed to CRs have presumed the existence of a functional value to response plasticity in *both* instrumental and classical preparations. Whereas there may well be other potential distinctions between classically conditioned and instrumentally acquired memories than the adaptiveness of the responses they each support, for the remainder of this discussion we plan to focus on possible adaptive differences in the processes underlying classical conditioning and instrumental learning, that is, ultimate differences between the two processes rather than the proximal ones to which we have alluded thus far. During this discussion, it should be kept in mind that ultimate causes of behavior, whether or not voiced in terms of adaptiveness, are not meant as substitutes for explanations at the proximal level of analysis. A common adaptive basis for classical conditioning and instrumental learning would suggest, but not assure common proximal mechanisms for the implementation of this shared adaptiveness. However, a lack of shared adaptiveness would make common proximal mechanisms most unlikely.

CONSIDERATIONS CONCERNING THE ADAPTIVENESS OF CLASSICAL CONDITIONING

Instrumentally acquired memories support behaviors that ordinarily have rather clear benefits for the performing animal in terms of survival and ultimately procreation. Surely there are exceptions to this rule; examples of dysfunctional behavior include such phenomena as negative automaintenance (Williams & Williams, 1969) and vicious-circle behavior (Gwinn, 1949), but these effects are ordinarily the result of presenting contingencies diametrically opposed to expectations that are either inherent due to conditions in the species' evolutionary past or a product of past experience. Moreover, the benefits of at least some instrumental behavior often are easier to view as "local adaptations" than as factors contributing to genetic propagation. This distinction between local adaptations and reproduction of the fittest is worthy of detailed consideration; however, we give short shrift to this problem here by simply noting that there is a high positive correlation between behavior immediately resulting in improved affect and behavior yielding a reproductive advantage.

Whereas the adaptiveness of instrumentally modified behavior is generally apparent, the functional value of most classically conditioned associations is far less obvious. There is little difficulty in seeing the advantage of being able to develop a conditioned eyelid response in anticipation of an air puff, or being able to develop a conditioned salivary response in expectation of dry food, but what about the majority of conditioned responses? For example, where is the evolutionary advantage in a conditioned knee flexion in anticipation of a patellar blow, in a conditioned galvanic skin response in expectation of electric shock, or in a swallowing response in anticipation of food?

By definition, a CR does not change the physical properties of the subsequent US, but it is possible that a component of the CR syndrome changes the biological consequences of the US. Such a notion has a long history. Pavlov (1927) among others seems to have been favorably predisposed to the idea, but he never emphasized it in his theorizing. In fact, his theory of stimulus substitution is often erroneously offered as a competing hypothesis when in fact it could be viewed as a method of modulating the consequences of the US. Schlosberg, in some of his writings (e.g., 1937), gave great weight to the possiblity of the CR influencing the effective US. In more recent times, Perkins' Preparatory Response (RT) Hypothesis (1955, 1968) and Lykken's Perception Hypothesis (Lykken & Tellegen, 1974) have again focused on the influence of the CR upon the biologically effective US. The PR Hypothesis appears clearly applicable to some classical conditioning preparations such as eye blink and salivation, but can it be applied to most classical conditioning preparations? (A few failures would be tolerable, as there are occasional examples of dysfunctional instrumental behavior.)

A number of observations provide support for, but not conclusive proof of, the PR Hypothesis. For example Scott and Barber (1977) found that pain tolerance in humans is increased when an aversive US is preceded by a CS. Consistently there are numerous reports that URs to aversive USs decrease as a result of conditioning (Kimble & Ost, 1961; Kimmel, 1966; Kimmel & Burns, 1975). Assuming that unconditioned response (UR) magnitude reflects the biological impact of the US, this observation suggests that the conditioned animal finds the US less noxious than the unconditioned subject. Moreover, after asymptotic acquisition the peak magnitude of the CR has been found ordinarily to occur immediately prior to the US (Martin & Levey, 1969; Prokasy, 1965), consistent with the notion that the CR helps prepare the animal for the US.

Arguments favoring a common adaptive view of both classically conditioned and instrumentally acquired responses have sometimes, especially in the 1930s, 40s, and 50s, taken the form of defending "response shaping" as prescribed by the Strong Law of Effect as the basis for both types of learning (Schlosberg, 1937). This particular position has been subject to much criticism (Coleman & Gormezano, 1979) on the grounds that it cannot account for the generation of the first CR, and more generally it has been demonstrated with both restrained and curarized animals that responding per se is not necessary for the acquisition of a conditioned response (Solomon & Turner, 1962). However, both of these issues pose equal problems to a Strong Law of Effect interpretation of instrumental learning. This is not the place to go into a lengthy discussion of the current status of the Law of Effect; however, we believe that the idea of reinforcement being necessary for any acquisition to occur has been obsolete ever since Tolman's (1932) critique, which correctly noted that the primary consequence of response reinforcement is not acquisition of associations, but rather is alteration of the likelihood and perhaps the patterning of the response. Notably, there are a few studies that pose problems for a reinforcement view of classical conditioning whether reinforcement is regarded as necessary for acquisition or as merely a motivating performance variable. For example, Prokasy and Kumpfer (1969) performed separate analyses of the immediate consequences of CR trials as opposed to non-CR trials, and found that the probability of a conditioned eyelid response increased more following a non-CR trial than following a CR trial. Such data appear to present serious problems for the PR Hypothesis; however, in principle one could argue that the putative response-shaping benefit of a CR trial was more than counteracted in this instance by the CS having been paired with an effectively less intense US owing to the preparatory value of the CR.

Early research seeking support for a role of preparatory responding in classical conditioning often sought to identify the preparatory response and its specific benefits. These endeavors proved rather fruitless primarily because of the complexity of most CR syndromes, of which the traditionally measured CR is only one component, and an *arbitrary* one at that. Possible mechanisms for preparing for the delivery of the US include gross postural adjustments (Wagner, Thomas, & Norton, 1967), local preparations such as muscle tensing or modified receptor sensitivity, and central nervous system preparations such as modulation of the affective pathways or the conditioned release of endorphins (Fanselow, 1979).

Our own research, in an effort toward producing a uniprocess theory of learning and memory, sought support for the PR Hypothesis, not in identifying the preparatory response, but in documenting its beneficial consequences. In truth, we never attempted to measure survival or procreative value, but assumed that the animal was prewired as a result of natural selection such that there was a high correlation between affective value and survival value. Essentially we asked, does classical conditioning make the world more pleasant for the animal?

PREFERENCE FOR SIGNALED SHOCK

The Nature and Importance of the Phenomenon.   As an experimental preparation, we first sought a situation that on the one hand did not appear to be especially amenable to the PR Hypothesis, but on the other hand did seem to lend itself to an analysis of the affective consequences of a CR. With these considerations in mind, we selected the preference-for-signaled-shock (PSS) phenomenon (Badia, Culbertson, & Harsh, 1973; Lockard, 1963). PSS consists of an animal choosing to receive a signaled shock in preference to an unsignaled shock despite the shock being overtly unavoidable and unmodifiable. In essence the subject is apparently electing to be conditioned, an impressive phenomenon that should make the heart of every Darwinian beat a little faster. (Preference for information about unmodifiable appetitive reinforcement is less interesting because it can be attributed to the acquired positive reinforcement value of the signal; in the case of aversive reinforcement the secondary reinforcement value of the signal would be expected to produce a preference for the unsignaled situation in contradiction to the observed PSS.)

The three theories traditionally offered to explain the PSS phenomenon are illustrated in Fig. 2.1. This figure also indicates the different temporal elements of the PSS paradigm during which each hypothesis posits the critical change in affect to be occurring. The temporal sequence consists of a variable time inter-trial interval, followed by a warning signal that is present or absent depending on the behavior of the animal, after which the inevitable shock occurs. In various demonstrations of the PSS effect, different experimenters have chosen in the unsignaled condition to present the signal explicitly unpaired with the shock, to present the signal truly randomly with respect to the shock, to have the signal occur immediately following the shock, or to omit the signal entirely. Each of these variations appear to produce equivalent results (Miller, Marlin, & Berk, 1977).

PREFERENCE − FOR − SIGNALED − SHOCK

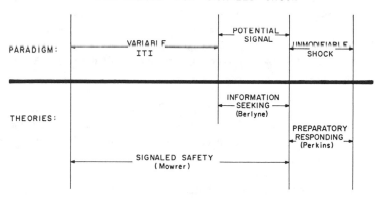

FIG. 2.1.   The temporal sequence of events giving rise to the PSS phenomenon is illustrated above the heavy line. Three traditional explanations of the PSS effect, the researcher who originally stated the hypothesis, and the temporal interval in which the signaled condition is alleged to be more desirable than the unsignaled condition are represented below the heavy line. Fanselow's (1980) explanation stressing the acquired aversiveness of apparatus cues in the unsignaled condition is a variation of Mowrer's (1960) Signaled-Safety Hypothesis in that it emphasizes differences in conditioned aversiveness during the intershock interval.

The PR explanation of PSS, at least in its early form (Perkins, 1968; but see Perkins, 1971 for a more general version of the PR position), posits that the PSS effect arises as a result of the preparatory response rendering the shock less aversive. As the shock in PSS is defined to be unavoidable and unmodifiable, the preparatory response presumably occurs inside the organism somewhere between the receptors sensitive to shock and the pathway in the brain whose activity is the essence of aversiveness. Alternate interpretations of the PSS phenomenon include Mowrer's (1960) and Seligman's (1968) Signaled-Safety Hypothesis, which argues that animals prefer the signaled conditioned, not because the shock is made less aversive, but because of a reduction in the aversive anxiety experienced during the intertrial interval. In the unsignaled condition the animal is condemned to sit in fear and trembling waiting for the unpredictable shock, whereas in the signaled condition the animal can relax until the warning signal is presented. Fanselow (1980) has recently proposed an explanation of the PSS effect, based on the Rescorla–Wagner (1972) theory of differential conditioning, that, like the Signaled-Safety Hypothesis, is concerned with differences in conditioned aversiveness between the apparatus cues of the unsignaled condition and those of the signaled condition. A third distinctive interpretation of the PSS phenomenon arises from Berlyne's (1960) Information-Seeking Hypothesis, which was developed in a very broad framework without specific reference to the PSS effect. Perhaps oversimplifying a bit, Berlyne believed that due to the occasional reproductive advantages of having general knowledge about one's environment, animals have evolved as generalized information seekers. The notion is intriguing, but in a world overly abundant with information, one would think that indiscriminate information gathering would overload an animal's processing and perhaps storage capacity. And once one begins generating selection rules for information, the Information-Seeking Hypothesis degenerates into one or another of the competing hypotheses as a function of the particular selection rules that are adopted.

Reliability of Preference for Signaled Shock.   Before attempting to differentiate between these competing but not necessarily exclusive explanations of the PSS phenomenon, we felt the need to convince ourselves that the effect was real, as there was some question concerning this in the literature (Biederman & Furedy, 1970, 1976). Initially we elected to use a two-compartment shuttle box preparation in which freely ambulatory rats received 0.5-sec footshock on a variable time schedule. A 5-sec tone preceded the footshock when the animals were in one compartment but not the other. A number of studies determined that it made no difference to the outcome if in the unsignaled condition the tone was presented immediately following the footshock, on a truly random schedule in respect to the footshock, or not at all. In each case, a distinct preference was established for the signaled shock condition within a few hundred pairings typically distributed over 2 to 4 days. After the rats established a distinct preference for the compartment in which signaled shock was given, we ordinarily reversed the signal conditions associated with the two compartments of the shuttle box. The resultant reversal in the animals' preference behavior assured us that their preferences were under the control of the tone–shock relationship rather than merely a preference for one compartment over another due to factors other than the tone–footshock relationship (Miller, Marlin, & Berk, 1977). In other studies we counterbalanced across animals for which of the two distinctive compartments would be associated with the signaled shock rather than doing successive reversals within animals. Typical of the consistent preference we found for signaled shock over unsignaled shock are the data presented in Fig. 2.2. These results are consistent with numerous other studies using footshock (Badia et al., 1973).

Although we had no trouble in obtaining a preference for signaled footshock, observation of the animals determined that during the warning tone they frequently made small postural adjustments (Marlin, Berk, & Miller, 1978). These modifications of posture ordinarily took the form of raising the forepaws a few millimeters off the floor and placing more of their total body weight on their rear legs. Measurements of total current flow through the animal on any given foot-

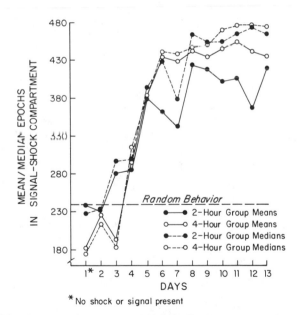

FIG. 2.2.   Representative example of the PSS effect in two groups of rats receiving 96 scrambled footshocks a day. The two groups differed only in whether each daily session was 2 or 4 hr long. Each session was divided into 480 epochs. Each group was counterbalanced for which compartment provided the signaled shock. (From Miller, Marlin, & Berk [1977], copyright of the Psychonomic Society, reprinted with permission.)

shock indicated that the postural adjustment did not change the net amount of current flowing through an animal; however, it clearly altered the current density distribution that the animal experienced, thereby making it extremely likely that the aversiveness of the shock had been modified. This subtle, but potentially important, *overt* modification of the scrambled footshock used in these studies suggested that the observed PSS effect was no more than a subtle form of instrumental behavior (i.e., a postural adjustment reinforced by a reduction in aversiveness of the footshock). To eliminate this problem and determine if we could obtain a PSS with the shock being truly unmodifiable, we developed a fixed electrode version of the shuttle box that eliminated many of the problems that arose in an earlier demonstration (Perkins, Seymann, Levis, & Spencer, 1966) of PSS using fixed electrodes. This apparatus is illustrated in Fig. 2.3. (For further detail, see Berk, Marlin, & Miller, 1977).

Using a fixed electrode tailshock, we obtained the PSS effect almost as easily as it had been with footshock (Miller, Daniel, & Berk, 1974). Therefore, it is

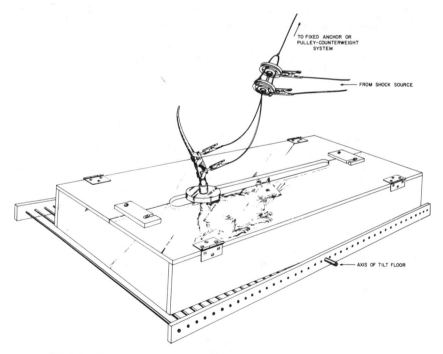

FIG. 2.3.   Fixed tail electrode preparation for rats in a shuttle box. The walls of each of the two compartments of the shuttle box were distinctly different from the other. The compartments were separated by a hurdle that added to the distinctiveness of the shuttle response and limited visibility of one compartment from the other compartment. (From Berk, Marlin, & Miller [1977], copyright of Brain Research Publications, reprinted with permission.)

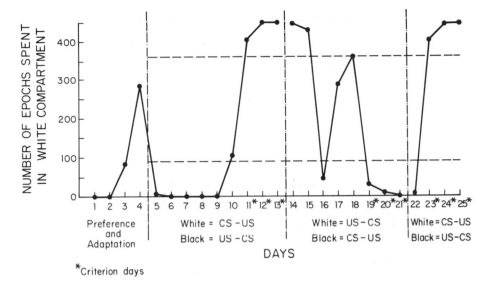

FIG. 2.4. Representative example of the PSS effect in one rat receiving 112 tailshocks from fixed electrodes during each 90-min daily session, which was divided into 450 epochs. Neither signals nor shocks were presented on Days 1–4; arbitrarily, time on the white side is illustrated for these sessions. Each time the animal showed a preference of 80% or better for one side on three consecutive days, the signal conditions correlated with the two compartments were reversed, with the exception of the strong black compartment preference that appeared on Days 5–9. These sessions corresponded to the first 5 days of tailshocks, which probably produced a stress-induced preference for darkness. Dashed lines denote the 80% criterion. (From Miller, Marlin, & Berk [1977], copyright of the Psychonomic Society, reprinted with permission.)

likely that the subtle changes in posture that we observed during signals that announced footshock contributed little to the PSS effect obtained with footshock. However, to eliminate any possibility whatsoever of the animals overtly modifying the shock, we decided to perform all subsequent experiments using fixed electrode tailshock rather than footshock. Typical of the PSS effect obtained with this preparation are the data presented in Fig. 2.4. Clearly, rats will repeatedly alter their positions in the shuttle box in order to maintain the signaled condition.

Basis of Preference for Signaled Shock.   Having established to our own satisfaction the validity of the PSS effect, we attempted to differentiate between the contending explanations. One such study was designed to minimize the contribution of Signaled Safety to choice behavior (Marlin, Sullivan, Berk, & Miller, 1979). This was done by signaling all shocks given in either compartment of the shuttle box. However, rather than have all the tailshocks of the same intensity we now used two randomly interspersed shock intensities, with each

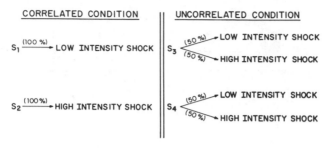

P (SHOCK | $\bar{S}_i$) = O IN BOTH CONDITIONS

FIG. 2.5.   Stimulus contingencies for the experiment in which all tailshocks were signaled, but rats had the option of receiving information about the intensity of impending shock. (From Marlin, Sullivan, Berk, & Miller [1979], copyright of Academic Press, reprinted with permission.)

intensity presented on 50% of the trials. Additionally, rather than having a single tone we now used four. Two of the tones were presented only in one compartment and the other two tones were presented only in the other compartment. In the first compartment one tone always preceded low intensity tailshock (.6 mA for all animals), whereas the other tone always preceded high intensity tailshock (1.3 mA for half the animals and 1.8 mA for the other half). In the other compartment each tone was followed by low intensity tailshock 50% of the time and high intensity tailshock the remaining 50% of the time. Across animals we counterbalanced as to which tones meant what, thereby avoiding the possibility that any observed preference behavior was due to unconditioned differential affective value of the auditory signals. As all shocks in this study were signaled, this was not a true PSS experiment. Instead we were giving rats an opportunity to display a preference for information about the intensity of the impending tailshock. The paradigm for this study is outlined in Fig. 2.5.

Prior to our actually performing this study, we established that all the tailshock intensities to be used in the experiment would support a significant PSS. With this information in hand, we proceeded with the experiment outlined in Fig. 2.5. The results of this experiment are illustrated in Fig. 2.6.

As is evident in Fig. 2.6, the animals for whom the tailshock was 0.6 mA half of the time and 1.8 mA the other half of the time displayed a clear preference for information concerning the intensity of the impending shock. As all shocks were signaled, there was no difference between the two compartments in the availability of signaled safety. Thus, the observed preference suggests that the PR Hypothesis and/or the Information-Seeking Hypothesis are valid and capable of contributing to choice behavior. This is not to imply that there is no validity to the Signaled-Safety Hypothesis, but rather that when it is eliminated as a factor contributing to preference behavior based on information about tailshock, there are still other factors remaining that cause an animal to prefer the more informa-

tive condition. It should be mentioned that D'Amato and Safarjan (1979) performed a similar study, only they used footshock and varied shock duration
rather than using tailshock and varying intensity as we did. Despite these differences their data are entirely consistent with ours.

An unexpected windfall of our study was the lack of preference exhibited by
animals given .6-mA tailshock half of the time and 1.3-mA tailshock the other
half of the time. Other shuttle box studies in our laboratory had determined that if
rats were given a choice between .6 mA and 1.3 mA, they would consistently
elect to receive the .6-mA tailshock; therefore, these two shock levels were both
discriminable and differentially aversive. As such, information regarding which
of these two shocks was about to be administered was meaningful to the animals;
yet, they did not choose to obtain this information when it was available. This
finding is directly contradictory to the Information-Seeking Hypothesis. Of
course the Information-Seeking Hypothesis can be made compatible with the
data if one applies selection rules to differentiate between different types of
information, information that will be sought and information that will not be
sought. However, this would no longer be the Information-Seeking Hypothesis,
but rather on the basis of the specific selection rule used it would constitute one
or another of the alternate explanations of the observed choice behavior. The
indifferent behavior of the group receiving the .6 and 1.3-mA tailshock is no

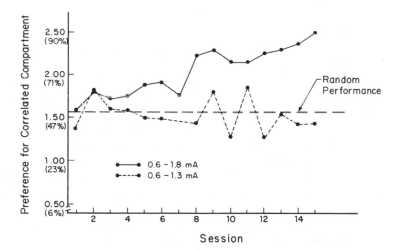

FIG. 2.6.   Mean square-root arc sine of percentage of 1200 30-second epochs
spent in the compartment in which tailshock intensity was signaled. The untrans-
formed percentages of epochs per session represented by these values are given in
parentheses. Each session consisted of 1200 epochs with shock occurring on a
random 300 of them. Half of the shocks were of high intensity and half were of
low intensity. Neither shocks nor signals were presented during Session 1. (From
Marlin, Sullivan, Berk, & Miller [1979], copyright of Academic Press, reprinted
with permission.)

problem for the PR Hypothesis if it is assumed that these two levels of shock, although differentially aversive, maximally benefit from the same preparatory response. The joint behavior of the two groups in this study caused us to conclude that the Information-Seeking Hypothesis, in its unmodified form, was incorrect, and that the Signaled-Safety Hypothesis might be correct but was inadequate to explain all the observed choice behavior.

We published these dual-intensity tailshock studies (Marlin et al., 1979) with a conclusion supportive of the PR Hypothesis based on our rejection of the two traditional competing explanations. However, arguments by negation are notoriously weak due to their dependence on a fixed and exhaustive list of alternative explanations, and in short order, Michael D'Amato pointed out to us that our data, in rejecting Signaled Safety and Information Seeking as explanations, did not leave the PR Hypothesis uncontested. Using the Rescorla–Wagner (1972) model of conditioning to calculate the acquired aversiveness of each of the four tones, we found that the mean acquired aversiveness for the two tones both signaling high and low intensity is more than the mean acquired aversiveness of the two tones when one tone consistently signals high intensity shock and the other consistently signals low intensity shock. Hence, our tailshock intensity data did not provide unambiguous support for the PR Hypothesis in the PSS phenomenon.

CONDITIONED TAIL FLEXION: CR-CONTINGENT MODIFICATION OF TAILSHOCK INTENSITY

Schlosberg (1934, 1936), in his efforts to obtain support for a Strong Law of Effect in classical conditioning, performed a series of omission experiments. These studies were predicated on the reasoning that, if classical conditioning was supported by covert reinforcement, the addition of an overt reinforcement contingency ought to summate with the covert reinforcement. Schlosberg used an aversive US, specifically electric shock, that for some animals was withheld whenever a CR was produced in response to the immediately preceding CS. It is important to note that the enhanced responding that Schlosberg expected could have been attributed, not only to superior acquisition (or performance) owing to the summation of reinforcement, but also to a number of other factors, including response summation based on two different underlying associative processes. However, a failure to observe improved performance as a result of the omission procedure would be a distinct embarrassment to either a Strong Law of Effect interpretation of classical conditioning or its modern equivalent, the PR Hypothesis.

If covert reinforcement was necessary for the continued generation of classically conditioned responses, augmented reinforcement in the form of the omission contingency should have yielded improved performance. Yet, Schlosberg found that superimposing an overt instrumental avoidance contingency on a classically conditioned preparation using an aversive US either failed to alter responding or actually diminished it. One of his studies (1936), which used a leg flexion measure, can be discounted because the data suggest that his preparation was inadequate to produce classical conditioning. However, a second experiment measuring tail flexion in rats (1934) cannot be so easily dismissed.

The problem with this latter study of Schlosberg's, and for that matter all experiments in which an aversive US is omitted whenever a CR is made, is that withholding the US not only reinforces the CR but also serves as an extinction trial. Gormezano and Coleman (1973) recognized this problem and modified the omission procedure, taking advantage of the fact that instrumental conditioning requires not that the instrumental response determine the presence or absence of reinforcement, but only that the response modulate the degree of reinforcement (Bersh & Alloy, 1980). Coleman (1975) performed one experiment using rabbits in which a conditioned nictitating membrane response attenuated, but did not fully eliminate, the subsequent shock serving as the US. Based on the observation that CRs tend to increase with US intensity when there is no CR contingency, traditional conditioning theory would predict that the occasional reduction in shock intensity resulting from Coleman's manipulation would if anything *reduce* overall conditioned responding; however, if classical conditioning is sensitive to reinforcement principles, response-contingent reduction of shock should *increase* conditioned responding. In fact Coleman found no increase in responding and concluded that CRs were relatively impervious to instrumental reinforcement, a position inconsistent with covert instrumental reinforcement being the basic mechanism underlying classical conditioning. Moreover, using the same paradigm in a human eyelid conditioning preparation with an air puff as the US, Clark and Prokasy (1976) obtained similar results.

Because of our strong intuition about the correctness of the PR Hypothesis, we here hesitant to accept the implications of Coleman's (1975) and Clark and Prokasy's (1976) results. Moreover, neither of these two reports provided or cited evidence that the changes in US intensity employed in these studies were able to support choice behavior in a traditional instrumental situation. Additionally, the shock electrodes on Coleman's rabbits were sufficiently far from the eye that the UR may have been more of a facial twitch than a readily discriminable nictitating membrane response (Salafia, Martino, Cloutman, & Romano, 1979). These reservations prompted us to perform a similar series of studies employing response-contingent modification of shock (Miller, Greco, & Vigorito, 1981), only we used restrained rats in a tail-flexion preparation similar to Schlosberg's. A small magnet tied to each rat's tail was suspended in an induction coil in order to sense tail flexions, and tailshock was applied through fixed electrodes.

We designed our first experiment in this series to determine if the observed tail flexions did indeed reflect an underlying associative process. One group of animals received 100 tone–tailshock pairings each day, whereas a truly random control group received the tone and tailshock independent of one another.

Indicative of the associative basis of tail flexions in our preparation, we found a difference in response frequency between these groups (Fig. 2.7). Moreover, after asymptotic responding was achieved, tailshock was discontinued, thereby extinguishing associations to the tone. The subsequent decrement in responding speaks for the postasymptotic sensitivity of our preparation to changes in stimulus contingencies.

In a second preliminary study we exposed independent groups of rats to three different tailshock intensities to ascertain if these shock intensities, despite their differences, were sufficiently similar to yield equivalent degrees of conditioning when US delivery was independent of the occurrence of the CR. Again we gave animals 100 variable time CS–US pairings per day. The conditioning asymptotes were in fact similar and assured us that later response-contingent switching between shock intensities would not result in changes in responding merely because one shock intensity was able to support more or less conditioning than another. The data from this study are presented in Fig. 2.8.

Whereas it was essential that the CR-contingent tailshock intensities we planned to use support equal degrees of classical conditioning, it was also necessary that the different shock intensities be differentially aversive so as to allow

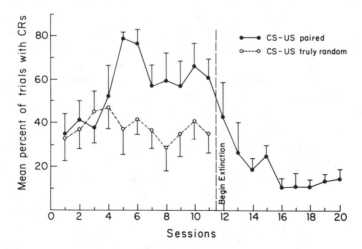

FIG. 2.7.   Mean percentage of conditioned tail flexions during 100 daily CS-tailshock presentations. The CS was an auditory signal and the US was a tailshock. Brackets indicate standard errors. The CS–US Paired group was conditioned to asymptote with a 1.6-mA US, after which the US was discontinued (extinction). The Truly Random group was run for the duration of conditioning of the Paired groups. (From Miller, Greco, & Vigorito [1981], copyright of the Psychonomic Society, reprinted with permission.)

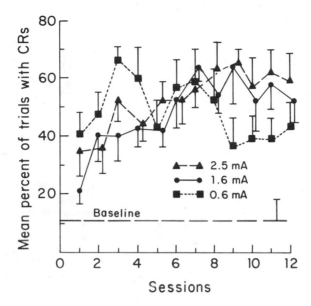

FIG. 2.8.   Mean percentage of conditioned tail flexions during 100 daily CS–tailshock presentations as a function of tailshock (US) intensity. Brackets indicate standard errors. Baseline reflects responding to the first CS in Session 1. (From Miller, Greco, & Vigorito [1981], copyright of the Psychonomic Society, reprinted with permission.)

reinforcement of CRs. Therefore, we performed a series of shuttle box studies in which rats were found to display consistently a preference for the reduced tailshock (.6 mA) over the standard tailshock (1.6 mA), and a preference for the standard tailshock (1.6 mA) over the increased tailshock (2.5 mA).

In the central study in this series, we presented rats with 100 CS–US pairings a day (US = 1.6-mA tailshock) until responding was asymptotic. After reaching asymptote, we subjected different groups to either a tailshock omission contingency, a tailshock increment contingency, or a tailshock decrement contingency. There was also a response-independent control group, and a yoked-decrement group that received USs reduced from 1.6 mA to .6 mA as frequently as shock was reduced for the average .6-mA CR-contingent tailshock decrement animal.

As can be seen in Fig. 2.9, overt reinforcement superimposed on a classical conditioning baseline did not alter responding in a fashion consistent with operant expectations. US omission impaired responding, and neither response-contingent US decrements nor increments had much effect. Thus, using a preparation quite dissimilar to that of Gormezano and Coleman (1973), our data fully supported their conclusions and made these conclusions more compelling

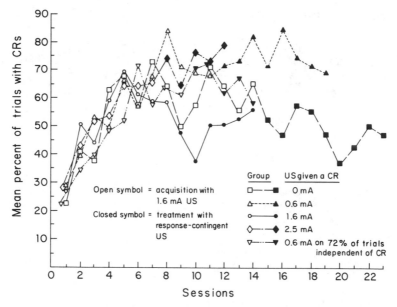

FIG. 2.9. Mean percentage of conditioned tail flexions during 100 daily CS–tailshock presentations. Prior to an acquisition asymptote (open data points), all USs were 1.6 mA of shock. After reaching acquisition asymptotes (closed data points), US intensity became contingent on the occurrence or absence of a CR, except for Group 0.6-I, which had a random 72% of its postacquisition USs reduced from 1.6 mA to 0.6 mA, thereby matching the overall daily shock experience of Group 0.6. If an animal in a response-contingent group did not produce a CR on a given trial, tailshock remained at the 1.6 mA used in acquisition. (From Miller, Greco, & Vigorito [1981], copyright of the Psychonomic Society, reprinted with permission.)

through the inclusion of additional control groups. In summary, both classically conditioned tail flexion and nictitating membrane responses appear relatively impervious to instrumental contingencies, a state of affairs seemingly inconsistent with covert instrumental reinforcement underlying classical conditioning.

CHANGES IN AFFECTIVE VALUE
OF THE US AS A FUNCTION OF SIGNALING

To date each of our tests of the PR Hypothesis of classical conditioning was based on indirect measures (i.e., preference for a signal given an unmodifiable US, and the influence of instrumental contingencies superimposed on classically conditioned associations). Any final decision concerning the validity of the PR Hypothesis would require a more direct test. Specifically, psychological tests in which the subject must rate the affective quality of the US are required to determine if an unpleasant US decreases in aversiveness as a consequence of its being signaled and a pleasant US increases in appetitive value as a consequence of its being signaled. A number of researchers using human subjects have attempted to answer this question, but the results have been equivocal. For example, D'Amato and Gumenik (1960) reported that anticipated shock is less aversive than unanticipated shock, whereas Furedy and Doob (1972) found no such reduction in aversiveness of shock. Notably, Furedy and his colleagues have been presenting both indirect and direct evidence contrary to the PR Hypothesis for many years, evidence to which we would be inclined to give greater weight if they were able to replicate certain effects consistently seen by others. Over a multitude of published studies (Biederman & Furedy, 1970, 1976), they have not been able to obtain the basic PSS phenomenon with scrambled footshock that has been witnessed in over a dozen other laboratories without any difficulty. Perhaps part of the inconsistency in the human experimental literature arises from the influence of the situational demand characteristics present in these studies. We intended our last series of studies to be a direct test of the PR Hypothesis using rats as subjects. Essentially, we wished to know if, given parameters that supported PSS, those tailshocks that followed a signal were less detrimental than unannounced shocks. Again we made the assumption that aversiveness is directly related to the damage that shock was capable of producing.

The apparatus that we used in these psychophysical studies of aversiveness consisted of twelve specially modified two-lever operant chambers. On the chamber wall opposite the operant levers was a horizontal slit running the length of the chamber, through which the animal's tail passed. Two electrodes were attached to the tail on the far side of this slit such that the animal could not chew on the electrode. Each chamber was also equipped with a water dipper, a houselight, and a speaker. Water-deprived rats were shaped to obtain water on most of 200 daily discrete trials occurring on a variable time schedule during each daily 6-hour session. Every trial consisted of the houselight going on for 5 sec, announcing that pressing one of the two levers would yield water. Trials ended as soon as one lever had been pressed. If the correct lever was selected, the rat received a dipperful of water. If the incorrect lever was depressed first, the rat was subjected to a correction trial following a delay. We provided the rat with information as to which of the two levers was correct in the form of a tailshock that immediately preceded the onset of the houselight. If the tailshock was weak (initially 0.4 mA), as was the case in half the trials, one lever was correct; if it was strong (initially 1.0 mA), the other lever was correct.

Teaching rats this discrimination was not as difficult as we had expected. In shaping, we first taught the rats to discriminate between cue lights over each of the levers, and then we slowly increased tailshock intensity while fading out the cue lights. The high and low tailshock intensities were adjusted until the average animal was correct about 85% of the time. By this stage of shaping we found that the correction trials were not necessary to maintain performance, this being indicative of performance being motivated by water reinforcement rather than avoidance of the tailshock on correction trials. Not only could the rats discriminate the two levels of tailshock, but in a separate shuttle box study, rats made choices indicating that both our high and low intensity tailshocks were aversive relative to no shock. Finally, when animals achieved the 85% discrimination criterion, an intermediate intensity tailshock was presented on 20% of the daily trials. A randomly selected half of all the lever presses in response to the intermediate level shock were reinforced. We titrated the intensity of the intermediate level tailshock until animals responded to it by pressing each of the two levers on roughly half of these trials. This behavior was obtained with an intermediate level tailshock of .8 mA. Fig. 2.10 illustrates the hypothetical psychophysical functions for these three intensities of tailshock. Incidentally, we reconfirmed the classical finding that the function relating sensation to shock intensity has an exponent greater than 1. Fig. 2.11 represents the average responding to each of the three intensities of tailshock on the last few days during which the intermediate level shock was titrated.

Now that we had our subjects shaped, the basic experimental manipulation consisted of presenting a tone immediately before half of the shocks of each intensity. The central question was whether the signaled intermediate intensity tailshock would be rated as being of low aversiveness more often than the unsignaled intermediate intensity tailshock. We signaled half of the high and low intensity tailshocks as well as half of the intermediate level tailshocks in order to prevent the signal from denoting a trial on which each bar was reinforced 50% of the time, a condition that would have led to arbitrary responding on signaled trials. The basic paradigm is illustrated in Fig. 2.12. We anticipated that the affective value of signaled shocks would be displaced toward lower aversiveness relative to unsignaled shocks of the same intensity if and only if the PR Hypothesis was correct. The hypothetical psychological functions for the three

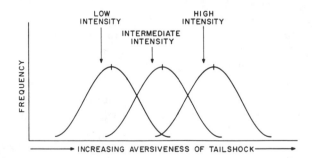

FIG. 2.10.   Hypothetical psychophysical functions for the three intensities of tailshock. The ordinate represents the relative frequency with which a given degree of aversiveness was assumed to be experienced as a consequence of a shock of a specific intensity.

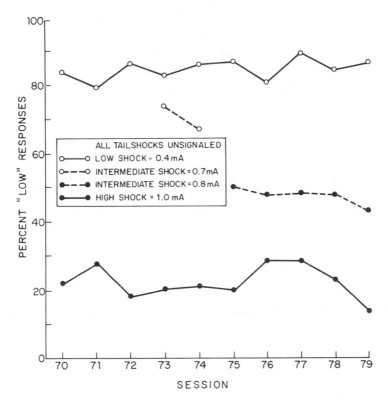

FIG. 2.11.   Mean percentage of total response on the "low intensity shock" lever as a function of tailshock intensity. The data represent choice performance over the last 10 days of titration of the intermediate shock intensity. Each daily session included 80 high intensity shocks, 80 low intensity shocks, and 40 intermediate intensity shocks.

tailshock intensities with and without the auditory signal are illustrated in Fig. 2.13.

Much to our surprise we found that signaled intermediate intensity tailshock was rated as being significantly *more* aversive than unsignaled intermediate intensity shock. This relationship is illustrated in Fig. 2.14. Moreover, similar significant shifts in responding toward the lever associated with the high intensity tailshock as a consequence of the signal being present were seen for both the low and high intensity shocks. These relationships are illustrated in Fig. 2.15.

These results are clearly contradictory to the PR Hypothesis that we had initially found so appealing. We briefly entertained the idea that our subjects may have been responding to the intensity of the tailshock (e.g., high intensity press left, low intensity press right) rather than its aversiveness (e.g., high aversiveness press left, low aversiveness press right). If aversiveness but not intensity

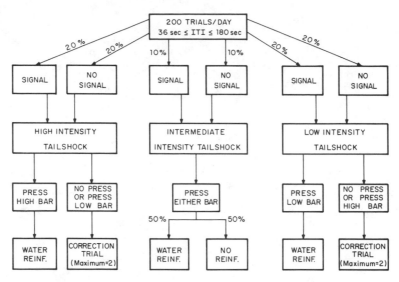

FIG. 2.12.   The paradigm for determining if signaled tailshocks are differentially aversive relative to unsignaled tailshocks. Elimination of the correction trials after initial shaping did not alter behavior.

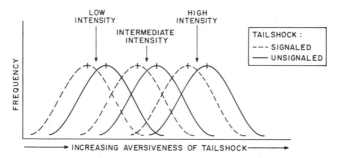

FIG. 2.13.   Hypothetical psychophysical functions for the three intensities of tailshock with and without a prior warning signal. The ordinate represents the relative frequency with which a given degree of aversiveness was assumed to be experienced as a consequence of a shock of a specific intensity. The downward shift in aversiveness on signaled trials presumes the occurrence of an effective preparatory response.

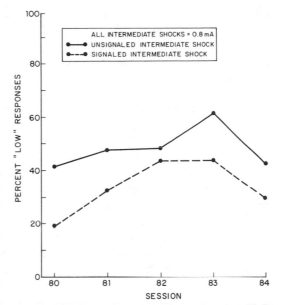

FIG. 2.14.   Mean percentage of responses on the "low intensity shock" bar for intermediate intensity tailshock trials as a function of the presence or absence of a warning signal. The data represent choice performance on the first 5 days during which the signal was presented. Each daily session included 20 signaled intermediate shocks and 20 unsignaled intermediate shocks.

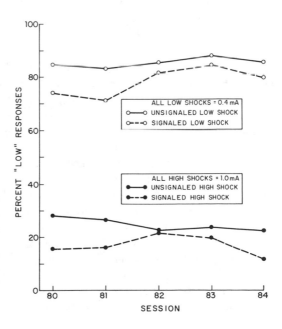

FIG. 2.15.   Mean percentage of responses on the "low intensity shock" bar for high and low intensity tailshock trials as a function of the presence or absence of a warning signal. The data represent choice performance on the first 5 days during which the signal was presented. Each daily session included 40 signaled shocks of each intensity.

judgments are influenced by PRs, our study would have been insensitive to PRs. However, we rejected this possibility because significant differences in lever selection did occur as a function of the signal condition given the same tailshock intensity. If the animals had been responding as a function of tailshock intensity independent of the signal, the signal would not have influenced choice behavior.

Our disturbing results prompted us to perform numerous additional studies in which most of the initial parameters were varied in an attempt to obtain a reduction in aversiveness as a function of the signal being present. Among the variables that we manipulated were the duration of the signal, the absolute intensities of the tailshocks, and the difference between the low and high intensity tailshocks. Our best efforts notwithstanding, the increased aversiveness of signaled shocks over unsignaled shocks remained. Sometimes this effect was reduced in magnitude but we never managed to reverse it.

Finally, despite our initial parameters being the same as we had used previously to obtain PSS in a shuttle box, we questioned whether the present preparation would yield a PSS effect. Therefore, we added a third manipulandum, specifically a chain, that when pulled provided the animals with 6 minutes of all shocks being signaled and a cue light that informed the animal that it was in the signaled condition. Outside of this period, all shocks were unsignaled. Following achievement of asymptotic performance, the contingency was reversed so that all shocks were signaled except those following within 6 minutes of a chain pull. *The rats displayed a significant preference for trials on which shocks were signaled, but then rated shocks on those very same trials as being more aversive than shocks on trials lacking a warning signal.*

Clearly the PR Hypothesis is unable to explain these findings. The actual basis for the behavior that we did observe is not relevant to our thesis, which is concerned with the PR Hypothesis and the adaptiveness of classically conditioned responses. However, digressing for a moment, it appears that the signal in our last set of studies acquired aversive value that summated with the aversiveness of the tailshock, and it was this combined aversiveness that guided the animals' choice of levers. This explanation does not salvage the PR Hypothesis in our situation. Even if the aversiveness of the signal had masked an attenuation in the aversiveness of the shock, the signal and the shock being rated as *more* aversive than the shock alone leads to the PR-based prediction that the unsignaled shock condition would be preferred to the signaled shock condition, which is contrary to the observed PSS effect. To explain the PSS phenomenon as well as the affective-rating data, we feel a hybrid theory is required, incorporating for the PSS effect the Signaled-Safety Hypothesis and the acquired aversiveness of contextual cues in the *absence* of a discrete signal (Fanselow, 1980), and to explain the present lever press data we favor the acquired aversiveness of the signal. Notably absent from this list of contributing factors is the PR Hypothesis.

DISCUSSION

Although our data are based on only three responses and but one US, they appear consistent with several other recent reports (e.g., Klemp & Rodin's [1976] findings with humans). Collectively, these several sets of studies make a strong case against the importance of PRs in providing covert reinforcement of classically conditioned responses. In light of these findings, one might expect us to have grown skeptical concerning the adaptiveness of classically conditioned responses. However, there are surely other ways in which classical conditioning could be adaptive besides the CR serving a preparatory role. For example, classical conditioning could be of value by virtue of its contribution to instrumental behavior as proposed by two-factor theory (Mowrer, 1960), or by virtue of its integration at the response level with instrumental behavior as discussed in Hearst and Jenkins' (1974) monograph on "sign-tracking." Alternatively, classical conditioning may be a nonadaptive epiphenomenal offshoot of instrumental learning or some other adaptive process. Although none of these possibilities can be rejected, the pervasiveness of classical conditioning across species and situations suggests that classical conditioning evolved in its own right and therefore ought to be more adaptive than our data suggest.

Zener, in 1937, noticed that his dogs, when released from their conditioning harnesses, responded to the CS by approaching the food tray and generally behaving in a highly functional manner. He concluded that CRs in the laboratory were fragments of a larger behavioral act that animals would perform were it not for the restraining apparatus in which many classical conditioning studies with animals are performed. Human subjects in classical conditioning experiments are less apt to be physically restrained, but the demand characteristics of the situation are often as effective as a harness or a restraining cage. The potential to be classically conditioned evolved in the natural habitat of animals, a set of circumstances in which bodily restraint is notably absent. Therefore, we see considerable merit in regarding a CR as a small segment of the entire behavioral syndrome that would occur in an animal's natural habitat. Such a position makes a lack of adaptive function on the part of classically conditioned associations in the laboratory less incongruous in respect to Darwinian thinking because evolutionary theory recognizes that adaptations are best suited to the ecological niche in which they arose. This is not to suggest that the interrelationships of most traditional variables of classical conditioning cannot be profitably studied in preparations using restrained animals; however, such preparations may be inappropriate for the functional analysis of classical conditioning. Despite our data, these considerations cause us to doubt the validity of differentiating between classical conditioning and instrumental learning on the basis of differences in their adaptiveness. In conjunction with our earlier evaluation of other potential differences between classical conditioning and instrumental learning, this leads us to conclude that at the present time there is insufficient reason to assume that different processes underlie the two associative learning paradigms.

SUMMARY

Some of the more commonly cited differences between classical conditioning and instrumental learning are reviewed briefly and generally are found to be inadequate as a basis for distinguishing either separate acquisition or separate retention processes. The adaptiveness of instrumentally acquired responses is contrasted with the frequent apparent lack of adaptiveness of classically conditioned responses. A possibly adaptive role of CRs is suggested by Perkins' (1955, 1968) Preparatory Response Hypothesis, which posits that a component of the CR syndrome serves to modify the effective US to the animal's benefit. Discounting overt (i.e., external) modification of the US, which constitutes traditional instrumental behavior, consideration is given to the likelihood of critical aspects of the CR syndrome serving to modify covertly the state of the animal in anticipation of the US, an act that would alter the consequences of the US for the animal.

Towards evaluating the Preparatory Response Hypothesis, we carried out three converging lines of research using rats. The first sought evidence of preparatory responding as the basis of the preference-for-signaled-shock phenomenon. Although we found no direct evidence contrary to the occurrence of preparatory responding in this series, all aspects of the data could be explained in terms of well-established factors without recourse to preparatory responding. The second series examined variations on the omission paradigm, explicitly CR-contingent increments and decrements in US intensity, to determine if classical conditioning was sensitive to overt reinforcement. No reinforcing effect of overt reinforcement was observed. We concluded that, if classical conditioning is impervious to overt reinforcement, it is probably also insensitive to the covert reinforcement that is the essence of the Preparatory Response Hypothesis. The third line of research directly measured the affective value of an aversive stimulus, specifically tailshock, as a function of whether or not it was signaled. Contrary to the prediction of the Preparatory Response Hypothesis, signaled tailshocks were judged to be more aversive than unsignaled tailshocks. In toto, we obtained no evidence supporting the Preparatory Response Hypothesis.

Given the lack of applicability of preparatory responding across the three distinct classical preparations described in this report, the direct adaptive value of CRs as a general principle is rejected. Consideration is given to the three not necessarily mutually exclusive possibilities: (1) that classical conditioning is epiphenomenal; (2) that its function is indirectly adaptive in that it mediates instrumental behavior (e.g., two-factor theory); and (3) that the CR syndrome seen in the laboratory is only a truncated and perhaps distorted element of the response to the same CS that would be seen in the unrestrained animal in its natural habitat. Although more research is needed before these possibilities can be evaluated, we tentatively favor the last owing to its plausibility and the parsimony that it offers in not distinguishing between classical conditioning and instrumental learning. We conclude that there is little reason at this time for believing that fundamentally different processes underlie classical conditioning and instrumental learning.

ACKNOWLEDGMENTS

The preparation of this chapter and all the experimental work therein were supported by NSF Grant BMS75-03383 and NIMH Grant MH33881. Ralph R. Miller was supported by NIMH Research Scientist Development Award K2-MH00061. We are indebted to Alvin Berk, Carolyn Greco, Nancy Marlin, John Sullivan, and Michael Vigorito for their assistance in conducting the research. Thanks are also due Wesley Kasprow, Charles C. Perkins, and Stanley Scobie for their critical reading of an early draft of the manuscript.

REFERENCES

Bacon, W. E. Partial-reinforcement extinction effect following different amounts of training. *Journal of Comparative and Physiological Psychology*, 1962, *55*, 998-1003.

Badia, P., Culbertson, S., & Harsh, J. Choice of longer or stronger signalled shock over shorter or weaker unsignalled shock. *Journal of the Experimental Analysis of Behavior*, 1973, *19*, 25-32.

Berk, A. M., Marlin, N. A., & Miller, R. R. A system for delivering tailshock to freely ambulatory rats. *Physiology and Behavior*, 1977, *19*, 815-818.

Berlyne, D. E. *Conflict, arousal, and curiosity.* New York: McGraw-Hill, 1960.

Bersh, P. J., & Alloy, L. B. Reduction of shock duration as negative reinforcement in free-operant avoidance. *Journal of the Experimental Analysis of Behavior*, 1980, *33*, 265-272.

Biederman, G. B., & Furedy, J. J. The preference-for-signalled-shock phenomenon: Signalling shock is reinforcing only if shock is modifiable. *Quarterly Journal of Experimental Psychology*, 1970, *22*, 681-685.

Biederman, G. B., & Furedy, J. J. Operational duplication without behavioral replication of changeover for signaled inescapable shock. *Bulletin of the Psychonomic Society*, 1976, *7*, 421-424.

Bloch, S., & Bello, M. Differential instrumental learning with food reward after extensive neocortical lesions in rats. *Acta Neurobiologiae Experimentalis*, 1974, *34*, 603-613.

Clark, C. G., & Prokasy, W. F. Manipulation of response-contingent unconditional-stimulus intensity in human eyelid conditioning: A two-phase model analysis. *Memory & Cognition*, 1976, *4*, 277-282.

Coleman, S. R. Consequences of response-contingent changes in the unconditioned stimulus intensity upon the rabbit (*Oryctolagus cuniculus*) nictitating membrane response. *Journal of Comparative and Physiological Psychology*, 1975, *88*, 591-595.

Coleman, S. R., & Gormezano, J. Classical conditioning and the "Law of Effect": Historical and empirical assessment. *Behaviorism*, 1979, *7*, 1-33.

D'Amato, M. R., and Gumenik, W. E. Some effects of immediate versus randomly delayed shock on an instrumental response and cognitive processes. *Journal of Abnormal and Social Psychology*, 1960, *60*, 64-67.

D'Amato, M. R., & Safarjan, W. R. Preference for information about shock duration in rats. *Animal Learning and Behavior*, 1979, *7*, 89-94.

DiCara, L. V., Braun, J. J., & Pappas, B. A. Classical conditioning and instrumental learning of cardiac and gastrointestinal responses following removal of neocortex in the rat. *Journal of Comparative and Physiological Psychology*, 1970, *73*, 208-216.

Fanselow, M. S. Naloxone attenuates rat's preference for signaled shock. *Physiological Psychology*, 1979, *7*, 70-74.

Fanselow, M. S. Signaled shock-free periods and preference for signaled shock. *Journal of Experimental Psychology: Animal Behavior Processes*, 1980, *6*, 65-80.

Furedy, J. J., & Doob, A. N. Signalling unmodifiable shocks: Limits on human informational cognitive control. *Journal of Personality and Social Psychology*, 1972, *21*, 111-115.

Gibbs, C. M., Latham, S. B., & Gormezano, J. Classical conditioning of the rabbit nictitating membrane response: Effects of reinforcement schedule on response maintenance and resistance to extinction. *Animal Learning and Behavior*, 1978, *6*, 209-215.

Gormezano, J., & Coleman, S. R. The law of effect and CR contingent modification of the UCS. *Conditional Reflex*, 1973, *8*, 41-56.

Gwinn, G. T. The effects of punishment on acts motivated by fear. *Journal of Experimental Psychology*, 1949, *39*, 260-269.

Hearst, E., & Jenkins, H. M. *Sign-tracking: The stimulus-reinforcer relation and directed action*. Austin, Tex.: Psychonomic Society, 1974.

Hilton, A. Partial reinforcement of a conditioned emotional response in rats. *Journal of Comparative and Physiological Psychology*, 1969, *69*, 253-260.

Holland, P. C. Differential effects of omission contingencies on various components of Pavlovian appetitive conditioned responding in rats. *Journal of Experimental Psychology: Animal Behavior Processes*, 1979, *5*, 178-193.

Kimble, G. A., & Ost, J. W. P. A conditioned inhibitory process in eyelid conditioning. *Journal of Experimental Psychology*, 1961, *61*, 150-156.

Kimmel, H. D. Inhibition of the unconditioned response in classical conditioning. *Psychological Review*, 1966, *73*, 232-240.

Kimmel, H. D., & Burns, R. A. Adaptational aspects of conditioning. In W. K. Estes (Ed.), *Handbook of learning and cognitive psychology* (Vol. 2). Hillsdale, N.J.: Lawrence Erlbaum Associates, 1975.

Klemp, G. O., & Rodin, J. Effects of uncertainty, delay, and focus of attention on reactions to an aversive situation. *Journal of Experimental Social Psychology*, 1976, *12*, 416-421.

Lewis, D. J., Misanin, J. R., & Miller, R. R. Recovery of memory following amnesia. *Nature*, 1968, *220*, 704-705.

Lockard, J. S. Choice of a warning signal or no warning signal in an unavoidable shock situation. *Journal of Comparative and Physiological Psychology*, 1963, *56*, 526-530.

Lykken, D. T., & Tellegen, A. On the validity of the preception hypothesis. *Psychophysiology*, 1974, *11*, 125-132.

Mackintosh, N. J. *The psychology of animal learning*. London: Academic Press, 1974.

Mackintosh, N. J., & Dickinson, A. Instrumental (type II) conditioning. In A. Dickinson & R. A. Boakes (Eds.), *Mechanisms of learning and motivation: A memorial volume to Jerzy Konorski*. Hillsdale, N.J.: Lawrence Erlbaum Associates, 1979.

Marlin, N. A., Berk, A. M., & Miller, R. R. Modification and avoidance of unmodifiable and unavoidable footshock. *Bulletin of the Psychonomic Society*, 1978, *11*, 203-205.

Marlin, N. A., Sullivan, J. M., Berk, A. M., & Miller, R. R. Preference for information about intensity of signaled tailshock. *Learning and Motivation*, 1979, *10*, 85-97.

Martin, J., & Levey, A. B. *The genesis of the classical conditioned responses: International Series of Monographs in Experimental Psychology* (No. 8). Oxford, Eng.: Pergamon Press, 1969.

Miller, N. E. Learning of visceral and glandular responses. *Science*, 1969, *163*, 434-445.

Miller, N. E., & Dworkin, B. R. Visceral learning: Recent difficulties with curarized rats and significant problems for human research. In P. A. Obrist, A. H. Black, J. Brener, & L. V. DiCara (Eds.), *Cardiovascular psychophysiology*. Chicago: Aldine, 1974.

Miller, R. R., Daniel, D., & Berk, A. M. Successive reversal of a discriminated preference for tailshock. *Animal Learning and Behavior*, 1974, *2*, 271–274.

Miller, R. R., Greco, C., & Vigorito, M. Classically conditioned tail flexion in rats: CR-contingent modification of US intensity as a test of the Preparatory Response Hypothesis. *Animal Learning and Behavior*, 1981, *9*, 80–88.

Miller, R. R., & Kraus, J. N. Somatic and autonomic indexes of recovery from ECS-induced amnesia in rats. *Journal of Comparative and Physiological Psychology*, 1977, *91*, 434–442.

Miller, R. R., & Marlin, N. A. Amnesia following electroconvulsive shock. In J. F. Kihlstrom & F. J. Evans (Eds.), *Disorders of memory function*. Hillsdale, N.J.: Lawrence Erlbaum Associates, 1979.

Miller, R. R., Marlin, N. A., & Berk, A. M. Reliability and sources of control of preference for signaled shock. *Animal Learning and Behavior*, 1977, *5*, 303–308.

Miller, R. R., Ott, C. A., Daniel, D., & Berk, A. M. ECS-induced amnesia and recovery of memory for classically conditioned fear in the rat. *Physiological Psychology*, 1976, *4*, 57–60.

Miller, R. R., & Springer, A. D. Induced recovery of memory in rats following electroconvulsive shock. *Physiology and Behavior*, 1972, *8*, 645–651.

Moore, B. R. The role of directed Pavlovian reactions in simple instrumental learning in the pigeon. In R. A. Hinde & J. Stevenson-Hinde (Eds.), *Constraints on learning*. New York: Academic Press, 1973.

Mowrer, O. H. *Learning theory and behavior*. New York: Wiley, 1960.

Oakley, D. A. Learning with food reward and shock avoidance in neodecorticate rats. *Experimental Neurology*, 1979, *63*, 627–642.

Oakley, D. A. Improved instrumental learning in neodecorticate rats. *Physiology and Behavior*, 1980, *24*, 357–366.

Oakley, D. A., & Russell, I. S. Performance of neodecorticated rabbits in a free-operant situation. *Physiology and Behavior*, 1978, *20*, 157–170.

Pavlov, I. P. *Conditioned reflexes*. Oxford, Eng.: Oxford University Press, 1927.

Pearce, J., & Hall, G. Overshadowing the instrumental conditioning of a lever press response by a more valid predictor of reinforcement. *Journal of Experimental Psychology: Animal Behavior Processes*, 1978, *4*, 356–367.

Perkins, C. C., Jr. The stimulus conditions which follow learned responses. *Psychological Review*, 1955, *62*, 341–348.

Perkins, C. C., Jr. An analysis of the concept of reinforcement. *Psychological Review*, 1968, *75*, 155–172.

Perkins, C. C., Jr. Reinforcement in classical conditioning. In H. Kendler & J. T. Spence (Eds.), *Essays in neobehaviorism*. New York: Appleton–Century–Crofts, 1971.

Perkins, C. C., Jr., Seymann, R. G., Levis, D. J., & Spencer, H. R., Jr. Factors affecting preference for signal-shock over shock-signal. *Journal of Experimental Psychology*, 1966, *72*, 190–196.

Prokasy, W. F. Classical eyelid conditioning: Experimenter operations, task demands, and response shaping. In W. F. Prokasy (Ed.), *Classical conditioning: A symposium*. New York: Appleton–Century–Crofts, 1965.

Prokasy, W. F., & Kumpfer, K. L. One and two-factor versions of a two-phase model applied to the performance of Vs and Cs in human eyelid conditioning. *Journal of Experimental Psychology*, 1969, *80*, 231–236.

Rescorla, R. A., & Wagner, A. R. A theory of Pavlovian conditioning: Variations in the effectiveness of reinforcement and nonreinforcement. In A. H. Black & W. F. Prokasy (Eds.), *Classical conditioning II: Current research and theory*. New York: Appleton–Century–Crofts, 1972.

Salafia, W. R., Martino, L. J., Cloutman, K., & Romano, A. G. Unconditional-stimulus locus and interstimulus-interval shift in rabbit (*Oryctolagus cuniculus*) nictitating membrane conditioning. *Pavlovian Journal of Biological Science*, 1979, *14*, 64–71.

Schlosberg, H. Conditioned responses in the white rat. *Journal of Genetic Psychology*, 1934, *45*, 303–305.

Schlosberg, H. Conditioned responses in the white rat: II. Conditioned responses based upon shock to the foreleg. *Journal of Genetic Psychology*, 1936, *49*, 107–138.

Schlosberg, H. The relationship between success and the laws of conditioning. *Psychological Review*, 1937, *44*, 379–394.

Schneider, A. M., Tyler, J., & Jinich, D. Recovery from retrograde amnesia: A learning process. *Science*, 1974, *184*, 87–88.

Scott, D. S., & Barber, T. X. Cognitive control of pain: Effects of multiple cognitive strategies. *The Psychological Record*, 1977, *27*, 373–383.

Seligman, M. E. P. Chronic fear produced by unpredictable shock. *Journal of Comparative and Physiological Psychology*, 1968, *66*, 402–411.

Shettleworth, S. J. Constraints on learning. In D. S. Lehrman, R. A. Hinde, & E. Shaw (Eds.), *Advances in the study of behavior, IV*. New York: Academic Press, 1972.

Solomon, R. L., & Turner, L. H. Discriminative classical conditioning in dogs paralyzed by curare can later control discriminative avoidance responses in the normal state. *Psychological Review*, 1962, *69*, 202–219.

St. Claire-Smith, R. J. The overshadowing and blocking of punishment. *Quarterly Journal of Experimental Psychology*, 1979, *31*, 51–61.

Tolman, E. C. *Purposive behavior in animals and men*. New York: Appleton–Century–Crofts, 1932.

Twitmyer, E. B. A study of the knee jerk. *Journal of Experimental Psychology*, 1974, *103*, 1047–1066.

Wagner, A. R., Thomas, E., & Norton, T. Conditioning with electrical stimulation of motor cortex: Evidence of a possible source of motivation. *Journal of Comparative and Physiological Psychology*, 1967, *64*, 191–199.

Weinstock, S. Acquisition and extinction of a partially reinforced running response at a 24-hour intertrial interval. *Journal of Experimental Psychology*, 1958, *46*, 151–158.

Williams, D. R., & Williams, H. Auto-maintenance in the pigeon: Sustained pecking despite contingent non-reinforcement. *Journal of the Experimental Analysis of Behavior*, 1969, *12*, 511–520.

Zener, K. The significance of behavior accompanying conditioned salivary secretion for theories of the conditioned response. *American Journal of Psychology*, 1937, *50*, 384–403.

3

Within-Event Learning
In Pavlovian Conditioning

Robert A. Rescorla
Paula J. Durlach
Yale University

It has become common to describe Pavlovian conditioning as the learning of relations among events. In the context of that description, our knowledge of conditioning has expanded considerably in recent years. We now have a rich empirical base for understanding which relations among events are actually learned. The notions of excitatory and inhibitory relations have become principal tools for integrating such knowledge. Moreover, we know a considerable amount about the conditions that are responsible for such relational learning. And there are available several theoretical frameworks that, although still rivals, nevertheless share many ideas about the manner in which relations among events are learned.

Relatively more neglected in recent studies of Pavlovian conditioning has been the study of learning about the events themselves. How does the organism represent the individual events that Pavlovian theories describe as entering into learned relations? Presumably most events have multiple features that are somehow integrated into a memory representation. What is the nature of that integration and what are the conditions that promote its occurrence?

This chapter describes one research approach to that set of questions. The strategy of the approach is to model events that have multiple features by artificially creating stimuli with experimentally separable components. One can then ask about the organization of those components in the event memory representation. This statement of the problem of event representation has a decidedly associative bias. It assumes that one can usefully think of events as having multiple features that are somehow put together (by ''associations'') to form the event representation. This assumption, which has a long history, will in fact prove a useful one with which to describe initially some of the research we have done. But we will later have occasion to question it.

The organization of this chapter is as follows: First, we ask whether the events that enter into Pavlovian relations in fact form organized memory representations. We provide evidence of such internal organization primarily for one of the important Pavlovian events, the conditioned stimulus (CS). Second, we discuss some of the implications of that internal organization for interpretation of relational learning in Pavlovian conditioning. In that context we show its occurrence in several theoretically important paradigms. Third, we describe some preliminary evidence on the rules that govern the formation of these memory representations. Although only the simplest of circumstances have been examined so far, some of the results are surprising. Finally, we briefly mention several theoretical frameworks in which such event memories can be conceptualized. Throughout the discussion, we draw on the results of various Pavlovian preparations. Our intention is to explore the generality of within-event learning across a variety of stimulus modalities and reinforcer values.

DEMONSTRATION OF WITHIN-EVENT LEARNING

In this section we give some evidence for the occurrence of organization within the primary individual events used in Pavlovian conditioning. At the simplest level, the question is whether the organism learns about the co-occurrence of multiple features of an event. We describe here two examples of such learning for events that are relatively neutral and therefore might serve as CSs in typical Pavlovian experiments. The first example explores an event with multiple-flavor features that might be used to signal illness in a flavor-aversion preparation; the second uses a multifeature visual event such as might signal food for a pigeon in an autoshaping procedure. We also cite some evidence that animals develop an internal organization for affectively valued stimuli.

Within-CS Learning

Rescorla & Cunningham (1978) have provided a clear demonstration that exposure to multifeatured flavor stimuli results in learning that those features co-occur. Those authors used a variation on the standard sensory preconditioning paradigm, in which rats were initially exposed to a multifeatured flavor and subsequently made ill following consumption of one of those features presented separately. Then the rats were tested for their willingness to consume water flavored with the other feature. The assumption was that to the degree that the organism had organized (associated) the two features, subsequent changes in the value of one might be reflected in the value of the other.

In order to provide a well-controlled demonstration of such learning, Rescorla & Cunningham (1978) actually employed a somewhat more complex procedure in which each rat was exposed to two compound stimuli. Those stimuli were

TABLE 3.1
Design of Rescorla and Cunningham (1978)

Group	Phase 1	Phase 2	Test
1	SH-, NQ-	H+, Q-	S, N
2	SH-, NQ-	H-, Q+	S, N
3	SQ-, NH-	H+, Q-	S, N
4	SQ-, NH-	H- , Q+	S, N

Note: S = sucrose, H = hydrochloric acid, N = salt, Q = quinine
+ = toxin and - = nonreinforcement.

constructed from four elementary flavors, intended to represent what have often been described as the four primary tastes: sweet (sucrose), salty (NaC1), bitter (quinine), and sour (hydrochloric acid). As indicated in Table 3.1, some rats were presented with simultaneous compounds of sucrose and hydrochloric acid (*SH*) and of salt and quinine (*NQ*); others received the alternative compounds of *SQ* and *NH*. Then half of each set of animals received presentations of *H* followed by .5% body weight injections of .6M LiCl; they also received nonreinforced presentations of *Q*. The other half of the animals received poisoned presentations of *Q* but not of *H*. Finally, all animals were given a choice between *S* and *N*. The expectation was that if the organism has learned about the way in which the features of the events co-occur, then the intakes of *S* and *N* should reflect the current values of their co-features, *H* and *Q*.

Figure 3.1 shows the principal data from this experiment, the intakes of *S* and *N* during the test. The left panel displays the results for those animals that received the *SH* and *NQ* compounds. To the far left are their consumptions of sucrose. Notice that sucrose consumption was less in those animals that had been poisoned with hydrochloric acid (*H*+) compared with those that had been poisoned with quinine (*Q*+). By contrast, the consumptions of salt were least in those animals poisoned with quinine rather than hydrochloric acid. That is, the intakes of *S* and *N* indeed reflected the current values of the other features of their compounds. The data from those animals that had been exposed to *SQ* and *NH*, displayed in the right-hand panel, show an analogous pattern. Again, intakes of *S* and *N* were specifically affected by the conditioning of *H* and *Q*. These results provide strong evidence that the organism has knowledge of the co-occurrence of the various event features. Apparently, with flavor features of ingestive stimuli, rats do develop within-event organizations.

The conclusions of the Rescorla & Cunningham experiment appear applicable both to a variety of event features and to several techniques for revealing the integration of those features. Results like these are not confined to flavors used in a poisoning procedure. For instance, Heth (personal communication, 1979) has found that rats integrate not only flavor but also temperature features of fluid events. Rescorla (1980a) has reported the integration of auditory and visual features of a compound event for rats that were tested with a conditioned sup-

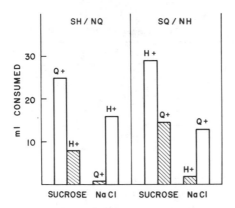

FIG. 3.1. Consumption of sucrose (S) and NaCl (N) in animals that had been exposed to either the sucrose–hydrochloric acid (SH) and salt–quinine (NQ) or the SQ and NH compound events and then poisoned to either H or Q. Consumption of the element whose partner was subsequently poisoned is indicated by cross-hatching (from Rescorla & Cunningham, 1978).

pression procedure. Moreover, such learning can be revealed by making one of the features attractive rather than aversive. We describe in the following section the use of food in an autoshaping procedure to reveal integration of visual stimuli by pigeon subjects. Later in the chapter we report the use of a motivational procedure to enhance the value of one feature of an event; that too can be used to reveal within-event learning.

To illustrate this generality, we display in Fig. 3.2 the results of an autoshaping study that is analogous to the Rescorla and Cunningham experiment. Although this study uses the same basic design, it differs from that experiment along three dimensions: modality of the stimulus features being integrated, the value of the reinforcer used to reveal that learning, and the species in which the learning occurs. Nevertheless, the same basic results were obtained.

In this study 16 pigeon subjects were first trained to peck at a white key illuminated for 5 sec in a standard autoshaping procedure that used 5 sec of grain as the reinforcer. The pigeons then received 12 nonreinforced presentations of each of two compound stimuli on each of 3 days. These compound stimuli were composed of a color (either blue (B) or yellow (Y)) and an orientation of black grids on white backgrounds (either 45 or −45 degrees from the vertical). The colors were projected on the bottom half of a standard response key in an operant chamber; the orientations were projected on the top half. Mixed with those compound presentations were 6 reinforced presentations of the full key illuminated with white. This procedure was intended to produce continued attention to the response key and thus ensure exposure to the color-orientation compounds. By analogy with the Rescorla–Cunningham experiment, half the birds received one pairing of color-orientation compounds (B/45, Y/−45) and the other half received the other pairing (B/−45 and Y/45). Then all birds received 3 days of discrimination training with the orientations alone. On each day, each orientation was presented 12 times and one was reinforced (with 5 sec of grain), whereas the other was nonreinforced. Finally, all birds received 6 nonreinforced test presentations of each of the colors. The issue was whether responding to the colors would reflect the autoshaping of the orientations with which they had previously been paired.

In Fig. 3.2 the results of the final test session are displayed in terms of the number of responses per minute elicited during the colors. The elaborate counterbalancing has been ignored and the data are plotted separately for that color whose orientation had been reinforced (labeled ''+'') and for that color whose orientation had been nonreinforced (−). It is clear that more responding occurred to the former color (Wilcoxon $T = 5$, $p < .01$), indicating knowledge of the particular color-orientation pairings. The results of these experiments thus provide strong evidence for the integration of multiple features of stimuli like those used as CSs in Pavlovian conditioning experiments.

Within-Reinforcer Learning

Although the main emphasis of this chapter is on integration of the CS memory, it is worth mentioning that there is also evidence for within-event learning with reinforcers. For instance, using a logic similar to that employed here, Rescorla (1980a) found that in the course of a second-order conditioning experiment, the organism not only learns to associate the two events, but also integrates the multiple features of the reinforcer. Moreover, notice that the flavor stimuli that we have here described as CSs can additionally be thought of as reinforcers. Although these substances are neutral in the sense that thirsty rats consume them in amounts similar to water, they are surely capable of serving as reinforcers for antecedent CSs or operant behaviors. Thus the Rescorla and Cunningham (1978) experiment also provides evidence that events that can serve as reinforcers develop within-event integration. Indeed, the important property of the stimuli used in that study is not that they lack any particular intrinsic value, but rather that they are susceptible to change in that value by various experimental manipula-

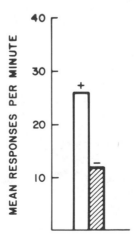

FIG. 3.2.   Mean rate of pecking to one element of a compound visual event as a function of whether the other was subsequently autoshaped (+) or not (−).

tions. It is that susceptability that allows us to detect the within-event learning of interest here.

INVOLVEMENT IN PAVLOVIAN PARADIGMS

The previous section showed that events that are typically used in Pavlovian paradigms sometimes form internally integrated memories. The intention of this section is to illustrate that they actually do so in the context of Pavlovian conditioning experiments. We discuss three common Pavlovian paradigms: simple reinforced presentation of a stimulus, blocking, and conditioned inhibition.

Simple Reinforced CS Presentation

Perhaps the simplest question one can ask is whether a multifeatured CS becomes integrated when that CS is used as a signal for a more significant US. Despite the evidence that such integration occurs when the CS is presented alone without important consequence, one might still suspect that within-event learning is a luxury that the animal foregoes when there are important events to be predicted.

An illustration that this is not the case was provided in an experiment reported by Speers, Gillan, & Rescorla (1980). That experiment employed a design essentially identical to that illustrated in Table 3.1, except that during the first phase of the experiment all compound flavors were followed by a mild LiCl injection. The question was whether that injection, which was sufficient to produce a moderate level of aversion to the compound flavors, would prevent the within-event learning. The answer was clearly negative. When H or Q was subsequently followed by a more substantial poison, consumption of S and N showed evidence of that poisoning in a manner that revealed that considerable within-event learning had occurred. Consequently, one may expect this within-CS learning to occur in the course of normal acquisition of an excitatory response.

One way to view the procedure employed by Speers et al. is as an example of an overshadowing experiment. In many Pavlovian procedures when a signal with separable elements is followed by a US the question of interest is the degree to which those elements compete for the association with the US. For instance, one may ask whether the conditioning of a target element is reduced by the simple presence of another stimulus at the time of reinforcement. Will the additional element overshadow the first? Although the Speers et al. experiment did not contain the comparisons appropriate for evaluating such a possibility, such overshadowing is a commonly reported outcome for many Pavlovian preparations. That observation, in fact, has had an important impact on modern theories of Pavlovian conditioning.

However, there also have been reports describing the opposite outcome. In some studies, the addition of a second element does not overshadow conditioning of the first but instead potentiates that conditioning (Clarke, Westbrook, & Irwin, 1979; Rusiniak, Hankins, Garcia, & Brett, 1979). Because it turns out that this potentiation is at least partly a result of the kind of within-event learning of concern here, we describe one example and provide some analysis of its basis.

A good illustration of potentiation is an experiment by Durlach and Rescorla (1980, Exp. 1). Following the earlier report of Rusiniak et al., they employed compound events composed of odors and tastes. The principal taste was the sweetness of .06% saccharin; the odors were dilute (1.5%) solutions of commercially available flavorings, banana (B) and almond (A), delivered in water available through a drinking tube. There is evidence that these latter substances are primarily olfactory in character (Rusiniak et al., 1979) but our present use of the term "odor" is only for expositional convenience. Each animal was exposed to a single conditioning trial with each odor, a 10-min presentation of banana and almond, in each case followed 15 min later by a .5% body weight injection of a .6M LiCl solution. However, for each subject, one of these odors was compounded with saccharin; for half of the animals (Group BS) the banana solution was sweetened and for the other half (Group AS) the almond was sweetened. Subsequently, all animals were given a choice test with A and B. The data of interest are the relative aversions of A and B as a function of which was conditioned alone and which was conditioned in compound.

Figure 3.3 shows the consumption data from this test for the two groups. In Group BS, banana was rejected in favor of almond. By contrast, in Group AS, almond was rejected relative to banana. In each case, animals exhibited a stronger aversion to the odor conditioned in compound than to the odor conditioned alone. That is, potentiation, rather than overshadowing, was obtained.

Durlach & Rescorla (1980) considered a variety of interpretations of this outcome, but two are of particular interest here. One possibility is that potentiation is to be interpreted as the opposite of overshadowing—as due to differential

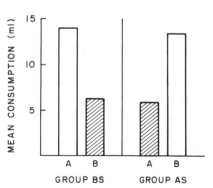

FIG. 3.3.   Consumption of almond (A) and banana (B) odors in animals poisoned to almond alone and banana presented in compound with saccharin (Group BS) and in animals poisoned to banana alone and almond presented in compound with saccharin (Group AS) (from Durlach & Rescorla, 1980).

strength of the association with the US. Just as most theories of overshadowing view the role of the added element as attenuating the association between the target CS and the US, one might view potentiation as a case in which the added element enhances the association between the target CS and the US. It is this interpretation that has led Garcia and his collaborators (Palmerino, Rusiniak, & Garcia, 1980) to identify potentiation as evidence for a fundamental difference between the conditioning rules for flavor-aversion learning and other instances of Pavlovian conditioning.

However, one can give an alternative interpretation that views potentiation as the product of within-event learning. The results described in the previous section would lead one to suspect that responding to the odor might depend not only on its association with the poison but also on its association with any co-occurring taste. In the simplest associative terms, the potentiated odor might be more aversive not because it has a stronger association with the US but because it has an additional association with a taste that is also aversive by virtue of its own pairing with the US. Those two sources of aversion (odor–taste and odor–US) may combine to produce greater rejection of the tasty odor than of the odor that has only the direct association with poison.

One way to choose between these alternatives is suggested by noting the different roles they assign to the aversiveness of the taste. According to the second interpretation, the odor uses its association with the taste to "borrow" some of the latter's aversion, thus enhancing its own rejection. Consequently, potentiation should be critically dependent on the current aversiveness of the taste. If that taste were to lose its aversiveness, there would be nothing for the odor to borrow and potentiation should disappear. On the other hand, if the role of the taste is only to act as a sort of catalyst, enhancing the direct association between the odor and LiCl, then potentiation should be relatively insensitive to any subsequent changes in the value of the taste.

A second experiment by Durlach and Rescorla (1980, Exp. 4) examined these differential predictions. In this experiment, each animal was exposed to three odors (the almond and banana used before plus a 1.5% solution of strawberry) and two tastes (saccharin and salt). In a counterbalanced fashion, each animal received one odor ($O1$) presented alone, one presented with sucrose and one presented with salt. During conditioning, one 10-min presentation of each type was given and on each occasion solutions were followed 15 min later by a LiCl injection. As a result of these procedures, one would anticipate being able to observe potentiation (i.e., that $O1$ would be preferred to each of the other odors [which had been poisoned in conjunction with a taste]). However, prior to testing, one of the tastes (salt for half of the animals, saccharin for the other half) was repeatedly presented alone without poisoning so as to extinguish its aversiveness. The odor that had been poisoned in conjunction with the subsequently extinguished taste was designated $O3$; the odor whose taste was left unextinguished was designated $O2$. Both of the foregoing views of potentiation antici-

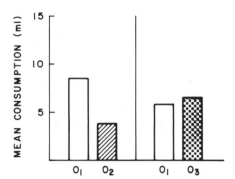

FIG. 3.4. Consumption of an odor that had either been poisoned alone (O1) or in conjunction with a taste. The taste was subsequently extinguished for O3 but not O2 (from Durlach & Rescorla, 1980).

pate that the animals would reject O2 relative to O1 when given the choice. However, the interpretation in terms of an odor–taste association expects that O3 should no longer be rejected relative to O1, because its associated taste is no longer aversive.

Figure 3.4 shows the results of those choice tests. For those animals tested with O1 versus O2, potentiation was again observed. Simply extinguishing some taste did not eliminate the preference for a previously unaccompanied odor (O1) relative to one poisoned in conjunction with a taste (O2). However, there is no evidence of such potentiation in those animals given a choice between O1 and O3. Extinguishing the taste that had been paired with O3 during conditioning selectively attenuated the aversiveness of O3. This specificity of action on O3 but not on O2 provides strong evidence for the role of the odor–taste association in producing potentiation. It suggests that potentiation does not result from an enhanced odor–US association.

Additional evidence on this point comes from a recent experiment that attempted to model the phenomenon of potentiation. The idea behind the experiment was to produce potentiation by separately giving the odor each of the associations presumed necessary, one with LiCl and one with the taste, but without ever having the taste accompany a poisoned presentation of the odor. If the role of the taste is to enhance the odor–LiCl association, one would anticipate that its presence at the time of their pairing might be important. On the other hand, if the taste simply provides an alternative associative source of aversiveness, one should be able to mimic potentiation by separately establishing that association.

In this experiment two odors (banana and almond) were each presented four times for 10 min; one of these odors (designated O2) was accompanied by salt on each occurrence. On these trials no poisoning was given; but one would anticipate on the basis of results reported previously that O2 would become associated with salt. Then each animal received a single presentation of each odor alone followed by poison. This phase provided the opportunity for each odor to become associated with the US. Next all animals received an initial choice test with O1

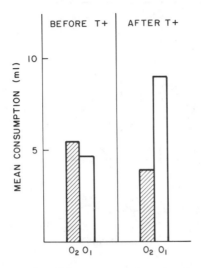

FIG. 3.5.   Artificially produced potentiation. Consumption of odors presented alone ($O1$) or in conjunction with salt ($O2$) before and after poisoning of the salt taste (T).

and $O2$. The results of that test are shown to the left of Fig. 3.5. It is clear from those data that the animals displayed little preference. Apparently, a history of joint presentation with a taste is not in itself sufficient to enable subsequent separate poisoning of an odor to produce potentiation. That observation is of interest because one might entertain the attractive thought that with joint presentation the taste could change the character of the odor and make it more conditionable.

Subsequent to this initial test, which should leave the animal with associations between each of the odors and LiCl as well as an association between $O2$ and salt, all animals received poisoned presentations of salt. According to the present interpretation of potentiation, that conditioning should complete the set of sources for aversiveness of $O2$ that are normally responsible for potentiation. In this case, however, the $O2$-LiCl, $O2$-taste, and taste-LiCl associations have all been established on separate trials, whereas in potentiation they occur on the same trial. Nevertheless, we should see potentiation-like rejection of $O2$ relative to $O1$. The right-hand panel of Fig. 3.5 shows the results of the final choice test between $O1$ and $O2$. Consumption of $O1$ was greater than on the initial test, presumably because that test produced some extinction of the aversion previously conditioned to the odors. However, the result of primary interest is the rejection of $O2$ relative to $O1$ (Wilcoxon $T = 25.5$, $p < .05$). Apparently, we can produce a result that looks like potentiation without ever having the taste accompany the odor on the poisoned trials. All that is needed is to set up the individual odor-taste, taste-poison, and odor-poison associations. This result conforms to an interpretation of potentiation in terms of the importance of within-event learning.

There are several important points to be made from these experiments on overshadowing and potentiation. First, it is clear that within-event learning occurs during simple excitatory conditioning of a CS. Second, within-event learning can sometimes be so powerful as to reverse the normally observed phenomenon of overshadowing. Third, that learning can often be extremely rapid; in the present experiments a few joint occurrences were sufficient to produce substantial learning. Finally, it is important to note that in the case of potentiation, attending to within-event learning as an alternative source for responding prevented us from misinterpreting a theoretically important phenomenon. In fact, it is difficult to see how one could generally hope to make detailed sense out of Pavlovian conditioning experiments that involve compound stimuli without attention to the role of within-event learning in generating responding to the individual stimuli.

Blocking

One of the most widely discussed phenomena of Pavlovian conditioning is the blocking of conditioning of one CS by the presence of another, previously conditioned CS. In the pardigmatic case (Kamin, 1968), prior conditioning of the form A—US allows A to reduce greatly the conditioning of X by the US on subsequent AX—US trials. In the present context, one may note that the AX compound can be viewed as a single stimulus with multiple features for which the organism may form a memory representation. It then becomes of interest to ask whether that AX undergoes any integration that allows the organism to record the fact that the A and X features have co-occurred. Speers et al. (1980) provided some initial evidence that such learning occurs when a blocking paradigm is carried out in a flavor-aversion preparation. We here describe an experiment showing more complete evidence for the case of autoshaping.

The experiment contained two groups, the first of which was designed simply to demonstrate the presence of blocking in an autoshaping preparation. This group was deemed necessary because of the uncertainty surrounding the occurrence of blocking in autoshaping (see Jenkins, 1981). The second group was designed to enable detection of within-event learning.

The experimental design is outlined in Table 3.2. During Phase 1 the eight birds in Group 1 received a discriminative autoshaping procedure in which one of

TABLE 3.2
Design of Blocking Experiment

	Phase 1	Phase 2	Phase 3	Test
Group 1	01+, 02-	01C1+, 02C2+	omitted	C1, C2
Group 2	01,+ 02+	01C1+, 02C2+	01+, 02- 01-, 02+	C1, C2

Note: 01 and 02 are line orientations, C1 and C2 are colors, + and - indicate reinforcement and nonreinforcement, respectively.

the two line orientations (O1) previously described was followed by food and the other (O2) was nonreinforced. After three days during each of which they received 12 trials of each type, the birds began Phase 2. During this phase each bird received two color-orientation compounds, both reinforced. Again 12 trials of each of the two types were given on each of 3 days. Notice that the consequence of these procedures is that both colors are reinforced in conjunction with an orientation, but one of those orientations has previously received excitatory conditioning and the other has not. If blocking occurs, one would anticipate greater conditioning of the color reinforced in conjunction with O2.

Testing the colors in Group 1 resulted in the data displayed in the left-hand panel of Fig. 3.6. As expected, there was more responding to the color reinforced in the presence of O2, giving evidence for blocking (Wilcoxon $T = 2$, $p < .05$). It may be noted that this blocking result seems smaller than that often observed in other preparations, such as conditioned suppression. However, the present design may provide a more accurate estimate of blocking than that gained from the conventional designs most often used in other preparations. The most frequently used designs actually confound both familiarity with the reinforcer and a history of some prior conditioning with the intended difference in conditioned strength of A at the time of AX trials. Using a within-subject design like that employed here avoids such confoundings. But in any case, the important point is that Group 1 demonstrates blocking with the present experimental procedures.

The eight birds in Group 2 received the same treatment as those in Group 1, with two exceptions. First, during Phase 1 both orientations were reinforced. Consequently, both colors should be blocked in Phase 2. Second, in order to reveal the within-event learning expected to occur in Phase 2, they received discriminative training with their orientations prior to testing of the colors. The intention was to assess whether responding to the colors would reflect the current status of the jointly presented orientations, as would be expected on the basis of within-event learning.

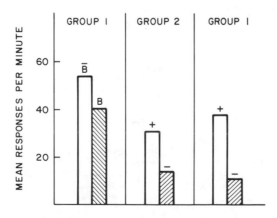

FIG. 3.6.   Within-compound learning during blocking in an autoshaping preparation. The left panel shows responding to a color whose conditioning with food was carried out in a blocking (B) or nonblocking (B⁻) procedure. The middle and right panels show responding to a color for which the blocking stimulus was subsequently reinforced (+) or extinguished (−).

The middle panel of Fig. 3.6 shows that the data confirmed that expectation. Responding to that color whose orientation was reinforced (labeled "+") was greater than to that color whose orientation was nonreinforced ("−") ($T = 3$, $p < .05$). The right-hand panel of Fig. 3.6 shows further confirmatory data. Following their test for blocking, the animals in Group 1 were also subjected to the Phase 3 discrimination and test procedures given Group 2. As the right-hand panel shows, they yielded similar results. Thus the same animals that had previously shown blocking also developed within-event learning.

These results suggest that even when one feature of an event has become sufficiently valuable, by prior conditioning, to produce blocking of conditioning to an added feature, the organism still learns the relation between the two features. Apparently neither the fact that one feature has value nor the fact that it is an alternative predictor of the US prevents its integration with other features. A recent experiment in our laboratory has found analogous results in a conditioned suppression setting. In that instance, greater blocking (less suppression) was obtained when the blocking CS was extinguished prior to testing the blocked CS. Holman (1980) has used a motivational, rather than a conditioning manipulation to make a similar point. He found evidence for equivalent within-event learning whether or not one feature of the event was made valuable by a deprivation technique.

The contribution of within-event learning to responding to the stimuli in a blocking experiment expands a point made previously. Within-event learning greatly complicates the use of standard Pavlovian experiments for inferring basic facts about the formation of inter-event associations. Clearly, not all of the responding to a stimulus is governed by its association with the US; its association with other stimuli or features of stimuli is also important. In fact, within the context of blocking experiments, manipulations that are intended to vary the strength of CS–US associations actually might produce differential behavior instead by varying the contribution of within-CS learning to behavior.

Conditioned Inhibition

Another popular Pavlovian procedure that presents a stimulus with multiple features is the conditioned inhibition paradigm. In that paradigm the organism receives two interspersed kinds of trials which may be described as A—reinforced and AB—nonreinforced trials. The most frequently observed outcome is that A becomes excitatory whereas B becomes inhibitory. There is reasonable evidence available to suggest that A and B have separately formed excitatory and inhibitory associations with the reinforcing US. But it also turns out that there is some form of learning within the AB compound that allows the organism to know that A and B have co-occurred.

A recent autoshaping experiment illustrates that point. The logic of the experimental design was similar to that of previous experiments. Each pigeon was given two concurrent conditioned inhibition treatments in each of which an orientation presented alone was reinforced whereas the combination of that orientation with a particular color (blue or yellow) was nonreinforced. The orientations should become excitatory and the colors inhibitory. After 14 days on each of which each orientation was reinforced six times and each compound nonreinforced 24 times, the birds showed substantial responding to the orientations but little behavior during the compounds. That constitutes one kind of evidence that the colors are inhibitory—they interfere with the responding that the excitatory orientations would otherwise have produced.

Although the identities of the events were counterbalanced, for any given bird each color was inhibitory only by virtue of its nonreinforcement in conjunction with a particular orientation. The question of interest is then whether or not the color-orientation learning has taken place. To answer that question, each bird received discrimination training with the two orientations. On each of 4 days the birds received six reinforced presentations of one orientation and 24 nonreinforced presentations of the other. Finally, the birds were tested by receiving 15 reinforced presentations of each of the colors. At issue was whether the acquisition of responding would be more rapid to that color whose paired orientation had been maintained as excitatory compared with one whose paired orientation has been extinguished. Such a result would indicate knowledge of the particular color-orientation pairings.

Figure 3.7 shows the course of this acquisition of excitation for the colors, separated according to the previous treatments of the paired orientations. Although the effect was small, in fact acquisition was faster for a color whose orientation had not been extinguished. This constitutes evidence that in a conditioned inhibition paradigm there may develop some integration of the excitor and inhibitor. A parallel set of outcomes has been observed for the flavor-aversion preparation (Speers et al., 1980).

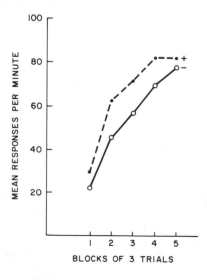

FIG. 3.7.   Acquisition of responding to a stimulus previously presented in a conditioned inhibition paradigm. The stimuli differ in whether their jointly presented excitor was subsequently extinguished (−) or not (+).

As a set, these data constitute a powerful argument that one must attend to the integration within events in interpreting Pavlovian conditioning. Such integration is apparently pervasive and sometimes powerful in its ability to control behavior.

RULES GOVERNING WITHIN-EVENT LEARNING

The previous sections have given some feeling for the involvement of within-event learning in Pavlovian settings. In this section we report some preliminary evidence on the circumstances that promote such learning. We deal with four topics: initial acquisition, extinction and retraining, the role of temporal relations, and the interaction between within-event learning and the formation of associations between events.

Acquisition

As the previous sections have made clear, the organism's knowledge of multiple features of an event depends on the joint occurrence of those features. But none of those experiments gives any evidence about the course of acquisition of that knowledge with exposure to the event. Here we report some data that suggest that this formation of within-event memories follows a systematic course.

For this experiment we chose an experimental procedure not yet described in this chapter. This procedure differs from those previously employed not in its manner of producing within-event learning but in its manner of detecting it. The experiment shares with previous ones the general logic of detecting that learning by modifying the value of one feature of an event and looking for consequent modification in responding to another feature. It differs from those experiments in not using a conditioning operation to modify the value of a feature. Rather it uses what might be called a motivational operation—it creates a specific hunger for one feature.

To accomplish this, we followed Fudim (1978) in exploiting the well-known ability of formalin injections to produce a strong increase in salt intake. We have found in earlier experiments that when an animal has previously consumed a fluid consisting of salt and quinine mixed, the subsequent induction of a sodium deficiency produces an increase not only in the intake of salt but also of quinine. Moreover, that increase is specifically dependent on the prior experience with those flavors in joint compound. Consequently, this procedure can be used to index the strength of the within-event memory when salt is one of the relevant features.

One advantage of this technique is that it does not require the separate presentation of either of the features during a conditioning procedure in order to modify its value. As we see later, such separate presentation can have a marked decremental effect on our ability to detect within-event learning. Moreover, in the context of studying the course of acquisition, one necessarily varies the or-

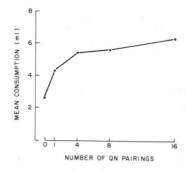

FIG. 3.8.   Mean consumption of quinine in sodium-deficient animals as a function of the number of prior quinine–salt (QN) pairings.

ganism's familiarity with the individual features, and that variation can have profound effects on the ability of a conditioning operation to modify successfully the value of the features. This, of course, would complicate the interpretation of any acquisition study.

Using this sodium deficiency technique, we exposed four groups of eight rats each to either 1,4,8, or 16 10-min presentations of a quinine–salt (QN) mixture, delivered at a rate of one per day. The manner of presentation was such that the animals received the appropriate number of QN trials at the end of the 16-day period; water was presented on the initial days to those subjects receiving fewer than 16 presentations of QN. A control group received four separate 10-min presentations each of Q and N over the last 8 days of this phase of the experiment. Then all animals received a 3-day procedure designed to induce a sodium deficit. On each day they had ad lib access to water and a salt-free diet (matzos). On the last day, they additionally received a 2.5-ml injection of .06M formalin. On the next day, their water was removed and 3 hours later they were given 30-min access to quinine, with a water alternative. The question of interest was how the quinine intake would vary with the number of QN presentations. Presumably, such variations are indicative of the strength of the within-event learning.

Figure 3.8 shows the quinine consumption over the 30-min test, plotted as a function of the number of QN pairings. The point plotted as zero is the control group, which had received four separate presentations each of N and Q. It is clear that there is an orderly increase in consumption over trials. Each of the paired groups consumed more than did the unpaired group ($Us < 14$, $ps < .05$), but the only differences among the paired groups were that Groups 8 and 16 combined consumed more than did Group 1 ($U = 30$, $p < .05$).

This reasonably straightforward acquisition function contains only two points that require further comment. First, acquisition is extremely rapid. The bulk of the learning was completed with one exposure and performance was essentially asymptotic after four exposures. Of course, the rate of within-event learning will likely vary with such parameters as the modality, salience, and duration of the event components. But in the present instance, it was very rapid indeed. Second, the learning curve is apparently monotonic. This is of interest because some experiments that have used a sensory preconditioning procedure for measuring associations between sequentially presented stimuli have reported nonmonotonic functions (cf. Thompson, 1972). In those experiments, the best learning occurred when only a few *AB* presentations preceded the conditioning of *B* and testing of *A*. It seems possible that those results are partly attributable to the damage that repeated *AB* presentation can do to the conditionability of *B* and hence measured responding to *A*. One advantage of the present sodium deficit procedure is that it does not use a conditioning operation to change the value of *B* and consequently is not subject to such difficulties. For that reason, it may provide a superior measure of the course of *AB* acquisition, less encumbered by necessarily confounded changes in the conditionability of the elements. In any case, the major fact to be learned from this experiment is that the acquisition of within-event learning is orderly and rapid.

Extinction and Retraining

Just as one expects joint presentation to promote within-event learning, one would anticipate that separate feature presentation would undermine it. Moreover, subsequent joint presentation should reestablish the memory. It turns out that the former expectation is correct but the latter is not. Figure 3.9 displays some relevant data collected in our laboratory by Freberg (1979).

That figure shows the consumption of quinine from an experiment that used the sodium deficit procedure. Four groups of rats (*P*, *EP*, *PE*, and *R*) had received four 10-min exposures to the *QN* solution whereas the fifth (*U*) had received four separate presentations each of *Q* and *N*. For Groups *P* (paired) and

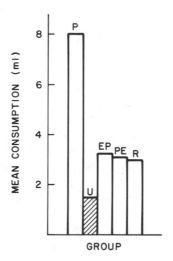

FIG. 3.9. Consumption of quinine in sodium-deficient animals for which quinine and salt had simply been paired (*P*), unpaired (*U*), or who had received exposure (*E*) to quinine alone either before or after pairing. Group *R* received retraining exposures to the quinine–salt compound following a treatment identical to Group *E* (from Freberg, 1979).

U (unpaired) those were the only experiences with flavors prior to the induction of a salt need and test for quinine consumption. The fact that Group P showed more consumption of quinine than did Group U is evidence that the procedure was adequate to establish within-event learning. Two of the other groups that had received QN trials additionally received six separate presentations of Q. For Group PE (paired-extinguished) those separate presentations followed QN training; for Group EP (extinguished-paired) they preceded it. It is clear from Fig. 3.9 that those separate presentations markedly reduced Q consumption in a manner consistent with the hypothesis that the within-event learning had been reduced. Moreover, in this experiment the magnitude of the reduction was quite similar whether the separate Q presentations followed or preceded joint exposure. In fact, other experiments in our laboratory have found that any separate presentation of an element, either alone or in compound with other elements, equivalently undermines within-stimulus learning. In the present experiment this "extinction" was purposefully incomplete, but in other experiments Freberg (1979) has found that an even greater number of separate presentations can reduce the level of responding to that of Group U.

What is of most interest in this experiment, however, is the results of Group R (retrained). That group was treated exactly like Group PE, receiving QN trials, then separate presentations of Q; but, before it was tested, it additionally received four more QN presentations in an effort to retrain the within-event learning. However, those retraining trials were without detected effect. Despite the fact that the same number of QN presentations was quite adequate to establish strong QN learning in Group P, and was found to produce almost asymptotic levels of learning in Fig. 3.8, it was essentially without effect as a retraining procedure. This is especially surprising inasmuch as the extinction had been purposefully incomplete so as to maximize sensitivity to any retraining. Group R remained reliably different from Groups P and U but indistinguishable from Groups PE and EP.

This failure of retraining is not an isolated result. Using a somewhat more complex design we have obtained essentially the same results in a recent autoshaping experiment. In that experiment, 16 pigeons initially received 60 reinforced presentations of a white keylight each day for 3 days. That pretraining was intended to ensure attention to the response key. Then on each of the next 3 days they received 12 nonreinforced presentations of each of two color–pattern compounds, mixed with six reinforced presentations of white. The compounds were composed of one of two colors (orange and magenta) and the patterns were sets of either black dots or sine waves on a white background. The compounds were presented by dividing the response key into quadrants by a black X; the colors could be presented on the top and bottom quarters whereas the patterns could appear on the left and right quarters.

After this training, eight birds received simple extinction for 3 days. On each day the birds received 24 separate presentations of one color together with six

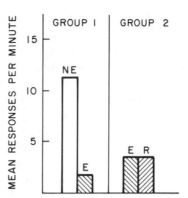

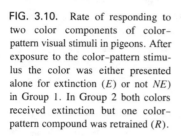

FIG. 3.10. Rate of responding to two color components of color–pattern visual stimuli in pigeons. After exposure to the color–pattern stimulus the color was either presented alone for extinction (*E*) or not *NE*) in Group 1. In Group 2 both colors received extinction but one color–pattern compound was retrained (*R*).

reinforced presentations of white; the other color was not presented. On each of the next 3 days they received 12 reinforced presentations of each of the patterns. Finally, they were tested for their response to the colors. The question of interest was whether the color that had been presented separately would yield a lower response rate, thus indicating attenuation of its association with the pattern. The left-hand side of Fig. 3.10 shows that this indeed was the case. Responding to the extinguished color was specifically depressed, relative to responding to the nonextinguished color (Wilcoxon $T = 1$, $p < .02$).

The other eight birds received a treatment intended to extinguish both of the color–pattern associations but then were retrained on one. On each of the 3 days following their initial exposure to the compounds, they received 24 separate nonreinforced presentations of each color, mixed with six reinforced presentations of white. Then for the next 3 days, they received 12 nonreinforced presentations of one of their original compounds, but no presentations of the other. Finally, they received 3 days of training on both patterns and were tested for their response to the colors. It was anticipated that responding to the colors would be low, indicating loss of the within-event learning. However, there was the opportunity to observe retraining in one of those compounds. The right-hand side of Fig. 3.10 shows the data from the test session. Those data confirm the former expectation on extinction but not the latter on retraining.

One related result is worth mentioning. In both of the previously described experiments "extinction" was accomplished through separate presentations of the eventually tested feature of the event. But we have elsewhere (Rescorla & Freberg, 1978) reported that similar decrements can be produced by separate presentations of the other feature. More recent experiments have suggested that presentation of the alternative feature is less powerful in reducing our ability to detect within-event learning, but it is nevertheless effective. This result is of special interest because standard sensory preconditioning experiments demand a stage in which *B* is presented repeatedly and reinforced between exposure to *AB* and testing of *A*. The implication is that too extensive conditioning of *B* could reduce our ability to observe within-event integration. That implication has been confirmed in a recent conditioned suppression experiment (Rescorla, 1980a).

This pattern of results suggests that separate presentation of the features of an event undermines the observation of within-event learning in a manner that is largely independent of the manner of that presentation. Disruption occurs whether the feature is given alone or in combination with other features, whether it occurs before or after the joint presentation, and whether it is the tested or reinforced element that is separately presented. Although these different modes of presentation might be interpreted in terms of various theoretical concepts, such as extinction, counterconditioning, and latent inhibition, the similarity of their impact suggests instead the possibility of a common basis. Moreover, the relative stability of the detrimental effect, as evidenced by ineffectiveness of attempts at retraining, might encourage a rejection of several currently available theoretical alternatives. This is a point to which we shall return.

Finally, the detrimental effect of separate element presentation upon the observation of within-event learning has an implication for the phenomenon of potentiation. Because that phenomenon was viewed as dependent on within-event learning between odor and taste, one would expect it to be attenuated if separate odor presentations were given prior to the compound conditioning trial. Recent experiments in our laboratory have confirmed that implication.

Temporal Relations

All of our previous discussion has dealt with learning about simultaneously presented stimulus features. Such a mode of presentation is natural when using the language of learning about features of a single event. Indeed, at some level the singleness or multiplicity of events is tied up with temporal extension; it is exactly in the case of simultaneous occurrence that one might be tempted to talk of forming a memory of the features of a single event. But studies of the learning of relations among events, such as Pavlovian conditioning experiments, typically have used sequential rather than simultaneous presentation. Moreover, simultaneous presentation apparently does not result in very good learning in those paradigms. Thus it is of interest to investigate the relative merits of simultaneous and sequential presentation of the event features studied here.

Such comparisons have, of course, been made many times before. In the main they employ a relatively straightforward between-group comparison in which various groups receive presentations of two stimuli but with varying temporal relations among those stimuli. One might, for instance, compare the learning that results from simultaneous AB presentation with that resulting from sequential presentation of A then B. In a setting in which A and B are relatively neutral, one must engage in a subsequent step, such as pairing B with a US, but eventually both groups are tested for some response to A.

However, it has not seemed to us that this kind of comparison is adequate. Notice that groups like these differ not only in the temporal relation between A and B but also in the context of A's presentation. For a simultaneous group, A is never presented alone until the final test, whereas sequential presentation naturally involves the occurrence first of A and then of B. One could imagine various consequences of this difference, but two especially bothered us. First, in the simultaneous group the presence of B may adversely affect the organism's processing of A; at the time it is asked to process A, it also must process B. In the sequential group, the organism can inspect A alone without explicit competition. The result may be that, in the simultaneous group, A is less well processed and therefore less able to become associated with other stimuli, whatever their temporal relation to it. Second, in the final test, A is a novel stimulus for the simultaneous group but not for the sequential one. Even if learning had been excellent under both conditions, one might anticipate differential generalization decrement between training and test in the two groups. Both of these consequences of the different context of A's presentation could result in our underestimating the relative power of simultaneous presentation to establish an association.

With these difficulties in mind, we have come to use a somewhat more complex design, which involves presenting each animal with three stimulus elements in a relation that may be described as $AB—B'$ (Rescorla, 1980b). Each animal receives trials that involve simultaneous presentation of A and B followed by B'. Then half the animals receive pairings of B with the US and half receive pairings of B' with the US. When the animals are finally tested for their response to A, the former animals provide an index of the strength of the simultaneous A–B association whereas the latter provide an index of the strength of the sequential A–B' association. Notice that the context of A's presentation has been matched for both groups, thus equating the difficulty of processing A and the amount of stimulus generalization decrement from training to test. Consequently, this procedure may provide a more balanced assessment of the merits of the two modes of stimulus presentations.

Figure 3.11 shows the results of one application of such a paradigm to a flavor-aversion procedure. The elements used in this experiment were sucrose (S), quinine (Q), and hydrochloric acid (H). Two groups of animals received 5-min presentations of S mixed with either H or Q, followed immediately by a 5-min presentation of Q or H. During subsequent conditioning half of each group received two poisoned presentations of Q and the other half received two poisoned presentations of H. In this way, half of the animals were poisoned with the flavor previously presented simultaneously with S and half poisoned with the flavor that had followed S. The animals were then given a 10-min choice test involving simultaneous access to S and water. A third, control group received 5-min presentations of S followed by water on some days and either the H–Q or

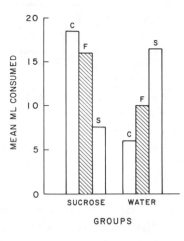

FIG. 3.11.   Consumption of sucrose and water in animals that had received sucrose and hydrochloric acid presented simultaneously (*S*), in a forward (*F*) relation, or had received an unpaired control (*C*) treatment (from Rescorla, 1980b).

the *Q*–*H* sequence on other days, so as to present *S, H,* and *Q* for the same durations in the experimental groups. Half of the animals in this group were then poisoned following *H* and half following *Q*.

The results for those control animals are not surprising. We knew from previous work with these concentrations that they would prefer sucrose to water in a ratio of about 3 to 1. That is the result to be expected if there are no associations between *S* and a poisoned flavor. The results for the animals poisoned on the flavor presented simultaneously with sucrose (labeled *S* here) are also consistent with earlier results. That treatment reversed the ordinary preference relation and resulted in a marked reduction in sucrose consumption. The most interesting results are those of the animals that were poisoned on the flavor that had a forward conditioned relationship with sucrose (labeled *F* here). They showed only slight signs of rejecting sucrose compared with the control animals. Certainly they evidenced less rejection than did the animals of Group *S*. Consequently, with the present technique, it appears as though there is more learning of the co-occurrence of features when they are simultaneous than would normally occur if they were properties of a single event.

It is not entirely clear how general one can expect this conclusion to be. We have applied the same design to auditory and visual stimuli with rats in a conditioned suppression setting and observed similar results. However, the procedure is clearly best adapted to cases in which *A, B,* and *B'* are all relatively neutral so that one can assess the associations of *A* with *B* and *B'* under conditions where *B* and *B'* can be thought of as identical in value. In the case in which *B* and *B'* have values not under experimental control, as when they are USs, the interpretation of responding to *A* would be considerably more difficult. But in any case, with the kind of events used here, within-event learning is clearly promoted by simultaneous rather than sequential presentation.

It is worth pausing for a moment to note an implication of that conclusion for a phenomenon we described earlier, potentiation. Recall that we gave a particular interpretation to that phenomenon: the greater aversion to an odor poisoned in conjunction with a taste compared with one poisoned alone was attributed to the within-event odor–taste learning. Consequently, experimental variations that manipulate that association should likewise manipulate the magnitude of potentiation. An implication of the present data is that if the odor and taste were applied sequentially rather than simultaneously, the within-event learning would be substantially less and consequently should produce less potentiation.

A recent experiment tested that implication. Two groups of thirsty rats received a single 3-min presentation of each of two odors (banana and almond). Each odor was followed 15 min later by a .5% body weight injection of .6M LiC1. For each animal one odor ($O1$) was presented alone but the other odor ($O2$) was accompanied by a taste (saccharin). However, half the animals had the saccharin mixed in the solution with $O2$ and half received a 3-min saccharin presentation 2 min after the presentation of $O2$. To match fluid intakes the animals receiving simultaneous odor and taste received 3 min of access to water 2 min after the presentation of their odor–taste compound. For all animals, the relation between the odors and poison was constant; they differed only in whether the taste was presented simultaneously or sequentially with $O2$. After recovery from poisoning, the animals were given a choice test between $O1$ and $O2$.

The results of that test are shown in Fig. 3.12. To the left are the data from the animals given simultaneous odor and taste presentation. Their data pattern is like that previously reported for potentiation: they consumed more $O1$ than $O2$. To the right are the results of those animals given sequential odor–taste presentation, which show quite a different pattern. Those animals consumed more $O2$ than $O1$ (Wilcoxon $T = 10.5$, $p < .01$). Not only was potentiation destroyed by this

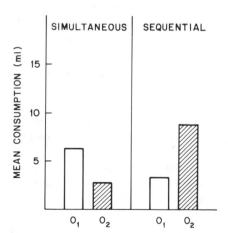

FIG. 3.12.   Consumption of fluids with odors that had been presented and poisoned alone ($O1$) or in simultaneous or sequential compound with saccharin ($O2$).

manipulation, but the commonly observed phenomenon of overshadowing was restored. Manipulation of the temporal relation between odor and taste clearly had a profound effect on the outcome. These results can be interpreted naturally in terms of the role of within-event learning in converting an overshadowing outcome into one of potentiation. Moreover, they confirm the superiority of that learning with simultaneous presentation.

Interaction with Between-Event Learning

The final determinant of within-event learning on which we present evidence concerns its interaction with learning associations between events. We earlier described evidence that the embedding of an event presentation in the context of ongoing Pavlovian conditioning does not prevent the occurrence of within-event learning. But it remains to be decided whether the two kinds of learning interact or simply occur independently. There are a variety of ways in which they might interact, but in the present section we are concerned with one possibility—that the concurrent learning of Pavlovian associations might affect the course of within-event learning. In particular, we wish to know whether following an event with a Pavlovian reinforcer interferes with integration of the event. Is there competition between the two types of learning as might be expected from a variety of limited-capacity models? (see Cheatle & Rudy, 1978).

That apparently simple question turns out to be reasonably difficult to address experimentally. A straightforward approach would be to present each animal with two events, designated AB and CD, but follow only one of these with a US. Then we might inspect the AB and CD learning by differentially conditioning B and D and then testing A and C. The difficulty is that A and C will have different likelihoods of evoking a response simply as a result of the prior differential conditioning of the compounds, so that not all their responding during the test will be attributable to their associations with B and D. That makes it virtually impossible to use those test results to infer the strength of the AB and CD memories.

We have been exploring various alternative designs that solve this problem. We report the results of one still inadequate design that has the virtues of solving this problem and also of being sufficiently simple to allow brief presentation. In this design, animals are exposed to two types of trials, $AB+$ and $AC-$; the issue is whether A becomes better associated with B or C. That issue is addressed by subsequently reinforcing B or C in different groups and asking which group shows a greater response to a tested A. Notice that the target stimulus, A, has the same relation to the US in both groups, so that although that relation will affect responding during the test, it will do so equivalently whether the test is otherwise measuring the AB or AC learning.

One application of this design has been made in an autoshaping experiment with pigeon subjects. The stimulus A was a dot pattern projected on two opposite

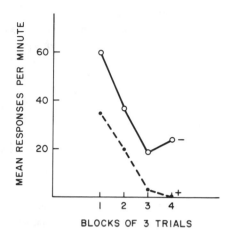

FIG. 3.13.   Mean rate of responding to a color component of a color–pattern visual stimulus in pigeons. The presentation of the color–pattern stimulus had either been followed by food (+) or not (−).

MEAN RESPONSES PER MINUTE

BLOCKS OF 3 TRIALS

quadrants of a response key; *B* and *C* were orange and magenta colors that could simultaneously be projected on the other quadrants. After 3 days on each of which the animals received 12 *AB*+ and 12 *AC*− trials, in which "+" designates 5-sec access to grain, the birds received 3 days of discrimination training with *B* and *C*. Half the animals received 12 *B*+ and 48 *C*− trials per day; half received the reverse discrimination. Finally, all birds received 12 nonreinforced test presentations with the dot pattern (*A*).

Figure 3.13 shows the results of that test session. The figure displays the mean rate of responding during the dot pattern over the course of extinction testing. It is clear that responding was greater for those animals who were subsequently reinforced following *C* but not *B* (labeled "−" to indicate that this treatment should expose the learning that was not followed by the US).

These results suggest that there is a kind of interference with the formation of within-event learning when the event is followed by a US. However, that interference need not mean that there is a commonality in the underlying learning processes. It may only imply that the organism has a limited processing capacity that prevents it from accomplishing both the within-event and between-event simultaneously without loss.

Two final points should be made about this competition. First, it suggests that under some circumstances the impact of within-event learning on conditioning paradigms may be reduced. For instance, in a normal overshadowing experiment the delivery of a reinforcer immediately following CS presentation may reduce the amount of within-event learning. In that case one would anticipate that delaying the delivery of that reinforcer would allow time for the within-event learning to occur and thus make especially likely the observation of potentiation, rather than overshadowing. Experiments both in our laboratory and that of Garcia (Palermino, et al. 1980) confirm this prediction of potentiation, rather than overshadowing, with delayed delivery of the US.

Second, that some manipulations known to affect the success of between-event learning also modulate the magnitude of simultaneously occurring within-event learning particularly complicates interpretation of many Pavlovian experiments. For instance, when one changes the magnitude of the US intensity during a compound conditioning experiment, that change may affect the progress of within-event learning but be incorrectly interpreted as producing a change in the between-event associations.

Conclusions on Rules Governing Within-Event Learning

The results of this section have identified a variety of determinants of a within-event memory. That memory grows rapidly with repeated occurrences of the event. It is especially strong with simultaneous presentation of the features of the event. Within-event learning occurs whether or not a US follows the event, but is more successful when no US is given, perhaps suggesting posttrial processing. Finally, separate presentation of the features of an event in other contexts reduces evidence of integration of those features. That reduction occurs whether the separate presentation precedes or follows exposure to the event and is not easily reversed by reexposure to the event.

These results offer a prescription for maximizing the observation of within-event learning. One should present the elements simultaneously, minimize the events immediately after that presentation, and avoid separate presentations of the elements. Following these guidelines should enhance one's chances of seeing sensory preconditioning just as we have seen it enhance one's chances of seeing potentiation.

THEORETICAL INTERPRETATIONS

There are various theoretical frameworks within which to consider the kinds of learning described here. Throughout the preceding discussion we have employed a variety of languages that differ in their theoretical commitments: within-event integration, within-stimulus learning, formation of event memories, associations among event features, and associations among co-occurring stimuli. That range of languages was partly intended to prevent the assumption of a particular theoretical framework; but it also reflects our own real ambivalence about which framework might be most appropriate. We here describe two possibilities, neither of which seems entirely satisfactory.

Within the context of American psychology, the most natural language in which to describe any learning process is associative. In its most blatant form, an associative account of our results would describe within-event learning as the formation of associations between the stimulus components. According to this account, when the organism receives a complex stimulus, it decomposes it into its component parts and then (judging by the present data) forms associations among those parts. That is, the animal first performs an analysis of the stimulus and then resynthesizes it in terms of an associative structure.

There are certainly obvious advantages to this approach. Associative theory has been highly successful and provides the most widely accepted account of learning processes. Describing this particular learning as associative would allow one to bring to bear all the highly developed empirical and theoretical literature already available for associations between events. No new learning processes or laws would be necessary. It was precisely this approach, of course, that the British associationists took to the problem of within-event learning. They envisioned the organism as perceptually dissecting the stimulus into its elements and then representing objects as clusters of associations among those elements. Moreover, they supposed the rules applicable to this form of learning to be the same as those appropriate for describing associations between events.

Such an approach could deal with much of the data reported here. It makes understandable the growth of within-event learning as a function of number of exposures to the event. It anticipates the loss of that learning when features are presented outside the event. It provides a natural language in which to discuss potentiation.

However, any attempt to deal with within-event learning using the same principles of associative learning that apply to Pavlovian conditioning also has empirical difficulties. First, it is embarrassed by the superiority of simultaneous, compared with sequential, presentation of stimuli. Of course, that disagreement with the Pavlovian literature may be due partially to differences in assessment technique. However, some recent results (Freberg, 1979) indicate that simultaneous within-event learning may be superior even when more traditional comparisons are made. Perhaps more seriously, the absence of substantial retraining of within-event associations by additional presentations of the event is at odds with the rapid retraining observed with Pavlovian conditioning.

An attempt to force within-event learning into the conventional Pavlovian mold also meets with intuitive objections. First, most modern views of Pavlovian conditioning view it as emerging from a predictive relationship between the two events being associated. The functional role of conditioning usually is seen as providing a means by which the animal can correctly anticipate the subsequent occurrence of emotionally significant events. But that does not seem to be the function of within-event learning, especially among simultaneously presented features. When the features of an event are integrated, one feature does not predict the future occurrence of another. Second, several authors have argued for distinguishing between a stimulus object and a feature of that object. For instance, Asch, Ceraso, and Heimer (1960) have suggested that the relation between features of a stimulus is more intimate than the relation between two separate stimulus objects. They have pointed out that for many features it makes little sense even to think of their occurrence apart from some object. Neither of these essentially intuitive notions is sufficient to reject an associative account, but neither do they seem well captured by that account.

There is, however, another approach to within-event learning that may capture those intuitions. That approach, which has been described in various ways by an assortment of authors (e.g., Gibson, 1969; James, 1890; Kohler, 1941; Robinson, 1932), suggests that events are not represented in terms of analyzed and reassociated components. Instead, when the organism receives a complex event, it forms a representation of that event as a unit. New perceptual experiences are then evaluated for their similarity to preexisting unitary memories. To the degree that those experiences are similar to existing memories, they activate those memories; to the degree that they are discrepant, they result in the formation of their own memory representations.

We have described previously how such an alternative approach might deal with the sort of data reported here (Rescorla, in press). Consider the case of presentation of an *SH* compound. According to this account, the stimulus is not analyzed into its components; rather a unitary *SH* representation is formed. Then, should *H* subsequently be presented, it would reactivate the *SH* memory because of their similarity. Poisoning of *H* would effectively result in the conditioning of an aversion to the memory of *SH*. Subsequent test presentations of *S* would also reactivate the similar *SH* memory and result in rejection of *S*. It is not that the organism analyzes *SH* into its components, which it then reassociates. Rather, the organism confuses *S* and *H* each with the similar *SH* memory representation. Failure to discriminate the compound from its component parts results in association-like performance.

This approach has advantages in dealing with some of the data we have described. First, one might expect simultaneous presentation to result in a unitary *SH* memory representation but sequential presentation to establish separate *S* and *H* representations. It seems possible that with the kinds of stimuli used here the formation of associations between separately represented *S* and *H* events might not be especially good. But with simultaneous presentation there is no need for such associative learning. Perhaps that would result in superior performance with our test procedures.

Second, this approach provides a natural account of the "extinction" and "reconditioning" data. When either *S* or *H* is separately presented (or presented in the context of other features), alternative memory representations would be established. As a result, their subsequent occurrence would be less likely to activate the *SH* memory, and evidence for the presence of that within-event learning would be reduced. If test presentations of *S* have both *SH* and *S* memories to contact, and there is some limitation on the contacting process, then no matter how strong the *SH* representation or its association with the US, rejection of *S* would be reduced. Moreover, once the *S* representation had been established, additional presentations of *SH* (reconditioning) might have little impact. According to this account, the difficulty in our "extinction and retraining'' experiments is not one of destruction of the within-event learning but rather of the ability of the individual components to retrieve that memory. The difficulty lies not in the learning itself but rather in our ability to detect that learning. Consequently, manipulations that are intended to reestablish the within-event learning cannot be of much help.

But there are also disadvantages to this approach. They center around the notion of generalization between the compound and its component parts. If we are to deal with the available phenomena of Pavlovian conditioning, many of which concern responding to elements after compound conditioning or responding to the compound after element conditioning, such generalization is critical. Specifying when such generalization will or will not occur is, of course, the sort of problem typically faced by holistic approaches to stimulus processing.

One way to reconcile these two approaches might be to acknowledge the presence of a stimulus unique to the joint presentation of two elements. Such a notion has proved useful in other settings for allowing a basically associative theory to deal with apparently configural findings (Rescorla, 1973, 1980a). If such a unique stimulus were acquired with exposure to the event, it might provide the basis for the within-event learning observed here.

But we do not propose here to chose between these alternative theoretical approaches. Each approach has its attractions and drawbacks. At the present state of our knowledge it may be best simply to keep the possibilities before us. In our own experience, they have each proven heuristic in generating experimental outcomes.

CONCLUSIONS

One may identify three interesting questions in the analysis of within-stimulus learning. First, does such learning occur? In our view, the kinds of data reported here permit a reasonably positive yes to that question. We have shown various illustrations of the occurrence of such learning and have identified its operation in various popular Pavlovian paradigms. Such learning indeed seems powerful and widespread. Classical theoretical approaches that assume that components of the CS operate independently (Bower, 1967; Estes, 1951; Rescorla & Wagner, 1972) clearly need to be modified. Second, what are the rules of that learning? We have provided some initial description of a few of the circumstances that promote within-event learning. At the present state of our knowledge that description gives a picture of a systematic learning process, but one which does not appear to follow the same rules that are commonly accepted for between-event learning. Third, is there a hierarchical organization such that within-event learning provides the units that are then associated by Pavlovian conditioning? In many ways this is the most interesting question. The present experiments only provide a foundation upon which to begin to search for its answer.

ACKNOWLEDGMENT

The research reported in this chapter was supported by NSF Grant BNS 78-02752.

REFERENCES

Asch, S. E., Ceraso, J., & Heimer, W. Perceptual conditions of association. *Psychological Monographs: General and Applied.* 1960, *74*, 1-48.

Bower, G. A multicomponent theory of the memory trace. In K. W. Spence & J. T. Spence (Eds.), *The psychology of learning and motivation.* New York: Academic Press, 1967.

Cheatle, M. D., & Rudy, J. W. Analysis of second-order odor-aversion conditioning in neonatal rats: Implications for Kamin's blocking effect. *Journal of Experimental Psychology: Animal Behavior Processes,* 1978, *4*, 237-249.

Clarke, J., Westbrook, R. F., & Irwin, J. Potentiation instead of overshadowing in the pigeon. *Behavioral and Neural Biology,* 1979, *25*, 18-29.

Durlach, P. J., & Rescorla, R. A. Potentiation rather than overshadowing in flavor-aversion learning: an analysis in terms of within-compound associations. *Journal of Experimental Psychology: Animal Behavior Processes,* 1980, *6*, 175-187.

Estes, W. K. Toward a statistical theory of learning. *Psychological Review,* 1951, *51*, 94-107.

Freberg, L. *Evidence supporting a perceptual learning model of the sensory preconditioning of flavors.* Unpublished PhD dissertation, University of California, Los Angeles, 1979.

Fudim, O. K. Sensory preconditioning of flavors with a formalin-induced sodium need. *Journal of Experimental Psychology: Animal Behavior Processes,* 1978, *4*, 276-285.

Gibson, E. J. *Principles of perceptual learning and development.* New York: Appleton–Century–Crofts, 1969.

Holman, E. W. Irrelevant-incentive learning with flavors in rats. *Journal of Experimental Psychology: Animal Behavior Processes,* 1980, *6*, 126-136.

James, W. *Principles of psychology,* New York: Holt, 1890.

Jenkins, H. M. Why autoshaping depends on trial spacing. In C. M. Locurto, H. S. Terrace, & J. Gibbon (Eds.), *Autoshaping and conditioning theory.* New York: Academic Press, 1981.

Kamin, L. J. Attention-like processes in classical conditioning. In M. R. Jones (Ed.), *Miami Symposium on the Prediction of Behavior: Aversive Stimulation.* Miami: University of Miami Press, 1968.

Kohler, W. On the nature of associations. *Proceedings of the American Philosophical Society,* 1941, *84*, 489-502.

Palmerino, C. C., Rusiniak, K. W., & Garcia, J. Flavor–illness aversions: the peculiar roles of odor and taste in memory for poison. *Science,* 1980, *208*, 753-755.

Rescorla, R. A. Evidence for a "unique stimulus" account of configural conditioning. *Journal of Comparative and Physiological Psychology,* 1973, *85*, 331-338.

Rescorla, R. A. *Pavlovian second-order conditioning: Studies in associative learning.* Hillsdale, N.J.: Lawrence Erlbaum Associates, 1980. (a)

Rescorla, R. A. Simultaneous and successive associations in sensory preconditioning. *Journal of Experimental Psychology: Animal Behavior Processes, 1980, 6,* 207-216. (b)

Rescorla, R. A. Simultaneous associations. In P. Harzem & M. Zeiler (Eds.), *Advances in analysis of behavior* (Vol. 2). New York: Wiley, in press.

Rescorla, R. A., & Cunningham, C. L. Within-compound flavor associations. *Journal of Experimental Psychology: Animal Behavior Processes,* 1978, *4*, 267-275.

Rescorla, R. A., & Freberg, L. The extinction of within-compound flavor associations. *Learning and Motivation,* 1978, *9*, 411-427.

Rescorla, R. A., & Wagner, A. R. A theory of Pavlovian conditioning: Variations in the effectiveness of reinforcement and nonreinforcement. In A. H. Black & W. F. Prokasy (Eds.), *Classical conditioning II: Current theory and research*. New York: Appleton-Century-Crofts, 1972.

Robinson, J. S. *Association theory today*. New York: Century, 1932.

Rusiniak, K., Hankins, W., Garcia, J., & Brett, L. Flavor–illness aversions: Potentiation of odor by taste in rats. *Behavioral and Neural Biology*, 1979, *25*, 1–17.

Speers, M. J., Gillan, D. J., & Rescorla, R. A. Within-compound associations in a variety of compound conditioning procedures. *Learning and Motivation*, 1980, *11*, 135–149.

Thompson, R. F. Sensory Preconditioning. In R. F. Thompson & J. S. Voss (Eds.), *Topics in learning and performance*. New York: Academic Press, 1972.

4

Long-Delay Conditioning and Instrumental Learning: Some New Findings

M. R. D'Amato,
William R. Safarjan,
David Salmon
Rutgers University

The emphasis on learning phenomena that characterized animal behavioral research during the period 1940-1970 has been partially supplanted by a lively interest in memory mechanisms. Much of this recent research has been concerned with memory for events of varying complexity or for associations between two events formed under conditions of minimal memorial burden (i.e., under immediate reinforcement). Learning with delayed reinforcement, one of the oldest problems in learning theory, involves memory mechanisms as well as learning, inasmuch as the animal must remember, at the time of reinforcement, certain critical features of the earlier training event if the required association is to be formed, a point clearly recognized almost 50 years ago. Although some advances have been made in recent years, the problem of learning with delayed reinforcement remains unresolved. Unresolved in the sense that the controlling variables are poorly understood, particularly in the case of instrumental learning.

When considering delayed reinforcement as a controlling variable in behavior, it is important to keep in mind the distinction between classical and instrumental conditioning. Some forms of classical conditioning, in particular taste aversions, seem capable of enduring substantial reinforcement delays, whereas instrumental learning is often severely impeded in animals by reinforcement delays of only a few minutes. Thus, under appropriate experimental conditions a strong conditioned taste aversion can be obtained within a single trial and with a reinforcement delay (CS-US interval) of 30 min or longer, whereas when reinforcement is delayed for even a few minutes a simple instrumental response will require many trials before any sign of learning is evident. Whether this striking difference reflects the existence of specialized learning mechanisms in the case of taste aversions or whether it is indicative of the operation of different variables in the case of classical and instrumental conditioning is an issue of some importance.

To provide a brief overview of what follows, in the first part of the chapter we describe recent results which suggest that conditioned taste aversions may represent one instance, though a powerful one, of a more general category—classically conditioned affective responses—that encompasses attractions as well as aversions. In the second part of the chapter we identify two variables that have a dramatic impact on the ability of monkeys to acquire a simple instrumental response under delayed reinforcement, variables that play little, if any, role in conditioned taste aversions and related phenomena. When these variables take on favorable values, monkeys are capable of efficient instrumental learning with substantial reinforcement delays (30 min). When unfavorable, the animals show no signs of learning despite intensive training.

ONE-TRIAL, LONG-DELAY CONDITIONED ATTRACTIONS IN MONKEYS AND RATS

We have recently reported that under appropriate experimental conditions cebus monkeys are capable of acquiring a conditioned attraction for a spatial location within a single trial and with a 30-min reinforcement delay (D'Amato & Buckiewicz, 1980). The experiment, which employed a T-maze scaled up to accommodate our monkeys, was quite simple. On Day 1 all animals were allowed to explore the maze for 5 min, and the amount of time spent in the left, striped arm and in the right, black arm of the T-maze were recorded. Percent preference for an arm of the maze was defined as the amount of time spent in that arm divided by the amount of time spent in both arms multiplied by 100, analogous to the two-bottle preference test given in conditioned taste-aversion studies.

Twelve monkeys, which varied in sex, age, and previous experimental experience (none in the T-maze or in similar apparatuses), were assigned to an experimental, a CS-only, and a US-only group (N = 4 per group) on the basis of the Day 1 spatial preference test. On Day 2 the experimental animals were placed in the nonpreferred arm of the T-maze (as determined by the Day 1 preference test) for a 1-min period, a treatment that will be referred to as "exposure to the CS." They were then removed from the T-maze and placed in a holding cage in the test room for a 30-min delay interval. At the end of the delay interval they were introduced into the startbox of the T-maze, where they found 10 raisins, a highly preferred food. After consuming the raisins (the US), they were removed from the startbox for a short interval of time, then reintroduced into the startbox and given a 3-min preference test conducted in the same manner as the baseline preference test of Day 1. It was assumed that if the animals associated the CS (the nonpreferred arm) with the food (US) given 30 min later, they would show an increase in preference for the CS arm on the second preference test. In parallel with conditioned taste-aversion studies, we might therefore conclude that a conditioned attraction for the CS arm had been established.

The CS-only control group was exposed for 1 min to the nonpreferred arm, just as the experimental subjects, and they also spent a 30-min delay interval in the holding cage. However, when introduced into the startbox of the T-maze, they found it empty. This group, then, constituted a control for alterations in spatial preference due to exposure to the CS alone. The US-only group received the raisin reward without being first exposed to the CS. These animals were brought into the test room and placed directly in the holding cage, where they spent the 30-min delay period. They were then introduced into the startbox, which contained the raisin reward, and shortly thereafter they were given the 3-min preference test. Any alterations in spatial preference that might result from exposure to the US (food) alone, would be reflected by the performance of this group.

On Days 3 and 4 the experimental, CS-only, and US-only groups received precisely the same training–test sequence as occurred on Day 2.

Approximately 120 days later a retention test was given to all animals, which consisted of a single 3-min spatial preference test, identical in all respects to those given on Days 2–4. During the intervening 120 days the animals were housed in group living cages and received no experimental manipulations whatever.

Figure 4.1 summarizes the results for the percent preference measure. The three groups were, of course, closely comparable on the baseline preference measure, as the groups were assigned on this basis. However, as a result of a single pairing of CS and US, separated by a 30-min delay, the experimental animals displayed a sharp reversal of preference on Day 2 (Test Trial 1), now showing a preference for the CS arm. The two control groups maintained their baseline preferences. A simple analysis of variance on the preference data of Test Trial 1 showed that the differences among the groups were reliable [$F(2,9) = 5.16$, $p < .05$]. Subsequent t-tests indicated that the experimental group was significantly different from each of the control groups ($p < .02$ in both cases). Moreover, a t-test comparing the preference scores on the first test trial with a chance, 50%, baseline indicated that the experimental animals developed a significant preference for the arm that was originally nonpreferred [$t(3) = 3.95$, $p < .05$]. During Test Trials 2 and 3 (Days 3 and 4) the experimental animals maintained their newly formed preference, whereas the CS-only animals ($C1$), which were placed but not rewarded, maintained their original preference. On the other hand, the US-only animals ($C2$) lost their original preference.

Although impressive, the percent preference scores do not reveal whether the experimental animals actually increased the amount of time spent on the originally nonpreferred side, as they are relative preference measures only. The

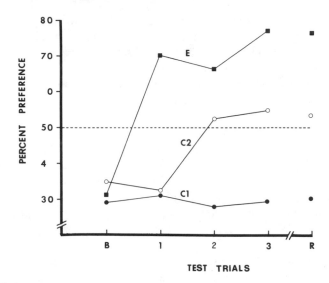

FIG. 4.1.   Percent preference scores for the experimental (E), the CS-only $(C1)$, and the US-only $(C2)$ groups obtained during baseline (B), the three test trials, and retention (R). (From D'Amato & Buckiewicz, 1980.)

absolute duration of time spent in the originally nonpreferred arm of the T-maze is shown in Fig. 4.2. The baseline scores of Day 1 were multiplied by .6 to account for the fact that a 5-min preference test was given during baseline whereas subsequent preference tests were 3 min in duration. It is clear that as a result of the single pairing of CS and US the experimental animals more than doubled the amount of time spent in the originally nonpreferred arm. On the other hand, there was virtually no change in the two control groups. The Test Trial 1 differences are significant $[F(2,9) = 4.58, p < .05]$, as is the difference between the experimental group and each of the control groups considered separately. The time duration scores show essentially the same pattern as the percent preference scores over Test Trials 2 and 3.

Figure 4.1 also shows that, with regard to the percent preference measure, there was excellent retention of the conditioned spatial attraction over the 4-month retention interval. Although an analysis of variance based on the data from the three groups was not significant, the difference between the experimental and CS-only groups was statistically significant $(p < .05)$. As revealed by Fig. 4.2, retention was also excellent when measured in terms of absolute time. In this case the overall F was significant $[F(2,9) = 7.17, p < .05]$.

We were rather surprised by the robustness of the conditioning and retention results, considering that there were only four animals in each group and that the backgrounds of the animals varied enormously, although we tried as much as possible to equate for the latter factor. Although one-trial appetitive conditioning has been reported before (Albert & Mah, 1972; Tenen, 1965), we know of no case where appetitive conditioning has been attained in a single training trial with a 30-min delay of reinforcement. Among the factors that might be responsible for our success is the use of a simple response already present in the animal's repertoire (approaching either the striped or black arm), just as conditioned taste-aversion studies capitalize on the strong propensity of thirsty animals to lick fluid from familiar drinking tubes. That the experimental apparatus constituted a novel environment for the animals was probably also important, as well as the fact that the delay interval was spent in the quiet test room, which may have served both to facilitate poststimulus processing and to isolate the training experience from potentially interfering events. Whatever the nature of the variables responsible for our results, the latter suggest to us that affective responses, whether positive or negative, whether based on taste or exteroceptive cues, are capable of being conditioned very rapidly and with substantial reinforcement delays.

Having just about exhausted our monkey colony, it was necessary that we turn to a more abundantly available animal if we wished to investigate one-trial, long-delay conditioned attractions further. After a considerable amount of pilot work, in which a variety of parameters were manipulated, we finally uncovered conditions that were capable of producing a similar phenomenon in rats.

Conditioned Spatial Attraction in Rats.   Safarjan and D'Amato (1981) used a T-maze very similar to that employed by D'Amato and Buckiewicz (1980). Each arm of the T-maze could be made black or striped by removable inserts that were

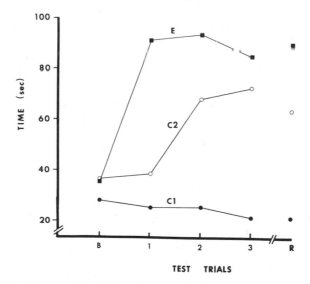

FIG. 4.2. Amount of time spent in the originally nonpreferred arm during baseline (*B*), the test trials, and the retention test (*R*), for the experimental (*E*) and control groups. (From D'Amato & Buckiewicz, 1980.)

applied to the three walls and floor of an arm. The training procedure, on the other hand, was rather different from that used with the monkeys. The animals of the present study were maintained on a strong water-deprivation schedule, being allowed 10 min access to water daily. Days 1 and 2 were devoted to obtaining baseline preference scores. The important point to note is that during these 5-min baseline preference sessions *both* arms of the T-maze were black, so that the preference measure obtained on these days was a preference for the left or right side of the T-maze, unrelated to arm color. On the basis of these preference scores, the 192 animals, female Sprague–Dawley rats, were assigned to 16 groups of 12 animals each. Twelve of the 16 groups formed a factorial design based on the following three variables. The first variable was experimental versus control. Experimental animals were exposed to the CS (the striped arm of the T-maze), and after a delay interval they were given 15 min access to a sucrose solution (7%, w/v), the unconditioned stimulus, in a different location. The control animals were really CS-only controls, in that they were exposed to the CS but not to the sucrose solution. The second variable was the duration of exposure to the CS, which was 10, 30, or 40 min. Note that these durations are considerably longer than the 1-min CS exposure used in the monkey study. The third variable was the duration of the reinforcement delay, either 30 or 120 min.

The single conditioning trial, which occurred while the animals were 44 hours water deprived, proceeded as follows. The animal was placed in the startbox of the T-maze with the door leading to the arm on the preferred side closed, thus forcing the animal to the nonpreferred arm. In all cases the nonpreferred arm was now striped and served as the CS. After the animal was confined in the CS arm for the appropriate duration, it was removed to a delay area where it remained during the reinforcement delay. It was then placed into a wastepaper basket and, if it were an experimental animal, it received 15 min access to the sucrose solution. A control animal was confined to the wastepaper basket for 15 min without the sucrose solution.

A single test session was administered 2 days later, when the animals were once again approximately 44 hours thirsty. The test consisted of a 5-min preference test, with the striped arm on one side of the T-maze and the black on the other, as they had been during the conditioning trial.

The results are summarized in Fig. 4.3, which presents the mean percent preference scores for each of the 12 groups plotted as a function of exposure duration and reinforcement delay. With increasing CS exposure, the controls tended to decrease the percentage of time spent in the striped, CS arm of the T-maze whereas the experimental animals increased somewhat the percentage of time spent in the CS arm. An analysis of variance yielded a highly significant result for the experimental versus control comparison [$F(1,132) = 17.95$, $p < .001$], indicating that an overall conditioning effect was obtained. The only other significant effect was for the interaction between experimental versus control and the CS-exposure variable ($p < .01$). The basis of this interaction was that

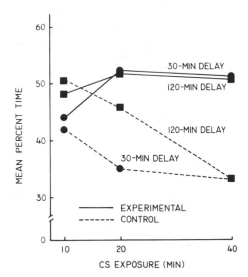

FIG. 4.3. Mean percent preference (time) scores for the 12 experimental and control groups as a function of CS-exposure duration and reinforcement delay (CS–US interval). (From Safarjan & D'Amato, 1981.)

the experimental subjects differed from their controls when CS exposure was 20 or 40 min, but not when it was only 10 min.

We can make better sense of the results by plotting them as difference scores between corresponding pairs of experimental and control groups, as is done in Fig. 4.4. Positive difference scores indicate that the experimental group spent a greater percentage of time in the striped, CS arm than did its associated control group. It is clear that at the shortest CS exposure, 10 min, there was no sign of conditioning in either the 30-min or the 120-min reinforcement delay groups. At the 20-min CS-exposure duration, the difference between the experimental and control groups was highly significant in the 30-min reinforcement delay condition ($p < .01$), but not in the 120-min delay groups ($t = 1.05$). With the 40-min CS exposure, however, the difference between the experimental and control groups was significant for both reinforcement delays ($p < .01$). Thus, CS duration was a critical variable determining the degree of conditioning and, to some extent, could offset the deleterious effect of extended reinforcement delay.

When similar difference scores were calculated for the absolute time spent in the CS arm, the same overall pattern of results was obtained. All the comparisons that were significant with the percent preference difference scores were also significant with the absolute time measure.

To get some idea of how conditioned spatial attraction varies as a function of reinforcement delay, two other groups of subjects, one experimental and one control, received 20 min exposure to the CS but experienced only a very short delay of reinforcement, approximately 10 sec. In other words, reinforcement was virtually immediate in these groups. Fig. 4.5 presents the percent preference data from these groups plotted as a difference score, along with the difference scores from the groups of the previous analysis that received a 20-min CS exposure with

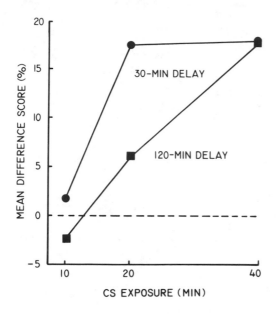

FIG. 4.4. The data of Fig. 4.3 plotted as difference scores between corresponding pairs of experimental and control groups at the various values of CS exposure and reinforcement delay. (From Safarjan & D'Amato, 1981.)

a reinforcement delay of either 30 or 120 min. The resulting delay-of-reinforcement gradient is virtually flat between 10 sec and 30 min, falling off sharply at the 120-min delay interval. It will be recalled that the difference between the experimental and controls was significant at the 30-min delay but not at the 120-min delay of reinforcement. Separate comparison of the experimental and control animals that received ''immediate'' reinforcement was also significant ($p < .02$). These data indicate, then, that with CS duration fixed at 20 min, the strength of conditioned spatial attraction produced by a single conditioning trial is little affected by reinforcement delay up to at least 30 min.

One other variable was investigated, the locus in which reinforcement occurred. All the experimental groups discussed thus far received reinforcement in the wastepaper basket and their controls were confined to the basket for an equal duration of time. It will be recalled that in the monkey study, reinforcement occurred in the startbox, a procedure similar to that employed by Lett in her demonstrations of instrumental learning with delayed reward (Lett, 1973, 1975). We employed the startbox as the reinforcement location in earlier pilot studies and got the impression that it resulted in weaker conditioning than reinforcing the animals away from the apparatus, although our major reason for using the wastepaper basket was expediency. We simply could run more animals by using this procedure and it avoided the problem of having to insure that no residue of reward was present in the startbox on subsequent trials. In any case, we attempted to compare the startbox and wastepaper basket loci of reinforcement by running an experimental and control group in the 20-min CS exposure and 30-min delay of reinforcement. Although the conditioning effect was substantially greater in the wastepaper basket animals than in the startbox subjects, a 2×2 ANOVA produced a significant result ($p < .01$) for the experimental versus control comparison, but not for the interaction ($F = 1.17$). Nevertheless, a t-test performed on the startbox animals' data did not prove significant, so we are inclined to conclude tentatively that the wastepaper basket was a more efficient locus of reinforcement than the startbox.

Such a conclusion is not difficult to justify theoretically. During preconditioning, the animals twice experienced the sequence of startbox followed by black arm. It seems possible that for an animal reinforced in the startbox, the cues of the startbox could have served to retrieve memories of the black arm rather than, or in addition to, memories of the striped, CS arm.

Returning to Figs. 4.3 and 4.4 for a moment, it is clear that the significant conditioning that emerged in the 40-min CS exposure, 120-min delay condition was not the result of an increase in percentage of time spent in the CS arm by the experimental animals (compared to the comparable experimental subjects of the 20-min CS exposure condition). Rather, it was due to a reduction in percentage of time spent in the striped arm by the control animals, a finding that requires some comment. Is it possible that the results of the present experiment can be accounted for without appeal to conditioning, in terms of differential habituation to the striped arm or similar nonassociative mechanisms? One might argue, for example, that the reward experienced by the experimental animals simply served to decrease the habituation to the striped arm caused by the previous CS exposure. The difficulty with this and related explanations is that, although the same reward was given to all experimental subjects, Fig. 4.3 shows that the experimental animals that received 20 and 40 min of CS exposure spent a greater

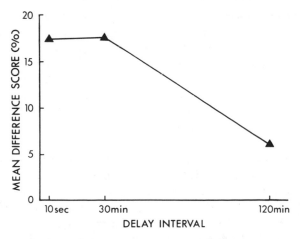

FIG. 4.5. Delay-of-reinforcement gradient in the 20-min CS-exposure condition based on differences between experimental and control groups. (From Safarjan & D'Amato, 1981.)

percentage of time in the CS arm than the experimental animals that received only a 10-min exposure. Moreover, if the reward acted to reduce habituation (or stimulus satiation) it should have been more effective the sooner it occurred after the CS-exposure experience. However, there was virtually no difference in the amount of conditioning observed in the groups that received immediate reinforcement or reinforcement after a 30-min delay (Fig. 4.5).

Still, the considerable difference in percentage of time spent in the CS arm by the 30- and 120-min delay control groups exposed to the CS for 10 or 20 min deserves attention. One possible explanation for the difference is that because the delay interval was spent in dim surroundings in the test room, this experience may have generalized to the subsequent preference test, causing some degree of generalized satiation (or habituation) for the dimmer black arm. Assuming this to be the case, it follows that the longer the delay interval the greater the degree of such generalized habituation, which in turn implies that the control animals in the 120-min delay condition ought to have spent more time in the CS arm than the corresponding animals in the 30-min delay condition. On the other hand, a very long (40-min) CS-exposure duration might be expected to cause so much "primary" stimulus satiation or habituation for the striped arm as to completely overpower any differences that might arise from generalized sources. Although post hoc, this analysis nicely accounts for the preference functions obtained in the 30-min and the 120-min delay control groups (Fig. 4.3).

The results of the present experiment and those of the monkey study suggest to us that one-trial, long-delay conditioning of affective responses may be a much more general phenomenon than hitherto thought. From this point of view, conditioned taste aversions may simply be a special case of this larger category. It appears that affective responses, whether positive or negative, whether based on interoceptive or exteroceptive cues, are conditionable in a single trial and with substantial delays of reinforcement. Although the boundaries of this generalization remain to be established by future research, the results already in hand prompt the following question. If positive affective responses (as revealed by preference for a spatial location and the like) are so readily established and so resistant to delay of reinforcement, why is it that even a modest delay of reward causes such interference with acquisition of instrumental behavior? It is true that even with conditioned reinforcement cues largely eliminated, rats can learn a spatial discrimination response with delays up to a few minutes, a fact that has been known for a long time. However, the evidence for spatial discrimination learning with longer delays, say in the neighborhood of 20 min or longer, is scarce and not yet compelling. The situation is far worse in the case of visual discrimination learning, where there currently is some question whether rats can learn a simple black–white discrimination when reward is delayed for as little as one minute (Lett, 1977; Roberts, 1976, 1977). Although monkeys appear capable of efficient visual discrimination learning with delays of a minute or so (D'Amato & Cox, 1976a), we were unable to obtain evidence of visual discrimination learning with delays of 16 min (D'Amato & Cox, 1976b; cf. Riesen, 1940). It appears that if appropriate affective responses are conditioned in these situations, some factor or factors inhibit expression of this conditioning in terms of the target instrumental behavior.

DIFFERENTIAL EFFECT OF REINFORCEMENT DELAY ON AFFECTIVE AND INSTRUMENTAL RESPONSES

In the next experiment we tried to obtain direct evidence for the notion that affective and instrumental responses are differentially susceptible to delay of reinforcement. We used an experimental situation that allowed us to assess concurrently the rates of conditioning of both types of responses. The apparatus was the same T-maze as employed in the previous experiment. However, the left arm was always striped and the right arm always black. Before providing details, an overview of the experiment (D'Amato & Safarjan, 1981) may be useful.

Thirsty rats were given a water reward after entering the left, striped arm of the T-maze and a saccharin solution (.1%, w/v) reward after entering the right, black arm. Following each saccharin solution reward some animals were poisoned with lithium chloride shortly thereafter whereas others were poisoned 30 min later. Following the water reward, saline solution was injected either immediately or 30 min later, as required. Three dependent variables were assessed, two being indicators of affective responses. Consumption of saccharin versus consumption of water reflected the aversion conditioned to the saccharin solution. Spatial preference tests provided an assessment of the aversion conditioned to the arm of the maze correlated with the saccharin solution, namely the black arm. The third dependent variable was acquisition of the instrumental response of choosing the arm that contained water, that is, learning to choose the left, striped arm. With regard to the instrumental behavior, then, for some animals the choice was between immediate reward in the left, striped arm versus immediate saccharin solution reward plus poisoning 1 min later in the right, black arm. For other animals the choice was similar except that poisoning was delayed for 30 min. The hypothesis under test was that delay of reinforcement, poisoning in this case, would have a greater impact on acquisition of the instrumental response than it would have on acquisition of the taste or the spatial aversion. We made no attempt in this study to determine whether aversion for the black, saccharin, arm of the T-maze, if obtained, was in some way mediated or potentiated by the saccharin aversion. This issue was not directly related to our primary concern, which was whether the instrumental behavior and the spatial aversion, whatever its genesis, differed substantially in the degree of their dependence on the delay-of-poisoning variable.

As for the procedural details of the experiment, in Session 1 the subject was confined for 5 min in the left, striped arm of the T-maze, which contained water, and in Session 2 it was confined for 5 min in the black arm of the maze, which contained the saccharin solution. Session 3 was devoted to a 5-min baseline spatial preference test, during which no fluids were present in the T-maze. There then followed 16 training sessions, consisting of one trial per session. Eight of the 16 trials were free-choice trials and eight were forced.

On forced trials, which alternated with free-choice trials, the animal was forced to the arm not chosen on the previous free trial. On both free and forced trials an animal was confined to the entered arm for 5 min.

In addition to the delay-of-poisoning variable, there was a second manipulation, uncontrolled versus controlled water intake. The uncontrolled animals were allowed to drink as much water and saccharin solution as they wished during the 5-min confinement periods. Because poisoning followed ingestion of the saccharin solution, it was of course to be expected that the animals would reduce their intake of this fluid. To take this factor into account, the controlled-intake animals were allowed to drink an amount of water approximately equal to the amount of saccharin consumed on the previous saccharin trial.

Animals in the 1-min delay-of-poisoning group were taken from the T-maze to the colony room where, if they had previously chosen the black, saccharin arm, they were injected with an isotonic (.15 M) lithium chloride solution at a dosage of 4 ml/kg. If the animals had previously chosen the striped, water arm they were injected with a comparable volume of isotonic saline. Subjects in the 30-min delay groups were placed in their home cages for 30 min before receiving lithium chloride or saline injections. Training sessions were spaced two days apart, and on nontraining days the animals received their usual 10-min water ration but were otherwise undisturbed.

Aversion for the black, saccharin, arm was assessed by a 5-min spatial preference test administered after Training Trials 4 and 12. *No fluid was available in the T-maze during these tests.*

Turning to the results, we first consider the effect of delayed poisoning on the conditioning of affective responses. Because the uncontrolled-intake groups were free to drink as much water as they wished during the 5-min confinement in the striped arm, these animals provided a saccharin preference measure based on the amount of saccharin consumed divided by the amount of saccharin plus the amount of water consumed on a pair of successive trials. Each pair of successive trials generated one such score. Figure 4.6 presents these data for the 1-min and 30-min delay groups. It is clear that there was little difference between the groups with regard to the aversion developed for the saccharin solution over the 16 trials, which inflicted 8 poisonings.

To evaluate the degree of saccharin aversion in the controlled-intake groups, the amount of saccharin solution consumed on later trials was expressed as a percentage of the amount consumed on the first exposure during training. Surprisingly, the difference between the 1-min and 30-min controlled-intake groups was significant (greater suppression in the 1-min delay group). As with the

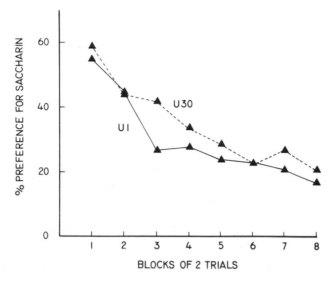

FIG. 4.6.   Percent preference for the saccharin solution over the 16 training trials in the uncontrolled-intake groups that received lithium chloride injections either 1 min (U1) or 30 min (U30) after ingestion of the saccharin solution. (From D'Amato & Safarjan, 1981.)

previous measure of saccharin aversion, however, there was no difference between the corresponding uncontrolled-intake groups. We have no convincing explanation why delay should affect the degree of conditioned saccharin aversion in the controlled-intake groups but not in the uncontrolled groups.

The conditioned spatial aversion produced a more consistent pattern. Figure 4.7 presents the results of the spatial preference tests given after Trial 4 and Trial 12 as well as the baseline preference scores obtained during pretraining. All groups were comparable on the baseline preference test, as group assignment was made on that basis. Baseline preference for the black arm, which averaged 59.5% over the 32 subjects, was significantly greater than chance expectation (p < .001), indicating an initial preference for the black, saccharin arm. However, after four training trials, on only two of which saccharin was paired with lithium chloride, all four groups changed their preference from the black to the striped arm of the T-maze. The mean preference for the black side, 40.3%, was now significantly below chance expectation (p < .001). Preference for the black arm was even lower on the Trial-12 test (35.9%), but this was not significantly different from the Trial-4 preference test. The same pattern of results was obtained when absolute amount of time spent in the black arm of the T-maze was considered rather than percent preference. Thus, the two poisoning experiences had a strong effect on spatial preference, resulting in a distinct conditioned aversion for the black, saccharin arm. Moreover, the strength of the aversion was comparable for the 1-min and the 30-min delay-of-poisoning conditions.

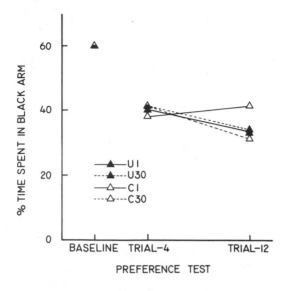

FIG. 4.7.   Results of the baseline, Trial-4, and Trial-12 spatial preference tests, which were conducted with no fluids in the T-maze. The experimental conditions were controlled (*C*) versus uncontrolled (*U*) intake and 1- versus 30-min delay of poisoning. (From D'Amato & Safarjan, 1981.)

In order to evaluate the instrumental behavior, the percentage of correct responses was calculated for each group over blocks of four free trials. The resulting group means are presented in Fig. 4.8, collapsed over the controlled-versus uncontrolled-intake variable. It is apparent that, whereas the 1-min delay groups showed clear signs of learning to go to the striped (water) arm by the end of the free-choice trials, there was no evidence of acquisition in the 30-min delay groups. An ANOVA based on the three factors of reinforcement delay, type of intake, and trial blocks, produced a significant result for delay [$F(1,28) = 5.68$, $p < .03$], and a marginally significant effect for the delay-by-blocks interaction [$F = 3.92$, $p < .058$]. In view of the difference in the saccharin aversion observed in the two controlled-intake groups (C1 and C30), it is worth noting that over the last four free-choice trials the difference in percentage of correct responses between Groups U1 and U30 was somewhat greater than the difference between Groups C1 and C30. Thus, delay of poisoning significantly interfered with acquisition of the instrumental response in both the controlled-intake and the uncontrolled-intake conditions; in contrast, it had no observable effect on the conditioned spatial aversion and influenced the conditioned taste aversion only in the case of the controlled-intake groups.

As noted previously we cannot assess from the present results the degree to which the conditioned spatial aversion was mediated (or potentiated) by the saccharin aversion, if at all. The difference in saccharin aversion observed in the controlled-intake groups taken in conjunction with their comparable spatial aversion suggests some degree of uncoupling of the two. Nevertheless, this interesting issue deserves further attention (cf. Lett, 1980).

We can conclude from this series of experiments that affective responses, both positive and negative, are remarkable in their ability to be conditioned extremely rapidly and under the burden of a substantial delay of reinforcement, or in Pavlovian terms, a lengthy CS–US interval. Although conditioned taste aversions are in some respects more powerful than the conditioned spatial attractions and aversions that we have produced, this may be more a matter of parameter values than of basic structural differences. Novelty of the CS is an important variable in allowing an association to overcome a lengthy CS–US interval. Not only are the taste stimuli employed in conditioned taste aversions usually novel in the sense that the animals have had little previous experience with the CS fluid, but they often also enjoy a high degree of relative novelty. By the latter we mean that the novel taste is superimposed on a past history of depressingly homogenous foods and fluids, usually nothing more than Purina Lab chow and water. Mitchell, Winter, and Moffitt (1980) have recently shown that taste aversion learning and neophobia are much stronger when a novel taste CS is experienced within well-adapted contextual cues than when it occurs in a context that is poorly adapted. Another important parameter is the strength of the US. Perhaps conditioned attractions would be much stronger if they were established with appetitive USs that rivaled in intensity the poisoning agents used in taste aversions. Imaginative and careful parametric studies are needed to clarify these issues.

It may be appropriate to comment briefly on how affective responses are assumed to be related to preference behavior and instrumental responses. To begin with, conditioned affective responses are inferred entities; they are not to be equated with the preference behavior by means of which they are detected. In

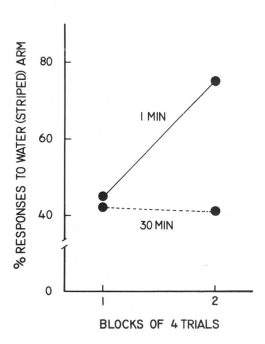

FIG. 4.8.   Mean percentage of responses on the 8 free-choice trials to the water (striped) arm of the T-maze in the combined 1-min and 30-min delay (CS–US) groups. (From D'Amato & Safarjan, 1981.)

the case of a conditioned saccharin aversion, for example, the preference be-havior (reduced consumption of saccharin) is not itself the conditioned aversion but rather a manifestation of an association developed between saccharin and some consequence of the poison US. Whether the conditioned aversion (i.e., the negative affective response) is, at bottom, a change in the taste value of saccharin or an anticipatory nausea response is unclear, but the problem is by no means intractable (cf. Krane, 1980). The food US employed in the first two experiments is similarly assumed to result in the conditioning of a positive affective response to the CS arm—a conditioned attraction—that manifested itself in the spatial preference behavior of the monkeys and rats.

Preference tests (taste and spatial) are extremely sensitive indicators of con-ditioned affective responses because they instantly reveal the animal's tendency to maintain contact with an attractive stimulus or break off contact with a stimulus that elicits a negative affective response; intervening processes are reduced to a minimum. Instrumental responses can also be used to detect con-ditioned affective responses but they generally will be far less sensitive than preference behavior (Garcia, Kovner, & Green, 1970; Holman, 1975). It is true that a conditioned taste aversion may be revealed by a simple runway response, but apparently only if the response is not strongly entrenched (Chen & Amsel, 1980). Perhaps one reason why instrumental responses are less sensitive in this regard is that, compared to preference behavior, they usually are more distal in time and space from the CSs that elicit the relevant affective responses. Con-sequently, the individual must somehow come to anticipate the relevant affective response before the latter can exert control over the instrumental behavior.

The differential effect of delayed poisoning on affective and instrumental responses observed in the present experiment may be related to this factor. A moderate delay of reinforcement might result in the conditioning of an affective response that is only slightly weaker than that conditioned with immediate rein-forcement. Where reflected by the instrumental behavior, this small difference could become substantially amplified if the required anticipatory process is strongly dependent on the strength of the relevant affective response. Other possible mechanisms, addressed specifically to delayed reward, are discussed in the next section.

INSTRUMENTAL LEARNING WITH LONG DELAYS

Let us now leave affective conditioning and take a closer look at instrumental conditioning under substantial reinforcement delay. Given the rapidity with which positive affective responses can be conditioned even with lengthy rein-forcement delay, why is it that animals find it so difficult to learn a spatial discrimination when delay of reward exceeds several minutes or, in the case of a visual discrimination, exceeds a minute or so? The results of the last study suggest that appropriate affective conditioning may occur under delayed reinforcement but for some reason it is not very effective in guiding instrumental behavior.

Not that instrumental learning does not occur with delayed reward; rather, the issue is that such learning is remarkably paltry given the rapidity with which the underlying affective responses appear to be conditioned. As early as 1934, Wolfe reported that rats could learn a position discrimination in a T-maze with delays of at least 2½ min, although final performance was only at the level of approximately 70% correct responses. Perkins (1947) later published similar results, despite determined efforts to eliminate all sources of conditioned reinforcement cues. More recently Lett (1973), using different training procedures, has extended the reinforcement delay interval to 8 min. However, her report that rats are capable of learning with a 60-min reinforcement delay seems less convincing (Lett, 1975); the difficulty is that in Experiment 1 only the rats rewarded for choosing the black (presumably preferred) arm appeared to learn the task, and in Experiment 2 this tendency persisted, although it was not statistically significant. The question not answered in that study was whether the animals rewarded for going to their nonpreferred side learned the task, an issue that will later be seen to be an important one. In any case, the combined final performance of these animals was below 80% correct responses.

Turning to visual discrimination learning, we find much less evidence of learning with significant delays. In Grice's (1948) classic study, rats subjected to a 10-sec delayed reward failed to learn a simple black–white discrimination although given the benefit of some 1400 trials. In an earlier study with chimpanzees, Riesen (1940) reported that his animals were unable to learn a visual discrimination (actually a discrimination reversal) with delays in excess of 4 sec. These results, however, seem not to be characteristic of the ability of animals to learn visual discriminations under delayed reward. We have clearly shown that, even with all sources of conditioned reinforcement cues eliminated, cebus monkeys are capable of rather efficient visual discrimination learning with reinforcement delays on the order of 1 min (D'Amato & Cox, 1976a). Lett (1974) reported a similar result for rats, but Roberts (1976) was unable to reproduce her results (see Lett, 1977, 1978; Roberts, 1977). In a carefully controlled study, we were unable to obtain visual discrimination learning in monkeys with a delay of 16 min (D'Amato & Cox, 1976b). The important point is that the limits of learning with delayed reward seem far more constricted for visual than for spatial discrimination learning. We later offer a possible explanation for this difference.

After having achieved long-delay conditioned attraction in our monkeys in the T-maze apparatus, it naturally occurred to us that they might be capable of learning a cue-correlated spatial discrimination in the same situation with a substantial delay of reward. We therefore ran the indicated experiment in the T-maze used in the spatial attraction study. First, we employed a 3-min preference test to determine for each monkey (*Cebus apella*) the nonpreferred arm of the T-maze, either the left, striped arm or the right, black arm; the nonpreferred arm subsequently served as S+. Three animals were run in a virtually immediate-reward condition. After making its choice, the animal was confined in the arm for 1 min, then removed directly to the startbox where, if the animal had been correct, it received a reward of 10 raisins. If it had been incorrect, it was confined to the startbox for a 1-min period. One trial was given daily, except for the first 6 days, when a second trial, forced to the correct side, was given if the animal had been incorrect on the first trial. The other three animals were run with a 30-min delay of reward, which was spent in a holding cage located in the test room. It will be recalled that this was the procedure used in the preference study. We tracked changes in the animal's spatial preference by means of 3-min preference tests given after every 20 training sessions. Training continued until the criterion of at least 90% correct responses in two successive 10-trial blocks was reached or until a total of 100 free-choice trials (one per day) was accumulated.

Although the three subjects run in the virtually immediate-reward condition initially had rather strong preferences for S− (as revealed by the first 3-min preference test), all acquired the spatial discrimination rapidly, in 20, 40, and 40 trials (not including criterial trials).

The results of the animals subjected to the 30-min delay of reward are shown in Fig. 4.9. Note that Kip actually achieved 100% correct responses in the fourth block of 10 trials, which seemed extremely promising. However, his perfor-

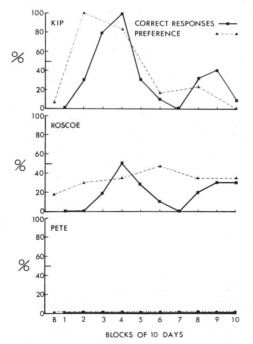

FIG. 4.9.   Percentage of correct responses and percent preference for the S+ arm in the 3 monkeys trained with a 30-min reinforcement delay.

mance deteriorated shortly thereafter, until it reached zero percent in the seventh block. Kip's spatial preferences closely tracked his instrumental behavior, leading it somewhat. Roscoe showed similar cyclic instrumental performance, although it never went beyond 50% correct, nor did his spatial preference behavior go beyond that value. Pete was a total failure. In the 100 free-choice trials distributed over approximately 4 months he made not a single correct response.

Discouraging as these results were, we decided not to abandon the problem, on the chance that Kip's rapid initial learning might not be an accident. We knew from earlier work that forcing the animal to remain in the experimental apparatus during the delay period suppressed discriminative performance because of the aversiveness of the delay interval (cf. Cox & D'Amato, 1977; D'Amato & Cox, 1976a). Requiring the animal to remain in the experimental situation, if not in the experimental apparatus itself, might also have a deleterious effect, even though it might allow for poststimulus processing. Thus, in the next study we evaluated this variable by having two animals spend the 30-min delay period in their home cages in the colony room and two in the test room, as in the previous study. We modified three other parameters. Rather than providing reinforcement in the startbox, reward and nonreward occurred in the center section of the T-maze and therefore in full view of the arms themselves. (Transparent Plexiglas doors separated the arms from the stem of the maze.) This modification, as well as the reduction in the time spent in an arm of the T-maze from 60 to 10 sec, was modeled after Lett's procedures. Finally, we increased the payoff from 10 to 20 raisins. Again a single trial was given each day, except for the first 6 days, when an animal was forced to the correct side on the second trial if it had been incorrect on the first. The animals received 100 free-choice trials, distributed over about 4 months. As with the earlier studies, a 3-min preference test determined the nonpreferred arm, which subsequently served as S+. No other preference tests were administered.

The results appear in Fig. 4.10. At first sight the data appear chaotic, as we seem to have obtained everything from bona fide learning to a complete failure of learning. But on closer examination a sensible pattern becomes discernible. First, it is clear that the top two animals performed better than the bottom two. As indicated in the figure, the top two animals spent the delay period in their home cages rather than in the test room; thus, their results favor the home-cage condition. Next note that the two animals on the left performed better than the two on the right. Also note that the two animals on the right had a far stronger initial preference for the incorrect alternative than did the pair on the left. In short, we seem to have a two-variable factorial experiment with one animal in each cell. The two variables are home cage versus test room and strength of initial preference for S−, strong versus weak. Apparently, spending the delay period in the home cage and having a weak initial bias for the incorrect arm both facilitate learning with delayed reward. When both these factors are operating in a favorable direction, learning occurs, as shown by Peewee's performance, which

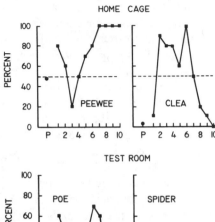

FIG. 4.10. Percentage of correct responses (filled squares) over the 100 free-choice trials and the initial percent preference for the S+ arm (filled circles). Peewee and Clea spent the 30-min reinforcement-delay interval in their home cages; Poe and Spider remained in the test room during the delay interval.

reached 100% correct. When both factors are operating in the wrong direction, as was the case with Spider, the situation is plainly hopeless. With only one factor in the advantageous direction, things are unstable, and though some evidence of learning might occur, as in the case of Clea, inexplicably, it can totally disappear.

After our previous failures to find evidence of long-delay learning, we were not particularly happy with these results. If they had been cleanly negative, we could have turned our backs on the whole business and concluded that when carefully done, animals, at least monkeys, are not capable of long-delay learning. But given Peewee's results, which seemed a clear case of reasonably efficient spatial discrimination learning, this conclusion was obviously premature. Moreover, unlike the rat data, where asymptotic performance with any sizable delay is considerably below 100%, Peewee did not make a single error during the last 40 trials.

We therefore decided to run four additional animals in the home-cage condition. The only differences between this experiment and the previous one were that: (1) the animals were removed from the arm of their choice within 7–10 sec of entering the arm; (2) for the first 15 trials, if an animal was incorrect, it was given a second, forced trial to the correct side; and (3) reward and nonreward were administered in the startbox rather than in the center section.

The results of this study appear in Fig. 4.11. The top two animals, Headly and Jodi, had only mild preferences for the arm that served as S−, and it is clear that both of these animals acquired the spatial discrimination very effectively;

Headly, in only 10 trials. Moreover, their final performance was at or close to 100%.

The situation was strikingly different for Hubert and Potato, both of which had a strong preference for the incorrect arm. At the end of 50 free-choice trials (65 trials including the 15 forced trials), Hubert had made only two correct responses, and Potato only one. Given the previous results, there seemed little point in training the animals further. Rather, we thought it more productive to try to alter the preference of one of the animals, to see whether this experimental manipulation would indeed result in some degree of long-delay learning. To bias the results against our manipulation, a 3-min preference test was conducted after the 50th trial to gauge each animal's preference for the incorrect arm. As indicated in Fig. 4.11, Potato's preference for the latter was 100%—he never ventured into the correct arm. We therefore chose Potato as our experimental subject, Hubert serving as the control.

We attempted to extinguish Potato's strong preference for S− simply by allowing the animal to freely explore the apparatus for a 10-min period on 20 separate daily sessions. During the first 3 min of these sessions, the animal's preference for the S+ and S− arms was measured and its initial choice was recorded. To avoid possible differential reinforcement arising from removal from the maze, on alternate days the animal was removed from the left and the right arms.

It is of some interest that during the 20 extinction sessions Potato's initial choice was always to the S− arm. However, his preference behavior, which initially was strongly biased toward the S− arm, reversed itself during the later

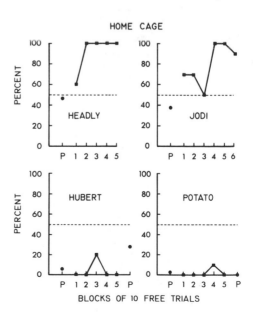

FIG. 4.11. Percentage of correct responses (filled squares) and percent preference for the S+ arm (filled circles) in four subjects that spent the 30-min reinforcement-delay interval in their home cages.

sessions, reaching a level of 31% by the last two extinction sessions. It must be remembered, however, that the preference tests were restricted to the first three of the 10-min extinction sessions, and we have no way of knowing how the animal distributed its time during the last 7 min of a session. At the termination of the 20 extinction sessions, training was reinstituted with the 30-min delayed reward and with the assignment of S+ and S− remaining as they were prior to the extinction sessions. As before, one free-choice trial was given daily, although until the first correct free-choice trial was made, the subject was given a forced trial if the free-choice trial was incorrect.

Hubert, the control animal, received a 20-day break in training, during which time he was not exposed to the experimental apparatus. The 20-day break occurred between trials 54 and 55, rather than after trial 50. Starting with trial 60, this animal also received a forced trial to the correct side if its free trial of that day was incorrect, the forcing procedure being terminated after the first correct free-choice trial.

As Fig. 4.12 shows, Hubert reached a level of only 30% correct responses and then returned to zero percent. His final preference score was extremely low. On the other hand, Potato's performance showed a steady increase up to 90% correct, and over the last 30 trials averaged about 87% correct. On his final preference test, Potato spent 98% of the time on the correct side, a remarkable reversal of preference over what it had been after Trial 50. Interestingly, the single correct response in the sixth block of free trials occurred on the very last trial of that block. Thus, after the first correct response was made, learning was extremely rapid, despite the fact that reward was delayed for 30 min.

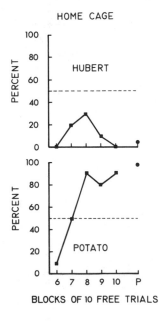

FIG. 4.12.   Percentage of correct responses (filled squares) and percent preference for the S+ arm (filled circles). Potato received 20 extinction sessions prior to Trial 60; Hubert did not receive this extinction experience.

INTERPRETATIONS AND CONCLUSIONS

That is the end of the empirical story. Let us now try to draw some conclusions from these results and see how they apply to previous relevant research. First, if conditions are favorable, animals, at least monkeys, are capable of remarkably efficient cue-correlated position learning though burdened by a substantial delay of reward. Given the results of the long-delay conditioned attraction experiments described earlier, this should come as no surprise. Unfortunately, however, it is easy to obliterate long-delay discrimination learning if the training conditions are not favorable. Requiring the animal to remain within the experimental apparatus during the delay interval, or perhaps even within the general experimental situation, can greatly impede learning, due to the aversiveness that develops as the animal begins to discriminate the delay contingency. The aversiveness induced by delay of reward can become associated with S+ and possibly supplant the positive affective response conditioned to S+ on earlier trials (cf. Cox & D'Amato, 1977). We have seen monkeys subjected to a substantial delay of reward in a visual discrimination task actually cover the S+ stimulus with their forepaws. Note that this factor cannot be of any importance on the first few trials, before the delay contingency has been discriminated, and thus played no part in the long-delay conditioned attraction studies.

A simple solution to the foregoing problem is to have the animals spend the delay interval in their customary living cages. It is interesting that Lett has consistently used this arrangement in her studies of long-delay learning, although she was motivated by different theoretical considerations. It is also of interest that Mischel (1974), in his studies of delay of gratification in children, found that young children could tolerate delays better if, during the delay interval, they thought of pleasant events other than the reward, a technique that serves to remove the subject cognitively, rather than physically, from the delay situation and its associated aversiveness.

Of perhaps greater significance for long-delay learning are the stimulus preferences and response biases that the subject brings to the experimental situation. A strong bias for an incorrect alternative seems almost impossible to abolish when response and outcome are separated by a substantial delay. Moreover, as we saw in the case of Kip and Clea, a strong bias for an incorrect response alternative that is overcome by a delayed reinforcement contingency can reappear in full strength. It seems likely that a preexisting preference for S− played an important role in the failure of Grice's animals to learn a black–white discrimination with only a 10-sec delay of reward. He reported that the animals either had no initial color preference or a preference for the black alley, and he deliberately eliminated three animals that had initial white preferences. Because S+ was the white alley, in many cases a preference for the black alley had to be overcome by the reinforcement contingency, which was easily accomplished by immediate reinforcement but not by the 10-sec delayed reinforcement.

Even if no preexisting biases for incorrect alternatives exist, visual discrimination learning by its very nature has the capacity to develop such incorrect response tendencies. The partial reinforcement that an animal receives for position responding often results in a strong position bias from which the animal has to recover before learning can occur. The implication, then, is that learning a visual discrimination with delayed reward will usually prove more difficult than learning a spatial discrimination, not necessarily because of any inherent difference between the two types of tasks, but because of the likelihood that a strong bias for an incorrect response tendency will develop in the visual discrimination task.

Riesen's (1940) failure to find visual discrimination learning in naive chimpanzees with delays beyond 4 sec seems attributable to an unusual amount of frustration induced by the reinforcement delays and to the strong position biases and color preferences that resulted from the repeated reversal of only two discriminative stimuli. It is not often reported that Riesen ran a second group of chimpanzees that was concurrently trained on hue discrimination tasks by a different experimenter in a different apparatus. These test-wise animals, for which one might think stimulus and response biases would have been attenuated, were far better at delayed-reward learning than the naive chimpanzees. Even so, the longest delay they could tolerate was only about 20 sec, a limitation probably attributable to the aversiveness of the delay interval.

Granting the importance of preexisting or concurrently developed interfering stimulus preferences and response biases in learning with delayed reward, the question arises as to why they are so resistant to modification. A number of theorists assume that in order for an animal to learn a delayed-reward contingency, some attribute or attributes of the animal's response on the previous trial must be active in the animal's memory at the time it experiences the delayed consequence. It is of interest that this ''retrieval'' interpretation of long-delay learning, which has considerable popularity today, was clearly articulated almost half a century ago by Wolfe (1934, p. 17). In any case, if this interpretation is correct, then one must assume that the existence of a strong bias or preference for an incorrect alternative prevents or greatly attenuates the necessary retrieval process.

To pursue this line of reasoning, consider what might occur in an animal with a strong bias for an incorrect alternative at the time that it experiences the delayed reward, whether as a result of a free or a forced choice. It is not unreasonable to assume that because the incorrect response tendency is strong the animal will anticipate its execution and its consequences even as the animal enters the experimental room and is placed in the startbox. If so, this anticipation represents retrieval of the incorrect response, which conceivably is reinforced by presentation of the reward object. Thus the animal might never associate the delayed-reward outcome with the correct response.

Another possibility, one that could work in conjunction with the retrieval interpretation, arises from the fact that when animals have completely learned the two contingencies, they frequently show a strong preference for a small immediate reward over a much larger delayed reward (Rachlin & Green, 1972). In our studies, the existence of strong stimulus or response biases suggests the operation of an unauthorized source of reinforcement in the experimental situation; an animal that has a strong position bias might be motivated by avoiding certain cues in the apparatus. Such a source of immediate reinforcement, though not considerable, could easily overwhelm the delayed reward, because of the strong propensity of animals (and humans) to prefer small immediate rewards over larger delayed rewards. This interpretation has the benefit of integrating long-delay learning with the more fundamental relationships that hold between the incentive value of a reinforcer and the delay associated with its presentation (cf. Ainslie, 1975). It also is less inconvenienced by the sharply nonmonotonic performance observed in some of the animals, particularly Kip and Clea. It is difficult to understand from a purely retrieval interpretation why an animal that once showed reasonable evidence of learning the delayed contingency would subsequently revert to virtually exclusive choice of the incorrect alternative, when nothing in the experimental situation has changed. Viewed as representing the consequence of choosing between a small immediate reward and a larger delayed reward, such an outcome is not farfetched if one assumes that the two alternatives are not markedly different in incentive value. In the absence of a substantial difference in the incentive value of the two alternatives, choice behavior might be expected to be unstable, particularly if consistent exposure to one alternative served to increase the attractiveness of the other.

If we combine the retrieval interpretation with the "incentive competion" view, we can account for most of our obtained results: (1) when no strong incorrect response tendencies exist, the animal, at the time that the delayed consequence occurs, is likely to have retrieved critical aspects of its previous instrumental behavior (e.g., direction of turn or color of arm entered), which become associated with the delayed outcome, reward or nonreward. As we know from the affective-conditioning studies, the cues associated with S+ can take on positive value very rapidly, in a single trial. Under such circumstances instrumental learning with even substantial delays can be extremely efficient if, in addition, the aversiveness that can be generated by the delay interval is prevented. An example of the efficiency possible in long-delay learning is seen in Headly's performance, which reached the 100% correct level in only 10 trials; (2) a strong preference for S− can completely suppress learning, particularly if no, or few, forced trials to S+ are given. The existence of a strong stimulus preference or response bias implies some source of immediate reinforcement, which may be sufficient to maintain uninterrupted responding to S−. In addition, it is likely that cues associated with responding to S− are retrieved at the time that the delayed consequence is applied, so that even if a moderate number of forced trials to S+ are administered, these might only serve to strengthen the incorrect response; (3) if in spite of a strong initial incorrect response tendency an animal nevertheless learns something about the delayed contingency, it will find itself faced with a conflict of incentives, namely, a small immediate reward versus a larger delayed reward. Performance is likely to be unstable in this case, possibly because responding to one alternative alters the incentive value of the other; (4) stimulus preferences and response biases will also play a role when reinforcement is delivered promptly. In this case, however, their negative impact will be much reduced because information regarding the previously executed response is still active or is easily retrieved at the time of reinforcement and because there is no conflict of incentives.

A number of predictions and interesting experiments flow from this analysis, incomplete though it is. First, our emphasis on the role of incorrect response tendencies (which are related to Harlow's "error factors," 1959) suggests that if all such tendencies are extinguished before training commences, long-delay instrumental learning should be greatly facilitated. Second, in animals that have no significant incorrect response tendencies, long-delay learning should be precluded if a small immediate reward is given for one response (S−) and a large delayed reward is given for the other (S+). For example, if in our situation the animal is immediately rewarded in the startbox with one rasin for going left, and rewarded after a 30-min delay with 25 raisins for going right, few animals should learn the delayed contingency. Those that do, ought to show the nonmonotonic performance functions produced by Clea and Kip. Third, long-delay instrumental learning should be facilitated by forced trials to S+, the reason being that such forced trials should interrupt the continuous control by the small immediate reward. If only free trials are given in a situation where the animal has a strong response bias toward S−, the small immediate reward associated with the latter might prevent adequate sampling of S+. It is interesting to note in this connection that although Lett did not use a forced-trial procedure in her long-delay studies, she often continued daily trials until the first correct response was made. Possibly a single forced trial to S+ after a single incorrect response would have been equally effective. Finally, the larger the delayed reward the better performance will be because preference will be tilted further in favor of the delayed reward in cases where the animal is assumed to be facing a choice between a small immediate reward and a larger delayed reward.

The importance assigned to preexisting stimulus preferences and response biases raises a serious methodological issue. What is the correct control for long-delay learning? If the animals enter an experimental situation with a strong bias toward one alternative and the latter is assigned to be S−, we have seen that learning will be greatly impeded. On the other hand, if the preferred alternative is assigned as S+, the bias will operate in the opposite direction and learning may be inferred where none really exists. For example, we tested two monkeys in the T-maze apparatus for their position and arm preferences on 4 separate days. On each day the position of the black and the striped arm was alternated, which enabled us to partial out position biases from arm preferences. One animal had a consistent left-turning bias and the other had a strong preference for the black arm. Visual discrimination training then followed with the striped arm assigned as S+ for the first animal and the black as S+ for the second; the black and striped arms appeared on the left and right sides of the T-maze in a quasi-random order. One free trial was given daily, except that if the animals were incorrect a forced trial to the correct side was given. This procedure was followed for 50 sessions, after which another 50 sessions were given with only one free trial per session.

The first animal maintained its left-turning bias for the first 30 trials at 100% after which it declined to 70%, only to return to the 100% level and remain there. More to the present point, the animal that began training with a strong preference for the black, S+ arm averaged 85% correct responses on the first 20 trials and 100% over the last 20. Its performance never fell below 80% correct in a block of 10 trials. It is unlikely that this sustained high performance level represents any significant degree of learning of the delayed contingency. Even if a significant linear trend were discernible in the animal's data, it need not reflect instrumental learning but merely an amplification of the initial preference. To rule out the latter possibility a control group is necessary in which animals with an equally strong initial preference for S+ are noncontingently rewarded (i.e., rewarded after S+ and S− choices with equal probability).

Nor is the methodological dilemma necessarily solved by identifying S+ with the preferred alternative for half the animals and with the nonpreferred alternative for the other half, for in such a case the first subgroup may show no evidence of learning whatever, whereas the second might produce evidence of learning that might not be genuine. This is the basis of our reservations concerning the purportive evidence of cue-correlation position learning in rats with a 60-min delay (Lett, 1975). Of course, if learning is obtained in spite of the fact that the animals are run against their biases, so much the better. But because this is a risky procedure, perhaps a better strategy is to train only those animals that show by pretraining tests no strong bias for any of the available response alternatives, animals that might be said to have an "open mind" with regard to the experimental task. The latter analogy may be more real than apparent, in the sense that where consequences are delayed in human affairs the connection between consequence and its antecedent conditions may be more readily perceived by someone who approaches the task with few preconceptions (incorrect response tendencies) than one more heavily burdened in this regard.

Our understanding of long-delay conditioning and instrumental learning is heightened by our knowledge of the critical roles played by such variables as novelty of the CS, CS duration, and strength of the US in the case of conditioning, and aversiveness of the delay and strength of biases for incorrect alternatives in the case of instrumental learning. We can understand how, through the manipulation of a few simple behavioral variables, intelligent creatures like chimpanzees can be made to look foolish in their inability to learn a simple discrimination under a reinforcement delay of a few seconds, whereas the far less intelligent rat can be made to appear superior in this regard. By virtue of being exposed to a simple behavioral extinction procedure, Potato became capable of rapid learning of the position discrimination that previously eluded him; deprived of this extinction experience, Hubert remained completely insensitive to the experimental contingencies. Anyone needing reassurance about the power of simple behavioral variables need look no further than long-delay learning, a problem area whose understanding has eluded us for so long perhaps in part because the solutions were too prosaic, too close at hand.

The controversy over general versus species-specific laws of learning, once rather vitriolic, has mellowed with the recognition that there is theoretical room for both points of view (cf. Logue, 1979). We have no desire to rekindle old passions, but it is apparent that some of the data described in the foregoing whittle away further at any existing support for the necessity of specialized learning mechanisms. One-trial, long-delay conditioning apparently is not restricted to taste aversions and related paradigms. Headly's and Jodi's T-maze performance shows that under favorable conditions instrumental learning with a 30-min delay of reward can be extremely efficient and asymptote at perfect or near-perfect levels. This is not to say that the physiological structure of an animal cannot favor some discriminative stimuli over others or cause some CS–US relationships to be more easily established than others, or that such differences are not important. Our results merely underscore the fact that simple behavioral variables can exert a profound influence on conditioning and learning. Before one assigns an observed difference in conditioning or in learning to structural or to species differences, the contribution of such variables should be assessed—not always an easy task.

SUMMARY

After a single exposure to a distinctive arm of a T-maze (the CS) followed 30 min later by a food reward (the US), monkeys subsequently showed a preference for the CS arm. In parallel with conditioned aversions, we referred to such alterations in spatial preference as "conditioned attractions." The previous conditioned attraction remained essentially intact after a 4-month retention interval. One-trial, long-delay conditioned attractions were also demonstrated in rats, with delays up to 2 hours.

These results raised the question of whether the poor instrumental learning that usually occurs with a substantial delay of reward is due to the failure of the supporting affective responses to become conditioned on early trials. An experiment addressed to this issue revealed that 1-min and 30-min delayed toxicosis produced approximately the same degree of taste aversion and spatial aversion, but instrumental learning was markedly impeded by the 30-min delay.

Subsequent experiments, which were motivated by the assumption that appropriate affective responses are also conditioned when reward is delayed, showed that if the aversiveness that can be generated by a delayed reward is minimized (by having the animals spend the delay period in their home cages) and if the animals do not have a strong bias for the incorrect alternative, monkeys are capable of learning a cue-correlated spatial discrimination extremely efficiently, in as few as 20 trials, despite a 30-min delay of reward. In marked contrast, animals that remained in the testing situation during the delay interval and had a strong bias for the incorrect alternative usually showed no sign of learning the spatial discrimination.

The indicated conclusion is that, given favorable experimental conditions, long-delay conditioning and learning are obtainable in a much wider context than previously suspected.

ACKNOWLEDGMENTS

Supported by NSF Grant 78-24644 and NIMH Grant MH32424. We wish to thank Jay Buckiewicz and M. Puopolo for assistance in data collection.

REFERENCES

Ainslie, G. Specious reward: A behavioral theory of impulseveness and impulse control. *Psychological Bulletin*, 1975, *82*, 463–496.

Albert, D. J., & Mah, C. J. An examination of conditioned reinforcement using a one-trial learning procedure. *Learning & Motivation*, 1972, *3*, 368–388.

Chen, J. S., & Amsel, A. Recall (versus recognition) of taste and immunization against taste anticipations based on illness. *Science*, 1980, *209*, 831–833.

Cox, J. K., & D'Amato, M. R. Disruption of overlearned discriminative behavior in monkeys (*Cebus apella*) by delay of reward. *Animal Learning & Behavior*, 1977, *8*, 359–362.

D'Amato, M. R., & Buckiewicz, J. Long delay, one-trial conditioned preference and retention in monkeys (*Cebus apella*). *Animal Learning & Behavior*, 1980, *8*, 359–362.

D'Amato, M. R., & Cox, J. K. Delay of consequences and short-term memory in monkeys. In D. L. Medin, W. A. Roberts, & R. T. Davis (Eds.), *Process of animal memory*. Hillsdale, N.J.: Lawrence Erlbaum Associates, 1976. (a)

D'Amato, M. R., & Cox, J. Long-delay discrimination performance and acquisition in monkeys. Paper presented at Psychonomic Society Convention in St. Louis, Mo., November 13, 1976. (b)

D'Amato, M. R., & Safarjan, W. R. Differential effects of delay of reinforcement on acquisition of affective and instrumental responses. *Animal Learning & Behavior*, 1981, in press.

Garcia, J., Kovner, R., & Green, K. F. Cue properties vs palatability of flavors in avoidance learning. *Psychonomic Science*, 1970, *20*, 313–314.

Grice, G. R. The relation of secondary reinforcement to delayed reward in visual discrimination learning. *Journal of Experimental Psychology*, 1948, *38*, 1–16.

Harlow, H. F. Learning set and error factor theory. In S. Koch (Ed.), *Psychology: A study of a science* (Vol. 2). New York: McGraw-Hill, 1959.

Holman, E. W. Some conditions for the dissociation of consummatory and instrumental behavior in rats. *Learning and Motivation,* 1975, *6,* 358–366.

Krane, R. V. Toxiphobia conditioning with exteroceptive cues. *Animal Learning & Behavior,* 1980, in press.

Lett, B. T. Delayed reward learning: Disproof of the traditional theory. *Learning and Motivation,* 1973, *4,* 237–246.

Lett, B. T. Visual discrimination learning with a 1-min delay of reward. *Learning and Motivation,* 1974, *5,* 174–181.

Lett, B. T. Long delay learning in the T-maze. *Learning and Motivation,* 1975, *6,* 80–90.

Lett, B. T. Regarding Roberts' reported failure to obtain visual discrimination learning with delayed reward. *Learning and Motivation,* 1977, *8,* 136–139.

Lett, B. T. Long-delay learning of a black–white discrimination: Effect of varying the length of delay. *Bulletin of the Psychonomic Society,* 1978, *12,* 307–310.

Lett, B. T. Taste potentiates color-sickness associations in pigeons and quail. *Animal Learning & Behavior,* 1980, *8,* 193–198.

Logue, A. W. Taste aversion and the generality of the laws of learning. *Psychological Bulletin,* 1979, *86,* 276–296.

Mischel, W. Processes in delay of gratification. In L. Berkowitz (Ed.), *Advances in experimental social psychology* (Vol. 7). New York: Academic Press, 1974.

Mitchell, D., Winter, W., & Moffitt, T. Cross-modality contrast: Exteroceptive context habituation enhances taste neophobia and conditioned taste aversions. *Animal Learning & Behavior,* 1980, *8,* in press.

Perkins, C. C., Jr. The relation of secondary reward to gradients of reinforcement. *Journal of Experimental Psychology,* 1947, *37,* 377–392.

Rachlin, H., & Green, L. Commitment, choice, and self-control. *Journal of the Experimental Analysis of Behavior,* 1972, *17,* 15–22.

Riesen, A. H. Delayed reward in discrimination learning by chimpanzees. *Comparative Psychology Monographs,* 1940, *15,* 1–54.

Roberts, W. A. Failure to replicate visual discrimination learning with a 1-min delay of reward. *Learning and Motivation,* 1976, *7,* 313–325.

Roberts, W. A. Still no evidence for visual discrimination learning: A reply to Lett. *Learning and Motivation,* 1977, *8,* 140–144.

Safarjan, W. R., & D'Amato, M. R. One-trial, long-delay conditioned preference in rats. *Psychological Record,* Submitted 1981.

Tenen, S. S. Retrograde amnesia from electroconvulsive shock in a one-trial appetitive task. *Science,* 1965, *148,* 1248–1250.

Wolfe, J. B. The effect of delayed reward upon learning in the white rat. *Journal of Comparative Psychology,* 1934, *17,* 1–21.

5 Actions and Habits: Variations in Associative Representations During Instrumental Learning

Christopher Adams
Anthony Dickinson
University of Cambridge

A complete analysis of learning and memory must address three separate, but interrelated, questions: What do we know? How do we come to know it? How do we retain and use this knowledge? The first is concerned with characterizing the knowledge representations set up by a learning experience, whereas the second two focus on the mechanisms controlling the formation and subsequent deployment of these representations. Although the question of "what is learned?" aroused great interest forty or so years ago, the bulk of contemporary research, at least in the field of animal behavior, has concentrated on elucidating learning and memory processes rather than the representations on which these processes act. One reason for this disenchantment with theories of animal knowledge was the feeling that this issue was not open to empirical analysis (Kendler, 1952). The subsequent decades, however, have given us new techniques that allow the debate to be reopened with profit.

ASSOCIATIVE REPRESENTATIONS

Traditionally theories of associative learning have assumed that knowledge about a relationship between events in the environment is stored in the form of a structure consisting of representations of the constituent events joined by associative links. Specifically, stimulus–response theory argues that associative learning results in the formation of an internal structure consisting of some representation of the stimulus context in which the target behavior is reinforced joined by a link to the behavior-generating mechanism (S–R representation). In the case of instrumental learning, there has been a persisting dissatisfaction with this account,

143

primarily because the S-R representation does not allow the animal any knowledge about the outcome of its behavior. The alternative view argues that the associative representation encodes information about the relationship that is actually set up by the instrumental contingency, namely that between the instrumental behavior and the reinforcer. Tolman (1932) attempted to capture the properties of such a representation with his concept of a "sign-gestalt expectation", and subsequently similar theories of instrumental knowledge have been espoused by a number of authors (Bolles, 1972; Irwin, 1971; Mackintosh, 1974; Mackintosh & Dickinson, 1979; Maier & Seligman, 1976; Mowrer, 1960a). This type of associative structure can be regarded as consisting of representations of the instrumental behavior and reinforcer conjoined by an associative link, although the properties of this link are often left unspecified. Such an associative structure is typically referred to as a response-reinforcer association. We agree, however, with Skinner (1938) that characterizing the instrumental behavior as a response prejudges certain important theoretical issues by implying that it is a reaction to some unidentified stimulus; rather, in the context of this theory, which does not specify such an eliciting stimulus, the instrumental behavior is more appropriately referred to as an action, so that we can view instrumental learning as setting up an action-reinforcer (A-Rfr) representation. On the other hand, instrumental behavior that is controlled by a learned S-R representation is typically referred to as a habit.

The contrast between S-R and A-Rfr theories of instrumental knowledge can be seen as an example of a more general distinction between different types of knowledge structures, namely that between procedural and declarative representations (Anderson, 1976). The S-R structure is a particular form of procedural representation that specifies the conditions under which a behavior or operation is to be performed. The A-Rfr structure, however, is an example of a declarative representation that serves to describe a relationship between events in the animal's environment.

THE INTEGRATION OF KNOWLEDGE

Procedural and declarative representations have various general merits and disadvantages (Winograd, 1975). Let us consider the case of a hungry rat pressing a lever for sucrose pellets. We might argue that this learning experience sets up a procedural representation of the form "when in the operant chamber, press the lever." Of course, we are not suggesting that the rat encodes information in a medium resembling natural English, but rather we shall employ English statements and commands to indicate the general form of the representation. If we accept that, at one level, a psychological explanation of performance ends with a command for the appropriate behavior, the advantage of the procedural representation is that it is in a form that allows the encoded knowledge to be translated directly into behavior. By contrast, a declarative representation, such as "lever pressing causes sucrose delivery," does not contain any form of behavioral command and thus requires the operation of some form of knowledge-action translation process to derive a command for the appropriate action.

Although it may be more difficult to account for the production of instrumental behavior from an underlying declarative representation, the knowledge is stored in a form that can be employed with greater flexibility. For instance, knowledge about separate, but relevant, event associations can be integrated using the declarative form. To illustrate such integration, let us consider a case in which lever pressing is first reinforced by the delivery of sucrose pellets, and subsequently the reinforcer is devalued by pairing the consumption of sucrose with an aversive event. Alternative procedural and declarative representations set up by such experiences are illustrated in Table 5.1. We could then test the animals' ability to integrate their knowledge about the two relationships by giving them an opportunity to press the lever in extinction. As stated, there is no obvious inference rule for integrating the two procedural representations, for they have no terms in common. On the other hand, the declarative representations have the "sucrose" term in common and thus provide the animal with a basis for inferring that "a lever press causes the delivery of an aversive agent." If the event relationships are stored in a declarative form, and therefore susceptible to such integration, we should expect the animal to be less ready to press the lever in an extinction test following devaluation of the sucrose reinforcer.

The significance of this integration test for the problem of "what is learned?" has long been recognized (Rozeboom, 1958), and studies employing this test, some successful (Miller, 1935; Tolman & Gleitman, 1949) and others not (Rozeboom, 1957; Tolman, 1933), have been reported spasmodically over the last few decades. At the time, however, a potent technique for devaluing the primary reinforcer directly was not available, and in these studies the integration test was implemented by altering the significance of stimuli that were simply

TABLE 5.1
Integration of Associative Representations

Event Relationship	Procedural Representation (S - R)	Declarative Representation (A - Rfr)
Lever press → sucrose	"when in the operant chamber, press the lever"	"a lever press causes sucrose delivery"
Sucrose consumption → aversive event	"when in the operant chamber, do not eat sucrose"	"eating sucrose causes an aversive event"
Integration	- - - - - - - - - - - - - - - - - - - -	"a lever press causes the delivery of an aversive agent"

correlated with the reinforcer during training, such as the goal box cues or magazine stimuli. As a result, we cannot be sure that the integration test tapped directly the associative representation underlying the initial acquisition of the target behavior, namely, that set up by the presentation of the reinforcer itself. Failures of integration may have arisen simply because these incidental stimuli were not incorporated in the representation set up by the initial training. Conversely, successful integration, while indicating encoding of the incidental stimulus, does not establish that the animal had any knowledge about the relationship between its behavior and the primary reinforcer itself. A potent procedure for devaluing positive reinforcers directly became available with the discovery of food-aversion learning (Garcia, Kimmeldorf, & Koelling, 1955), and although Holland and his colleagues (Holland & Rescorla, 1975; Holland & Straub, 1979) have demonstrated successful integration in classical conditioning using this technique, there have been few comparable studies of instrumental conditioning. In this chapter we report attempts to investigate whether instrumental behavior is also susceptible to reinforcer devaluation by food-aversion learning.

BEHAVIORAL AUTONOMY—FAILURES OF INTEGRATION

We started out with a strong prejudice in favor of the declarative theory and so were surprised to learn that instrumental performance in both the operant chamber (Holman, 1975; Morrison & Collyer, 1974) and T-maze (Garcia, Kovner, & Green, 1970) is unaffected by postconditioning devaluation of the food reinforcer. In these three studies, initial instrumental training was followed by food-aversion conditioning, in which consumption of the reinforcer in the home cage was paired with the administration of an illness-inducing agent. Although this procedure successfully suppressed consumption of the reinforcer, the animals' readiness to perform the instrumental response in extinction appeared to be completely unaffected. On closer inspection, however, we decided that none of these three studies was a fair test of integrative capacity. We should expect extinction performance to be depressed only if the devaluation procedure was successful in attenuating the reinforcing properties of the food. In fact, Garcia et al. (1970) found that their reinforcer was perfectly capable of sustaining instrumental performance following food-aversion conditioning, whereas Morrison and Collyer (1974) and Holman (1975) did not test for reinforcing properties, as opposed to consumption of the reinforcer following devaluation. Consequently, Adams decided to perform an integration test that included an assessment of the capacity of the food to act as a reinforcer following devaluation.

Initially the rats were trained to lever press for single sucrose pellets in an operant chamber. The experimental group then received a series of trials in which the consumption of sucrose pellets in a separate cage was immediately followed by an injection of lithium chloride (LiC1) until consumption was completely suppressed. The animals were then returned to the operant chamber for a session in which responding was measured in extinction. Finally, in a second test session lever pressing was once again reinforced with sucrose pellets to test the effectiveness of the devaluation procedure. A control group received exactly the same procedure except that access to sucrose pellets and LiC1 injections occurred on alternate days during food-aversion training. In agreement with the previous studies, the extinction test revealed identical levels of responding in the experimental and control groups. The reacquisition test, however, reinstated responding in both groups, albeit at a slightly lower level for the experimental animals. It appeared that the reinforcer devaluation was largely context-specific (Archer, Sjödén, Nilsson, & Carter, 1979) and had failed to generalize from the aversion cage to the operant chamber. Clearly this study, and by implication the previous ones in the literature, do not represent an appropriate test of integrative ability.

Adams (1980) sought to overcome the problem of context specificity by training the food aversion in the operant chamber. Following a session of magazine and continuous reinforcement training, lever pressing was reinforced by single sucrose pellets on a variable interval (VI) 60-sec schedule for four 30-min sessions. The animals were then divided into four groups for food-aversion training. The paired group (Group P) was averted from the sucrose by experiencing sucrose–LiC1 pairings, whereas the remaining three groups acted as controls against which to assess the effects of this aversion training. The unpaired group (Group U) received unpaired sucrose presentations and LiC1 injections and the no-lithium group (Group NLi) sucrose presentations but no LiC1 injections. Finally, the no-treatment group (Group NT) experienced neither sucrose presentations nor LiC1 injections. This training was conducted over three 2-session cycles in the operant chambers with the levers withdrawn. In the first daily session of each cycle Group P received 30 sucrose pellets on a variable time (VT) 60-sec schedule, following which the animals were immediately given an injection of 13-ml/kg body weight 0.15 M LiC1 before being returned to their home cages. The animals in Groups U and NLi were randomly matched to subjects in Group P and received, on the same schedule, the number of pellets consumed by their Group P counterparts. After 30 min they were removed from the operant chamber and given a saline injection. On the second session of each cycle, the rats in these three groups were placed in the operant chamber for 30 min without any food, after which Groups P and NLi were injected with saline and Group U with LiC1. The final group, Group NT, remained in their home cage throughout this period. Twenty-four hours later all subjects were given a 30-min extinction test in which the lever was reinserted, followed the next day by a reacquisition test in which responding was once again reinforced with sucrose pellets on a VI 60-sec schedule.

Figure 5.1 displays the response rates during both the extinction and reacquisition tests. The first point to note is that the food-aversion procedure successfully attenuated the reinforcing properties of the sucrose pellets; whereas the control

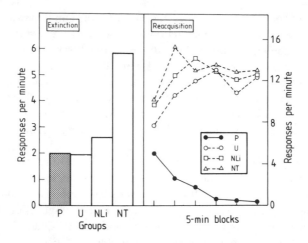

FIG. 5.1. Mean response rates of groups receiving paired (P), unpaired (U), no-lithium (NLi), and no-treatment (NT) food-aversion treatments during the extinction and reacquisition tests (in 5-min blocks).

groups showed a progressive increase in responding, the output of Group P declined across the reacquisition session. As result we can be confident that the devaluation procedure successfully reduced that property of the sucrose pellets that was responsible for establishing instrumental responding in the first place. Even so, there was no evidence that the current value of the reinforcer in any way controlled responding in extinction. Although Group P responded at a lower rate than Group NT, its output was identical to that of Groups U and NLi. Why animals in Group NT, which were not exposed to the operant chamber and injection procedure during food-aversion training, should respond more in extinction is not clear. The effect appears to be similar to Pearce and Hall's (1979) observation that postconditioning nonreinforced exposure to an operant chamber reduces subsequent instrumental responding. In addition, the association between exposure to the operant chamber and the injection procedure itself in Groups P, U, and NLi may have contributed to the difference.

Be that as it may, the outcome of this experiment clearly favored the procedural theory in that the animals appeared to be incapable of integrating information about the instrumental training with that from the food-aversion conditioning. But theoretical prejudices die hard, and we were consoled by the thought that response rate measures are not really very sensitive indicators of reinforcer value. Perhaps a devaluation effect would show up if we used a preference measure. So Adams then trained a set of rats to lever press in two different chambers with an interconnecting door. One chamber was black and dark, and the other white and illuminated. Furthermore, lever pressing was reinforced by sucrose pellets in one chamber and mixed-composition food pellets in the other. For the first six sessions the interconnecting door was locked and the subjects were given alternating daily sessions in each chamber, with the order counterbalanced across animals. During these six sessions all animals received in each chamber one session of magazine training, one in which lever presses were continuously reinforced, and a session of training on a VI 60-sec schedule. For the next three sessions the interconnecting door was unlocked and the animals allowed free access to both chambers, with the respective reinforcers programmed by independent VI 60-sec schedules. At the end of this stage the animals responded at approximately equivalent rates in the two chambers and distributed their time equally between them.

Following this instrumental training, the levers were removed and the interconnecting door once again locked. For half the animals the sucrose reinforcer was devalued in the appropriate chamber, using the food-aversion procedure employed for Group P of the previous study. The remaining animals received the unpaired control procedure used for Group U. Half the animals of each group (Groups P–S and U–S) were then confined to the sucrose chamber for an extinction and reacquisition session as in the previous experiment. The remaining subjects (Groups P–C and U–C) received similar test sessions, except that they had free access to both chambers. During the extinction session neither reinforcer was available, whereas both were programmed in the appropriate chamber during reacquisition.

The pattern of responding for animals confined to the sucrose chamber was essentially similar to that seen in the previous experiment, except that, if anything, the animals for which the sucrose reinforcer had been devalued, Group P–S, showed more responding during extinction than the appropriate control group, Group U–S. Our hope that a reinforcer devaluation effect might be evident with a choice procedure was not fulfilled; the pattern of extinction responding in the sucrose chamber for rats given free access to both chambers, Groups P–C and U–C, were essentially similar to that exhibited by the rats confined to the sucrose chamber during testing. Furthermore, the way in which the animals allocated their time between the two chambers during testing just served to confirm this picture. Figure 5.2 shows that Groups P–C and U–C spent similar amounts of time in the sucrose chamber during the extinction test, although interestingly there was a bias away from this chamber in both groups relative to the equal distribution observed during the final instrumental training session. During reacquisition, the control group, Group U–C, reestablished an equal distribution of time between the two chambers, whereas the paired group, Group P–C, rapidly gave up visiting the sucrose chamber at all, thus providing further confirmation of the success of the devaluation procedure.

Faced with these data, we were forced to abandon our cherished notion that instrumental performance is always controlled by the current value of the reinforcer. Under certain circumstances, at least, animals appear to act in ignorance of detailed knowledge about the consequences of their behavior, a fact that must provide prima facie support for the procedural theory. Before accepting this unpalatable conclusion, however, we decided to address a theoretical weakness of the integration test. The ability to integrate two declarative representations requires that they contain a common term, such as "sucrose" (Table 5.1). Consequently, the basis for integration will be absent if exposure to two event relationships leads to different encoding of the common event in the respective associative representations. So our failure to observe integration would be compatible with the declarative theory if exposure to the lever press–sucrose and the sucrose–LiCl relationships led to different encodings of the "sucrose." Holland and Straub (1979) have recently presented some evidence that is consistent with this idea. They found that LiCl-induced devaluations of a Pavlovian reinforcer attenuated predominantly conditioned responses that were consummatory in nature, occurring during the terminal periods of the conditioned stimulus, while leaving the more appetitive responses, evident during the initial periods of the stimulus, unaffected. By contrast, another devaluing agent, high-speed rotation, mainly affected the initial appetitive responses. This pattern of results can be understood if it is assumed that only aversion training with rotation, but not LiCl, leads to an encoding of the reinforcer that is similar to that embodied in the associative representation underlying appetitive responses. As our target behavior, lever pressing, is appetitive in character, our failure to observe a devaluation effect perhaps is not surprising. As a result, Adams decided to employ the devaluing agent, high-speed rotation, which Holland and Straub reported to be effective in attenuating appetitive responses and to compare its effectiveness with that of LiCl.

The initial training procedure was identical to that employed in the choice experiment. Subsequently, half of the animals received pairings of sucrose consumption with the devaluation agent (Groups R–P and L–P), and the remaining animals unpaired presentations of the opportunity to consume sucrose pellets and the devaluation agent (Groups R–U and L–U). For one set of animals (Groups

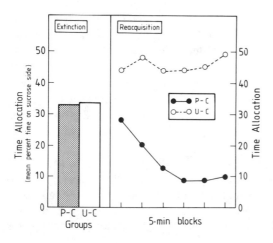

FIG. 5.2.   Mean percentage of time spent on the sucrose side of the choice box by the paired (P–C) and unpaired (U–C) groups during the extinction and reacquisition tests (in 5-min blocks).

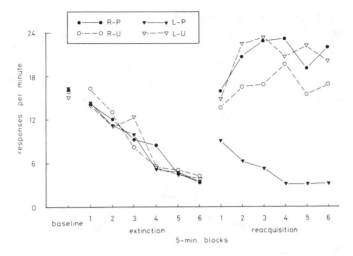

FIG. 5.3. Mean response rates of the groups receiving the paired and unpaired lithium (L–P and L–U) and rotation (R–P and R–U) food-aversion treatments during the final instrumental training (baseline) session and during the extinction and reacquisition tests (in 5-min blocks).

R–P and R–U) the devaluation agent was 15-min rotation at 100 rpm in a small box mounted 15 cm from the center of a turntable inclined at 20 degrees to the horizontal. The devaluation agent employed for the remaining animals (Groups L–P and L–U) was an injection of 6-ml/kg body weight of 0.15 M LiCl. The quantity of LiCl administered was reduced in an attempt to equate the strength of the sucrose aversion supported by the two agents. The devaluation procedure was basically the same as that used in the previous studies except that four 2-session cycles were given to the animals in the LiCl condition and six to those experiencing high-speed rotation, again in an attempt to equate the strength of the aversion. Finally, all animals were given an extinction session with free access to both chambers, followed by a reacquisition session in which they were confined to the sucrose chamber. As Fig. 5.3 shows, responding on the sucrose lever in extinction was totally unaffected by reinforcer devaluation with either LiCl or high-speed rotation. Thus, with instrumental conditioning, at least, the nature of the devaluing agent does not appear critical. In addition, there were no differences between the time the various groups spent in the sucrose chamber during extinction. This conclusion, however, must be qualified by the fact that we were unable to demonstrate that high-speed rotation, unlike LiCl injections, reduced the reinforcing properties of the sucrose during reacquisition (Fig. 5.3). But this does not mean that high-speed rotation was totally ineffective as an aversive agent. In a consumption test, given a day after reacquisition, the rats had 5-min access to 100 sucrose pellets preloaded into the magazine. The animals in Group R–P ate an average of 34.3 pellets, which was significantly lower than the mean of 53.3 pellets consumed by Group R–U. Holland and Straub (1979) reported a comparable consumption pattern following aversion training with rotation in a similar test.

The cumulative impact of these experiments led us to the conclusion that instrumental performance can be autonomous of the current value of the reinforcer. Given this conclusion, a simple S–R procedural representation appears to provide an adequate basis for the control of instrumental behavior, at least under certain circumstances, in that it does not permit integration with other knowledge about the reinforcer.

THE TRANSITION FROM ACTION TO HABIT

Perhaps we should not have been surprised by these failures of integration, for it is often assumed that the processes controlling instrumental behavior can vary. Tolman (1932), for instance, argued that under certain conditions an animal becomes what he called "fixated" upon a particular instrumental activity so that the behavior is autonomous of the original goal. For Tolman (1932): "Fixations must be conceived, then, as both the *antithesis* and the *nemesis* of sign–gestalt-expectations. They overtake the latter with certain conditions [p. 154]." In our terminology the idea is that an instrumental behavior starts out as a true action, under control of the goal or reinforcer via a declarative representation, but that with training the behavior becomes independent or autonomous of the goal by the transfer of control to a procedural representation. In the state of behavioral autonomy the instrumental activity is simply a habit that occurs in the appropriate situation independently of the current value of the reinforcer.

Although there is little evidence about the conditions that are necessary for establishing behavioral autonomy, a general view is that habits result from extended practice with an instrumental activity (Kimble & Perlmuter, 1970). If this is so, the amount of baseline training given in Adams' (1980) studies may have been sufficient to establish lever pressing as a habit. Restricting the amount of initial training may prevent the onset of behavioral autonomy, thus rendering the instrumental activity susceptible to reinforcer devaluation. To investigate this idea, Adams varied the amount of initial instrumental training received by different groups, using a simple continuous reinforcement schedule, prior to reinforcer devaluation.

After magazine training, two groups of rats were allowed to make either 100 or 500 lever presses, each of which was reinforced with a single sucrose pellet. Training occurred at the rate of 50 lever presses per daily session, so that this training was distributed over only two sessions for rats in the 100-response condition, but over 10 sessions for animals in the 500-response condition. Following the last session of instrumental training, the levers were withdrawn and half the animals in each training condition (Groups 500-P and 100-P) received pairings of sucrose consumption and LiC1 injections, while the remaining animals (Groups 500-U and 100-U) received unpaired presentations of sucrose and LiC1 injections. This devaluation procedure was similar to that used in the paired and unpaired conditions of the initial study (Adams, 1980), except that 50 sucrose pellets were preloaded into the magazine before the start of the session. In order to produce a complete suppression of consumption, the animals in the 500-response condition required five 2-session cycles of food-aversion training, whereas those in the 100-response condition needed only three 2-session cycles. This difference probably reflects the fact that the rats in the 500-response groups had received more exposure to the sucrose pellets during initial instrumental training and therefore probably showed greater latent inhibition during food-aversion learning. Following the last session of food-aversion training, the levers were reinserted for a 20-min extinction test followed by a 10-min reacquisition session on the next day.

As Fig. 5.4 shows, for the first time we observed successful integration in that in the 100-response condition the group averted from sucrose, Group 100-P, showed less responding in the extinction test than the control group, Group 100-U. Furthermore, the amount of initial instrumental training appeared to have a dramatic effect on the development of behavioral autonomy. In contrast to the 100-response condition, the response output of Group 500-P was unaffected by reinforcer devaluation. It is unlikely that this significant interaction between the amount of instrumental training and reinforcer devaluation was due to differing strengths of the sucrose aversion in the two conditions. Although it is true that the

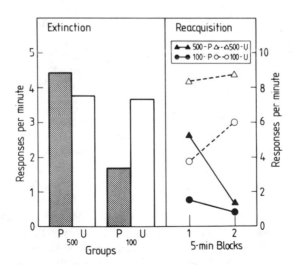

FIG. 5.4.   Mean response rates in the paired and unpaired aversion conditions for animals experiencing 100 (100-P and 100-U) and 500 (500-P and 500-U) reinforced training responses during the extinction and reacquisition tests (in 5-min blocks).

rats in the 500-response condition acquired the sucrose aversion more slowly, their training was extended until a comparable aversion was seen in the two conditions. Moreover, the reacquisition performance shows that the sucrose appeared to be ineffective as a reinforcer in both Group 100-P and Group 500-P. Although Group 500-P responded more during the first 5 min of the reacquisition session, probably reflecting a carry-over of the difference in extinction performance, by the second 5-min block neither group exhibited significant responding.

This study established two important points. First, an instrumental behavior can be sensitive to reinforcer devaluation and, by implication, can be a true action based on some form of declarative representation. Secondly, the results confirm the intuition that extending initial training can render an instrumental activity impervious to reinforcer devaluation. Although a behavior may start out under the control of the reinforcer, with further practice a transition appears to occur whereby the instrumental activity becomes autonomous of the current value of the goal. These conclusions raise a number of important theoretical questions. One of the most pressing concerns the conditions that are necessary for the development of behavioral autonomy. If we assume that such autonomy reflects the formation of a habit under procedural control, then traditional S–R theories of learning should identify the important factors for its development. These theories have argued for two potentially important influences (Kimble, 1961). On the one hand, contiguity theories maintain that habit strength should be a function of the number of occasions on which the response has occurred contiguously with the appropriate eliciting stimulus, and as a result we should expect behavioral autonomy to increase simply with the number of responses emitted prior to devaluation. By contrast, "law-of-effect" theories point to the number of response–reinforcer pairings as the major determinant of habit strength so that the critical difference between the 100- and 500-response conditions is not just the variation in the number of response emitted but also the number of reinforcers presented.

As well as these standard accounts of habit formation, Rescorla (1977) has recently identified another potential mechanism of behavioral autonomy by pointing to the role of higher-order Pavlovian conditioning and analogous processes in maintaining instrumental responding via either incentive mechanisms or conditioned reinforcers. Starting from Holland and Rescorla's (1975) observation that higher-order, unlike first-order Pavlovian conditioning is not susceptible to reinforcer devaluation under certain conditions, Rescorla pointed out that instrumental behavior should show comparable autonomy to the extent that similar processes control the target behavior. In fact, he found that performance of an instrumental lever press, established solely with a conditioned reinforcer, was unaffected by subsequent extinction of the conditioned reinforcer. Given this observation and the assumption that the role of conditioned reinforcers and incentives depends on the number of primary reinforcers delivered, we might expect resistance to reinforcer devaluation to increase with the number of rein-forcers delivered during initial instrumental training.

As the previous experiment confounded the number of responses emitted with the number of reinforcers delivered, it is impossible to decide whether either of these factors is important in the development of autonomy. Consequently, in the next study Adams decided to dissociate these two factors. Following a single session of magazine training, 50 lever presses were consistently reinforced with sucrose pellets in a single session. Thereafter, the schedule was changed to a variable ratio (VR) 9, and the rats allowed to make 450 responses for 50 sucrose pellets. Thus, by the end of instrumental training all animals had emitted the same number of responses, namely 500, as those in the condition showing resistance to reinforcer devaluation in the previous study, while receiving only 100 reinforcers, which is equal to the number delivered to the group susceptible to reinforcer devaluation. If the number of responses is the critical determinant of the onset of behavioral autonomy, we should expect lever pressing in extinction to have been unaffected by food-aversion training. However, if the number of reinforcers delivered is more important, the animals should be susceptible to reinforcer devaluation after this instrumental training.

In addition, we decided to study the effects of another potentially important factor, the spacing of training, which was confounded with response and rein-forcer number in the previous study; Group 500-P received their instrumental training distributed over 10 daily sessions, whereas only two sessions of training were given to Group 100-P. As it is known that spaced practice can be more effective than equivalent massed practice in a variety of learning tasks (Bad-deley, 1976), it is possible that the distribution of training has an effect on the development of behavioral autonomy. Consequently, Adams gave half the rats in the present study massed practice and the remaining animals the equivalent amount of spaced practice. In the massed condition the rats were allowed to make the last 450 responses in a single session, whereas animals in the spaced condi-tion were required to emit the same number of lever presses at the rate of 50 responses per daily session across nine sessions. Thus, including the initial continuous reinforcement session, animals in the massed condition received two sessions of training and those in the spaced condition ten sessions. These distri-butions were the same as those experienced by animals in the 100- and 500-response conditions, respectively, in the previous study. The food-aversion pro-cedure was initiated on the day following the last instrumental training session. As the animals that received pairings of sucrose consumption and LiC1 injections acquired the aversion at the same rate in the massed and spaced condition, only three 2-session cycles of aversion training were given. Extinction and reacquisi-tion tests followed as in the previous experiment.

The results of the extinction test, illustrated in Fig. 5.5, suggest that neither the number of responses nor the number of reinforcers is a critical determinant of behavioral autonomy. In the massed condition, the paired group (Group M–P)

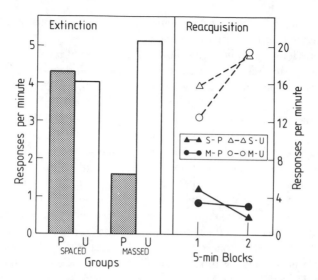

FIG. 5.5.   Mean response rates in the paired and unpaired aversion conditions for animals receiving spaced (S–P and S–U) and massed (M–P and M–U) training during the extinction and reacquisition tests (in 5-min blocks).

responded significantly less than the unpaired control group (Group M–U), even though their instrumental training was equivalent, in terms of the number of responses, to the group showing behavioral autonomy in the previous experiment (Group 500-P). Conversely, in the spaced condition the paired group (Group S–U) was insensitive to reinforcer devaluation, relative to the unpaired control group (Group S–U), after only 100 reinforcers, the number received by the group showing a devaluation effect in the previous study (Group 100-P). Clearly, the factor controlling behavioral autonomy in the present experiment was the distribution of training with animals averted from the sucrose showing a devaluation effect in the massed, but not the spaced condition. There is no reason why this significant interaction should be attributed to a difference in the degree of reinforcer devaluation; both Groups M–P and S–P failed to show sustained responding during the reacquisition test, although it must be acknowledged that such a difference may have been obscured by a "floor" effect.

Given the present results, the distribution of training, rather than the number of responses or reinforcers, may have been responsible for the pattern of autonomy observed in the previous experiment. Of course, this should not be taken to mean that these other factors have no effect. At present, we have little idea about the mechanism by which the distribution of training exerts its action on the development of autonomy. Although it is well known that training distribution can affect the strength of responding during acquisition, it is unlikely that this was an important factor in the present studies. In both experiments the unpaired control groups in the training conditions susceptible to reinforcer devaluation,

Groups 100-U and M-U, responded at least as vigorously in the extinction test as the equivalent groups in the conditions resistant to devaluation, Groups 500-U and S-U. It is possible, however, that the total response output is an amalgam of two relatively independent sources of responding, one reflecting the strength of the underlying declarative representation and the other that of the degree of procedural control. Although the total contribution from these two sources may not differ as a function of the training conditions, the relative contributions from each source may. Thus massed and restricted training may favor declarative control, whereas spaced and extended training may lead to dominance by procedural control and behavioral autonomy. Why this might be so remains to be investigated.

Even if we could isolate the conditions that are necessary for the development of behavioral autonomy, these experiments raise a number of other important issues. For instance, the study manipulating the extent of training suggests that an instrumental behavior passes from a state in which it is sensitive to reinforcer devaluation to one in which it is not. If we accept that this transition reflects a change from predominantly declarative to predominantly procedural control, an obvious question is whether the initial declarative control is a necessary prerequisite for establishing the behavior as a habit; perhaps the development of an action and habit formation proceed independently. Furthermore, what is the state of the declarative control when the instrumental behavior has become autonomous? Has such control declined from its strength during initial learning, and if so why, or has it simply been masked by a stronger habit? At present, we can do no more than raise these issues.

Finally, we should point out that other potential indices of behavioral autonomy and habit formation, such as resistance to satiation (Morgan, 1974) and the propensity of animals to perform an instrumental response when given free access to the reinforcer, the so-called "contrafreeloading" phenomenon (Osborne, 1977), also vary as a function of the training schedule (Capaldi & Myers, 1978; Tarte & Snyder, 1973). Whether or not evaluations of behavioral autonomy by reinforcer devaluation and these alternative measures show the same correlation with training parameters remains to be explored.

THE REPRESENTATIONAL BASIS OF ACTION

We have argued that the integration procedure employing reinforcer devaluation is the prime diagnostic test of the associative representations underlying instrumental performance. Its main advantage is that it correlates a change in performance with variations in the significance of the agent that was responsible for establishing that performance in the first place, and thus directly taps the mechanisms that maintain responding. Furthermore, the test for integration does not involve alterations in the drive state of the animals between training and testing. By contrast, other conventional tests of associative representations, such as latent learning and extinction, and irrelevant incentive learning, seek to change the significance of stimuli that were incidentally correlated with responding during training. As a result, absence of the appropriate behavioral change does not mean that the animal failed to learn about the relationship between its behavior and any reinforcing consequences during training. Knowledge about this relationship is simply not addressed by these procedures. We have chosen to interpret successful integration as indicating an underlying declarative structure, and failures of integration as reflecting a procedural form of representation. We have already suggested, however, that at least some cases of behavioral autonomy may be the consequence of declarative representations with no term in common, and similarly it must be acknowledged that the implications of successful integration are not as clear-cut as our discussion has so far assumed.

For instance, integration may be mediated by a procedural representation of the form "when I expect sucrose, press the lever," in which the reinforcer is encoded in the term specifying the conditions for the action. In fact, one of the most influential theories of instrumental learning and performance, two-process theory (Estes, 1969; Rescorla & Solomon, 1967; Trapold & Overmier, 1972), argues that the instrumental contingency sets up just such a procedural representation, which can then masquerade as its declarative counterpart. For instance, Trapold and Overmier (1972), in their development of the Hullian r_g-s_g mechanism, suggest that the presentation of a reinforcer in the presence of the stimuli comprising the instrumental context allows these stimuli to activate a mediator, or expectation, of the reinforcer via a Pavlovian conditioning mechanism. Reinforcing the instrumental behavior in the presence of the aroused expectation allows subsequent arousal of the expectation to activate the response-generating mechanism.

Although this associative representation is intrinsically procedural in form, it does encode the reinforcer and so could provide a basis for the reinforcer devaluation effect. Such a representation, however, does not give an animal true knowledge about the outcome of its action, for the relationship between the terms specifying the reinforcer and the action in the representation is not a reflection of the real correlation between the action and the reinforcer in the environment. Rather, it simply encodes the context in which the behavior is reinforced. Although in many situations this associative representation may suffice, two-process theory limits an animal's capacity to learn about the structure of an environment containing both response-contingent and noncontingent events. This point can be illustrated by considering an experiment in which the animals receive intermixed presentations of the contingent and noncontingent food pellets during instrumental training. Here, the contextual stimuli should arouse an expectation of both the contingent and noncontingent foods, so that lever presses should be reinforced in the presence of both these expectations. As a result, devaluation of either the contingent or noncontingent food would be expected to produce equivalent decrements in subsequent instrumental performance.

We (Adams & Dickinson, 1981) have recently attempted to investigate whether or not the reinforcer devaluation effect is sensitive to the actual contingency between the instrumental behavior and the reinforcer by comparing the effects of devaluing the reinforcer with that produced by establishing a comparable aversion to food pellets presented noncontingently during instrumental training. Initially the animals received two magazine training sessions. This training was similar to that employed in previous studies except that the VT 60-sec schedule delivered the reinforcer and noncontingent food pellets in alternation. In the next session 50 lever presses were reinforced. However, the session started with the delivery of a noncontingent food pellet, and thereafter the reinforcer and noncontingent food pellets were available in strict alternation. This was achieved by scheduling the delivery of a noncontingent food pellet 5 sec after the delivery and collection of a reinforcer. Furthermore, lever presses that occurred prior to the delivery and collection of a scheduled noncontingent food pellet were not reinforced and postponed noncontingent delivery by a further 5 sec. The structure of this basic schedule was preserved in the final instrumental training session during which 50 reinforcers were delivered on a VR 9 schedule. The previous experiment has already shown that such massed training yields a devaluation effect. In order to present the noncontingent food pellets, the schedule was suspended halfway through each ratio and was only reinstated once a noncontingent pellet had been delivered and collected. This noncontingent pellet was not delivered until 10 sec had elapsed without a lever press. Strictly speaking, the presentation of the noncontingent pellets was not independent of lever pressing. The fact that responding postponed the delivery of noncontingent pellets prevented fortuitous pairings with a lever press. Furthermore, the procedure of alternating the presentations of the reinforcer and the noncontingent pellet provided a simple way of ensuring a similar distribution of these events across each session and thus, hopefully, comparable conditioning of any expectation of these events to the general apparatus cues.

Following instrumental training, the rats in the paired condition were averted from the reinforcer and those in the unpaired condition from the noncontingent food during three 2-session cycles of food-aversion training. On the first session of each cycle the magazine was preloaded with 50 reinforcer pellets in the paired condition and 50 noncontingent food pellets in the unpaired condition. After 15 min the animals were removed and injected with LiCl before being returned to their home cages. On the second day of each cycle the magazines were preloaded with a number of the opposite pellets equivalent to that consumed on the first day. After 15 min the animals were now injected with saline of equivalent volume and molarity. For half the animals in each group the reinforcer was a sucrose pellet and the noncontingent food a mixed-composition food pellet. The remaining animals received the opposite allocation. On the day following the last food-aversion session, the levers were reinserted for a 20-min extinction test followed by two daily reacquisition sessions. The first employed the reinforcer and the second the noncontingent food.

If the devaluation effect is mediated by a declarative representation that directly encodes the contingency between lever pressing and the reinforcer, we should expect animals in the paired condition to have shown less responding in the extinction test than those in the unpaired condition. On the other hand, a similar response output should have been observed in the two conditions if the representation simply encodes an instruction to perform the response in a context that arouses expectations of events present during instrumental training, as two-process theory suggests. Our results, illustrated in Fig. 5.6, argue against the sufficiency of two-process theory. Lever pressing in the extinction test was lower in the paired condition when the reinforcer was either mixed-composition food pellets (Group P–F) or sucrose pellets (Group P–S) than in the appropriate unpaired control groups (Groups U–F and U–S, respectively). Moreover, the reacquisition tests clearly demonstrated that the food-aversion procedure had been effective in selectively attenuating the reinforcing capacity of the appropriate pellets. When reacquisition was conducted with the reinforcer employed during initial training, responding was rapidly reestablished in the unpaired, but not the paired, condition. A switch to reacquisition with the food pellets employed as the noncontingent food during instrumental training reversed this pattern, thus demonstrating that this food had been devalued only in the unpaired condition.

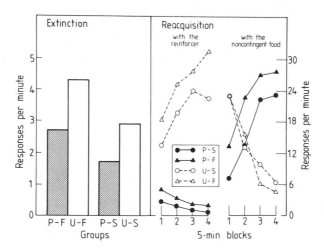

FIG. 5.6.   Mean response rates in the paired and unpaired aversion conditions when the reinforcer was sucrose (P–S and U–S) and mixed composition food (P–F and U–F) during the extinction test and the reacquisition tests with the reinforcer and the noncontingent food (in 5-min blocks).

It is difficult to account for the selective integration in our study without assuming that instrumental performance can be based on a representation that encodes the actual contingency between the behavior and reinforcer. It must be admitted, however, that two-process models could possibly account for the importance of the action-reinforcer contingency by appealing to the role of local features of either the operant chamber, such as the lever itself, or the schedule of reinforcer and noncontingent food delivery to which a specific expectancy of the reinforcer might have been selectively conditioned. The fact that our procedure selectively reinforced the instrumental behavior in the presence of such features may have allowed the expectancy of the reinforcer to exert a greater procedural control over lever pressing than that of the noncontingent food, thus rendering the behavior sensitive primarily to devaluation of the reinforcer rather than the noncontingent food. Given such assumptions, the present experimental paradigm probably cannot resolve the distinction between two-process accounts and theories that argue for a direct encoding of the contingency between the action and reinforcer.

The traditional reluctance to accept that an animal really knows about the consequences of its actions and can use this knowledge to control its behavior is readily understood. As Guthrie (1952) pointed out, the problem is that of explaining how this knowledge is translated into action. Associative theories of knowledge usually assume that an associative representation of a simple relationship consists of representations of each event and some form of connecting or relational term between these two event representations. The problem of how such associative knowledge can control behavior is usually solved by ascribing a particular property to the connection, which is typically that of transmitting excitation from one event representation to the other. Such an excitatory link can, of course, be considered on a number of different levels. For instance, Konorski (1948) viewed excitatory links in terms of neural connections, whereas others prefer to think of them as connections between elements in a memory store that allow for retrieval (Wagner, 1978). Be that as it may, the process of knowledge–action translation is surprisingly simple. Activation of one event representation will lead to arousal of the other, target representation via the excitatory link. Arousal of the target will in turn cause the behavioral output normally produced by activating this representation directly. In the case of temporal relationships, studies of backward and bidirectional conditioning (Gormezano & Tait, 1976) indicate that the transmission properties of excitatory links are largely unidirectional from the representation of the temporally prior, or predictive event to that of the subsequent, or contingent event.

Given this view of associative learning, we can immediately see the problem faced by declarative theories of instrumental knowledge. In no way can the presence of an excitatory link *from* the representation of the temporally prior event, the instrumental action, *to* that of the contingent event, the reinforcer, explain why the action is emitted, or how its emission can be modulated by changes in the significance of the reinforcer. If we are to subscribe to a declarative theory, as we believe the evidence for successful integration compels us to do, instrumental performance cannot be attributed just to the activation of an associative representation with a relational term consisting of a simple excitatory link.

How then should we conceive of instrumental knowledge and the processes involved in the deployment of this knowledge? Typically, adherents of the declarative theory are notably coy about characterizing the nature of the associative representation and are usually content to identify it as an "expectation" that an action produces a particular outcome (Bolles, 1972; Irwin, 1971; Maier & Seligman, 1976; Tolman, 1932). It is then assumed that this expectation can control behavior in a way that reflects the current value of the outcome; for instance, Bolles (1972) suggests that an expectancy of a particular outcome is conditioned both to the action and environmental stimuli, and that combination of these two declarative representations in a "psychological syllogism" is responsible for appropriate behavioral output. It seems to us that the hidden implication of this view is that, at one level of analysis, we should regard the associative representation as propositional in form and therefore open to manipulation by inferential processes (Mackintosh & Dickinson, 1979). To develop this idea, let us assume that, at this level of analysis at least, the sufficient condition for the performance of a particular action, say lever pressing, is the derivation of a command to perform that action, such as "press the lever." The only way in which this command can arise from a representation of the current value of an outcome, such as "I want food," and an act–outcome expectancy, for example "lever pressing causes food delivery," is through the operation of some form of inferential process. We might, for instance, choose to characterize the steps in this process in the following form:

	"I want food" ....motivational proposition
therefore	"perform an action that causes food delivery" ....motivational command
	"lever pressing causes food delivery" ....knowledge proposition
therefore	"press the lever" ....action command

Although the nature of the logical system mediating the type of practical inference underlying instrumental action is an issue of debate in action theory (Goldman, 1970), we really have little idea about an adequate formal characterization of practical inference, let alone about the processes mediating such inference. Mowrer (1960a, 1960b) clearly recognized the problems presented by the processes of action selection and initiation associated with an A-Rfr theory of instrumental knowledge. He appealed to a system by which action representations were "scanned" prior to the production of the appropriate action under the motivational control of feedback from the associated reinforcer representation (Mowrer, 1960b). Others have appealed to motivational modulation of S–R mechanisms by a reinforcer representation aroused via an A-Rfr structure (King, 1979; Sheffield, 1965).

Whatever the merits of these various process theories, the important point is that a declarative theory requires an associative representation with a form that can be used by processes mediating practical inference. It is the causal role of inferential processes in the production of behavior that endows instrumental actions with their rational and purposive character and distinguishes them from habits, reflexes, fixed-action patterns, and the like. Danto (1976) has succinctly expressed this point; a basic action can be: "decomposed into a representation on the one side, and a piece of operant behavior on the other, with the former causing the latter and the latter satisfying the former [p. 24]." If by learning we change our representations to fit the world, then by instrumental action we change the world to fit our representations.

SUMMARY

Instrumental behavior can take two forms. The first is that of a true action that is under the control of the current value of the reinforcer or goal, as evidenced by its susceptibility to postconditioning devaluation of the reinforcer. By contrast, in the second form, that of a habit, the instrumental activity appears to be insensitive to changes in the significance of the reinforcer and occurs automatically in the appropriate training context. In our hands, the same instrumental activity, reinforced by the same reward, appears to be capable of taking up both forms. We have argued that the distinction between actions and habits is best thought of in terms of a difference in the internal representations controlling the instrumental behavior. Actions are based on a declarative representation that encodes the actual contingency between the behavior and the reinforcer, whereas habits reflect the operation of a procedural representation that just specifies the conditions under which the behavior is to be performed.

Actions and habits are not mutually exclusive, and instrumental activity can undergo a transition from an action to a habit with extended training. With limited training the behavior is sensitive to reinforcer devaluation, whereas extended training leads to a state in which the activity is autonomous of the current value of the goal. At present, it is not clear what factors are critical in producing a transition between actions and habits, although at least one important factor may be the distribution of training. With massed training the instrumental behavior remains sensitive to goal devaluation, although the equivalent amount of distributed training leads to a state of behavioral autonomy.

ACKNOWLEDGMENTS

The preparation of this chapter was supported by grants from the U.K. Medical and Science Research Councils. We should like to thank John Pearce for commenting on the manuscript.

REFERENCES

Adams, C. D. Post-conditioning devaluation of an instrumental reinforcer has no effect on extinction performance. *Quarterly Journal of Experimental Psychology*, 1980, *32*, 447-458.

Adams, C. D., & Dickinson, A. Instrumental responding following reinforcer devaluation. *Quarterly Journal of Experimental Psychology: Comparative and Physiological Psychology*, 1981, *33B*, 109-121.

Anderson, J. R. *Language, memory and thought*. Hillsdale, N.J.: Lawrence Erlbaum Associates, 1976.

Archer, T., Sjödén, P., Nilsson, L., & Carter, N. Role of exteroceptive background context in taste-aversion conditioning and extinction. *Animal Learning and Behavior*, 1979, *7*, 17-22.

Baddeley, A. D. *The psychology of memory*. New York: Harper and Row, 1976.

Bolles, R. C. Reinforcement, expectancy and learning. *Psychological Review*, 1972, *79*, 394-409.

Capaldi, E. D., & Myers, D. E. Resistance to satiation of consummatory and instrumental performance. *Learning and Motivation*, 1978, *9*, 179-201.

Danto, A. C. Action, knowledge and representation. In M. Brand & D. Walton (Eds.), *Action theory*. Dordrect, Holland: D. Reidel, 1976.

Estes, W. K. New perspectives on some old issues in association theory. In N. J. Mackintosh and W. K. Honig (Eds.), *Fundamental issues in associative learning*. Halifax: Dalhousie University Press, 1969.

Garcia, J., Kimmeldorf, D. J., & Koelling, R. A. Conditioned aversion to saccharin resulting from exposure to gamma radiation. *Science*, 1955, *122*, 157-158.

Garcia, J., Kovner, R., & Green, K. F. Cues properties versus palatability in avoidance learning. *Psychonomic Science*, 1970, *20*, 313-314.

Goldman, A. I. *A theory of human action*. Princeton, N.J.: Princeton University, 1970.

Gormezano, I., & Tait, R. W. The Pavlovian analysis of instrumental conditioning. *Pavlovian Journal of Biological Sciences*, 1976, *11*, 37-55.

Guthrie, E. R. *The psychology of learning*. New York: Harper & Brothers, 1952.

Holland, P. C., & Rescorla, R. A. The effects of two ways of devaluing the unconditioned stimulus after first- and second-order appetitive conditioning. *Journal of Experimental Psychology: Animal Behavior Processes*, 1975, *1*, 355-363.

Holland, P. C., & Straub, J. J. Differential effects of two ways of devaluing the unconditioned stimulus after Pavlovian appetitive conditioning. *Journal of Experimental Psychology: Animal Behavior Processes*, 1979, *5*, 65-68.

Holman, E. W. Some conditions for dissociation of consummatory and instrumental behavior in rats. *Learning and Motivation*, 1975, *6*, 358-366.

Irwin, F. W. *Intentional behavior and motivation: A cognitive theory*. Philadelphia: Lippincott, 1971.

Kendler, H. M. "What is learned?"—a theoretical blind alley. *Psychological Review*, 1952, *59*, 269-277.

Kimble, G. A. *Hilgard & Marquis' conditioning and learning*. New York: Appleton-Century-Crofts, 1961.

Kimble, G. A., & Perlmutter, L. C. The problem of volition. *Psychological Review*, 1970, *77*, 361–384.

King, D. L. *Conditioning: An image approach*. New York: Gardner, 1979.

Konorski, J. *Conditioned reflex and neuron organisation*. Cambridge, Eng.: Cambridge University Press, 1948.

Mackintosh, N. J. *The psychology of animal learning*. London: Academic Press, 1974.

Mackintosh, N. J., & Dickinson, A. Instrumental (Type 2) conditioning. In A. Dickinson & R. A. Boakes (Eds.), *Mechanisms of learning and motivation*. Hillsdale, N.J.: Lawrence Erlbaum Associates, 1979.

Maier, S. F., & Seligman, M. E. P. Learned helplessness: Theory and evidence. *Journal of Experimental Psychology: General*, 1976, *105*, 3–46.

Miller, N. E. A reply to 'sign-gestalt or conditioned reflex'. *Psychological Review*, 1935, *42*, 280–292.

Morgan, M. J. Resistance to satiation, *Animal Behavior*, 1974, *22*, 449–466.

Morrison, G. R., & Collyer, R. Taste-mediated conditioned aversion to an exteroceptive stimulus following LiCl poisoning. *Journal of Comparative and Physiological Psychology*, 1974, *86*, 51–55.

Mowrer, O. H. *Learning theory and behavior*. New York: Wiley, 1960. (a)

Mowrer, O. H. *Learning theory and the symbolic processes*. New York: Wiley, 1960. (b)

Osborne, S. R. The free loading (contrafree loading) phenomenon: A review and analysis. *Animal Learning and Behavior*. 1977, *5*, 221–235.

Pearce, J. M., & Hall, G. The influence of context-reinforcer associations on instrumental performance. *Animal Learning and Behavior*, 1979, *7*, 504–508.

Rescorla, R. A. Pavlovian second-order conditioning: Some implications for instrumental behavior. In H. Davis & H. M. B. Hurwitz (Eds.), *Operant Pavlovian interactions*. Hillsdale, N.J.: Lawrence Erlbaum Associates, 1977.

Rescorla, R. A., & Solomon, R. L. Two-process learning theory: Relationships between Pavlovian conditioning and instrumental learning. *Psychological Review*, 1967, *74*, 151–182.

Rozeboom, W. W. Secondary extinction of lever-pressing behavior in the albino rat. *Journal of Experimental Psychology*, 1957, *54*, 280–287.

Rozeboom, W. W. "What is learned?"—An empirical enigma. *Psychological Review*, 1958, *65*, 22–33.

Sheffield, F. D. Relation between classical conditioning and instrumental learning. In W. F. Prokasy (Ed.), *Classical conditioning: A symposium*. New York: Appleton–Century–Crofts, 1965.

Skinner, B. F. *The behavior of organisms: An experimental analysis*. New York: Appleton–Century–Crofts, 1938.

Tarte, R. D., & Snyder, R. L. Some sources of variation in the bar-pressing versus free loading phenomenon in rats. *Journal of Comparative and Physiological Psychology*, 1973, *84*, 128–133.

Tolman, E. C. *Purposive behavior in animals and man*. New York: Century, 1932.

Tolman, E. C. Sign-gestalt or conditioned reflex? *Psychological Review*, 1933, *40*, 246–255.

Tolman, E. C., & Gleitman, H. Studies in learning and motivation: I. Equal reinforcements in both end-boxes followed by shock in one end-box. *Journal of Experimental Psychology*, 1949, *39*, 810–819.

Trapold, M. A., & Overmier, J. B. The second learning process in instrumental learning. In A. H. Black & W. F. Prokasy (Eds.), *Classical conditioning II: Current research and theory*. New York: Appleton–Century–Crofts, 1972.

Wagner, A. R. Expectancies and the priming of STM. In S. H. Hulse, H. Fowler, & W. K. Honig (Eds.), *Cognitive progresses in animal behavior*. Hillsdale, N.J.: Lawrence Erlbaum Associates, 1978.

Winograd, T. Frames representations and the declarative–procedural controversy. In D. G. Bobrow & A. Collins (Eds.), *Representation and understanding*. New York: Academic Press, 1975.

6 Working Memory and the Temporal Map

Werner K. Honig
Dalhousie University

"What's past is prologue"

—(Shakespeare, 1623)

THE TEMPORAL MAP

In this chapter I present the concept of a cognitive temporal map, with particular emphasis on the contribution of this concept to the analysis of working memory in animals. One may well ask whether it is justified to add yet another cognitive concept to the burgeoning list of such terms that have become popular for the theoretical analysis of animal behavior. I therefore try to justify the temporal map by elucidating the concept with some care and by supporting it with a set of experimental observations from the research literature. I then try to show that this kind of analysis is useful for the explanation of behavior that involves working memory in animals.

I elaborate on a view of working memory that has been proposed elsewhere (Honig, 1978; Honig & Wasserman, in press), namely, that the content of working memory need not be restricted to the retention of prior stimuli. We have suggested that working memory processes can be prospective as well as retrospective. In fact, the former appear to attenuate forgetting. In this chapter I describe some results that support this conclusion. The concept of a temporal map is particularly relevant because it provides a framework for the anticipation of events, including responses and trial outcomes. Such anticipations can provide the basis for response decisions, which are made and retained in the course of the memory interval. (Grant's chapter in this volume provides a related discussion of the retention of anticipated responses.)

Because working memory procedures are mentioned at various points in this chapter, it is useful to establish a terminology for events during a trial. Each trial begins with an *initial stimulus* that provides the information necessary for an appropriate *criterion response* to a *test stimulus* (or stimuli) following a *retention* or *memory interval* (MI). The *trial outcome* is normally food reward or its absence. The criterion response is based on an assumed *response decision*, which can be made either during the retention interval or the test stimulus.

Temporal and Spatial Maps

It may be easiest at the outset to elucidate the concept of the temporal map through a comparison with the cognitive spatial map, which is more familiar. Spatial maps have been discussed in detail in a number of sources, among them O'Keefe and Nadel (1978), Olton (1978), and Menzel (1978). I trust that spatial cognitive maps are well enough understood so that an analogy with the temporal cognitive map is feasible.

Temporal and spatial maps are both psychological structures that reflect stable relationships among objects and/or events. The spatial map is obviously based on the relationships among objects in space; the temporal map, on sequences of discriminable events that vary but little between repetitions. Both structures depend on extended past experience with these relationships. They are accessed within long-term (or "reference") memory, and both can be modified through experience. Because locations of objects and sequences of events change from time to time on a long-term basis, the psychological structures based on them change accordingly. Both temporal and spatial maps incorporate landmarks. For the spatial map, we may call them "space marks," which bear a fixed spatial relationship to each other. "Time marks," on the other hand, are events that occur in a fixed order and are separated by established intervals. In space, the animal's own behavior normally determines its location with respect to the "space marks," and it can remain immobile. On the temporal dimension, the subject does not usually enjoy this freedom. However, temporal contingencies like avoidance schedules permit a degree of behavioral control over future events. Such behavior, which necessarily bears a consistent relationship to future events, can itself become a "time mark." With respect to space, some animals, such as hikers and dogs, also provide their own "space marks."

Within the temporal or spatial map, the animal keeps track of its own position on any particular occasion. Changes in its location do not, however, alter the psychological structure in reference memory. Such temporary changes are presumably accessed in short-term, or "working" memory. These changes necessarily involve variables that are orthogonal to the dimensions of the psychological structure. If the animal moves in space, such movements take time. However, the temporal dimension as such is not part of the spatial map, although it is an aspect of behavior controlled by this psychological structure. For the hungry animal, the more distant goal is usually temporally more remote as well. Conversely, for the animal threatened by shock at regular intervals in the shuttle box, escape to a safe part of the box also involves a change in spatial location.

Finally, it should be clear that spatial and temporal maps do not have the status of stimuli. Perhaps the best term for them would be *representations,* based on previous experience but capable of influencing present behavior (Roitblat, 1980). Whereas available stimuli provide the current "location" in the temporal or spatial map, behavior is frequently governed by objects and events that are "out of range." For example, the forager finds its way to a distant spring and returns to its den by a route that is influenced by a predator it cannot see. On the dimension of time, all but perhaps the most recent events are out of range. Future events are not directly accessible, and if we can show that behavior is determined by the anticipation of such events, this will provide strong support for the representations that constitute the temporal map. In short, the spatial and temporal maps are psychological structures that help to explain the organization of sequences of behavior in space and time that are not under immediate stimulus control.

THE TEMPORAL FIELD

Like any other psychological structure, the temporal map cannot be studied directly. Its characteristics can be assessed indirectly to some degree by the study of the discrimination of duration and temporal order in what I will call the *temporal field.* The animal "moves" through this field on each occasion on which it encounters a particular sequence of events that provide the time marks for that field. At any moment, a portion of the field lies in the past, a small portion comprises the "apparent" (or "specious") present, and a portion lies in the future. These portions keep changing, of course, with the passage of time.

If events lie in the past, their temporal relationships are necessarily perceived retrospectively, and the research falls into the field of memory. A proper psychophysical analysis of order and duration can be carried out only on the basis of past events. If the animal is "moving through" a particular sequence of events, or a stimulus of a particular duration, patterns of behavior can be used to assess the apparent temporal location of the subject. Thus, while all time lies formally in the past or future, such a pattern can used to assess the "apparent present." Finally, a sequence of events, or a set of durations, may lie in the future. In this case, the discrimination between them is usually assessed by a choice that reflects a preference between alternatives. The order of two events is necessarily confounded with the anticipated duration to the onset of each. In this selective review, I describe evidence for discriminations of duration, temporal location, and temporal order. I emphasize those aspects of the data that suggest the retention of a decision as the basis for subsequent discriminative behavior.

The Discrimination of Duration

The discrimination of duration has been studied primarily with rats and pigeons with the use of standard psychophysical techniques. Much of the work is capably summarized by Stubbs (1979). A few examples will therefore suffice. In the method developed by Stubbs (1968), the center key of a pigeon box was illuminated with white for one of a set of durations on each trial. Two side keys were then displayed. Pecking at the red one was reinforced if the initial center key illumination was "long," whereas the green one was correct if the sample was "short." (These contingencies were reversed for half the subjects.) In some experiments, the center key illumination could assume several durations within a range (e.g., 1 sec, 2 sec, 3 sec, etc., to 10 sec). The 10 durations were equally divided between "short" and "long." In other experiments, only two extreme durations were used in training, such as 1 sec and 10 sec, and the intermediate durations were reserved for testing.

Results were similar for the two procedures. Quasi-ogival functions were obtained, which were almost identical for different ranges (e.g., 1–10 sec, 2–20 sec, and 4–40 sec) once they were multiplied by appropriate constants. When an entire range of values was presented in training, the pigeons "bisected" it (by responding "long" and "short" equally often) near the midpoint defined by the experimenter—for example, 5 sec in the range from 1–10 sec. However, when the range of durations was represented only by its extreme values in training, the pigeons defined the midpoint differently. They bisected the interval at its geometric mean (near 3 sec in the range from 1 to 10 sec), indicating that duration was perceived on a logarithmic scale.

Church and his associates (Church, 1980; Church & Deluty, 1977; Church, Getty, & Lerner, 1976; see also Church, 1978) have carried out comparable work with rats. The subjects had to discriminate between two durations of white noise, which preceded a choice between two levers introduced into the box after the noise ended. In one set of studies, Church et al. (1976) established that the difference limen for duration was roughly constant when the standard was equal to or greater than 1.0 sec. In a second experiment, Church and Deluty (1977) presented long and short durations in training and then introduced five intermediate test durations for a number of sessions. The function relating choice to test stimulus duration was ogival, as Stubbs had previously determined with pigeons. Furthermore, the point of bisection was at the geometric mean of the training durations. These findings were confirmed with a number of training and test conditions.

Church (1980) studied the retention of signal durations ranging from 1 to 16 sec with a similar procedure. All durations less than 4 sec were defined as "short," and the rest as "long," 4 sec being the geometric mean of the extreme values. In testing, a memory interval was inserted between the end of the signal and the opportunity for a choice response. Delays of 0.5 and 2.0 sec had no effect on the accuracy of the discriminations, as shown in the left and middle panels of

Fig. 6.1. A delay of 8 sec markedly flattened the psychophysical function, indicating a large proportion of errors. However, the function did not shift on the dimension of duration, and the point of bisection remained at 4 sec.

It would be reasonable to suppose that with the passage of time, the apparent duration of a prior stimulus might be "foreshortened," and the function would shift to the right, inasmuch as the number of "long" responses would be reduced for the various test durations. That this did not occur raises two possibilities: (1) The apparent duration of a prior interval does not change with the passage of time: (2) The subject makes a decision based on the duration of the interval as soon as it ends, and then remembers that decisive rather than the duration of the interval. However, either the duration or the decision may be forgotten, leading to the flattening of the psychophysical function.

The Discrimination of Temporal Order

Because animals can discriminate the duration of prior intervals, it is reasonable to suppose that they can also discriminate the temporal order of prior events. The work of Weisman and Dodd (1979) is typical of a number of experiments on temporal order (e.g., Weisman, Wasserman, Dodd, & Larew, 1980). In one study (Experiment 2 in Weisman & Dodd, 1979), they trained pigeons to peck at a white test stimulus after the offset of a sequence of houselight colors, which they called *AB*. For some birds this sequence was yellow-red; for others, red-yellow. Then they gave a generalization test that included all possible sequences of these colors and a novel color. The sequence *BA* was responded to less than *AB*. However, the birds responded as much to *BB* as they did to *AB*, and to *AA* as much as they did to *BA*. Thus, the temporal proximity of a particular stimulus to reinforcement seemed to control responding. In order to provide stronger evidence for the discrimination of temporal order as such, Weisman and Dodd successfully carried out multiple discrimination training in which only AB signalled reinforcement, while all other sequences were negative.

A further refinement of this general design is presented as Experiment 3 of Weisman et al. (1980), based on a study by Larew (1978). Pigeons were trained

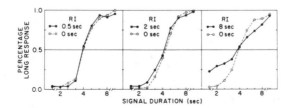

FIG. 6.1.   Mean proportions of "long" responses emitted by rats following various signal durations, where 4 sec is the geometric mean of a set of test values ranging from 1 to 16 sec. Retention intervals of 0.5, 2.0, or 8.0 sec followed the signal. Only the longest of these affected the psychophysical function (From Church, 1980)

with the sequences orange-orange, orange-green, green-orange, and green-green. These were followed after 0.5 sec by a test stimulus that was a horizontal or a vertical line. Orange-green preceded reinforcement only if the vertical test stimulus was presented. Conversely, green-orange preceded reinforcement only with the horizontal test stimulus. The subjects mastered this discrimination. Because the temporal interval between a specific color and the test stimulus was not confounded with reinforcement and extinction, the subjects were forced to discriminate and remember the stimulus sequence as such.

Larew (1978) also studied the memory for stimulus order by increasing the retention interval between the second item in the sequence and the test stimulus. All birds were tested with intervals up to 4 sec and one bird with intervals up to 12 sec. The retention interval had little or no effect when the two stimulus items were identical. However, when the stimuli differed, performance deteriorated. For example, they would respond wrongly to the horizontal test stimulus following the sequence orange-green. Representative data are shown in Fig. 6.2.

One interpretation of these findings is interesting in the present context: Sequences of identical stimuli never preceded reinforcement; thus the pigeon could "decide" at the time of second stimulus not to respond to the test stimulus and could remember that decision during the MI. However, when two different stimuli were presented, the memory for at least the second was critical, as reinforcement depended on the relationship between that stimulus and the test

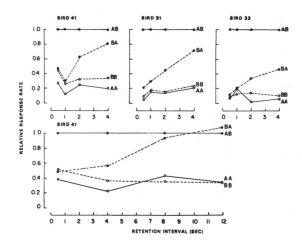

FIG. 6.2. Discrimination ratios obtained after sequences of two stimuli and a retention interval. Responding after sequence AB was always correct, and the ratio is by definition 1.0. Responses following all other sequences were errors. A low ratio is correctly maintained following a sequence of identical stimuli, even with intervening retention intervals. When different stimuli were presented in the wrong order (BA), the discrimination deteriorated as the retention interval increased. (From Larew, 1978)

stimulus. The pigeon could make a response decision only at the time of the test stimulus and had to remember stimulus information during the MI. In a further study, Larew increased the interval between the two colors, and the discrimination deteriorated for all types of trials. Clearly, in order to make a decision at the time of the second item, the first item always had to be remembered as a stimulus. Thus, this research supports the notion that memory for a decision is more robust than memory of a stimulus.

Devine, Burke, and Rohack (1979) used a more direct approach to the discrimination of temporal order in a series of studies with monkeys. In a matching-to-sample paradigm, two samples were presented in immediate succession at the beginning of each trial. The monkey then had to respond to the comparison stimuli in the order in which the samples were presented. The monkeys accomplished this task, and with some decrement they could remember the stimulus order for periods up to half a minute. However, the monkey could have treated this procedure as a simple matching study, attending only to the first-presented sample. The experiment was therefore repeated, and a distractor that matched neither sample was added to the two comparison stimuli. The subject had to respond to the correct comparisons in the order in which they were presented. They did discriminate these stimuli from the distractor.

Shimp (1976) carried out a study with pigeons that was similar in principle to that reported by Devine et al. (1979). The birds had to use the temporal location of a stimulus to report its previous spatial location. At the beginning of each trial, a dim X was projected three times onto the side keys in a three-key box. This X could appear in any of eight possible left–right sequences. Then the middle key was illuminated with red, blue, or white. Once the pigeon pecked at that, the two side keys were illuminated with the same color. If the color was red, then the pigeon was reinforced for pecking at the side key on which the first of the three X's had been displayed. With blue, pecking at the location of the second X was correct, whereas white signaled that the pigeon should peck at the location of the third X. The pigeons mastered this task, although, as one can gather even from this description, it was far from easy. The discrimination was remarkably accurate: about 100% for the position of the item presented third, 90% for that presented second, and 80% for that presented first. When Shimp inserted a retention interval up to 4 sec following the third X, this greatly reduced accuracy for the memory of the location of the first- and second-presented items, although accuracy for the third remained quite high.

Presumably, objects and locations that are highly discriminable can be more easily located and remembered in the spatial cognitive map. One may ask whether enhancing the discriminability of events would also improve the retention of their temporal order. For example, Shimp could have used three different stimuli as his first-, second-, and third-presented cues. Devine et al. (1979) did use different sorts of stimuli in their matching studies. They presented two colors, or two shapes, or one shape and one color, as their successive samples

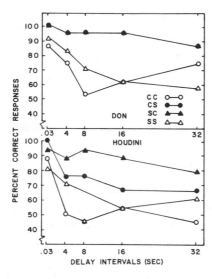

FIG. 6.3.   Performance of two monkeys in a delayed matching task in which they had to reproduce the sequence of the sample stimuli as they selected the comparison stimuli. The filled symbols are taken from data obtained when one stimulus was a color and the other a shape (CS and SC); the open symbols are taken from data based on two colors (CC) or two shapes (SS). The memory for sequences was better when stimuli from different categories were presented as samples. (From Devine, Burke, & Rohack, 1979)

(and their comparison stimuli). In both of the relevant experiments, they found that performance was better when a shape and a color were presented, than when two shapes or two colors were used. The difference was rather small in the absence of a retention interval, but it increased markedly when the order had to be remembered for as little as 4 sec. This result is shown in Fig. 6.3.

The Discrimination of Current Temporal Location

The ability to discriminate prior intervals and prior stimulus orders is probably of more interest to the psychologist than to his animal subjects. Of greater ecological benefit to the latter would be the discrimination of current location in a temporal interval or in a fixed sequence of events. Location within an interval has been studied by Stubbs (1979, 1980) with methods similar to those described earlier for the discrimination of duration. In one set of studies, he used an explicit changeover procedure. Pecking at one key provided food. This key was orange at the onset of each interval. A second, changeover key permitted the subject to change the color of the food key to green. Reinforcement was provided once during each trial, either during the first half if the food key was orange, or during the second half if it was green. Ogival functions were obtained for the probability of time spent in the stimulus appropriate to the latter half of the interval, and for the corresponding food-key response measure.

Stubbs carried out several experiments with this procedure. In one, he varied the rates of reinforcement in green and in orange. If the probability of reinforcement in green was relatively low, the birds tended to shift from orange to green late in the interval, although the available reinforcements in green were scheduled at random during the second half. If the probability of reinforcement in green was high, this shift occurred earlier. It is of some interest that the change in response bias (toward green or orange) was not accompanied by a change in sensitivity; the slope of the psychophysical function was independent of the probability of reinforcement in green.

Fixed-interval (FI) and fixed-time schedules of reinforcement were not designed as psychophysical procedures for the study of elapsed time. However, it is reasonable to assume that the systematic changes in behavior that occur in the course of each interval are directly determined by the time elapsed since the last reinforcement. Although more molecular interpretations are possible, the repeated interruption of fixed intervals, a procedure initiated by Dews (1962), supports the notion of a temporal discrimination. Several times in each interval, time-out periods alternated with the stimulus in which reinforcement was ultimately obtained. Responding during the time-outs was close to zero, but during the "time-in" stimulus, rate increased sequentially. In a further study, Dews (1966) presented the "time-in" stimulus only twice during the interval, once before reinforcement, and once at a variable earlier location. Rate during the isolated stimulus increased as a function of its proximity to the end of the FI. Thus the subjects must have discriminated the temporal location of the stimulus.

It could be argued that the FI scallop does not represent an "estimate" of the interreinforcement interval. Perhaps response rate just increases until reinforcement is delivered. If the subject could not estimate the time of delivery, then the rate ought to increase after the normal end of the interval. In this regard, Roberts (1979) developed a simple but incisive procedure with rats (see also Maricq, Roberts, & Church, 1981). On some trials, a reinforcement was delivered on a fixed-interval basis after 40 sec had elapsed. On others, the trial ended after 80 sec with no reinforcement. This resulted in a gradual increase in rate until about 40 sec, and then a gradual decrease if no food was delivered at that time. The rats seemed to estimate the time of food delivery at slightly greater than 40 sec.

A Temporal "Route"

If animals can discriminate their current location in an interval, it is reasonable to suppose that they can also master the passage through a fixed order of stimuli. An experiment by Straub, Seidenberg, Bever, and Terrace (1979) was addressed to the acquisition of a "temporal route" in pigeons. The pigeons were presented with four keys on each trial, illuminated simultaneously with four colors. They had to peck each key once in the order green–white–red–blue to be reinforced. (Repeated successive pecks to a given stimulus were allowed.) Of the 24 possible linear arrays of four colors, 15 were used in training, and four were presented after training as transfer arrays.

The pigeons achieved a level of performance that was well above chance. They came to respond in the correct sequence on 40% to 70% of the trials in a session. (Random choice would have resulted in a performance below 1% correct.) Furthermore, the probability of a correct transition between two colors (e.g., green–white, white–red, and red–blue) considered separately was very high (above 80%). On a session that included the novel arrays, responding on transfer trials was 32% correct, still well above chance, but below the level of accuracy on the training displays (55%).

This work was extended to situations with more keys and a greater variety of transfer tests (Straub & Terrace, 1980). Of particular interest was good transfer to sets of stimuli in which one or two values were missing (e.g., BD, AD, ACD, BC, etc.). Transfer to these sequences shows that the mastery of the original sequence did not involve a simple chaining procedure. Clearly, there must have been some internal organization of the sequence that permitted a correct succession of responses even when some of the "route marks" were absent.

Anticipated Temporal Location

There have been few attempts to demonstrate directly that animals can discriminate between the temporal locations of future events. Presumably this is considered a difficult problem. However, Gibbon and Church (1981) have approached it with the so-called "time-left" experiment. In the first procedure, rats were trained to press the left lever in the presence of a white houselight to obtain food, which was set up 60 sec after the lever was inserted (a discrete-trials FI 60-sec schedule). Similarly, food was made available for pressing the right lever 30 sec after it was inserted and a white noise was turned on. After independent training with these two FI schedules, the rats were tested with both levers and both signals presented concurrently. The right lever was inserted, on different trials, either 15, 30, or 45 sec after the insertion of the left lever. Thus food became available for responding to the right lever either 15 sec before it was set up on the left lever, at the same time, or 15 sec later. The authors recorded preference for the right lever as a function of time of insertion.

The mean data were unequivocal: When the right lever was inserted after 15 sec, the rats showed a 75% preference for responding to it. When it was inserted after 30 sec, the animals were indifferent. When it was inserted after 45 sec, the rats showed a 75% preference for the left lever. The simplest interpretation of these data is that the rats could estimate the time left to reinforcement within each alternative when the right lever was inserted.

These results were extended with a procedure that closely resembles concurrent chained schedules. Pigeons were used in this study. Each trial lasted for duration C, and began with two keys illuminated, the left one white and the right one red. At some variable point in the trial called time T, the right key was "primed" with a schedule that would produce reinforcement after time $C/2$. If the response following T was on the white key, the red key was turned off, and reinforcement was available after C. If the response was on the red key, the white key was extinguished. The red key then turned green for the rest of the interval, and the pigeon obtained reinforcement after time $C/2$ had elapsed. With this procedure, there was no external signal for the initiation of the shorter FI schedule. Reinforcement was initially closer for responding to the green key on each trial, but after half the trial had elapsed, it occurred sooner for responding to the white key. The pigeons shifted their preference very nicely from the red key to the white key in the course of trial, with the point of indifference not far from the middle of the interval. These results were replicated for a number of values of C.

If time left can be estimated by animals, it is reasonable to suppose that the discriminability of anticipated delays should vary with their duration, as does the discriminability of past durations (Church et al., 1976). The question has not been studied directly, as far as I know. However, an interesting study by Rachlin and Green (1972) can be brought to bear on the issue. The experimental procedure and some results are illustrated in Fig. 6.4. A concurrent chained schedule was used. In the first link, the pigeon could respond to either of two white keys. After the 25th peck, a blackout was imposed for time T, which varied in the course of testing. If the 25th peck occurred on the left key, the terminal link involved only one alternative. A green key was illuminated, and one peck at it produced 4 sec of blackout followed by 4 sec of grain presented automatically. If the peck occurred on the right key, the terminal link involved a choice between the green key and a red key. If the pigeon then pecked at the green key, the same consequences ensued. If it pecked at the red key, food was provided immediately for 2 sec, followed by 6 sec of blackout.

Whenever the pigeon entered the terminal link that offered a choice, it then pecked at the red key. This can be interpreted as a deplorable lack of self-control, as the bird preferred immediate delivery of a small reward over delayed delivery of a larger one. The main question of interest is the choice exhibited during the initial link as a function of T. As T increased, the pigeons increasingly chose the alternative that would force them to wait 4 sec before receiving the larger reward. The change in preference is shown in Fig. 6.4. Thus the pigeons "committed" themselves at an earlier time to an alternative that would look relatively unattractive later.

Although Rachlin and Green provide their own interpretation of this finding, the discriminability of the locations of future events may be relevant. At the time of the initial choice, there is always a difference of 4 sec in the time at which food will become available. At $T = 0$, this is the entire time of the delay (save for the response latency in the second link of the chain). As T increases, this difference of 4 sec decreases in relation to the total delay. At 16 sec, the largest value of T, 4 sec is only 25% more than the minimum delay to food. Thus the relative difference in time to the location of the anticipated reward decreases as T increases. If we can assume that the difference in the apparent magnitude of the rewards does not change with T, then the "cost" of waiting will appear less as the delay increases.

Although the number of studies that deal directly with the location of future events is small, they support the view that animals can discriminate such loca-

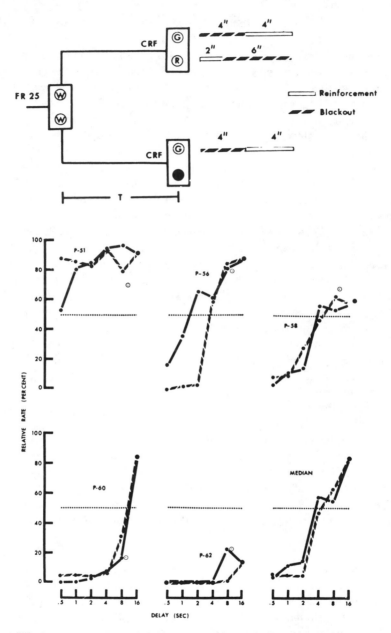

FIG. 6.4. Top: The procedure used by Rachlin and Green in a study on "self-control." An initial choice between two white keys led to a blackout for time T. If the right key was chosen, a peck at the single green key after the blackout led to a 4-sec reinforcement after a 4-sec delay. If the left key was chosen, the pigeon could then peck the green key with the same consequences, or choose the red key to obtain immediate reinforcement for 2 sec. Bottom: Relative rate of responding to the left key during the initial link as a function of the delay between that choice and the terminal link. Solid lines represent a series of ascending values of T; dotted lines, descending values. Circled points represent a set of isolated session with T = 10 sec. (From Rachlin & Green, 1972)

tions quite well, perhaps as well as they can discriminate the temporal locations of past events. If the immediate future is not a "tabula rasa" in the temporal field, then the anticipation of the future can guide response decisions and enter into memory processes. Such is the burden of much of my subsequent argument.

The Internal Clock

The concepts of the temporal map and the temporal field provide a framework for the temporal control of behavior, but no mechanism. We have seen that behavior is guided by current temporal location, but how is this sensed? How does elapsed time serve as a cue? Church and his associates (Church, 1978; Church & Deluty, 1977; Roberts & Church, 1978) have proposed the "internal clock" as such a mechanism. Church (1978) described the characteristics of the clock in some detail, as determined by behavioral studies. The clock times "up" rather than "down," and it times proportionally rather than arithmetically. Some relevant studies have been described earlier in connection with the discrimination of temporal duration. Many other experiments, which would require a lengthy exposition, do not directly contribute to our conceptualization of the temporal map.

The study of the internal clock involves procedures that also play a part in its definition. This is the fate of many cognitive concepts—their empirical specification is not entirely independent of the way in which they are defined. Fortunately, the operation of the clock can be examined with one method that is truly independent of the definition of its main characteristics. This is the injection of drugs, which may speed up the clock or slow it down. In a series of experiments, Maricq, Roberts, and Church (1981) injected rats with amphetamine during test sessions in which the behavior was controlled by the passage of time. For example, they used the discrimination of prior durations described previously. Rats had to press one lever following a short signal and another lever following a long one. The authors obtained the usual ogival functions for sets of test values contained within three different ranges of training durations (see Fig. 6.1 for an example). When amphetamine was injected, the functions were shifted to the left; rats tended to judge a given interval as "long" more often than in control conditions. For each range of test values, the point of indifference shifted to the left by about 10%. However, the slopes of the functions changed rather little. In other words, amphetamine accelerated the clock, but the reliability of time perception was not diminished.

ANALYSIS OF WORKING MEMORY PROCESSES

This discussion of the temporal map and the temporal field brings us to the point where we can appeal to these concepts in the interpretation of data from the area of animal working memory. Several kinds of working memory procedures are encompassed by the general paradigm sketched in the introduction to this chapter. In a delayed simple discrimination (DD), the initial stimulus is directly correlated with the trial outcome, and provides the information necessary to obtain it. A more traditional task is some form of the delayed conditional discrimination (DCD). In that paradigm, responding to one test stimulus is correct given one initial stimulus, whereas responding to the other test stimulus is correct given the other initial stimulus. If the same set of initial and test stimuli is used, such as red and green, then the DCD problem is true delayed matching to sample (DMTS). However, the task often takes the form of "conditional" matching; for example, a vertical line is the correct test stimulus if the initial stimulus is green, whereas a horizontal line is correct if the initial stimulus is red. In one variant of the DCD, only one test stimulus is presented at a time. Responding to it is rewarded or not, depending on its relation to the initial stimulus. This method, introduced by Nelson and Wasserman (1978), is important for the subsequent discussion.

I want to apply the concepts of the temporal map and the temporal field to the memory processes engendered by this general paradigm. In the course of training, the subject acquires a temporal map, or representation, of the sequence of events within each kind of trial used in the training procedure. On any particular trial, the initial stimulus establishes the temporal field for that trial. As the subject passes through the temporal field, it makes a response decision. This decision determines the response to the test stimulus, or the choice among test stimuli. There may be an interval between the response decision and the opportunity to make the response. In that case the decision has to be remembered.

Prospective and Retrospective Remembering

I want to suggest that the time of the response decision is critical for the interpretation of working memory processes. If this decision is made early in the trial, during the initial stimulus, then the memory process is prospective or anticipatory. Such a decision would most likely be based on the anticipated trial outcome, and information regarding the initial stimulus as such may be lost. If the decision is made late in the trial, at the time of the test stimulus, the memory process is retrospective. The decision would be based on information retained from the initial stimulus.

The widespread use of DMTS or some other form of the DCD has no doubt contributed to the predominance of retrospective models of remembering. Pigeons generally perform poorly with delays of more than a few seconds (but see Grant, 1976), which suggests that the process of retrospection is very imperfect. Roberts and Grant (1976) proposed a trace theory: The initial stimulus establishes a trace that fades rapidly and is subject to interference from events during the MI. (However, see Grant, this volume, for a substantial revision of this model.) D'Amato (1973) and his co-workers formulated a different retrospective account on the basis of extensive work with monkeys. If the subject can remember which of the initial stimuli occurred most recently, he or she can select the correct terminal stimulus. This model is therefore based on a temporal discrimination among the most recent initial stimuli. Forgetting results from proactive interference from prior initial stimuli.

The theoretical analysis of working memory should, in my view, be extended to include a third possibility, namely that the response decision is made at the time of initial stimulus. Such a process would seem particularly appropriate for the simple DD. In that paradigm, the initial stimulus indicates only whether or not a response to the test stimulus will be rewarded, or what form the response should take. The test stimulus does not provide information necessary to make a response decision. If the decision is made early, the content of the memory would involve the "intention" or "instruction" to make the appropriate response. The prior discussion suggests that much behavior is anticipatory in its function; such an intention or instruction may therefore be easier to remember than an initial stimulus. If some form of the DCD is used, a response decision at the time of the initial stimulus would have to be more complex, as it would have to include stimulus content. The subject would, for example, have to remember "respond to the green key" if green were the sample, and "respond to the red key" if red were the sample. If such stimulus content is hard to remember, the subject might adopt a memorial strategy that requires the least information to be retained over a delay, namely a memory of the initial stimulus itself.

Because the memorial processes that I have tried to describe have to be inferred rather than observed, the question arises how a claim for prospective memory can be supported. The strategy would at best be indirect. The simplest one is to develop experimental methods involving the DD, which we presume to be most likely to generate prospective remembering, and to show that retention is better than one normally obtains from DCD paradigms, where pigeons tend to respond at chance level with delays greater than 10–15 sec. A second strategy is the explicit comparison of memory functions in DD and DCD procedures. A third argument would be based on the manipulation of variables that are common to both procedures, and to show that memorial performance is differentially affected. These strategies are all exemplified in the research to be described.

Control over the Terminal Stimulus

A design that enables the subject to control the appearance or nature of the terminal stimulus may be particularly useful in revealing prospective memory processes. Such a procedure is described in considerable detail in a different chapter (Honig, 1978), and only the essential aspects are reviewed here. Each trial began with the exposure of a vertical line or a horizontal line on the bird's food key for 20 sec. The vertical line was S+, associated with a 30-sec variable interval (VI) reinforcement schedule. The horizontal line was S−, associated with extinction. Each trial ended with one of these as the terminal stimulus, which stayed on for one minute. If the trial began with the vertical S+, it ended with the horizontal S−, and vice versa. Thus the terminal stimulus and its associated schedule were signaled by the initial stimulus. A memory interval (MI) followed the initial stimulus. During this time the food key turned white, and a VI 2-min reinforcement schedule came into effect. When the MI was over, a side key was illuminated with red light. This was the advance key, and it served as the test stimulus in this procedure. If the pigeon pecked it, he immediately procured the terminal stimulus and its associated reinforcement contingency. If he did not, the white light stayed on the center key, and this was followed after 60 sec by the appropriate terminal stimulus. The latter was therefore inevitable; the pigeon could only advance the time of its onset.

It was to the pigeon's advantage to peck the advance key when the trial began with the horizontal S−, because this would procure the vertical S+. On the other hand, if the trial began with S+, a failure to make the advance key response maintained the VI 2-min schedule until it ended automatically with S−. Thus latencies to the advance key should be short if the trial began with S−, and long if it began with S+. The birds mastered this strategy without any MI; furthermore, they maintained an excellent performance even when MIs up to 30 sec were interposed following the initial stimulus. Some selected data are shown in Fig. 6.5.

In this procedure, the pigeon could control the time at which the terminal stimulus was presented, but could not determine the terminal stimulus and its associated trial outcome. Such an opportunity was offered in another design. Again the trial began with an S+ or an S−, this time blue and green respectively. After a retention interval in the presence of the white key, the side key (now called the "control key") was again illuminated with red. The trial ended with a vertical line as S+ or a horizontal line as S− for 60 sec; however, the contingencies associated with the response to the red key were somewhat more complex than before. If the trial began with S+ (blue) and the pigeon pecked the control key, he procured the terminal S− (horizontal) for 1 min. If he did not peck the control key, the terminal S+ (vertical) appeared automatically after 10 sec. If the trial began with S− (green), the opposite contingency was in effect: a response to the control key procured S+, whereas failure to respond resulted in S− as the terminal stimulus. Thus the optimal strategy was to peck at the control key when the trial started with green but not when it started with blue.

The pigeons also mastered this problem, and again, retention was very good with intervals up to 30 sec. It may be instructive to compare this second procedure with a DCD in which only a single terminal stimulus is presented on each trial. In such a method, the terminal stimulus also changes from trial to trial, but it is positive or negative in accordance with a conditional relationship to the initial stimulus. Thus the subject cannot anticipate the trial outcome until the terminal stimulus is presented. In the present procedures, the trial outcome can be anticipated, and in the second one, even controlled. Once the subject has learned the contingencies, he needs only to remember the appropriate behavior to the control key. In fact, the "feedback" provided by the terminal stimulus may

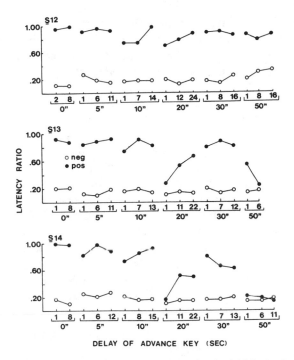

FIG. 6.5.   Latency ratios that indicate memory for the initial stimulus in the advance key procedure. The ratio should be high on positive trials and low on negative trials. The memory intervals, presented successively, are shown on the abscissa. Data points represent means from the first, middle (where applicable), and last blocks of five consecutive sessions at a given memory interval. Numbers on the abscissa represent the first session from each block. (From Honig, 1978)

no longer be essential. This possibility was examined in an extension of the second, control key, procedure.

The terminal stimulus on all trials was changed to orange in the place of a horizontal or vertical line. However, the differential outcome schedules remained in effect. When this change was introduced, the performance of only one of three subjects was adversely affected, and even that recovered after some sessions. What is more remarkable is that the pigeons did not appear to discriminate positive and negative trial outcomes. On a certain proportion of trials they made errors and procured extinction as the trial outcome. However, they pecked as quickly in the presence of the orange terminal stimulus on those trials as they did on trials in which they responded correctly in the presence of the control key. In a sense then, they showed no sign of "knowing" that they were in extinction. Yet even without evidence of functional feedback, they maintained the proper behavior to the control key very well with a 20-sec MI. It seems then, that with enough training, the response decision with regard to the control key is a simple one, and devoid of stimulus content with respect to trial outcome.

In this research, several aspects of the initial stimuli were confounded: their physical appearance, their associative value (positive or negative), the occasional delivery of reinforcement (only in S+), and response rate to the stimuli. This confounding made it possible to determine whether physical appearance was critical for performance with an extended MI. Two pigeons were trained with horizontal lines (S−) and vertical lines (S+) as initial stimuli in the advance key procedure until they reached a stable performance with a MI of 20 sec. They were then given simple discrimination training, off baseline, with a blue key as S+ (associated with a VI 30-sec reinforcement schedule) and a green key as S− (associated with extinction). In transfer tests, these stimuli were substituted for the vertical and horizontal lines as initial stimuli. Performance was but little affected by this change. Thus the pigeons remembered some aspect of the initial stimulus period other than the physical appearance of the initial stimuli. They may have remembered a response decision, or they may have used one of the confounded aspects of these stimuli as a cue. It would be of interest to determine whether a similar result would be obtained with a DCD. As far as I know this has not been done, although Maki, Moe, and Bierley (1977) showed that reinforcers and their absence can serve as initial stimuli in the DCD paradigm.

Performance in Delayed Simple Discriminations and Delayed Conditional Discriminations

The advance key and control key procedures differ in many ways from traditional DCD paradigms, such as delayed matching. In those methods, for example, the criterion response cannot be performed before the terminal stimulus appears, as that stimulus is critical for the subject to determine the trial outcome. There have been some efforts to make a direct comparison of performance in DD and DCD paradigms with pigeons. Perhaps the first was published by Smith in 1967. In that study, if a trial began with an inverted triangle on a key located on the front wall of the chamber, then a response to a key on the left wall was correct after the delay. If an upright triangle was initially displayed, then the correct key was on the right wall, In delayed matching, the pigeon had to match a vertical or a horizontal line initially displayed on the front wall with the appropriate comparison stimulus on one of the side keys. The location of the correct stimulus was an irrelevant cue. The matching problem was acquired more slowly with no delay, but to the same level of accuracy. Performance was poorer on the matching problem when MIs from 1 to 7 sec were introduced. During the MI, the center key was illuminated with white light. The first peck following the interval produced the test stimuli. This procedure discouraged obvious spatial mediating responses that might facilitate the simple discrimination.

Aside from differences in the specific stimuli used in this study, there is a problem of interpretation: In the DD, the discrimination is obviously spatial, and the pigeon must decide to turn to the right or to the left wall. Formally, this is also true of the DCD once the terminal stimuli have been presented. But functionally, the pigeon may be looking for the matching stimulus and approach it as a stimulus, rather than making a decision to turn right or left. This problem can be overcome with a design in which only one test stimulus is presented on each trial, and where the response is either to peck to it or not.

Honig and Wasserman (in press) carried out this comparison with the use of a procedure developed by Nelson and Wasserman (1978). Two experiments were run, one with independent groups, and one within subjects. In Experiment 1, each trial began with red or green presented on the key for 10 sec, and ended with vertical or horizontal lines for 5 sec. For the DD birds, the initial color alone determined whether responding to the lines would be reinforced at the end of the 5-sec period. For example, all trials beginning with red ended in reinforcement, whereas all trials beginning with green ended in a blackout, independently of the test line orientation. For the DCD birds, trial outcome was conditionally determined by the relationship between colors and lines; for example, if a trial began with red, the vertical lines were a cue for reinforcement, whereas horizontal lines signaled a blackout. The measure of discrimination was a ratio based on the rates of responding to a given line orientation on trials when that orientation signaled reinforcement and when it did not.

In Experiment 2, the procedure was similar, except that, for all subjects, two colors (e.g., red and blue) initiated DD trials, while two other colors (violet and yellow) signaled the DCD discrimination. In both experiments, the DD was acquired more quickly than the DCD with no MI, but similar levels of performance were achieved. In the principal phases of both experiments, three MIs were presented on different trials in each session. These are represented in Fig. 6.6. They are taken from the last block of sessions run at a given set of MIs. Two features of the data are particularly interesting. First, it is clear that the discrimination ratios were higher in the DD condition than in the DCD. This difference increases as a function of the MI. In fact, when 20 sec was the longest interval tested in Experiment 1, rather little forgetting was shown by the DD birds. The same can be said for the 10-sec MI in the DD condition in Experiment 2. Second, the data reveal a sensitivity to the distribution of MIs. In Experiment 1, performance deteriorated generally when the MI distribution was changed from 1, 10, and 20 sec to 1, 20, and 30 sec. The same effect can be seen for Experiment 2, when the distribution was changed from 0, 5, and 10 sec to 5, 10, and 25 sec. Purely retrospective interpretations would not cope with this latter finding. There is no reason why the rate of decay of a trace during retention intervals of a given duration should be affected by the distribution of retention intervals of other durations.

The method used by Honig and Wasserman permits pigeons in the DD problem to anticipate either the trial outcome or the appropriate response to the test stimulus. If the pigeon anticipates the former, then responding to the test stimulus may be cued by this anticipation. Whalen (1979) obviated this cue with

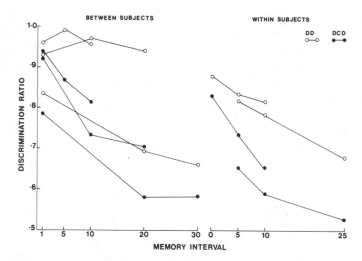

FIG. 6.6.   Left panel: Discrimination ratios obtained from independent groups of
pigeons run on the DD and DCD procedures. The data points are based on the
means of the last six sessions run with a particular set of delay intervals in each
session. These intervals were 1, 5, and 10 sec; 1, 10, and 20 sec; and 1, 20, and 30
sec. Right panel: Similar data obtained from a single group of pigeons run with the
DD and DCD procedures. They are based on the last block of four sessions (out of
60) with memory intervals of 0, 5, and 10 seconds, and a subsequent single block
of sessions with intervals of 5, 10, and 25 seconds. (Adapted from Honig &
Wasserman, in press)

a DD procedure method where the outcome could be positive on all trials.
However, the initial stimuli signaled different response patterns for gaining reinforcement. Red or green initial stimuli were presented for 5 sec on a center key,
and all trials ended with blue. If the trial began with (say) red, the bird could
receive grain for the first response to the test stimulus after it was on for 10 sec;
this is a FI 10-sec schedule. If the trial began with green, grain was presented as
soon as the bird let 10 sec elapse with no response (DRO 10 sec). Obviously, the
birds should not respond on DRO trials, but they would be likely to respond even
before 10 sec elapsed on FI trials. Whalen used responses from the first 10 sec in
the test stimulus for data analysis.

Whalen compared performance on this procedure with DMTS. Trials also
began with red or green on the center key, but they ended with a choice between
these colors shown on the two side keys. The measures of discrimination are
different with these procedures. For delayed matching, it is a choice measure.
For the delayed discrimination, it is a discrimination ratio based on differential
rates of responding. Whalen converted the latter measure to "proportion correct" by rank ordering response rates to all trials in a session. Then he determined the proportion of FI trials that were above the median. A comparison

based on the same set of data indicated that this conversion barely altered the values based on the discrimination ratio.

In several experiments in which the DD and the DMTS were compared, memory was better for the former. Two examples are shown in Fig. 6.7. One is taken from research with independent groups (filled symbols). Although the memory functions are clearly separated, there is not a clear difference between their slopes. This may indicate that the DMTS subjects failed to master the discrimination as well as the DD subjects. Results from a within-subjects study are not as striking but perhaps more convincing. Each pigeon received both kinds of trials; all of them began with red or green. The unfilled symbols again show superior performance on DD trials. In this case the difference emerged only with a substantial memory interval. Thus the difference can be attributed to differences in memory and not acquisition.

The DD and the DMTS differed in several procedural details. Therefore, it is not clear whether better retention in the former could be attributed to the task demanded of the pigeon. Where confounding of this sort is hard to avoid, it is useful to determine whether a given independent variable affects performance differently Whalen compared abrupt and gradual introduction of memory intervals. The latter procedure provided "memory practice." He used four groups of four birds each. All birds were first trained on both discriminations with no MI.

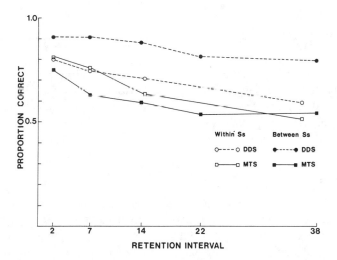

FIG. 6.7. Discrimination data obtained from pigeons run on delayed matching (MTS) and on a delayed discrimination (DDS) in which the initial stimulus signaled different appropriate response patterns to the test stimulus. Filled symbols are based on data obtained from independent groups; unfilled symbols represent data obtained from a single group of pigeons trained with both discriminations concurrently. (From Whalen, 1979)

The same initial stimuli were used for both problems; only the test stimuli and the task demands distinguished them. All groups were eventually tested with a 15-sec MI on both problems. Between the acquisition of the discriminations and the final test, one group was trained with two distributions of MIs on both problems. Ten sessions with a mean MI of 5 sec were followed by 15 sessions with a mean MI of 15 sec. For a second group, these distributions of the MIs were used only for DMTS trials, whereas the DD trials were run with no MI. A third group received the reverse conditions; memory practice was provided only on DD trials. The fourth group was simply run with no MIs on any trials for 25 sessions.

The results were unequivocal: DD performance ranged from 70 to 75% correct for all groups. DMTS performance was 65% correct for the group that received memory practice only on DMTS trials, and 70% correct for the group that received memory practice on both kinds of trials. The other two groups performed only at 55% correct on the DMTS problem. This last figure differed significantly from all the others; otherwise there were no significant differences. It thus appears that working memory in the DD procedure with a MI of about 15 sec is not assisted by memory practice, but for DMTS performance such training is essential. One reasonable interpretation of the results is that the anticipation of the correct response pattern in the DD persists through the MI. In DMTS, such mediation based on anticipated differential responding is not available.

TRIAL OUTCOMES AND MEMORY PROCESSES

In this section I discuss the effects of manipulating trial outcomes on working memory processes. I am not referring to the obvious fact that the trial outcome as a reinforcer determines the criterion response. I refer to variables that appear to influence the memory process itself in a more general way. The study of such variables will shed some light on working memory processes.

Differential Outcome Expectancies

Differential outcome expectancies may emerge when the DD procedure is used. In the Honig and Wasserman (in press) study, for example, all trials that began with one color ended with reinforcement, whereas all trials that began with the other color ended with no reinforcement. Such expectancies may have mediated the discrimination performance. Recent research by Peterson and his associates has shown that differential outcome expectancies will facilitate delayed conditional matching (Peterson, Wheeler, & Armstrong, 1978; Peterson, Wheeler, & Trapold, 1980). The initial stimulus was one of two colors, whereas the terminal stimuli were horizontal and vertical lines displayed simultaneously. In the study by Peterson, Wheeler, and Armstrong, the trial outcomes were grain and water. The differential outcome group received grain for all correct choices following (say) the red initial stimulus, and water for correct choices following green. The mixed outcome group received the same rewards randomly associated with the two initial stimuli. The general result was that, when MIs were introduced, performance was considerably better in the differential outcome condition.

This result was replicated by Peterson, Wheeler, and Trapold with a variant of special interest in the present context: When a correct response followed one initial stimulus, the trial ended with food and a tone; when it followed the other stimulus, the trial ended with no reinforcement. In some procedures the tone alone was presented instead, but in others, the correct choice led only into the inter-trial interval (ITI). Apparently, behavior in the no-reinforcement trials was maintained by advancing the program: A correct choice led to the next trial, whereas an error led to a repetition of the trial. Again, there was a comparison condition in which the two outcomes were randomly associated with the initial stimuli. A second comparison procedure provided grain reinforcement for all correct choices following either initial stimulus. Performance with a memory requirement was better with the differential outcome condition, although this provided primary reinforcement only half as often as the second comparison procedure. The difference between outcome conditions was replicated in various ways, including within-subject reversal of conditions. Representative data are shown in Fig. 6.8.

Differential outcome expectancies in effect constitute a delayed discrimination. The outcome of the trial is signaled by the initial stimulus. Without this association, the memory is not robust enough to cue the delayed choice between line orientations. Thus the outcome expectancy serves a memorial function. However, this does not imply that the pigeon made a response decision at the time of the initial stimulus. The discrimination was conditional, and the subject would have had to encode the correct choice at the time of the initial stimulus. It is more reasonable to suppose, as do Peterson and his associates, that the expectancy served as a cue on the basis of which the response decision could be made when the test stimuli appeared.

The study by Peterson et al. (1980) and the DD procedures from the Honig and Wasserman study (in press) can be interpreted in similar ways: In each case, the pigeon could anticipate reward or not, given the initial stimulus. In each case the effect of the anticipation was the enhancement of performance of a delayed discrimination. When the predictive relationship was eliminated, memory performance was much poorer. In the differential outcome studies, this was accomplished by a random association between the initial stimuli and the outcomes, while maintaining the format of the delayed discrimination. Honig and Wasserman effected the same change by requiring a conditional discrimination in which reward and no reward were associated equally with both initial stimuli. This was,

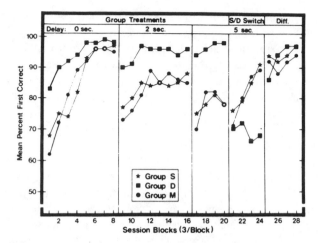

FIG. 6.8. Acquisition and memory data from three groups of pigeons run on delayed conditional matching with different outcome procedures. Group D received grain following one initial stimulus (and a correct response) and no reward following the other initial stimulus. For Group M, these trial outcomes were randomly associated with the two initial stimuli. Group S received grain following correct responses after either initial stimulus. The panel marked "S/D Switch" depicts the result of switching Group D to the single outcome procedure and the other groups to the differential outcomes procedure. The rightmost panel is based on data obtained when all groups were run with the differential outcomes procedure. (From Peterson, Wheeler, & Trapold, 1980)

of course, confounded with increased complexity of of the problem. It is therefore of interest to determine whether memory in the DCD procedure of the Honig and Wasserman experiment could be enhanced by differential outcomes as well.

DeLong and Wasserman (1980) have recently completed just such a study. Pigeons were trained with retention intervals of 0, 5, and 10 sec presented concurrently. For their differential outcome group, the probability of grain reinforcement was 1.0 on positive trials beginning with one color and 0.2 on positive trials beginning with the other color. For the nondifferential group, the probability of reinforcement was 0.6 on all positive trials beginning with either color. The problem was learned more quickly by the differential outcome group, particularly with the longer retention intervals. When the outcome probabilities associated with the two initial stimuli were reversed for the differential outcome group, this produced a marked reduction in accuracy for many sessions, followed by a gradual recovery.

This study is of particular interest because in this procedure, the outcome of any trial is not fully predictable from the initial stimulus. Half of the trials are negative and end with no reinforcement. (In the differential outcome experiments discussed previously, all trials are in principle "positive" unless the subject makes an error.) Thus, the maximum probability of reinforcement was 0.5 on any trial. For the differential outcome condition this probability was in fact 0.5 on those trials beginning with one stimulus, and 0.1 on the remainder. For the nondifferential condition, the probability of reinforcement was 0.3 on all trials. However, in spite of the uncertainty regarding the "sign" of the trial at the time of the initial stimulus, the subjects were still sensitive to one of the parameters governing the outcome of those trials that were positive.

Discriminability of Terminal Stimuli

The discriminability of trial outcomes can vary on dimensions other than the nature of the reinforcer. In an interesting experiment by Lawrence and Hommel (1961), the discriminability of the stimuli associated with reward and nonreward was manipulated. Their study concerned delay of reinforcement in the acquisition of a discrimination. (Thus, their paradigm dealt with associative memory rather than working memory; cf. Honig, 1978.) Grice (1948) had shown very poor memory for a discriminative cue in a study in which rats had to choose a black tunnel or a white tunnel between the start box and a gray delay chamber. If they chose the correct tunnel, they could enter a goal box that contained food; otherwise, the goal box was empty. Grice had found that a delay of only a few seconds prevented a development of the discrimination; in other words, associative memory appeared to be deplorably brief.

Lawrence and Hommel replicated this work with distinctly different goal boxes. For one group, one goal box was white and the other was black. (The authors provided reinforcement in the black goal box if the correct tunnel was white, and vice versa.) Another pair of goal boxes differed in shape and in floor texture. For groups that encountered distinctly different goal boxes, the memory function was much more robust. The rats could learn the discrimination with a delay of 10 sec, and this could be extended even to 1 min once the discrimination was acquired. By contrast, rats that ran into identical boxes following correct choices and errors had great difficulty with the 10-sec delay.

It is certainly difficult to interpret this finding within the context of retrospective memory processes. It is not clear why the rat should better remember which tunnel it chose when it later enters one of two discriminable goal boxes than when it enters a single goal box and does or does not find food. Within the context of prospective mediation, the finding makes a good deal of sense. If the rat can anticipate two very different terminal stimuli, then it may be much easier to associate these with reward and no reward at the time of the choice of tunnels. This anticipation could bridge the delay between the choice and the trial outcome. Again, this interpretation points out the importance of the discriminability of events that lie in the future portion of the temporal field.

Stimulus Control over Remembering

Trial outcome expectancies are involved in a different way with interesting procedures that demonstrate stimulus control over remembering. Such procedures are discussed in detail in two chapters in this book; Maki refers to the method as "directed forgetting," whereas Grant calls it "stimulus control over stimulus processing." I therefore treat this research area briefly. In a DCD paradigm, one of two cues is presented during the MI. The "remember" cue signals that the trial will end with a test stimulus (or stimuli). Following the "forget" cue, the test stimulus is omitted.

The general finding is that such cues exert control over remembering. This is demonstrated on probe trials in which the "forget" cue is actually followed by the test stimuli. Performance is generally poorer on such probe trials than it is when the test stimuli follow the "remember" cue. Grant's procedure is particularly appropriate to the present context, because his method employed the delayed conditional discrimination procedure with a single test stimulus, described previously in connection with the Honig and Wasserman (in press) study. Trials began and ended with red or green on the pigeon's key; the task was true delayed matching. Horizontal and vertical lines, displayed during the memory interval, when the key was otherwise dark, served as the "forget" and "remember" cues.

Grant (in press) ran a series of experiments that dealt with the temporal location of the stimuli that controlled remembering. First he established that the duration of the forget cue had little effect; a half second within a 3-sec MI had as great an effect as filling the MI interval. However, the temporal location within the interval was important; the later it came, the less effect it had. The failure to remember was much less severe when the forget cue immediately preceded the test stimulus than when it followed the sample directly. Furthermore, Grant established that in the absence of any control cue, the pigeons remembered as well as they did after the "remember" cue; in other words, the "default" process was remembering, and the active cue was the one that preceded omission of the test stimulus.

This procedure, which demonstrates control over remembering, involves differential trial outcomes. These appear to provide the basis for an expectancy that, if a forget cue is presented, is reflected in poor performance. The subject appears to be able to adopt a mnemonic strategy early in the MI and retain it. In fact, the forget cue is less effective if it immediately precedes the test stimulus than if it occurs early in the MI. All this suggests that the subject, anticipating the test stimuli, normally initiates rehearsal or some similar process at the beginning of the MI, but terminates it or reduces it when the forget cue is presented.

The elimination of the test stimulus involves three confounded changes: The test stimulus (or stimuli) is omitted, a criterion response cannot occur, and there is no reinforcement. Which of these is responsible for the effects of the forget cue? There has been some effort to sort them out. Grant ran half of his pigeons with a "dot test" procedure, where a black dot on a white ground replaced the normal green or red test stimulus on forget trials. After 5 sec, food was presented in a random relationship to the initial stimulus on half the trials. The results differed but little from those in which the test stimuli were simply omitted. Thus, it appeared that the omission of a terminal stimulus and of reinforcement did not cause the forgetting observed after the forget cues. Rather, the failure to require a response decision was critical.

This conclusion is very attractive in supporting the interpretation that the pigeon can anticipate a memory requirement and adopt an appropriate strategy. Unfortunately, similar control procedures run by Maki and his associates have not led to the same conclusions. In Maki's work, the test discrimination was a choice between two stimuli. In the "forget" trials, he substituted a simple simultaneous discrimination as the test task, rather than a choice based on the memory of the initial stimulus. This procedure obviated the deleterious effects of the forget cues. A detailed evaluation of the discrepancy must be left to the reader; Maki's chapter should be consulted for systematic comparisons.

CONCLUDING REMARKS

This chapter illustrates the use of a cognitive concept—the temporal map—to provide a framework for the interpretation of diverse findings in a particular research area working memory in animals. The discussion suffers from limitations of scope and detail. For one thing, the concept of the temporal map is not as well developed as the spatial cognitive map; with the exception of the experiments on the internal clock by Church, Gibbon, and their associates, there is no set of integrated studies on temporal processing that corresponds to those by Olton (1978) and Menzel (1978) on spatial mapping. Also, there has been no attempt to identify a neural structure that may underlie the temporal map, corresponding to the presumed role of the hippocampus in spatial location and orientation (O'Keefe & Nadel, 1978). Second, I have reviewed only those selected studies that directly address the processes and capacities required for temporal mapping. For example, I have omitted much of the work on time-based reinforcement schedules and patterned reinforcement. These may support the notion of the temporal map partly because many of the findings could in turn be interpreted by that concept. Such material may also provide clues on the conditions governing the establishment of a temporal map, its limitations, and its flexibility in reflecting changing temporal contingencies. Such aspects of the temporal map, although they should not remain unrecognized, have not been discussed here.

An enriched conceptualization of the temporal map could also enhance the understanding of memory processes not treated in this chapter. I have elsewhere distinguished "working memory," discussed here at length, from "associative memory," which is required for the acquisition of discriminations and behaviors in paradigms involving delay intervals. The sole example treated here is the delay of reinforcement in the work of Lawrence and Hommel (1961). But this area of memory also encompasses phenomena as different as "long-delay learning" (Lett, 1978; Revusky, 1971) and sequential patterns of reinforcement (Capaldi, 1971). In such procedures, the animal has to remember particular stimuli within or between trials in order to establish a performance appropriate to environmental contingencies.

Because such paradigms involve learning, the procedures may also incur the concurrent establishment of appropriate temporal maps. In the present discussion, I have assumed that the map is formed during initial training with no memory requirement; it is then "activated" to provide a temporal field as a cue to performance. It remains to be seen whether the concept of the temporal map can also assist the study of acquisition of problems involving retention intervals. The effort may founder on the problem of the conceptual "bootstrap." The temporal map may be supported by the very data it is then invoked to explain. I hope that I avoided this error in this chapter by separating the exposition of the concept from its application to the analysis to working memory processes. Whether a corresponding strategy can be carried out with any success in the area of associative memory still remains to be seen.

SUMMARY

The temporal map is proposed as a conceptual framework for the analysis of working (or "short-term") memory in animals. This is defined as a psychological structure accessed in long-term memory, based on experience with recurring sequences of events separated by consistent intervals. The temporal field is the perception of the current temporal situation, including the events in the immediate past, the current temporal location, and anticipated future events. This is accessed in working memory and provides the basis for response decisions. Selected evidence in support of these concepts is reviewed: the discrimination of stimulus duration and of the order of past stimuli, the control of behavior by current temporal location, and the anticipation and discrimination of future events.

The temporal map provides a theoretical framework for the postulation of prospective or anticipatory processes in working memory. Current research supporting this notion is reviewed. Several paradigms are described in which the subject can in principle make a response decision early in a retention interval, and remember it until the time of the test stimulus to obtain a favorable trial outcome. These methods are contrasted to the more traditional procedures in which retrospective memory for a particular stimulus is required on each trial to make a response decision. The notion of a prospective memory process suggests that differential trial outcomes will support working memory within trials. In the final section, recent research on differential outcome expectancies is reviewed in support of this notion.

ACKNOWLEDGMENTS

The preparation of this chapter was supported by Grant AO-102 from the National Sciences and Engineering Research Council of Canada, and by National Research Service Award No. 1-F32-MH08057 from the National Institute of Mental Health to the author. The Psychology Department at Brown University provided facilities and support that contributed to the writing of this chapter. I am particularly indebted to Donald S. Blough and Russell M. Church at Brown for many stimulating discussions. Research carried out at Dalhousie and described in this chapter was supported by the aforementioned granting agency. I thank Barbara Vavasour for extensive technical assistance, and Peter Dodd for a great deal of help, particularly in the development of computer programs for running the research and preparation of the manuscript.

REFERENCES

Capaldi, E. J. Memory and learning: A sequential viewpoint. In W. K. Honig & P. H. R. James (Eds.), *Animal memory*. New York: Academic Press, 1971.

Church, R. M. The internal clock. In S. H. Hulse, H. Fowler, & W. K. Honig (Eds.), *Cognitive processes in animal behavior*. Hillsdale, N.J.: Lawrence Erlbaum Associates, 1978.

Church, R. M. Short-term memory for time intervals. *Learning and Motivation*, 1980, *11*, 208-219.

Church, R. M., & Deluty, M. Z. Bisection of temporal intervals. *Journal of Experimental Psychology: Animal Behavior Processes*, 1977, *3*, 216-228.

Church, R. M., Getty, D. J., & Lerner, N. D. Duration of discrimination by rats. *Journal of Experimental Psychology: Animal Behavior Processes*, 1976, *2*, 303-312.

D'Amato, M. R. Delayed matching and short-term memory in monkeys. In G. H. Bower (Ed.), *The psychology of learning and motivation: Advances in research and theory* (Vol. 7). New York: Academic Press, 1973.

DeLong, R. E., & Wasserman, E. A. *The effects of differential reinforcement expectancies on successive matching-to-sample performance in pigeons*. Unpublished manuscript, 1980.

Devine, J. V., Burke, M. W., & Rohack, J. J. Stimulus similarity and order as factors in visual short-term memory in nonhuman primates. *Journal of Experimental Psychology: Animal Behavior Processes*, 1979, *5*, 335-354.

Dews, P. B. The effect of multiple S-delta periods on responding in a fixed-interval schedule. *Journal of the Experimental Analysis of Behavior*, 1962, *5*, 369-374.

Dews, P. B. The effects of multiple S-delta periods on responding on a fixed-interval schedule: IV. Effect of continuous S-delta with only short S-D probes. *Journal of the Experimental Analysis of Behavior*, 1966, *9*, 147-151.

Gibbon, J., & Church, R. M. Time left: Linear vs. logarithmic subjective time. *Journal of Experimental Psychology: Animal Behavior Processes*, 1981, *7*, 82-108.

Grant, D. S. Effect of sample presentation time on long-delay matching in the pigeon. *Learning and Motivation*, 1976, *7*, 580-590.

Grant, D. S. Stimulus control of information processing in pigeon short-term memory. *Learning and Motivation*, in press.

Grice, G. R. The relation of secondary reinforcement to delayed reward in visual discrimination learning. *Journal of Experimental Psychology,* 1948, *38,* 1–18.

Honig, W. K. Studies of working memory in the pigeon. In S. H. Hulse, H. Fowler, & W. K. Honig (Eds.), *Cognitive processes in animal behavior.* Hillsdale, N.J.: Lawrence Erlbaum Associates, 1978.

Honig, W. K., & Wasserman, E. A. Performance of pigeons on delayed simple and conditional discriminations under equivalent training procedures. *Learning and Motivation,* in press.

Larew, M. B. *Discrimination and retention of stimulus order by pigeons.* Honors thesis, University of Iowa, 1978.

Lawrence, D. H., & Hommel, L. The influence of differential goal boxes on discrimination learning involving delay of reinforcement. *Journal of Comparative and Physiological Psychology,* 1961, *51,* 552–555.

Lett, B. T. Long delay learning: Implications for learning and memory theory. In N. S. Sutherland (Ed.), *Tutorial essays in experimental psychology* (Vol. 2). Hillsdale, N.J.: Lawrence Erlbaum Associates, 1978.

Maki, W. S., Moe, J. C., & Bierley, C. M. Short-term memory for stimuli, responses, and reinforcers. *Journal of Experimental Psychology: Animal Behavior Processes,* 1977, *3,* 156–177.

Maricq, A. V., Roberts, S., & Church, R. M. Methamphetamine and time estimation. *Journal of Experimental Psychology: Animal Behavior Processes,* 1981, *7,* 18–30.

Menzel, E. W. Cognitive mapping in chimpanzees. In S. H. Hulse, H. Fowler, & W. K. Honig (Eds.), *Cognitive processes in animal behavior.* Hillsdale, N.J.: Lawrence Erlbaum Associates, 1978.

Nelson, K. R., & Wasserman, E. A. Temporal factors influencing the pigeon's successive matching-to-sample performance: Sample duration, intertrial interval, and retention interval. *Journal of the Experimental Analysis of Behavior,* 1978, *30,* 153–162.

O'Keefe, J., and Nadel, L. *The hippocampus as a cognitive map.* Oxford, Eng.: Clarendon Press, 1978.

Olton, D. S. Characteristics of spatial memory. In S. H. Hulse, H. Fowler, & W. K. Honig (Eds.), *Cognitive processes in animal behavior.* Hillsdale, N.J.: Lawrence Erlbaum Associates, 1978.

Peterson, G. B., Wheeler, R. L., & Armstrong, G. D. Expectancies and mediators in the differential-reward conditional discrimination performance of pigeons. *Animal Learning and Behavior,* 1978, *6,* 279–285.

Peterson, G. B., Wheeler, R. L., & Trapold, M. A. Enhancement of pigeons' conditional discrimination performance by expectancies of reinforcement and nonreinforcement. *Animal Learning and Behavior,* 1980, *8,* 22–30.

Rachlin, H., & Green, L. Commitment, choice, and self-control. *Journal of the Experimental Analysis of Behavior,* 1972, *17,* 15–22.

Revusky, S. The role of interference in association over a delay. In W. K. Honig & P. H. R. James (Eds.), *Animal memory.* New York: Academic Press, 1971.

Roberts, S. *Isolation of an internal clock.* Unpublished PhD dissertation, Brown University, 1979.

Roberts, S., & Church, R. M. Control of an internal clock. *Journal of Experimental Psychology: Animal Behavior Processes,* 1978, *4,* 318–337.

Roberts, W. A., & Grant, D. S. Studies of short-term memory in the pigeon using the delayed matching-to-sample procedure. In D. L. Medin, W. A. Roberts, & R. T. Davis (Eds.), *Processes of animal memory.* Hillsdale, N.J.: Lawrence Erlbaum Associates, 1976.

Roitblat, H. L. *The meaning of representation in animal memory.* Unpublished manuscript, 1980.

Shakespeare, W. *The tempest.* First folio edition, 1623. (Based on an invited contribution to the repertory of the Globe Theatre, ca. 1611.)

Shimp, C. P. Short-term memory in the pigeon: relative recency. *Journal of the Experimental Analysis of Behavior,* 1976, *25,* 55–61.

Smith, L. Delayed discrimination and delayed matching in pigeons. *Journal of the Experimental Analysis of Behavior*, 1967, *10*, 529-533.

Straub, R. O., Seidenberg, M. S., Bever, T. G., & Terrace, H. S. Serial learning in the pigeon. *Journal of the Experimental Analysis of Behavior*, 1979, *32*, 137-148.

Straub, R. O., & Terrace, H. S. *Generalization of serial learning in the pigeon*. Unpublished manuscript, 1980.

Stubbs, D. A. The discrimination of stimulus duration by pigeons. *Journal of the Experimental Analysis of Behavior*, 1968, *11*, 223-258.

Stubbs, D. A. Temporal discrimination and psychophysics. In M. D. Zeiler & P. Harzem (Eds.), *Advances in analysis of behavior, Vol. 1: Reinforcement and the organization of behavior*. Chichester, Eng.: Wiley, 1979.

Stubbs, D. A. Temporal discrimination and a free-operant psychophysical procedure. *Journal of the Experimental Analysis of Behavior*, 1980, *33*, 167-185.

Weisman, R. G., & Dodd, P. W. D. The study of associations: Methodology and basic phenomena. In A. Dickinson & R. A. Boakes (Eds.), *Mechanisms of learning and motivation: A memorial volume for Jerzy Konorsky*. Hillsdale, N.J.: Lawrence Erlbaum Associates, 1979.

Weisman, R. G., Wasserman, E. A., Dodd, P. W. D., & Larew, M. B. Representation and retention of two-event sequences in pigeons. *Journal of Experimental Psychology: Animal Behavior Processes*, 1980, *6*, 300-313.

Whalen, T. E. *Support for a dual encoding model of short-term memory in the pigeon*. Unpublished PhD dissertation, Dalhousie University, 1979.

7 Directed Forgetting in Animals

William S. Maki
North Dakota State University

As Wagner (this volume) pointed out, current theories of human memory distinguish between automatic and controlled processing. An automatic process is thought to involve an associatively connected set of routines in long-term memory, the execution of which proceeds rather inflexibly once triggered and is largely beyond voluntary control (Shiffrin & Schneider, 1977). In contrast, according to Atkinson and Shriffrin (1968) controlled processes: "are not permanent features of memory, but are instead transient phenomena under the control of the subject; their appearance depends on such factors as instructional set, the experimental task, and the past history of the subject [p. 106]." The distinction between controlled and automatic processes actually has a long history in writings about animal behavior. It is therefore quite familiar even though most students of animal learning would employ different terms. Hobhouse (1915/ 1973), for instance, was careful to distinguish between habitual modes of processing and those that appeared to involve more "intelligence." Later researchers were divided with respect to how much importance to attach to the two kinds of processing in animals; it is well known that workers in the Thorndikian tradition relied on passive processes in their accounts of conditioning (Spence, 1937), whereas Tolman (1948) was inclined toward more active processes in his views of animal behavior. For himself, Thorndike chose to emphasize the direct and automatic effects of rewards on association formation and to discount the importance of "rehearsal or reconsideration" of events in conditioning situations (Thorndike, 1931).

Our strategic orientation toward the controlled–automatic distinction is more moderate, embracing neither extreme position and excluding neither set of processes in advance of experimental evidence that would force us to do so. We began our studies of animal information processing being convinced that there was much to be gained from applying what is known about human information processing to studies of animal subjects (see Riley & Leith, 1976, for a review). We are thus disposed to provisionally grant our animals the capabilities for both types of processing so as to avoid a priori philosophical restrictions that would unnecessarily narrow the scope of our investigations and thereby promote an impoverished view of animal memory and related processes (see Hulse, 1978, for a more detailed set of arguments).

The focus of the present chapter will be on a single controlled process that we suspect animals use to maintain memories of events over brief periods of time in relatively complex tasks. This process, rehearsal, was chosen from a longer list of controlled processes in human memory. The choice of rehearsal was guided by its importance in studies of human memory (Atkinson & Shiffrin, 1968) and by the theoretical and empirical attention that rehearsallike processes in animals have recently received (Kamin, 1969; Maki, Moe, & Bierley, 1977; Wagner, 1978; Wagner, Rudy, & Whitlow, 1973).

CHARACTERISTICS OF REHEARSAL

There are several defining characteristics of rehearsal: Rehearsal has been claimed to increase the length of time that items occupy short-term memory (STM), to strengthen those items' representations in long-term memory (LTM), to demand attention, and to be of limited capacity. Most of the ensuing coverage is devoted to recent research on another characteristic—the dependence of rehearsal on instructional set. Although it is thus not the purpose of this chapter to review exhaustively work on all the potential characteristics of rehearsal in animals, it will be instructive at the beginning to see why that one particular characteristic was chosen in preference to others.

Longer STM.   The first characteristic of rehearsal is that which agrees with our most frequent intuitions, namely that rehearsal serves to prolong the residence of some item(s) in STM. At this level, rehearsal serves as a repetitious operation that, for example, allows us temporarily to retain an infrequently used telephone number. In the absence of such a holding operation, it is generally assumed that items in STM spontaneously decay or are displaced by processing of new information (Atkinson & Shiffrin, 1968). The problem with inferring rehearsal from an exceptionally persistent trace is that the persistence could be attributed equally well to other processes. For example, the renewed interest in the interplay between expectancies and memory processing (see Wagner, 1978) led to the finding that surprising events are more memorable than are expected events (Maki, 1979b; Terry & Wagner, 1975). The general plan to those experiments called for the target event (e.g., a US) to be made surprising or expected through its relationship to a preceding event (e.g., a CS), a relationship established through prior conditioning. The finding of longer retention of the surprising event, however, could have resulted from a stronger "encoding" of that event because the expectancy manipulation was complete at the time of that event's physical occurrence (Maki & Hegvik, 1980). Moreover, variations in trace persistence can be accounted for by models of automatic processing that do not formally acknowledge controlled processes (e.g., the trace strength–decay theory proposed by Roberts & Grant, 1976; see also Wagner, this volume).

Stronger LTM.   The second characteristic of rehearsal is that it has an enhancing influence on the state of LTM. Theories of both human and animal learning and memory (Atkinson & Shiffrin, 1968; Wagner, 1978) concur that the strength of a long-term association varies directly with the length of time that the constituents of the association are maintained in STM. One of the major research tactics has been the manipulation of posttrial events in attempts to increase or decrease such maintenance. For example, a surprising CS–US pair has been shown to be an effective amnesic agent, decreasing the rate of conditioning of a preceding target CS by a paired US; further, the interference is time dependent, resembling the familiar so-called consolidation gradient (Wagner et al., 1973). But the data picture is now complicated by the observations that surprising posttrial events can, under some conditions, also yield enhanced conditioning in the form of unblocking (Dickinson & Mackintosh, 1979). At the theoretical level, it can be noted that Wagner et al. equated "rehearsal" and "consolidation," and that the latter posttrial process usually has been taken to be a "passive continuation of a self-limiting process" (D'Amato, 1977). It would therefore not be surprising to learn that models of automatic processing can accomodate consolidationlike phenomena without recourse to speculations about control processes.

Attentional Demands.   Because rehearsal is thought to demand attention, which is assumed to be a limited commodity, it ought to be reduced in the presence of other stimuli that also require active processing or otherwise attract attention. This characteristic of rehearsal has usually been examined in tests of STM that, in the animal laboratory, are most often versions of delayed matching to sample (DMTS). In this task, each of many daily trials begins with one of two (or more) "sample" stimuli. After a retention interval (delay), two "comparison" stimuli are presented; the response to the comparison that "matches" the sample is rewarded. A common finding is that incidental stimuli presented during the delay decrease matching accuracy. This effect has previously been claimed to result from diminished rehearsal due to the presence of an attentional distracter (Grant & Roberts, 1976; Maki, Moe, & Bierley, 1977). But there are two findings that are incompatible with such a simple account. A brief period of delay-interval illumination disrupts pigeons' DMTS performance more when it occurs at the end than when it occurs at the beginning of the delay (Roberts & Grant, 1978). There are some ways to preserve a rehearsal interpretation in the face of such data (Roberts & Grant, 1978), but the interpretations do not deal fully with the second empirical complication. Pigeons eventually learn to match accurately in the presence of originally disruptive delay-interval illumination, and then delay-interval *darkness* is interfering (Tranberg & Rilling, 1980). Maki, Olson, and Rego (1979) offered a different hypothesis to account for these findings. Following a rationale similar to that advocated by Gordon (this volume), they postulated that delay-interval stimuli provided a context that was incorporated into the functional trace controlling choices among comparison stimuli. Full explication of the theory is beyond the scope of the present review, but it can be noted that the theory was generally S-R in nature, relied on automatic strengthening effects of reinforcers, and attributed some of the delay-interval illumination effects to generalization decrement. The effects of so-called attentional distracters on animals' performances in DMTS tasks can then be explained by a model of automatic processing, just as were the other characteristics considered in the foregoing.

Limited Capacity.   Fourth, it is widely agreed in theories of both human and animal memory processing (Shiffrin & Schneider, 1977; Wagner, 1978) that STM is of limited capacity. Only a relatively few items therefore may benefit from rehearsal at any given time. However, this characteristic is not a unique feature of controlled processing; Wagner (this volume) made a similar assumption part of his automatic processing model. Any data that might be offerred in support of the limited-capacity characteristic cannot thus be used as an unequivocal argument for controlled processing.

Controllability.   The foregoing, frequently cited defining features of rehearsal now appear to be suspect, at least as they apply to the question of controlled processes in animals. Some can be faulted on logical grounds because tbey do not distinguish between those theories that might formally include controlled processes and those that do not. Most, if not all, of the available empirical work cited in support of those characteristics can be explained without recourse to speculations about any process other than purely automatic ones. We are then left to admit to a model of automatic processing as a complete account of animal memory (Wagner, this volume), or we must look elsewhere for a characteristic unique to controlled processing and supporting data that cannot be so easily explained by automatic process models.

As indicated previously, one characteristic of a controlled process is its flexibility, literally being under control by the subject. This means that any particular controlled process can be modulated by instructions provided by the experimenter. In contrast, an automatic process, once initiated, is executed inexorably and is beyond the subject's control. Consequently, an automatic process should prove much more difficult (or even impossible) to modify by instructions (Shiffrin & Schneider, 1977). The appropriate instructions should thus be effective in persuading a subject to begin, continue, or stop controlled processing; the same instructions should be without effect on automatic processing. This distinction between controlled and automatic processing suggests a novel approach to the investigation of processes of unknown characteristics in inarticulate organisms. If Process X proves to be susceptible to experimentally manufactured instructions, we would have some reason to hypothesize that X was a controlled process. The strategy is admittedly imperfect; finding that Process X was *not* modifiable by our instructions would not warrant automatically concluding in favor of automaticity because of all the problems associated with defense of the null hypothesis. Nevertheless, this strategy does offer a fresh way of examining the nature of mnemonic activities in animals.

STIMULUS CONTROL OF MNEMONIC PROCESSES

The idea that certain stimuli might exert control over the maintenance of memories in animals has become quite popular within the last few years (see Grant, this volume). Although conveyed by an assortment of labels and expressed without explicit commitment to controlled processing in animals, the core assumption has been similar to that made here. In most cases, however, the suggestion of stimulus control of memory processing has been applied post hoc as an explanatory construct. Consequently, until very recently there existed no empirical evaluations of the hypothesis. It will nevertheless be worth examining some of the precursors of the present chapter for their theoretical and methodological tutorial value.

Memory Resetting.   Olton and Samuelson (1976) reported a series of experiments, the results of which were used to characterize a "working memory" in the rat (Olton, 1978). In their basic procedure, rats searched for food in an 8-arm radial maze. The rats ran to the end of each arm, consumed the food pellet that had been placed there at the beginning of the trial, and returned to the center of the maze after each choice. Rarely did the rats make a mistake as defined by a repeated choice of an arm (that no longer contained food by virtue of the rat's previous visit). The finding of interest here was that high levels of accuracy were maintained even when as many as eight trials occurred sequentially, separated by short (1-min) intertrial intervals. Olton (1978) accounted for the apparent lack of proactive interference (PI) by postulating a reset mechanism; the rats' working memories for spatial locations formed within trials were claimed to be reset between trials. However, a close inspection of the errors made at each serial position (Olton, 1978, Fig. 7) reveals a tendency for choices to be particularly inaccurate near the end of each trial and especially so after a few preceding trials.

That PI does occur when spatial memory trials are repeated has more recently been confirmed in other laboratories (Maki, Beatty, Berg, & Lunn, 1980; Roberts, personal communication). The significance of PI in spatial memory studies should be obvious; if working memory was truly reset by end-of-trial events (as one would reset a flip-flop or zero a mechanical counter), then PI from prior trials should not be observed. The occurrence of PI would be expected, though, if memories established in one trial passively decayed over a time course long enough to include the time of the next trial.

Termination of an Instruction.   Both Honig (1978) and Maki, Moe, and Bierley (1977) proposed that the sample stimulus itself may not be remembered during a delayed matching trial, but rather that the sample stimulus is transformed into an "instruction." What is meant is that the subject remembers "what to do" at the end of a retention interval rather than which stimulus began the trial. Honig also proposed that the instruction was "terminated" once the to-be-executed response had occurred. It will be noted that the concept of termination is closely related to that of resetting and should therefore encounter the same kinds of problems. Honig observed that demonstrations of PI in DMTS experiments presented just such a problem. This difficulty led to his elaboration of the termination hypothesis; it was proposed that the instruction could well be terminated when no longer of use but that "some memory" persisted beyond the moment of cancellation. This hypothesis preserves the essence of the idea of stimulus control of memory processing while allowing a basis for PI. Honig's speculations can be translated into terms more familiar to human memory theorists. Instead of saying that an instruction is terminated, we can say that the act of rehearsing the instruction (or whatever the representation) is interrupted by end-of-trial events. Simply stopping rehearsal does not destroy the memory, but rather the memory decays in the absence of rehearsal; this would result in the persistence of "some memory" and the possibility of PI. Unfortunately there are other roles that may be assigned stimuli occurring at the ends of trials. For example, it could be equally well argued that mnemonic processes in DMTS are passive ones and that the end-of-trial events simply act to distort the memory trace or else displace it from STM.

Self-directed Remembering.   In spite of the difficulties associated with it, hypothesizing that end-of-trial events control cessation of an active maintenance process has an interesting implication. If it is assumed that such events serve as instructions communicating to the animal that it need not continue rehearsing, then the significance of those events must have been learned during the course of training. It would therefore be anticipated, according to Maki (1979b): "that animals can learn when to rehearse and also when *not* to rehearse information in STM [p. 36]." In one recent study, Tranberg and Rilling (1980) trained pigeons to perform a version of the DMTS task. In their experiment, delay-interval and intertrial-interval (ITI) illumination conditions were the same or different (i.e., the houselight was turned on or turned off in both intervals or was on in one and off in the other). Key pecking was recorded during both intervals. The birds responded at higher rates during delays than during ITIs when the delay-interval stimuli were the same as the ITI stimuli. It thus looked as if the birds generated their own behavioral cues for when to rehearse, but did so only when the delay-interval stimuli did not serve as valid cues. However, it can just as well be argued that delay-interval responses were reinforced by trial outcomes and that the visual stimuli correlated with trial outcomes overshadowed the behavioral stimuli in the "different" condition; that is, this result can be seen as an instance of a stimulus-reinforcer relation overshadowing a response-reinforcer relation (Pearce & Hall, 1978).

Learning When to Rehearse.   Maki (1979b) provided another possible example of "learning when to rehearse." That study was conducted for quite different reasons, but the results were interpreted in terms of stimulus control of rehearsal. Pigeons were trained in a "symbolic" matching task invented by Maki, Moe, and Bierley (1977).[1] Each trial began with a white disk presented on the center key of a three-key conditioning chamber. A peck at the key produced one of two samples: 2 sec of food (an illuminated grain hopper) or 2 sec of darkness (no food). After a delay of several sec also spent in darkness, the two side keys were illuminated with red and green disks (comparison stimuli). If the trial had begun with food, a peck at the red key was reinforced with an additional 2 sec of grain; if the trial had begun with no food, a peck at the green key was reinforced. After the task was well learned, one-half of the daily DMTS trials were replaced by an equal number of discrimination learning trials. In these trials, a peck on the initiating white center key produced one of two other stimuli on the center key. When a vertical line (S+) was presented, the first peck after 10 sec produced reinforcement and the normal 20-sec ITI. When a horizontal line was presented, the trial ended automatically in no food and the ITI. Key pecking rapidly came under control of the lines with over 90% of the pecks at lines occurring in the presence of S+.

At this point, infrequent probe trials were introduced. In probe trials, DMTS trials were chained to discrimination learning trials such that the terminal event in the discrimination trial (food or no food) was the initial event in the DMTS trial. In the "expected" probes, food was preceded by S+ and no food was preceded by S− (just as in discrimination baseline trials). In "surprising" probes, food was preceded by S− and no food was preceded by S+.

---

[1] For convenience of exposition, these tasks (and performance in them) will be henceforth referred to as "matching" or "DMTS." It should be noted, however, that the terms are used generically and thus without regard to specific procedures (i.e., regardless of whether the samples and comparisons actually do physically "match").

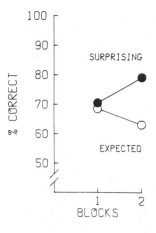

FIG. 7.1.   Accuracy of matching to "surprising" and "expected" samples. Data are plotted as a function of 20-day blocks. (Replotted from Maki, 1979b).

In general agreement with results of Terry and Wagner's (1975) Pavlovian conditioning study, accuracy of delayed matching to surprising samples was superior to accuracy of matching to expected samples. Of more interest, though, was the tendency for that effect to appear after quite a bit of experience with probe trial tests. The data in Fig. 7.1 show that there was no effect of the expectancy manipulation during the first 20 days of probe-trial testing. During the second 20 days, a surprise effect was noted and was due to the increased accuracy of matching to surprising samples.

Maki's (1979b) explanation of the effects depicted in Fig. 7.1 began with an observation about the structure of probe-trial sessions. During each day there were 32 DMTS trials, 32 discrimination baseline trials, 4 expected probes, and 4 surprising probes. Note that the events beginning expected probes were identical to those comprising discrimination baseline trials (S+/food or S−/no food). Thus, 32 of 36 occurrences of those sequences were never followed by comparison stimuli. In contrast, *every* occurrence of the events beginning a surprising probe (S+/no food or S−/food) was followed by comparisons. Therefore, it was argued, the birds could have learned which sequences would be inevitably followed by a test of sample memory and which sequences would generally not be followed by memory tests. Once again, however, we must admit that these kinds of results (see also Maki, Gillund, Hauge, & Siders, 1977) cannot be uncritically accepted as evidence for a kind of stimulus control of rehearsal because there exists at least one other hypothesis that is just as plausible if not more so. At the time of the sample all the information needed to predict how the trial would end was available to the bird (e.g., the sequence S+/food signaled the likely absence of comparison stimuli before the retention interval or ITI began). Therefore, these results can be attributed to variations in encoding of (attending to) the samples and not necessarily to variations in postsample processing (rehearsal).

Even though these results are theoretically ambiguous, they are still methodologically very useful. For one thing, omission of comparison stimuli is suggested as a possible way to persuade animals of the futility of maintaining sample memories. For another, we are now instructed that special care must be taken to insure equal attention to both to-be-remembered and to-be-forgotten samples.

STUDIES OF DIRECTED FORGETTING

The procedures that evolved for the study of stimulus control of memory in animals are close relatives of those used to study "directed forgetting" in humans (Bjork, 1972). In one kind of directed forgetting study (Woodward, Bjork, & Jongeward, 1973), subjects are presented with a list of words. Each word is followed by one of two cues, a cue to remember that word (R cue) or a cue to forget it (F cue). The validities of the cues are maintained by periodically testing retention of R-cued items while not testing retention of F-cued items. Ultimately, an unexpected final retention test is administered that covers both R-cued and F-cued materials. The standard finding is that recall of F-cued items is worse than recall of R-cued items. For present purposes it is not necessary to review all the varieties of directed forgetting procedures (e.g., Muter, 1980). It will be sufficient to abstract two of their most important shared features. First, retention tests following F cues are infrequent or nonexistent. Second, equal attention to (and hence equivalent storage of) both to-be-remembered and to-be-forgotten events is guaranteed by the practice of postinput cuing.

Procedures for Pigeons

The procedure that was developed in our laboratory for the study of directed forgetting in animals is outlined in general form in Fig. 7.2. At the beginning of each of many daily trials, a peck at the warning signal produces one of two samples, S1 or S2. After a brief interstimulus interval (ISI), one of two cues (R or F) occurs. Following the remainder of the delay interval, comparison stumuli (C1 and C2) are presented but only if an R cue followed the preceding sample.

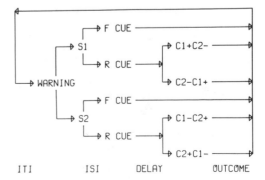

FIG. 7.2.   Flow-chart of comparison -omission procedure. S1 and S2 are sample stimuli and C1 and C2 are simultaneously presented comparisons; the correct and incorrect choices are marked by "+" and "−," respectively. Probabilities at each branching point are all .5.

When samples are followed by F cues, the comparison stimuli do not occur; rather the next trial is begun after an appropriate period of time has elasped (to control for durations of delays, reinforcers, and ITIs). This procedure captures the two essential methodological features of directed forgetting studies suggested earlier. First, the use of *comparison–omission* ensures a low probability of a retention test following F cues. Second, the use of *postsample cuing* guarantees equal attention to all samples regardless of eventual trial outcome.

The comparison–omission procedure actually involves omission of three end-of-trial events. First, there is no exposure to the comparison stimuli. Second, the usual act of discriminating and choosing among two stimuli is prevented. Third, the opportunity for reinforcement is denied. Pinpointing either response- or reinforcement-omission as the source of any effects of the F cue on performance would raise questions about whether the procedures schematized in Fig. 7.2 should be considered a true analogue of directed forgetting procedures used with humans. Consequently, the *comparison–substitution* procedure outlined in Fig. 7.3 was devised as a control for response- and reinforcement–omission. The sole difference between the omission and substitution procedures is how trials containing F cues end. In the omission procedure, all end-of-trial events are canceled, whereas in the substitution procedure, a different set of stimuli (D1 and D2 in Fig. 7.3) replace the true comparisons (C1 and C2). The different stimuli, however, permit a simple, unconditional simultaneous discrimination; choice of D1 is always defined as correct and inevitably reinforced. Thus, this set of stimuli insures that trials containing F cues always end in discriminated responding and (nearly) always in reinforcement. However, observe that performance of the different discrimination does not depend on the identity of the sample stimulus. Therefore, there is no reason to believe that a bird would benefit from rehearsal after F cues, a rationale that applies equally well to both omission and substitution procedures.

Cuing effects have been assessed in two ways. First, probe trials are inserted rather late in omission and/or substitution training. These trials typically contain F cues and end in the true comparison stimuli and reinforcement for correct

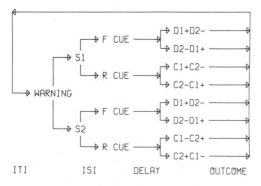

FIG. 7.3.   Flow-chart of comparison–substitution procedure. S1 and S2 are sample stimuli, C1 and C2 are simultaneously presented comparisons, and D1 and D2 are the simultaneously presented stimuli substituted for comparisons. The correct and incorrect choices are marked by ''+'' and ''−,'' respectively. Probabilities at each branching point are all .5.

choices. Probe frequencies are kept as low as economically possible (3–6% of a day's trials) to preserve the validity of the cues. Second, "return to baseline" tests have been employed in some experiments after probe-trial tests are completed. In these sessions, all trials end in comparisons and reinforcement for correct choices regardless of the identity of the cue.

Because of the performance decrements caused by even brief changes in intradelay stimuli (Maki, Moe, & Bierley, 1977), birds are routinely adapted to both R and F cues prior to introduction of the experimental procedures described previously. Adaptation simply consists of presentations of R and F cues in regular DMTS trials until accurate performance is recovered and an initial baseline established.

Finally, in all the experiments to be presented later, the basic task was matching to samples of food and no food (corresponding to S1 and S2 in Fig. 7.2) as outlined in connection with the surprise experiment (Maki, 1979b). A warning signal (a white center key) began each of 64 daily trials. A single response produced a 2-sec sample (food or no food). The ensuing delay (initially 0 sec) was gradually lengthened during each pigeon's preliminary training so as to maintain highly accurate matching. Thus, "long" delays were determined individually for each bird; "short" delays were always 2 sec. All delays (spent in darkness except for the cues noted in the following) ended in presentation of the comparison stimuli on the side keys; the comparisons were red and green disks that corresponded to C1 and C2 in Fig. 7.2. A peck on the correct key (red if the sample had been food, green if no food) resulted in reinforcement (2-sec food); a peck on the incorrect key resulted in 2 sec of darkness. Trials were separated by 20-sec ITIs.

To summarize the main aspects of the procedure, the experiments described subsequently all employed a symbolic version of delayed matching. Brief post-sample cues were intended to serve as instructions to remember (R cues) or forget (F cues). An R cue signaled that a trial would end in the usual comparison stimuli; an F cue signaled that those stimuli would be canceled or replaced by stimuli irrelevant to the matching task. The effectiveness of F cues was eventually tested in probe trials in which comparisons occurred following F cues.

Time-dependent Effects of F Cues

The first two experiments presented here were tests of the hypotheses that animals actively rehearse sample memories in tasks like DMTS and that those memories decay as a function of time spent in the absence of rehearsal. It was thus predicted that F cues should not only disrupt matching accuracy but that they should also prove most effective when the cue-comparison delay is long.

In one experiment (Maki & Hegvik, 1980), six birds were first given preliminary training and then adapted to the R and F cues. The cues were the presence and absence of a .5-sec white houselight (a concealed bulb mounted on the front panel above the center key); the ISI was 1 sec. For some birds the R cue was the light and the F cue was darkness; for other birds the cue functions were reversed. Short delays were the usual 2 sec and long delays averaged 7 sec (cue-comparison delays of 0.5 and 5.5 sec, respectively). A within-subjects design was employed in which all birds were first exposed to the comparison-substitution procedure and probe–trial tests. The substituted discriminanda were vertical and horizontal lines (D1 and D2 in Fig. 7.3) appearing on the side keys in place of comparison stimuli after F cues. Choice of vertical was always rein-forced regardless of the identity of the preceding sample. Then all birds were exposed to the comparison–omission procedure and more probe trials. Each treatment phase lasted 30 days, probe tests lasted 24 days (2 probes/day), and a return to baseline conditions (adaptation to R and F cues) occurred at the end of each probe test.

Mean percentages of correct matching obtained during probe tests are pre-sented in Fig. 7.4. The data are plotted separately by treatment condition (sub-stitution versus omission), sample (food versus no food), delay (short versus long), and cue (F-cue probes versus R-cue trials). The effects of F cues on matching accuracy were complexly dependent on all these variables. The effects only appeared during comparison–omission and then only for matching to sam-ples of food. Given these qualifications, the predicted time dependence was observed; the detrimental effect of the F cue was largest at long delays.

In another experiment (Maki, Olson, & Rego, in press), the cues were 1-sec orange and green lights (ISI = 0.5 sec) displayed from a transluscent panel mounted in the roof of the conditioning chamber. For half the birds, the R cue

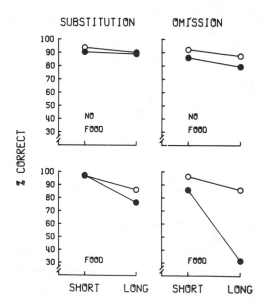

FIG. 7.4. Effects of postsample cues to forget and remember on match-ing accuracy during probe–trial tests. Open circles represent data from R-cue trials and filled circles represent data from F-cue trials. Data are plotted separately for each treatment condi-tion (substitution and omission), sam-ple (food and no food), and delay (short and long).

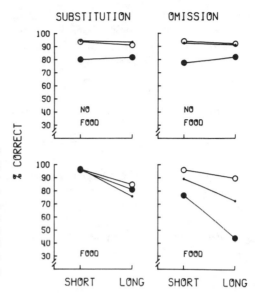

FIG. 7.5.   More effects of postsample cues on matching accuracy during probe-trial tests. Open circles represent data from R-cue trials, filled circles represent data from F-cue trials, and small dots represent data from probe trials containing no cue. Data are plotted separately for each group (substitution and omission), sample (food and no food), and delay (short and long).

was orange and the F cue was green (and for the other half, vice versa). All other temporal parameters were the same in this experiment except for the long delays, which averaged 9 sec. A between-groups design was used. After preliminary training and adaptation to the overhead lights, six birds were exposed to 30 days of comparison–omission and the other six birds were exposed to comparison–substitution. In this experiment, there was a single substituted stimulus (schematically, by omitting D2 in Fig. 7.3); in the substitution group a white cross was presented on a randomly chosen side key after F cues and a single response to it produced reinforcement. For both groups, the experiment ended with 40 more days of probe-trial tests (4 probes/day in the context of the treatment condition). Half of the probes contained F cues and the rest contained no cues (N cues); in N-cue probes, the delays were spent in darkness as they were early in preliminary training.

The results of this experiment's probe-trial tests are shown in Fig. 7.5. The data are displayed as before (Fig. 7.4) except for the addition of data from N-cue probes. With respect to the R-cue and F-cue comparisons, the results mirror those from the previous experiment (Fig. 7.4); and F cue produced poor matching accuracy at long delays but only after samples of food and only in the omission group. The effect of not presenting a cue (in N-cue probes) was not nearly as detrimental. In fact, unlike those of F cues, the effects of N cues did not differ between groups.

These two experiments establish both the reliability and generality of the time-dependent effects of F cues on delayed matching. They are reproducible in within-subjects and between-groups designs and do not depend on the specific stimuli chosen as cues. Unfortunately, the effects are also more complex than predicted by the rather simple rehearsal hypothesis stated earlier. There are two complications. First, the cuing effect is confined to matching to samples of food. Maki et al. (in press) suggested a reason for the asymmetry. They argued that pigeons might have a response bias in this task, treating "no food" not as an event in itself but rather as the *absence* of food. According to this view, a forgotten sample of food is treated as a memory of no food. It then follows that if the pigeon fails to remember a sample of food it will peck the "wrong" comparison stimulus (the one associated with no food), but if the pigeon forgets a sample of no food, it will still peck the comparison associated with no food (and will now be "right"). Therefore, the lack of an F-cue effect in the data from matching to samples of no food may not prove serious. The asymmetry between the different samples can be explained by the operation of a response bias unrelated to cuing; moreover, as reported by Grant (this volume), cuing effects are obtained with other (visual) samples in other versions of DMTS. The second complication, the lack of cuing effects during comparison–substitution, cannot be so easily dismissed. The data presented so far do not allow a firm determination of the reasons for the different results obtained with the omission and substitution procedures. However, a comparison of our results with those obtained in other laboratories provides grounds for rejecting some possible explanations.

Enough data have now been accumulated in different laboratories so that some of the grosser procedural differences between omission and substitution procedures can be evaluated. Table 7.1 summarizes the important procedural aspects and results of several experiments (Grant, 1981; Kendrick, 1980; Maki & Hegvik, 1980; Maki et al., in press; Stonebraker, 1980). The individual experiments are classified by treatment (omission versus substitution). For each experiment, proceeding from left to right, the type of task is first indicated. Second, the nature of events ending trials containing F cues are noted (varying from instrumental discriminanda through Pavlovian CSs to nothing at all). Third, the probability of reinforcement ending a trial containing an F cue is recorded. Finally, in the rightmost column, performance in F-cue probes has been classified as "high" or "low," with high being referenced to the high accuracy usually obtained in R-cue trials.

First of all, inspection of Table 7.1 reveals that the type of task (two-choice DMTS versus "go–no go" successive DMTS) does not determine the level of accuracy obtained in F-cue probes. Second, neither the type of samples nor the nature of cues is related to that performance. Third, neither the substituted stimuli nor the responses required to them seem to matter. Fourth, it seems difficult to argue that the "irrelevance" of sample retention to the nature of the end-of-trial events determines the performance in F-cue probes (cf. Grant, 1981); all the substitution procedures employed end-of-trial events that were irrelevant to the degree of sample retention on F-cue trials and yet only one of those procedures resulted in poor performance during F-cue probes (Grant,

TABLE 7.1

Summary of Methods and Results of Directed Forgetting Experiments

Experiment	Task	Substituted Stimuli	Response Requirement	Reinforcement Probability	Probe Accuracy
Substitution procedures					
Maki & Hegvik (1980)	DMTS[a]	S+ and S-[c]	Choice	1.0	High
Kendrick (1980; Experiment 1)	DMTS[b]	S+ and S-[c]	Choice	1.0	High
Maki, Olson, & Rego (in press)	DMTS[a]	S+ only[c]	Peck	1.0	High
Kendrick (1980; Experiment 2)	DMTS[b]	None[d]	None	1.0	High
Grant (1981)	Successive[b]	CS-[ ]	None	0.5	Low
Omission procedures					
Grant (1981)	Successive[b]	None	None	0.0	Low
Stonebraker (1980)	Successive[b]	None	None	0.0	Low
Kendrick (1980; Experiment 1)	DMTS[b]	None	None	0.0	Low
Maki & Hegvik (1980)	DMTS[a]	None	None	0.0	Low
Maki, Olson, & Rego (in press)	DMTS[a]	None	None	0.0	Low

Notes

[a] Samples of food and no food; diffuse cues (e.g., a houselight).

[b] Visual samples; localized (on key) cues.

[c] Responses to S+ followed by food.

[d] Noncontingent food.

1981). One variable that fares better in predicting whether high or low accuracy is obtained in F-cue probes is the probability of reinforcement ending trials containing F cues during both omission and substitution procedures. As Table 7.1 shows, probabilities of reinforcement of 0.5 or less are associated with poor performance in those probes.[2]

Reinforcement of Rehearsal

The results obtained so far indicate that postsample F cues decrease matching accuracy, and also that the cuing effect is time dependent; the detrimental effect of an F cue increases as a function of the time between the cue and comparison stimuli. Both findings are compatible with the original rehearsal hypothesis. However, these effects seem to depend on the probability of end-of-trial reinforcement, and the rehearsal hypothesis must be made to cope with the apparent importance of that variable. One possible modification is rather simple. The original hypothesis can be preserved; rehearsal can still be seen to maintain sample memories and forgetting can still be allowed to occur in the absence of rehearsal. The initial suspicion that rehearsal can be controlled by postsample R and F cues can similarly be preserved. All that then needs to be added is some specification of the action of end-of-trial reinforcers. It will be further assumed here that rehearsal is an instrumental response. It follows that, like other operants, rehearsal should be sensitive to the likelihood of its consequences. The "operant rate" of rehearsal should then be reduced when the probability of reinforcement is low (as in the omission procedures). On the other hand, when the probability of reinforcement is high (as in most of the substitution procedures listed in Table 7.1), rehearsal would still be followed by reinforcement and would therefore persist (regardless of the specific other behaviors that produced the reinforcer).[3]

---

[2]Grant (1981) employed a successive matching task. If two successively presented stimuli were the same (a matching trial), pecks at the second stimulus were reinforced; if the two stimuli were different (a nonmatching trial), pecks at the second stimulus were extinguished. Overall, the probability of end-of-trial reinforcement appears to be 0.5, even in the basic task and in R-cue trials. However, a reinforcement account can acknowledge sources of reinforcement other than food reward on matching trials. For example, it could be proposed that not responding is negatively reinforced in nonmatching trials. The functional probability of reinforcement is thus 1.0. Any procedure that eliminates food reward or that brings the animal into contact with nonreinforcement of responding reduces that probability of reinforcement.

[3]Huston and Mondadori (1977) recently proposed a similar notion; they argued that a reinforcer presented after a conditioning trial will prolong a "dynamic memory" (STM) and thus increase "the degree of fixation into LTM." Mondadori, Waser, and Huston (1977) reported that posttrial food reward enhanced passive avoidance learning in mice, but Marlin, Greco, and Miller (1978) failed to replicate the effect using water reward with rats. The theoretical links between the reinforcement of (postsample) rehearsal hypothesis proposed here and the reinforcement of (posttrial) dynamic memory hypothesis suggested by Huston are conceptually straightforward, but are complicated by the lack of understanding of the conditions under which posttrial reinforcement is effective and by the lack of evidence that would rule out alternative hypotheses (see Marlin et al., 1978).

As developed to this point, there is much that is left unsaid by the reinforcement-of-rehearsal hypothesis. Eventually, a more "determinate" theory (Wagner, this volume) will be desirable, but such an effort now seems premature in the absence of parametric data on the reinforcement–probability variable. It is clear from Table 7.1 that much more research needs to be done because all studies have used only two values, mostly 0.0 and 1.0, and it is difficult to assess interactions of this variable with others of potential importance.

Tests of Alternative Hypotheses

As the data base is enlarged, the reinforcement-of-rehearsal hypothesis may not turn out to be the best account of the origins of "directed forgetting" in animals. It is certainly not the only explanation of the effects of F cues reviewed so far. Therefore, having documented the cuing effects, some experimental efforts in our laboratory were directed at eliminating some other possible explanations of those effects.

Directed Forgetting as a Failure to Learn.   One class of explanations of the cuing effect holds that birds either might fail to learn to match or else might forget how to match in F-cue trials. Such hypotheses can be rejected on the basis of the time dependence of the cuing effect. For example, one automatic-process explanation of the effect would treat the comparison–omission (and substitution) procedures as rather complex forms of compound conditioning. It could be argued that birds learn new matching "rules" that are applied to compound stimuli composed of samples and R cues (e.g., "if food followed by orange light, peck the red side key") but do not have the opportunities to learn similar rules following compounds composed of samples and F cues (because of the omission of reinforcement). On this account, the F cue plays a benign role; the bird simply doesn't know what to do in probe trials. If this were the case, however, the bird should know just as little in short-delay probes as in long-delay probes. That expectation is not supported by the time-dependent effects of F cues portrayed in Figs. 7.4 and 7.5. In a similar fashion we can dismiss other hypotheses based on assertions about failures to learn. For example, if the pigeons did not expect comparison stimuli in probe trials and performance was disrupted by the novelty, that disruption should be just as severe after short cue-comparison delays as after longer delays (but it is not).

Recovery of Unconditioned Interference.   Another hypothesis, namely that cuing effects are related to the retroactive interference produced by delay-interval illumination (Grant & Roberts, 1976), can be rejected on the basis of data collected in the two experiments previously described (Maki & Hegvik, 1980; Maki et al., in press). Mean percentages of correct matching from 3-day baseline periods from the first and second experiments are summarized in Figs. 7.6 and 7.7. Consider Fig. 7.6 first. The leftmost top and bottom panels display data

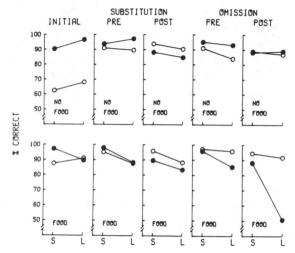

FIG. 7.6. Effects of postsample cues on accuracy during adaptation and baseline training. In the initial (adaptation) panels, dark circles represent data from DMTS trials with dark delays, and light circles represent data from DMTS trials containing a brief houselight. In the rest of the panels (pre- and postsubstitution and pre- and postomission baselines), dark circles represent F-cue trials and open circles represent R-cue trials. S and L refer to short and long delays.

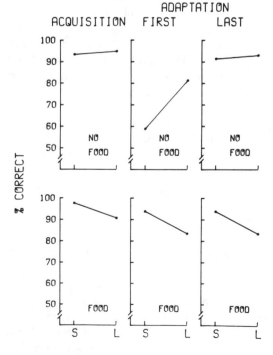

FIG. 7.7. Effects of postsample stimuli on matching during adaptation. Data are averaged over two intradelay stimuli (orange and green lights). S and L refer to short and long delays.

from the initial 3 days of adaptation (when the houselight was first introduced); in these panels, the open circles symbolize data from trials containing the houselight and the darkened circles symbolize data from trials with dark delays. It is clear that the effect of a novel light was to depress performance, but only for matching to samples of *no food*. The four sets (top and bottom) of panels to the right display data from 3-day baseline periods before and after substitution and omission treatment/test cycles; in these panels, open circles represent data from R-cued trials and filled circles represent data from F-cued trials. In agreement with the probe-trial results (fig. 7.4), these data show that F cues attacked performance after the omission training at long delays, but only for matching to samples of *food*.

The same kind of discrepancy between unconditioned interference effects and conditioned effects of F cues was noted in the second experiment. Fig. 7.7 displays the baseline data collected during the last 3 days prior to introduction of the overhead cue lights ("acquisition") and the first and last 3-day periods of adaptation. Again note that the unconditioned interference produced by the novel lights mostly affected matching to samples of *no food* at short delays. In contrast, the conditioned effects of F cues were most noticeable on matching to samples of *food* at long delays (see Fig. 7.5). We can therefore dismiss the possibility that the original, unconditioned interference from the stimuli used as cues recovered in the absence of continued adaptation because unconditioned interference effects were so different from the effects observed subsequent to omission training.

Proactive Effects on Performance.   It has been consistently assumed in this chapter that whatever F-cue effects were to be found would result from the influence of the cue on some process (like rehearsal) that was active at the time the cue was presented. However, in the absence of data to the contrary, it could just as well be assumed that the effects of F cues are proactive, disrupting performance at the time of choice between comparison stimuli. For example, stimuli that signal nonreinforcement (S−) produce emotional behaviors in pigeons, including turning away from the stimulus source (Terrace, 1972). In the omission procedure the F cue signals impending nonreinforcement (so is an S− by definition), and Kendrick (1980) reported that pigeons turn away from an F cue during the retention interval. If such disruptive effects of the F cue persist throughout the delay, it could be argued that a bird is not prepared to perform the simultaneous discrimination between comparison stimuli at the end of a probe trial containing an F cue. If that lack of preparation impairs just performance, then performance of *any* simultaneous discrimination should be harmed.

Maki et al. (in press) evaluated this alternative. Six pigeons had previously been given omission training (Fig. 7.5). These birds were trained to perform also a simple, unconditional simultaneous discrimination between two line orientations (vertical positive and horizontal negative). Two kinds of F-cue probe trials were then presented in the context of comparison–omission procedures. One kind

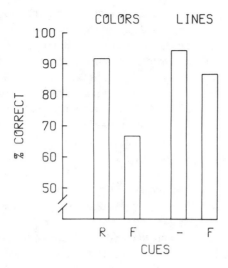

FIG. 7.8.   Matching accuracy as a function of the type of discrimination ending probe trials. For colors (true comparison stimuli), correct choices were conditional upon the preceding sample; for lines (a simple simultaneous discrimination), the correct choice was unconditional.

of probe ("colors") contained the usual comparison stimuli after long delays. The other kind of probe ("lines") contained the two line orientations. The results of this experiment are displayed in Fig. 7.8. From left to right, mean percentages of correct responses are first plotted for R-cue trials and F-cue probes that contained colors as comparisons. These data (averaged over matching to samples of food and no food) show the usual detrimental effect of F cues on DMTS performance. Next are plotted mean percentage of correct responses during line discrimination trials in which tbe presentation of the two lines as preceded by only an ITI. Finally, the data are plotted from those trials that began as DMTS probes containing samples and F cues but ended with the lines. There was almost no effect of the F cues on the accuracy of performing the simple line discrimination. These data therefore show that F cues do not proactively disrupt performance at the time of choice because performance of the unconditional discrimination was unimpaired. Put another way, the results of this experiment suggest that the effects of F cues are revealed when performance of a discrimination is based on (retention of) a preceding conditional stimulus. The results therefore support the contention that F cues interfere with transient memorial processes active during the retention interval rather than interfering proactively with performance of the simultaneous discrimination at the time of a retention test.

Motivated Forgetting Mediated by Classical Conditioning. The reinforcement-of-rehearsal hypothesis formulated earlier stresses a response-reinforcer relation. However, the directed forgetting effects described so far could also be explained by noting certain stimulus–reinforcer relations inherent in the omission and substitution procedures. For example, in the omission procedure, the R cue is paired with reinforcement and the F cue is paired with nonreinforcement. The stimulus–stimulus (CS–US) relations could allow for expectancies of trial outcomes to be formed during training and then elicited by the postsample cues. Following the reasoning of two-process theories (Rescorla & Solomon, 1967), it can be hypothesized that the classically conditioned expectancies motivate instrumental responding (in this case, rehearsing).

This two-process view can be made sufficiently explicit so as to generate testable predictions. For any particular sample, the omission procedure involves a discrimination of the form $AX + BX -$, where A corresponds to the R cue, B to the F cue, and the common element X to the sample. In discriminations of this sort, the elements signaling reinforcement (A) and nonreinforcement (B) can be assumed to take on excitatory and inhibitory properties, respectively (Rescorla & Wagner, 1972). Thus, in the analogy, the R cue excites and the F cue inhibits a conditioned expectancy of reward. Because the F cue is claimed to be Pavlovian conditioned inhibitor, considerable transfer between the omission procedure and other discrimination learning tasks can be anticipated. Following the logic underlying "transfer of control" experiments (Trapold & Overmeier, 1972), stimuli that have been trained as conditioned excitors and inhibitors by appetitive discrimination learning procedures should function as R and F cues in DMTS tasks.

Although this two-process view successfully accounts for the apparent dependence of cuing effects on reinforcement probability, it is probably not correct. We (Maki, Olson, & Rego, unpublished data) have now completed two transfer experiments; both failed to yield the predicted transfer. In the first experiment, we trained two groups of four pigeons each to perform delayed matching to samples of food and no food and adapted them to the postsample cue that would eventually be tested in probe trials. The birds were then trained on a discrete-trials operant discrimination. The stimuli were a horizontal line displayed on the center key (A) and a tone produced by an overhead "Sonalert" (B). When a particular stimulus was defined as S+, pecking at the center key produced reinforcement on an FI 10-sec schedule; when a stimulus was defined as S−, the trial ended automatically after 10 sec with nonreinforcement. One group learned an $AB + A -$ discrimination designed to render B (the tone) a conditioned excitor; the other group learned an $A + AB -$ discrimination designed to render B a conditioned inhibitor. After discrimination learning was complete (and the tone controlled responding in the $AB + A -$ group and little responding in the $A + AB -$ group), long-delay probe trials occurred in which the tone was tested for its potency as a postsample cue. The results are presented in the top two rows of Table 7.2. The effects of the tone on matching accuracy were extremely small. If anything, the tone slightly reduced accuracy of matching to samples of *no food* in the inhibitory group, an outcome quite unlike that noted with F cues made by omission training (Figs 7.4 and 7.5).

In the second experiment, we anticipated the objection that the efficacy of an auditory stimulus as an F cue had never been determined (in the omission procedure); perhaps the tone simply would not have made a good F cue under any

TABLE 7.2
Results of Transfer of Control Experiments

Discrimination	Stimuli	Design		Accuracy				
				Probe	DMTS		Probes	
			Group	cue	N	F	N	F
Instrumental	Auditory	Between	AB+A-	B	87	94	90	93
			A+AB-	B	93	91	86	92
Pavlovian	Visual	Within	A+B-	A	88	91	88	95
				B			78	95

Note: Data are percentage of correct matching displayed separately for samples of food (F) and no food (N).

circumstances. In this experiment we used the overhead colored lights that had been previously proven effective as R and F cues (Fig. 7.5). Four pigeons were trained as usual and adapted to both (orange and green) cues. Then, the pigeons were exposed to 416 Pavlovian trials spread over 13 days. Half of these trials $(A+)$ began with one of the lights for 3 sec and ended in reinforcement (2-sec food). The other half of the trials $(B-)$ began with the other light and ended in nonreinforcement (presentation of a 2-sec white houselight). During the last three days of Pavlovian training, two of the birds were observed by the three experimenters. Localized pecking at the front wall or the floor was consistently observed when CS+ (stimulus A) was presented. Behavior during CS− (stimulus B) was much more varied; rarely was directed activity observed, and the birds frequently oriented away from the front wall of the conditioning chamber. Finally, a series of long-delay probe trials was presented; some probes contained CS+ and some contained CS− as postsample cues. The results of this experiment are presented in the bottom two rows of Table 7.2. The pattern was very similar to that obtained in the previous experiment. There were small and nonsignificant effects that were most noticeable in the data from matching to samples of *no food* (again, cf. Fig. 7.5). The results of both experiments thus failed to provide evidence of the transfer predicted by the two-process hypothesis. As best as can now be determined, then, our directed forgetting results do not appear to be a case of "motivated" forgetting.

Mediating Behaviors.   One interpretation of the effects of F cues on matching would claim that delayed matching is based on sample-specific behaviors that occur during the delay and are acquired during delayed matching acquisition (Blough, 1959). According to such a hypothesis, the F cue interferes with those behaviors. The failure of postsample signals for food and no food to disrupt matching accuracy in the experiment just described allows some comment on this hypothesis. If the mediational hypothesis were true, matching accuracy should be decreased by introducing stimuli (F cues or not) that provoke other behaviors. As noted before, we took care to observe the birds' reactions to the visual CS+ and

CS− during Pavlovian training; conditioned appetitive responses (e.g., open-beak pecking at a wall) were evoked by CS+ and other behaviors were evoked by CS−. These activities should have competed with any sample-specific delay-interval behaviors and reduced matching accuracy during probe trials; no such accuracy losses were found. Unfortunately, a conclusion against the mediational hypothesis must be phrased more cautiously than we would like. Because the birds in our experiment were trained and tested with otherwise dark delays, delay-interval behavior was not directly observed during matching trials. However, Stonebraker (1980) also assessed the role of mediating behaviors in a directed forgetting experiment; he observed no sample-specific behaviors, reported rates of delay-interval key pecking that did not depend on the identities of preceding samples, and yet obtained the usual detrimental effect of F cues. Although meager, then, the available evidence fails to support an account of cuing effects in terms of overt mediation.

FUTURE DIRECTIONS OF DIRECTED FORGETTING

Even though the study of directed forgetting in animals is still in its infancy, it may not be too soon to speculate about where this line of research might lead our attempts to understand the nature of memory processes in nonhumans. In the immediate future, we can expect more experimental scrutiny of the cuing effects described in this chapter. We do not yet know with great confidence the origins of F-cue effects. The apparent importance of end-of-trial reinforcement was captured in the reinforcement-of-rehearsal hypothesis, but the obvious parametric studies of the reinforcement-probability variable are lacking. Such studies may reveal that the relationship between reinforcement probability and the cuing effect is one of mere correlation rather than causation.

Neither do we know with certainty the precise way that F cues adversely influence performance in tests of animal STM. An interpretation of cuing effects based on a rehearsal process was emphasized here; to-be-remembered information that was not maintained was assumed either to decay or to be displaced from STM. Sample memories not receiving rehearsal subsequent to F cues would then be unavailable to guide choices during a retention test at the end of a delay. In contrast, Rilling, Kendrick, and Stonebraker (in press) have argued for a retrieval interpretation. According to this hypothesis, the F cue changes delay-interval behaviors (Stonebraker, 1980) and thus produces an altered context at the time of the retention test. Information extracted from the sample stimulus is thus seen to become inaccessible (rather than unavailable) consequent to an F cue. Experimental evidence on which to base a decision between these two theoretical options is not now available (but hopefully it will soon become accessible).

Similarly, we do not yet have a full knowledge of the range of situations in which F cues operate. Perhaps the single most important experiment yet to be performed will test for the generality of F cues across tasks that presumably tap the same memory processes. If postsample cues truly control rehearsal, an F cue created by our standard procedures (matching to samples of food and no food, comparison–omission, etc.), for example, should instantly and without benefit of extraordinary measures transfer and function in the same way in the successive-matching task (Grant, this volume). If not, the failure would suggest an unfortunate task specificity that would be grounds to question the appropriateness of the analogy to human directed forgetting and that would pose a fundamental challenge to the conception of rehearsal as a controlled process in animals. But if such transfer can be demonstrated, we can then proceed to ask a question that originally prompted our work on directed forgetting described here. By use of other transfer designs (Maki, 1979a), we can ask whether the postsample processes we study in tasks like DMTS and call rehearsal are homologous to those posttrial processes studied in conditioning preparations (Wagner et al., 1973). If so, we ought to be able to establish F cues and find that they are effective retrograde amnesic agents, retarding associative learning. That we are sufficiently far along in the study of directed forgetting in animals to be able to entertain seriously such questions is indicative of the value of research on directed forgetting as a memory mechanism in animal behavior.

SUMMARY AND CONCLUSIONS

In this chapter, a general procedure for the study of directed forgetting in animals was described. The procedure mimics studies of directed forgetting in humans in two major ways. First, following cues to forget (F cues), retention tests are infrequent. Second, cues to remember (R cues) or forget occur during retention intervals, thus insuring equivalent degrees of attention to and learning about both to-be-remembered and to-be-forgotten events. In the research reported here, the general procedure was applied to delayed matching-to-sample tests of pigeon STM. F cues were found to decrease matching accuracy, particularly if the time between the postsample cue and the retention test (comparison stimuli) was long. The cuing effect appeared to be related to a low probability of end-of-trial reward in F-cue trials. The "reinforcement-of-rehearsal" hypothesis, calculated to account for such a relationship, treated rehearsal as an instrumental response, controlled by discriminative stimuli (R and F cues) that signaled different probabilities of reinforcement. Additional experimental evidence allows rejection of some alternative hypotheses, but three issues remain unresolved. First, the training conditions responsible for cuing effects are still not completely understood. Second, it is not known whether F cues interfere with performance by making traces of events less available or less accessible. Third, it is not known whether the R and F cues manufactured in these experiments function as "instructions" and thus have effects that generalize to situations beyond the original training context. In addition to being of inherent interest to students of animal memory, directed forgetting in animals may prove to be a valuable tool when applied to other questions of historical and contemporary theoretical interest (e.g., the role of active memory processes in associative learning).

ACKNOWLEDGMENTS

Preparation of this chapter and the author's research described in it were supported by National Institute of Mental Health Grant MH31432. The assistance of Donna Hegvik, Deborah Olson, and Susan Rego is gratefully acknowledged.

REFERENCES

Atkinson, R. C., & Shiffrin, R. M. Human memory: A proposed system and its control processes. In K. W. Spence & J. T. Spence (Eds.), *The psychology of learning and motivation: Advances in research and theory* (Vol. 2). New York: Academic Press, 1968.

Bjork, R. A. Theoretical implications of directed forgetting. In A. W. Melton & E. Martin (Eds.), *Coding processes in human memory*. Washington, D.C.: Winston, 1972.

Blough, D. S. Delayed matching in the pigeon. *Journal of the Experimental Analysis of Behavior,* 1959, *2,* 151–160.

D'Amato, M. R. Memory: Animal studies. In B. B. Wolman & L. R. Pomeroy (Eds.), *International encyclopedia of psychiatry, psychology, psychoanalysis, and neurology* (Vol. 7). New York: Aesculopius, 1977.

Dickinson, A., & Mackintosh, N. J. Reinforcer specificity in the enhancement of conditioning by posttrial surprise. *Journal of Experimental Psychology: Animal Behavior Processes,* 1979, *5,* 162–177.

Grant, D. S. Stimulus control of information processing in pigeon short-term memory. *Learning and Motivation,* 1981, *12,* 19–39.

Grant, D. S., & Roberts, W. A. Sources of retroactive inhibition in pigeon short-term memory. *Journal of Experimental Psychology: Animal Behavior Processes,* 1976, *2,* 1–16.

Hobhouse, L. T. *Mind in evolution.* London: Macmillan, 1915. (Reprint edition 1973 by Arno Press, Inc.)

Honig, W. K. Studies of working memory in the pigeon. In S. H. Hulse, H. Fowler, & W. K. Honig (Eds.), *Cognitive processes in animal behavior.* Hillsdale, N.J.: Lawrence Erlbaum Associates, 1978.

Hulse, S. H. Cognitive structure and serial pattern learning by animals. In S. H. Hulse, H. Fowler, & W. K. Honig (Eds.), *Cognitive processes in animal behavior.* Hillsdale, N.J.: Lawrence Erlbaum Associates, 1978.

Huston, J. P., & Mondadori, C. Reinforcement and memory: A model. *Activitas Nervosae Superioris,* 1977, *19,* 17–19.

Kamin, L. J. Selective association and conditioning. In N. J. Mackintosh & W. K. Honig (Eds.), *Fundamental issues in associative learning.* Halifax: Dalhousie University Press, 1969.

Kendrick, D. F. *Trace supraordinate stimulus control of delayed matching-to-sample performance.* Unpublished masters thesis, Michigan State University, 1980.

Maki, W. S. Discrimination learning without short-term memory: Dissociation of memory processes in pigeons. *Science,* 1979, *204,* 83–85. (a)

Maki, W. S. Pigeons' short-term memories for surprising versus expected reinforcement and non-reinforcement. *Animal Learning & Behavior*, 1979, *7*, 31-37. (b)

Maki, W. S., Beatty, W. W., Berg, B., & Lunn, R. *Spatial memory in rats: Temporal release from proactive interference*. Paper presented at the Psychonomic Society meeting, St. Louis, November 1980.

Maki, W. S., Gillund, G., Hauge, G., & Siders, W. Matching to sample after extinction of observing responses. *Journal of Experimental Psychology: Animal Behavior Processes*, 1977, *3*, 285-296.

Maki, W. S., & Hegvik, D. K. Directed forgetting in pigeons. *Animal Learning & Behavior*, 1980, *8*, 567-574.

Maki, W. S., Moe, J. C., & Bierley, C. M. Short-term memory for stimuli, responses, and reinforcers. *Journal of Experimental Psychology: Animal Behavior Processes*, 1977, *3*, 156-177.

Maki, W. S., Olson, D., & Rego, S. *The contribution of delay-interval stimuli to delayed matching performance*. Paper presented at the Psychonomic Society meeting, Phoenix, November 1979.

Maki, W. S., Olson, D., & Rego, S. Directed forgetting in pigeons: Analysis of cue functions. *Animal Learning & Behavior*, in press.

Marlin, N. A., Greco, C., & Miller, R. R. Effects of posttraining reinforcement upon retention of a passive avoidance task. *Bulletin of the Psychonomic Society*, 1978, *11*, 295-297.

Mondadori, C., Waser, P. G., & Huston, J. P. Time-dependent effects of post-trial reinforcement, punishment or ECS on passive avoidance learning. *Physiology & Behavior*, 1977, *18*, 1103-1109.

Muter, P. Very rapid forgetting. *Memory & Cognition*, 1980, *8*, 174-179.

Olton, D. S. Characteristics of spatial memory. In S. H. Hulse, H. Fowler, & W. K. Honig (Eds.), *Cognitive processes in animal behavior*. Hillsdale, N.J.: Lawrence Erlbaum Associates, 1978.

Olton, D. S., & Samuelson, R. J. Remembrance of places passed: Spatial memory in rats. *Journal of Experimental Psychology: Animal Behavior Processes*, 1976, *2*, 97-116.

Pearce, J. M., & Hall, G. Overshadowing the instrumental conditioning of a lever-press response by a more valid predictor of the reinforcer. *Journal of Experimental Psychology: Animal Behavior Processes*, 1978, *4*, 356-367.

Rescorla, R. A., & Solomon, R. L. Two-process theory: Relationships between Pavlovian conditioning and instrumental learning. *Psychological Review*, 1967, *74*, 151-182.

Rescorla, R. A., & Wagner, A. R. A theory of Pavlovian conditioning: Variations in the effectiveness of reinforcement and nonreinforcement. In A. H. Black & W. F. Prokasy (Eds.), *Classical conditioning II: Current theory and research*. New York: Appleton-Century-Crofts, 1972.

Riley, D. A., & Leith, C. R. Multidimensional psychophysics and selective attention in animals. *Psychological Bulletin*, 1976, *83*, 138-160.

Rilling, M., Kendrick, D. F., & Stonebraker, T. B. Stimulus control of forgetting: A behavioral analysis. In M. L. Commons, A. R. Wagner, & R. J. Herrnstein (Eds.), *Quantitative Studies in Operant Behavior: Acquisition*. Boston: Ballinger, in press.

Roberts, W. A., & Grant, D. S. Studies of short-term memory in the pigeon using the delayed matching to sample procedure. In D. L. Medin, W. A. Roberts, & R. T. Davis (Eds.), *Processes of animal memory*. Hillsdale, N.J.: Lawrence Erlbaum Associates, 1976.

Roberts, W. A., & Grant, D. S. An analysis of light-induced retroactive inhibition in pigeon short-term memory. *Journal of Experimental Psychology: Animal Behavior Processes*, 1978, *4*, 219-236.

Shiffrin, R. M., & Schneider, W. Controlled and automatic human information processing: II. Perceptual learning, automatic attending, and a general theory. *Psychological Review*, 1977, *84*, 129-190.

Spence, K. W. The differential response in animals to stimuli varying within a single dimension. *Psychological Review*, 1937, *44*, 430-444.

Stonebraker, T. *Stimulus control of active rehearsal processes in the pigeon using directed forget-*

ting techniques. Paper presented at the Association for Behavior Analysis meeting, Dearborn, May 1980.

Terrace, H. S. By-products of discrimination learning. In G. H. Bower (Ed.), *The psychology of learning and motivation: Advances in research and theory* (Vol. 5). New York: Academic Press, 1972.

Terry, W. S., & Wagner, A. R. Short-term memory for "surprising" versus "expected" unconditioned stimuli in Pavlovian conditioning. *Journal of Experimental Psychology: Animal Behavior Processes*, 1975, *1*, 122–133.

Thorndike, E. L. *Human learning*. New York: Century, 1931.

Tolman, E. C. Cognitive maps in rats and men. *Psychological Review*, 1948, *55*, 189–208.

Tranberg, D. K., & Rilling, M. Delay-interval illumination changes interfere with pigeon short-term memory. *Journal of the Experimental Analysis of Behavior*, 1980, *33*, 39–49.

Trapold, M. A., & Overmeier, J. B. The second learning process in instrumental learning. In A. H. Black & W. F. Prokasy (Eds.), *Classical conditioning II: Current theory and research*. New York: Appleton-Century-Crofts, 1972.

Wagner, A. R. Expectancies and the priming of STM. In S. H. Hulse, H. Fowler, & W. K. Honig (Eds.), *Cognitive processes in animal behavior*. Hillsdale, N.J.: Lawrence Erlbaum Associates, 1978.

Wagner, A. R., Rudy, J. W., & Whitlow, J. W., Jr. Rehearsal in animal conditioning. *Journal of Experimental Psychology*, 1973, *97*, 407–426.

Woodward, A. E., Bjork, R. A., & Jongeward, R. H. Recall and recognition as a function of primary rehearsal. *Journal of Verbal Learning and Verbal Behavior*, 1973, *12*, 608–617.

8 Short-term Memory In the Pigeon

Douglas S. Grant
University of Alberta

In many respects the present chapter represents a sequel to that of Roberts and Grant (1976). In that paper we outlined a theoretical conception of pigeon short-term memory (STM) as it evolved in the course of our empirical studies. It is my intent here to consider some of the work conducted following the appearance of that paper, with particular attention given to the implications of more recent findings for the model of STM espoused in 1976. Following initial description of that model, with its emphasis on trace strength, consideration will be given to more recent data that appear both to challenge that conception and to suggest the operation of certain previously unidentified processes in pigeon STM. The chapter concludes with a discussion of an alternative theoretical conception of pigeon STM.

THE TRACE STRENGTH CONCEPTION

Studies in STM in the pigeon generally have employed the delayed matching-to-sample task in which the pigeon is required to select between two different comparison stimuli the one that matches a previously presented sample stimulus. A peck to the matching comparison stimulus results in a reinforcer, whereas a peck to the nonmatching comparison stimulus results in a time-out. Over trials the stimulus serving as the sample and the position of the matching comparison stimulus are varied randomly. Accurate performance in this task thus requires the retention of information derived from the sample stimulus until the choice response occurs at the time of comparison presentation.

Our initial work employed the delayed matching preparation to investigate the effects of sample stimulus repetition and spacing on short-term retention (Grant, 1976; Roberts, 1972; Roberts & Grant, 1974). These studies revealed that matching accuracy was influenced primarily by three variables; (a) duration of exposure to the sample stimulus; (b) length of the retention interval separating sample termination and comparison presentation; and (c) degree of temporal spacing between successive sample presentations. Each of these variables influenced accuracy in an independent, noninteractive fashion. For example, *rate* of forgetting across a retention interval was influenced by neither duration of sample exposure nor degree of spacing between successive presentations of the sample.

To organize and account for findings on repetition and spacing effects, a simple trace strength conception of pigeon STM was formulated (Roberts & Grant, 1976). According to this view, presentation of the sample stimulus establishes an internal representation or memory trace that can vary in initial strength. The probability that the bird will select the matching comparison stimulus at testing is a monotonically increasing function of sample trace strength. The memory trace increases in strength as a negatively accelerated function of time in the presence of the sample and decreases in strength as a negatively accelerated function of time in the absence of the sample. Although all traces lose strength with the passage of time, the absolute rate at which a trace decays is independent of the current level of strength.

Investigations of proactive interference in pigeon STM (Grant, 1975; Grant & Roberts, 1973; Zentall & Hogan, 1974, 1977) resulted in additional assumptions being added to the trace strength conception. These studies demonstrated that the probability of choosing the matching comparison stimulus was reduced markedly if the nonmatching comparison stimulus had appeared recently as a sample. The interference effect increased with increased repetition of the sample corresponding to the incorrect comparison and decreased with increases in either repetition of the sample corresponding to the correct comparison stimulus or temporal separation between the samples.

To account for these findings within a trace strength conception, assumptions of trace independence and trace competition were incorporated into the model (Roberts & Grant, 1976). According to the trace independence assumption, different stimulus events that occur successively establish separate and independent memory traces. Although both traces decay with the passage of time, the presence of a trace in the system affects neither the initial strength nor the rate of decay of a second trace. The trace competition assumption embodies the notion that the probability of selecting the correct comparison stimulus is a function not only of the strength of the trace corresponding to the matching comparison, but is also a function of the strength of the trace corresponding to the nonmatching comparison. More specifically, the degree of interference resulting from a prior presentation of the incorrect comparison as a sample is a monotonically increasing function of the degree to which the trace strength distribution of the interfering stimulus overlaps or exceeds the trace strength distribution of the current sample stimulus.

The trace strength conception, bolstered by assumptions of trace independence and competition, proved reasonably successful in accounting both for repetition and spacing effects and for proactive interference effects. More recent findings have, however, posed something of a challenge. It is a consideration of these more recent findings, and concomitant theoretical implications, to which we now turn.

ACTIVE VERSUS PASSIVE INFORMATION PROCESSING

The trace strength conception views the pigeon as a rather passive participant in the processing of information. A stimulus event that impinges on the organism's receptors establishes a memory trace that subsequently grows in strength and then decays as a function of temporal parameters. Growth and decay of trace strength occur automatically and inevitably, permitting little in the way of active intervention by the organism. The data considered in the following sections suggest that the organism plays a more active role in information processing than previously suspected. Evidence implicating active participation in information processing comes from work on: (a) retroactive interference; (b) matching to surprising versus expected samples; and (c) stimulus control of information processing.

Retroactive Interference

Zentall (1973) was first to demonstrate that stimulation interpolated during the retention interval of a delayed matching trial decreases matching accuracy in the pigeon. Subsequent to Zentall's work, Roberts and I performed a series of experiments to determine the properties of interpolated stimuli that interfere with retention (Grant & Roberts, 1976). Of the dimensions of familiarity, saliency, complexity, and degree of illumination emitted, only the latter significantly influenced the amount of retroactive interference. Fig. 8.1, taken from an experiment in which we manipulated the intensity of a white light that appeared during the 5-sec retention interval, illustrates this effect. Matching accuracy was poorest when the light was at full intensity and improved regularly as the light was progressively dimmed.

In further work on retroactive interference effects (Roberts & Grant, 1978a), we discovered that a brief period of light more markedly decreased matching accuracy when presented at the end of the retention interval than when presented at the beginning of the interval. In a recent experiment, Tranberg and Rilling

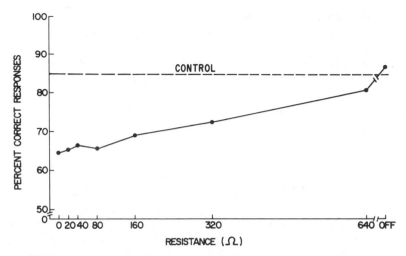

FIG. 8.1.   Percentage of correct responses as a function of the value of a dropping resistor in series with a white light interpolated during the 5-sec retention interval. Performance on control (dark retention interval) trials is shown as a dashed line (Grant & Roberts, 1976).

(1980) have shown that any change in illumination level from that which normally prevails, whether it involves an increase or a decrease, interfers with retention.

Although these findings are not necessarily antithetical to the strength and decay conception, they do appear more compatible with the view that the pigeon actively processes or rehearses the sample memory during the retention interval. In this view, the processing of interpolated stimulation commands a sufficient amount of the pigeon's processing capacity to reduce the level of processing devoted to maintenance of sample memory. The beginning–end effect could be accounted for by making the reasonable assumption that processes of maintenance rehearsal are more easily disrupted as the event that initiated that process becomes more temporally remote.

Surprising Versus Expected Samples

A recent experiment by Maki (1979) suggests further that the pigeon actively processes information in STM. Birds were trained initially in an arbitrary or symbolic delayed matching task in which the red comparison was correct given a sample of food and the green comparison was correct given a sample of no food. Subsequent training involved a simple, nonconditional discrimination between vertical (S+) and horizontal (S−) lines. Following acquisition of both tasks, the two types of discrimination trials were chained on infrequent probe trials such that the terminal event in the simple discrimination (reinforcement or nonreinforcement) served as the sample (food or no food) in the conditional discrimination. Maki's primary concern was whether delayed matching performance would be influenced by the degree to which the sample of food or no food was expected on chained trials. On "expected" trials, S+ was followed by reinforcement (expected food sample) or S− was followed by nonreinforcement (expected no food sample). On "surprising" trials, S+ was followed by nonreinforcement (surprising no food sample) or S− was followed by reinforcement (surprising food sample).

The data revealed that delayed matching accuracy given unexpected or surprising samples (81% correct) was significantly higher than accuracy given expected samples (67% correct). Maki interpreted this finding in terms of Wagner's (1978, 1979) model of STM, suggesting that surprising samples receive more processing or maintenance rehearsal than expected samples. This conclusion would have been strengthened considerably had retention interval been manipulated and a retardation in rate of forgetting as a function of sample surprisingness been demonstrated. In the absence of such a demonstration it is possible to argue that Maki's results are a product of an unexpected sample being better perceived: in the terminology of the trace strength conception, establishing a stronger trace. Even in the absence of retention interval manipulation, however, these results are certainly consistent with predictions derived from Wagner's active information-processing view of STM.

Roberts (1980), employing a preparation different from that of Maki, has shown recently that an unexpected sample is better remembered, and not merely better perceived, than an expected sample. Pigeons were tested on 12 delayed matching trials in each session, six trials involved a 0-sec retention interval and six involved a 6-sec retention interval. The 12 test trials were presented on each of two types of sessions, embedded sessions and control sessions. On embedded sessions the 12 test trials were presented in the context of 36 matching trials employing stimuli from a different dimension. The sequencing was arranged such that each line orientation test trial was preceded by three color trials (first replication), or each color test trial was preceded by three line orientation trials (second replication). On control sessions, on the other hand, the 12 test trials were presented in the absence of trials from the alternate dimension and the interval between test trials was equated to that on embedded sessions. Thus, embedded and control sessions differed in only one respect, whether or not test trials were preceded by three trials employing stimuli from the alternate dimension.

The data revealed that rate of forgetting was significantly reduced when test trials were embedded. That is, at the 0-sec retention interval test trial accuracy during embedded and control sessions was approximately equivalent. At the 6-sec retention interval, however, test trial accuracy was significantly higher during embedded sessions. Roberts suggested that enhanced retention as a function of embedding might be a product of differential sample rehearsal. He reasoned that the occurrence of the sample on test trials might be rendered somewhat novel or unexpected by virtue of being embedded in a sequence of trials employing samples from a different dimension. If so, Roberts maintained, Wagner's theorizing would suggest enhanced rehearsal of sample memory, and hence less rapid forgetting, on test trials that were embedded.

Stimulus Control of Information Processing

Although studies of retroactive interference and sample surprisingness are suggestive of a more active view of information processing than that embodied in the trace strength conception, they do not compel such a position. In a recent series of experiments an attempt was made to obtain more direct evidence relevant to the issue of whether pigeons actively process information in STM (Grant, 1981b). This was accomplished by determining whether the putative rehearsal process could be brought under stimulus control.

Birds were trained initially on the successive delayed matching task developed by Wasserman (1976), using red and green stimuli. In this preparation, sample presentation is followed by a retention interval and the subsequent presentation of a single test stimulus. If the test stimulus matches the previously presented sample, responding to the test stimulus is reinforced on a fixed interval 5-sec schedule. On nonmatching trials, responding to the test stimulus is not reinforced, and the test stimulus terminates automatically after 5 sec. As a function of these contingencies, birds come to respond to the test stimulus at a high rate on matching trials and at a low rate on nonmatching trials. A quantitative index of retention, the discrimination ratio, is obtained by dividing the number of responses on matching trials by the total number of responses on matching and nonmatching trials.

Following acquisition of successive delayed matching, all samples were followed by either a vertical or horizontal line. The vertical line is referred to as a "remember cue" and signaled that sample memory would be tested by the subsequent presentation of either the red or green test stimulus. The horizontal line is referred to as a "forget cue" and signaled that sample memory would not be tested on that trial (see Maki, this volume, and Rilling, Kendrick, & Stonebraker, 1981, for further discussion of stimulus control of forgetting).

As shown in Table 8.1, birds were exposed to one of two types of forget trials. For birds in the No Test Group, the pecking key remained dark during the test stimulus presentation period and no reinforcer was presented. For birds in the Dot Test Group, a black dot on a white background was presented in place of the red or green test stimulus. The dot stimulus terminated after 5 sec and was followed by a noncontingent reinforcer on 50% of the occasions. Three birds were trained on remember cued and forget cued–no test trials and the remaining three were trained on remember cued and forget cued–dot test trials.

TABLE 8.1
Illustration of Trial Types Employed to Study
Stimulus Control of Information Processing

	Trial Type		
Event	Remember Cued	Forget Cued-Dot Test	Forget Cued-No Test
Sample	Red or Green	Red or Green	Red or Green
Cue	Vertical Line	Horizontal Line	Horizontal Line
Test	Red or Green	Dot	None
Outcome	Reinforcement or Timeout	50% Noncontingent Reinforcement	Nonreinforcement

On the basis of the conception of the pigeon as an active processor of the sample stimulus memory, one might anticipate that with sufficient training the line stimuli would control the amount of processing devoted to the sample memory during the retention interval. That is, the remember cue might heighten or at least maintain processing, whereas the forget cue might terminate or at least dampen processing. This possibility was assessed by comparing test accuracy on remember cue trials with that on forget cue probe trials. On forget cue probe trials, a red or green test stimulus was presented rather than canceling the test or presenting a dot test. Less accurate retention on forget cue probe trials, relative to that on remember cue trials, would provide direct support for the notion that the pigeon actively processes information in STM.

In Fig. 8.2, test accuracy is shown on remember and forget cue probe trials as a function of cue duration during the 3-sec retention interval. Both groups demonstrated markedly higher accuracy on remember trials than on forget trials. In addition, there was a slight tendency for performance to decline as cue duration increased on forget trials, particularly from .5 to 1 sec. Response rate data, shown in Table 8.2, demonstrate that matching rates were stable across treatments, whereas nonmatching rates were markedly higher on forget trials. The equivalence of response rate on forget and remember matching trials suggests that the birds did not fail to notice the presentation of the test stimulus on forget cue trials.

TABLE 8.2
Mean Responses Per 5-Sec Test

	Dot Test Group		No Test Group	
Trial Type	Match	Nonmatch	Match	Nonmatch
Remember	12.3	2.7	9.4	1.7
Forget	12.4	9.5	8.8	4.8

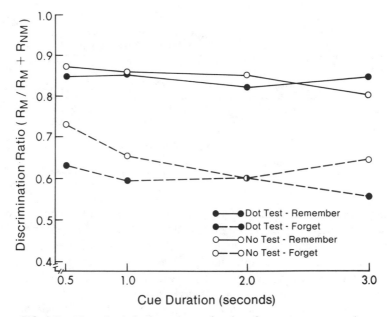

FIG. 8.2.   Mean discrimination ratio as a function of groups, cue type, and cue duration. R_M = responses on matching trials: R_{NM} = responses on nonmatching trials (Grant, 1981b).

Lower retention accuracy on forget trials than on remember trials provides direct support for the notion that pigeons actively process the sample memory during the retention interval. The present data do not permit comment, however, on the issue of whether a remember cue intensifies processing, a forget cue dampens processing, or whether both occur. Subsequent experiments in the series provided evidence consistent with the idea that a forget cue dampens the level of sample processing, whereas a remember cue has no effect on processing. In one of these experiments, 1-sec forget and remember cues were presented either in the beginning, middle, or end of a 3-sec retention interval. Retention on remember trials was unaffected by point of cue placement, suggesting that a remember cue does not influence information processing. On the other hand, forget cue effectiveness delined progressively as the temporal separation between sample offset and cue onset increased, suggesting that a forget cue reduces the intensity of sample processing. The latter finding also rules out the rather uninteresting possibility that the relatively poor performance obtained on forget cue probe trials might be a function of presenting an unexpected test. If this were the case, forget cue effectiveness should increase, rather than decrease, as the temporal contiguity of cue and test increased.

In a further experiment, employing retention intervals of 3 and 6 sec, retention on remember trials was found to be no better than that on noncued trials, whereas both types of trials produced higher test accuracy than did forget trials. Data from this experiment are shown in Fig. 8.3. One important aspect of these data is the fact that rate of forgetting was faster on forget trials than on the other trial types. Retention loss scores were calculated within each group and trial type by subtracting the mean discrimination ratio at 6 sec from that at 3 sec. In the Dot Test Group these scores were .02, .03, and .16 for remember, no cue, and forget trials, respectively, and were .04, .06, and .09 for the No Test Group. More rapid forgetting on forget trials is consistent with the hypothesis that a forget cue terminates, or at least reduces processing of the sample memory and further enhances confidence in the conception of the pigeon as an active processor of information.

Conclusion

Taken collectively, studies concerning retroactive interference, sample surprisingness, and stimulus control of information processing suggest rather strongly that pigeons actively process or rehearse the sample memory during the retention interval of a delayed matching trial. Thus, to speak of trace decay as a passive process that occurs spontaneously over time would appear to be something of a misnomer. The findings reviewed suggest instead that sample memory is maintained over a retention interval, albeit imperfectly, by an active process of maintenance rehearsal.

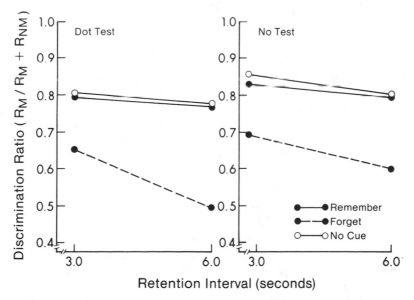

FIG. 8.3. Mean discrimination ratio as a function of retention interval for each group and cue type. R_M = responses on matching trials; R_{NM} = responses on nonmatching trials (Grant, 1981b).

NATURE OF THE MEMORIAL REPRESENTATION

We have now seen that recent empirical findings suggest that the concept of spontaneous decay of memory traces be abandoned and replaced by the notion that memories are maintained through active processes of maintenance rehearsal. Data considered in the present section suggest that the conception of the memory as a "trace" is likely in error.

The term *trace* connotes a memory that is isomorphic with the stimulus giving rise to the memory. Such a description of the memory in delayed matching agrees reasonably well with my earlier conception of pigeon STM. That is, I assumed that the pigeon, given a green sample, remembered "the color green" and, given a red sample, remembered "the color red," etc. I now believe that conceptualizing the memory as an instruction is preferable. On an instructional view of delayed matching, given a green sample the bird remembers the instruction "peck green" and given a red sample remembers the instruction "peck red," etc. (See Dickinson & Adams' chapter in this volume for further discussion of the conditions under which animal memory assumes an instructional format.)

Several lines of research are generating data that appear to converge in support of an instructional conception of pigeon STM. Evidence implicating an instructional memorial representation comes from work on retention and transfer in the advance key preparation and from studies of interference and sample repetition using samples from different dimensions.

Retention and Transfer in the Advance Key Procedure

An alternative preparation for studying short-term retention in the pigeon has been developed by Honig (1978). In this preparation a trial begins with a 20-sec prestimulus and terminates in a 60-sec poststimulus. The pre- and poststimulus were either a vertical line (S+) associated with a variable interval (VI) 30-sec schedule or a horizontal line (S−) associated with extinction. Trials beginning with S+ terminated in S− and trials beginning with S− terminated in S+. Interpolated between the pre- and poststimulus was a white interim stimulus associated with a VI 2-min schedule. At some point following onset of the interim stimulus a separate, advance key was illuminated with red light. In the absence of a response to the advance key, the advance key and interim stimulus remained illuminated concurrently for 60 sec and were then replaced by the single poststimulus. A single response to the advance key, however, terminated the interim component and procured the poststimulus immediately.

To the extent that the bird's behavior is controlled by these contingencies, latency to peck the advance key should be shorter on trials beginning with an S− prestimulus than on trials beginning with an S+ prestimulus. This is the case because responding to the advance key on an S− trial procures immediately S+, and a richer schedule of reinforcement (VI 30 sec versus VI 2 min). On an S+ trial, on the other hand, responding to the advance key procures immediately S−, and a reduction in reinforcement density (extinction versus VI 2 min).

Two of Honig's manipulations are particularly instructive with respect to the present concern with the nature of the memorial representation. The first involves the effect of length of retention interval on performance. This manipulation involves changes in the time interval separating termination of the prestimulus and the opportunity to peck the advance key. This may be accomplished easily by varying the length of time during which the interim stimulus is presented in isolation prior to illumination of the advance key.

In light of the fact that performance typically approaches a chance level at retention intervals of about 10 sec in delayed matching, we might anticipate rather rapid forgetting in the advance key preparation. Honig, however, has reported excellent retention in this preparation across a retention interval of 30 sec (see Figs. 3 and 4, pp. 223 and 224). Although I have reported above-chance retention at delays of 60 sec in the matching procedure (Grant, 1976), those birds required on the order of 17,000 preliminary delayed matching trials. Honig's animals, in contrast, performed rather well from the outset of training. Prior to discussing the theoretical implications of this discrepancy, another of Honig's findings will be considered.

A second of Honig's manipulations relevant to the issue of the nature of the memorial representation concerns transfer effects. In one such experiment birds were trained initially in the advance key procedure using vertical and horizontal lines as pre- and poststimuli. Subsequent treatment involved exposure to a multiple schedule (VI 30 sec/Ext) in which blue was positive and green negative. Once responding to blue and green had been stabilized, they were used as prestimuli in the advance key preparation in place of the lines. The interval between prestimulus offset and advance key onset, the retention interval, was 20 sec. In spite of the fact that the birds had had neither prior experience with these stimuli in the advance key procedure nor training to remember blue and green stimuli, advance key performance was as good, or slightly better, with blue and green prestimuli.

Although these findings do not deal a deathblow to the conception of the short-term memory as a trace, at a minimum a more liberal definition of the term "trace" appears required. Consider that in the typical delayed matching preparation the only aspect of the sample stimulus that can be used to control accurate test responding is wavelength in the case of colored fields or orientation in the case of lines, etc. In the advance key preparation, on the other hand, a number of properties of the prestimulus could control the advance key response in addition to wavelength or orientation. Such additional properties of the prestimulus include affective value, response rate, and possibly the occurrence or nonoccurrence of reinforcement. If one were willing to posit the existence of affective, behavioral, and consequent traces, Honig's findings would not be incompatible with the trace strength conception. The more robust retention seen in the advance key preparation might be viewed as a product of the existence of multiple, redundant traces at the time of advance key presentation, any one of which could control accurate performance. The transfer effects may be interpreted similarly within a liberalized conception of the trace. In this case, substitution of colored fields for line orientations as prestimuli would continue to establish affective, behavioral, and consequent traces. Because these traces should be established with equal efficacy by colored fields and line orientations, transfer performance would be expected to suffer little, if at all.

Although it is thus possible to account for these findings within a conception of the memory as a trace, Honig (1978) has advanced an alternative interpretation based on an instructional conception of the memory. In this view: "the pre-stimulus establishes an 'instruction', which is a state or process that determines the criterion response following the memory interval—whether the pigeon will peck or not peck at the ... advance key [p. 242]." The instructional view accounts rather nicely for the transfer data in that one would anticipate that an instruction could be established or activated by a number of independent events. To account for more robust retention in his preparation than in matching, Honig suggests that instructional encoding in the pigeon does not extend to situations in which particular physical characteristics must be retained. In this view, then, birds in the advance key situation remember an instruction to peck or not peck, whereas in delayed matching they must remember the physical characteristics of the sample. Instructional memories are presumably easier to encode and/or maintain than are traces of physical characteristics.

On the basis of the evidence presented to this point it would be difficult indeed to endorse confidently either the liberalized trace conception or the instructional conception. The following data, however, suggest that memories established in the delayed matching preparation are instructional in nature. These data tip the scale in favor of an instructional conception of memory, and it will be argued that memories in both preparations are instructional. In this view, differences in rate of forgetting in the two preparations result not from whether encoding occurs on an instructional basis but rather are a product of the efficiency with which the instruction can be encoded and/or maintained.

Samples from Different Dimensions

Interference Effects.   Maki, Moe, and Bierley (1977) employed delayed matching trials in which the comparison stimuli always consisted of one key illuminated with red light and the other with green light. The red comparison was correct if either of three types of samples had been presented previously on that trial; a red field, a white light to which 20 pecks were required to introduce the retention interval, or a 2-sec presentation of food. The green comparison was correct if either of three complementary samples had been presented; a green field, a white field requiring a single peck to introduce the retention interval, or a 2-sec time-out (no food).

Maki et al. found that whether samples involved colored fields, number of pecks, or food or no food, retention was affected similarly by both proactive and retroactive interference. Specifically, matching accuracy was significantly higher at a 20-sec intertrial interval than at a 2-sec intertrial interval within each sample dimension. In addition, retention of each type of sample was inhibited by house-light interpolated during the retention interval.

Although these findings do not compel the assumption that short-term memories are instructional, they do fit such a conception rather nicely, as Maki et al. pointed out. To the extent that the pigeon encodes a sample of green, 1 peck, or no food as the instruction "peck green," and a sample of red, 20 pecks, or food as the instruction "peck red," one would anticipate that the effect of basic memory variables would not interact with the nature of the sample stimulus. According to this view, although Maki et al. used nominally different samples, they may have been represented similarly because of the instructional nature of pigeon encoding.

Evidence from my laboratory is also consistent with the view of encoding on an instructional basis. Initial work involved an attempt to demonstrate "release from proactive interference" by employing interfering and target samples from different dimensions. Studies of human STM have demonstrated that proactive interference gradually builds up over trials, given that to-be-remembered items are drawn from the same category on successive trials, say all letter trigrams or all three-digit numbers. However, when the category of the to-be-remembered items is changed during the sequence, say letters to digits or vice versa, the class-shifted item is not subject to proactive interference.

In our first attempt to demonstrate release, birds were trained initially to match to sample using colored fields, red and green, and line orientations, vertical and horizontal. In the first experiment, each sample was presented for 4 sec and retention was tested at intervals of 0, 1, 3, and 6 sec. Interference trials involved the successive presentation of two different samples, S1 and S2, followed by the simultaneous presentation of S1 and S2 as comparison stimuli. The comparison corresponding to the more recent of the samples, S2, was designated correct. Control trials were identical to interference trials except that the initial, S1 sample was not presented. On interference-same trials, both S1 and S2 were from the same dimension, that is, both colors or both lines. On interference-different trials, one sample was a color and the other a line. A release from proactive interference would be demonstrated to the extent that less interference were obtained on interference-different trials than on interference-same trials.

The results of this experiment are shown in Fig. 8.4. The left panel displays performance when the target sample, S2, was a color and the right panel when

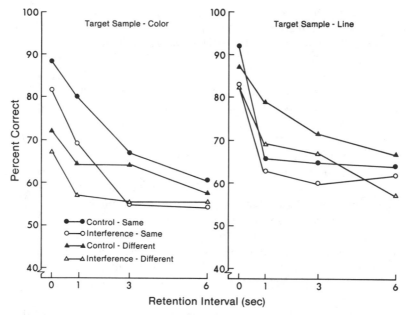

FIG. 8.4. Percentage of correct responses as a function of retention interval with conditions as the parameter. In the left panel the target sample, S2, was a color and in the right panel it was a line orientation. Same = both S1 and S2 were colors (left panel) or both line orientations (right panel); different = S1 was a line and S2 a color (left panel) or S1 was a color and S2 a line (right panel).

the target sample was a line. Although each interference condition reduced accuracy, and the amount of interference tended to increase across the retention interval, no evidence of a release from proactive interference was obtained. That is, the difference between control- and interference-different conditions was approximately equivalent to that between control- and interference-same conditions.

In a second experiment the possibility of obtaining a release from proactive interference was pursued further. Because both lines and colors are visual stimuli, perhaps the samples were not different enough to produce a release. On the basis of the notion that samples of food or no food contrast more markedly with samples of number of pecks, the second experiment employed such samples. Birds were trained initially to match to samples of food and no food and to samples of 1 and 20 pecks. Comparison stimuli always involved the presentation of a green field and a red field, with the red comparison correct given a sample of food or 20 pecks and the green comparison correct given a sample of no food or 1 peck.

The experiment was rather similar to the first except that the sample dimensions were numbers of pecks and food or no food rather than color and line orientation. On interference-same trials, S1 and S2 were drawn from the same dimension (both food and no food samples or both samples of numbers of pecks), whereas on interference-different trials they were drawn from different dimensions (a food or no food sample and a sample of number of pecks). Only a single control was required because the comparison stimuli always involved the simultaneous presentation of red and green. Release from proactive interference would be demonstrated if less interference were obtained on interference-different trials than on interference-same trials.

The results of this experiment are presented in Fig. 8.5. The left panel presents retention curves when S2 was a number of pecks sample and the right panel presents retention curves when S2 was a food or no food sample. Again there was no tendency for interference-different trials to produce a release from proactive interference. In fact, when target samples of food or no food were employed there was a strong trend in the opposite direction. Although the basis of the exaggerated interference obtained when samples of number of pecks were followed by food or no food is not entirely clear, it is possible to offer a tentative account. It may be that following a behavior (in the present case, 1 or 20 pecks)

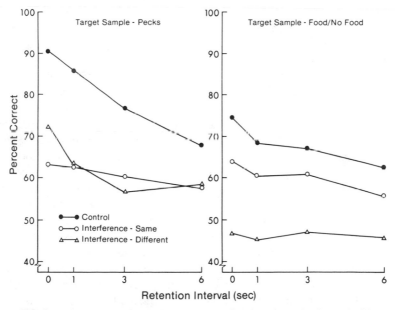

FIG. 8.5.   Percentage of correct responses as a function of retention interval with conditions as the parameter. In the left panel the target sample, S2, was either 1 or 20 pecks and in the right panel was either food or no food. Same = both S1 and S2 were a sample of number of pecks (left panel) or both were food/no food samples (right panel); different = S1 was a sample of food or no food and S2 a sample of number of pecks (left panel) or S1 was a sample of number of pecks and S2 a sample of food or no food (right panel).

by an outcome (food or no food) tends to enhance the memory of the event that preceded that outcome. If so, and if the pigeon's capacity for processing information is limited, such trials may have produced enhanced memory of the number of pecks sample and reduced memory of the food or no food sample. In any case it is clear that when samples from markedly different dimensions are employed interference is robust.

The failure to demonstrate release from proactive interference in these experiments may be accounted for in at least three ways. The first is the rather uninteresting possibility that the release phenomenon is restricted to humans, or at least is not a phenomenon produced by the pigeon information-processing system. Although this hypothesis is not testable directly, it would gain credence through repeated failures to obtain release under a variety of conditions and tasks.

The two remaining, more theoretically intriguing hypotheses both involve the notion that samples of color, food or no food, and number of pecks were coded in a common fashion at the time of presentation and thereby challenge the trace conception of the memorial representation. It would be necessary to speculate that the failure to obtain release when colors and lines were used as samples resulted from these stimuli not representing sufficiently different dimensions. To the extent that this argument is reasonable, hypotheses involving notions of common encoding, either on an instructional or noninstructional basis, could account for the second failure to obtain release.

Consider first the possibility suggested by Maki et al. (1977) that the pigeon codes samples of color, food or no food, and number of pecks in terms of the amount of illumination emitted. According to this view the pigeon remembers either "bright" or "dim" and employs response rules of the form "if bright peck red" and "if dim peck green" to generate accurate test performance. Such a strategy is feasible in that a red sample is brighter than a green sample, food (due to illumination of the magazine light) is brighter than no food, and 20 pecks (due to the white light remaining illuminated longer) is effectively brighter than 1 peck. Alternatively, the instructional coding hypothesis suggests that a sample of red, 20 pecks, or food is remembered as the instruction "peck red" and a sample of green, 1 peck, or no food as the instruction "peck green." Neither of these coding hypotheses would anticipate that amount of interference would be influenced by the manipulations employed in our second experiment reported earlier.

Current studies in my laboratory are pursuing further the question of release from proactive interference. One of these experiments has the potential to provide rather direct and convincing support for an instructional conception of memory. Although data is not yet available, a brief description of this work may provide additional insight into the way in which we conceptualize an instructional view. Birds are receiving concurrent training on two delayed conditional discriminations, one visual and the other spatial. The visual task is standard delayed matching, using red and green samples, whereas the spatial task involves vertical and horizontal line samples that indicate whether the right or left comparison is correct. One red field and one green field are presented as comparison stimuli on all trials. Thus, a color sample indicates to peck a particular color independent of position, whereas a line sample indicates to peck a particular position independent of color. If the memorial representation in pigeon STM is instructional, then color and line samples would be remembered as qualitatively different instructions: "peck red" or "peck green" versus "peck right" or "peck left." A release from proactive interference when S1 is a color and S2 a line, or vice versa, would bolster considerably our confidence in an instructional conception.

Repetition Effects.   Consider the now familiar situation in which birds have been trained to peck a green comparison given a sample of green, no food, or 1 peck and to peck a red comparison given a sample of red, food, or 20 pecks. The notion that the memory is an isomorphic representation of the sample, the trace conception, suggests that we are working with six distinct samples. The instructional view, on the other hand, suggests that we are working with two distinct samples: "peck green" and "peck red" samples.

In an attempt to differentiate empirically between these two views, the following sample repetition experiment was conducted recently in my laboratory. On each trial either one, two, or three sample presentations occurred prior to onset of the retention interval. Given either two or three sample presentations, the presentations involved either physical identity or instructional identity. Physical identity involved the presentation of the same nominal sample on each occasion, such as two repetitions of a red field or three repetitions of a sample of food, and so on. Instructional identity involved the successive presentation of nominally different samples, which were functionally equivalent in that each indicated the same comparison contigency. For example, a green field might be followed by a sample of no food, both indicating the choice of green, or a sample of food might be followed by a red field, which might be followed in turn by a sample of 20 pecks, each indicating the choice of red at the time of comparison presentation.

An instructional view would hold that but a single memory would be established on each trial, independent of the number of sample presentations and of whether the samples were the same or different. On trials with multiple sample presentations, each successive presentation would strengthen a unitary memorial representation of the instruction "peck green" or "peck red." Such a conception would predict that performance would improve as the number of sample presentations increased. More importantly, however, the instructional hypothesis would anticipate no difference between the presentation of nominally identical samples and nominally different samples.

According to the view that the memorial representation is isomorphic with the sample, the number of independent memory traces established on any trial would be a joint function of the number of sample presentations and of whether each presentation was nominally the same or different. Given a single presentation, or two or three presentations of the same nominal sample, a single memory would be established. Multiple presentations of the same sample would result in the growth of the strength of that memory according to a negatively accelerated function. On the other hand, two or three presentations of nominally different, although functionally equivalent, samples would establish multiple independent traces.

In contrast to the instructional conception, the trace conception does anticipate different levels of accuracy on same sample and different sample trials. On the assumption that the pigeon's choice behavior is governed by the strongest trace in the system (Grant & Roberts, 1973), performance should be less accurate on different sample trials. This is the case because successive presentation of physically different, although functionally equivalent samples would be expected to establish separate and independent traces, each having a strength equivalent to that accruing on the basis of a single sample presentation. A second or third presentation of the same physical sample, on the other hand, would boost the strength of the single trace of that sample (Roberts & Grant, 1976).

The data from this experiment are presented in Fig. 8.6. Although accuracy tended to increase as the number of sample repetitions increased, little difference

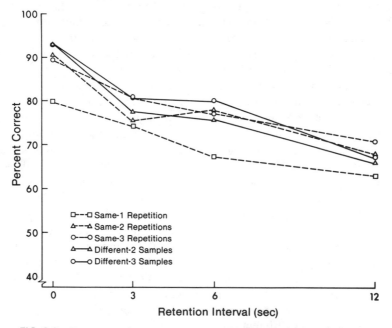

FIG. 8.6.   Percentage of correct responses as a function of retention interval with conditions of sample repetition as the parameter. Same = the physical characteristics of the sample remained constant on each repetition; different = physically different but functionally equivalent samples were presented on each repetition.

between same sample and different sample trials was obtained. In fact, collapsed across retention interval, the two conditions were identical (78% correct for both same and different at two repetitions and 80% correct for both same and different at three repetitions). These findings are, of course, inconsistent with the notion that the pigeon remembers an isomorphic representation of the sample. On the other hand, the findings are consistent with an instructional view of memory in which presentation of nominally different, although functionally equivalent samples strengthens a unitary memorial representation.

In a second experiment, we were interested in whether the manner of presentation of nominally different, although functionally equivalent samples would influence retention. Three samples were presented on each trial, either red, 20 pecks, and food or green, 1 peck, and no food. In the successive mode of sample presentation, the samples were presented successively with a white preparatory stimulus, requiring a single peck, separating each presentation. In the compound mode of sample presentation, a colored field sample was presented following a response to the preparatory stimulus. The sample remained illuminated until either 1 peck, if the sample were green, or 20 pecks, if the sample were red, were completed. The twentieth peck to the red sample resulted in a 2-sec presentation of food, whereas the first peck to green resulted in a 2-sec time-out.

It was anticipated that the successive mode of sample presentation might lead to better retention than the compound mode to the extent that encoding in the pigeon is not sufficiently rapid to permit all the information to be extracted from compound samples. This prediction was based on the finding that matching accuracy is reduced when compound, rather than element, samples are employed (Maki & Leith, 1973; Maki & Leuin, 1972; Maki, Riley, & Leith, 1976). In this preparation, birds were trained to match colored comparisons to colored samples, and line comparisons to line orientation samples. Following acquisition, birds were tested on element sample trials, either a color or a line sample, and on compound sample trials, a colored field with a line superimposed. The comparison stimuli always consisted of either two colors or two lines, but the bird could not predict which dimension would be tested on compound trials. One prominent interpretation of reduced accuracy on compound trials is that it reflects a deficit in the pigeon's ability to process or encode both dimensions of the sample (Maki & Leuin, 1972; Riley & Roitblat, 1978; but see Roberts & Grant, 1978b for an alternative interpretation). We therefore anticipated better accuracy on successive trials than on compound trials.

The results of our experiment are shown in the left panel of Fig. 8.7. The high levels of accuracy, even at a retention interval of 30 sec, suggest that the birds were indeed making use of all the information provided by the samples. However, there is little suggestion that mode of sample presentation influenced retention (collapsed across retention interval, 80% correct on successive trials and 79% correct on compound trials). Data in the right panel represent a replication of the experiment with one procedural modification. In this case we superim-

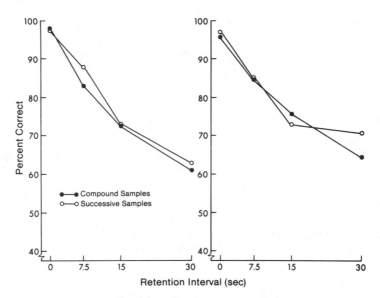

FIG. 8.7.   Percentage of correct responses as a function of retention interval with mode of sample presentation as the parameter. In the left panel the stimulus presented during a number of pecks sample was not superimposed on the color on compound trials, whereas in the right panel it was superimposed. Compound = the colored field remained illuminated until the associated number of pecks had been completed and the final peck was followed immediately by food or no food; successive = samples of color, number of pecks, and food or no food were presented as discrete samples and were separated by the interpolation of a white preparatory stimulus containing a small black dot.

posed the white circle, which was the stimulus presented for the peck samples, on the colored field during compound sample trials. Again, retention was excellent and no marked effect of mode of presentation was obtained (82% correct on successive trials and 78% correct on compound trials).

These data suggest strongly that the pigeon can rapidly encode information concerning comparison selection from three sources. In the face of these data, how can one maintain that the pigeon is incapable of encoding and processing information from two sources in the compound–element task of Maki and his associates? One obvious solution is to argue that my animals were exposed to the compound sample for a duration sufficient to permit all dimensions to be fully encoded. This possibility appears unlikely, however, in that the birds were exposed to the sample for a rather brief duration, about .5 sec when a single peck was required and about 2.5 sec when 20 pecks were required. Even when the 2-sec food or no food presentation is taken into account, sample duration was approximately 2.5 and 4.5 sec. Data obtained by Roberts and Grant (1978b) suggest that these durations are not sufficient to permit complete encoding in the element–compound task developed by Maki and his associates. In that study there was no tendency for the element–compound difference to be reduced as sample duration was increased from 1 to 6 sec.

A more adequate resolution of this paradox may involve recognition of pigeon encoding as occurring on an instructional basis. In my experiment each component of the sample was consistent with the same instruction and such samples were encoded rapidly and without deficit. In the element–compound task, on the other hand, the compound sample must be encoded as two different instructions. According to this view, the element–compound sample difference does not result from a limitation on the rate of encoding per se, but rather from a limitation on the efficiency with which the pigeon can encode and/or maintain multiple instructions.

Analysis of Error Patterns.   Although the findings from studies of interference and repetition effects are consistent with an instructional view of delayed matching, it may well be argued that such coding is of limited generality. That is, it may be suggested that the multiple sample preparation considered in the preceding sections induced instructional coding. As that preparation involved the association of three samples with a single choice response, efficiency of processing would be enhanced by coding the samples in terms of the choice stimulus. On the other hand, in more typical matching preparations in which there is a one-to-one correspondence between sample and correct comparison, instructional coding confers no obvious advantage in terms of processing efficiency. To the extent that encoding in the pigeon is viewed as a controlled process (see Maki, this volume for a discussion of controlled processes), instructional coding may be restricted to those situations in which such coding is beneficial. According to this view, pigeons might well retain an isomorphic representation of the sample in more typical matching preparations.

A recent experiment by Roitblat (1980, Exp. 3) obtained evidence consistent with the notion that instructional coding is a general property of pigeon STM. Three birds were trained in a symbolic matching task in which each of three samples was associated with the choice of a unique comparison stimulus. Two of the birds were trained with color samples and line orientation comparisons, whereas the remaining bird received line samples and color comparisons. The specific stimulus values along each dimension were selected such that two of the colors were more similar to each other (red and orange) than they were to the third color (blue), and two of the line orientations were more similar to each other (0° and 12.5°) than they were to the third orientation (90°). The specific pairings of samples and comparisons was accomplished such that the two similar colors were paired with the two dissimilar line orientations (orange with 12.5° line and red with 90° line), and the two dissimilar colors were paired with the two similar line orientations (blue with 0° line and orange with 12.5° line). The pairings were the same for all three birds regardless of whether samples were drawn from the color or line orientation dimension. On each trial sample offset was followed by a variable delay that terminated in presentation of all three comparison stimuli.

Although Roitblat's procedure is rather complex, the underlying logic is straightforward. He argued that if the pigeon maintains a memory isomorphic with the sample, forgetting over a retention interval should be manifest as an increased tendency to select the comparison stimulus that corresponds to the sample that is most similar to the presented sample. On the other hand, if the pigeon maintains a memory isomorphic with the correct comparison stimulus, forgetting should be manifest as an increased tendency to select the comparison stimulus that is most similar to the correct comparison. For example, given an orange sample with choice of a 90° line correct, birds will err by choosing either the 0° line associated with a blue sample or the 90° line associated with a red sample. If the birds are remembering "orange," they should tend to confuse orange with red and therefore should select the 90° line. If the birds are remembering "12.5° line," they should tend to confuse the 12.5° line with the 0° line and therefore should select the 0° line.

The data revealed that confusion between similar test stimuli increased faster across the retention interval than did confusion between similar samples. Although this trend was significant only for the two birds trained with color samples and line comparisons, these data nevertheless provide the most compelling evidence to date that pigeons code samples in terms of the test stimulus rather than in terms of the sample itself. As Roitblat concludes: "pigeons appear to store information about the sample, not in terms of an image of the presented sample, but more similarly to an image of the correct choice stimulus [p. 349]."

Conclusion

Studies of retention and transfer effects in the advance key procedure and studies of interference and sample compounding in delayed matching suggest that an instructional conception may prove more powerful theoretically than a trace conception. Although a number of the findings considered are equally compatible with hypotheses specifying either instructional or noninstructional sample coding, the weight of the evidence tends to support instructional coding. For instance, although it may be reasonable to suggest that samples of food or no food and number of pecks may be coded in terms of amount of illumination emitted, the idea that the pigeon, an organism with excellent color vision, also codes samples of red and green in this fashion is a bit strained. Moreover, the illumination coding notion can account for neither retention interval effects nor transfer effects in the advance key preparation. The instructional coding hypothesis, then, provides the most integrative account of these findings.

Additional findings considered provided further negative support for the notion that a memory is isomorphic with the event on which it is based. The finding that the successive presentation of nominally different, although functionally equivalent, samples appeared to establish or activate a unitary memorial representation argues against a trace conception and in favor of an instructional conception. Finally, recent work on error patterns in delayed matching suggests that associating a single comparison stimulus with multiple samples is not a necessary prerequisite for obtaining evidence consistent with an instructional conception of memory. Taken collectively, the findings reviewed in the present section suggest rather strongly that pigeons remember "what to do" rather than "what happened" in contemporary STM preparations.

THEORETICAL PERSPECTIVE

The data presented suggest that two fundamental changes in our, or at least in my thinking about pigeon STM are in order. First, the data suggest that the pigeon be viewed as an active processor of information, actively maintaining memory for short durations through processes of rehearsal. The second change in thinking suggested by the data involves the conception of the memorial representation. Rather than viewing the memory as an isomorphic representation of the event giving rise to the memory, a more accurate view involves the notion that to-be-remembered information is encoded instructionally in pigeon STM.

Consider first the implications of these notions for the trace strength model outlined earlier. Although the assumptions of memory strengthening and competition may remain intact, rather radical revision of the remaining assumptions is required. First, the notion that the memory is a "trace" of the physical stimulus now appears incorrect. Second, it would no longer appear accurate to speak of memories as spontaneously losing strength, decaying, or fading with the passage of time. Finally, the independence assumption requires modification in such a way that successive stimulus events are viewed as establishing independent memories only to the extent that those events have contrasting instructional properties.

Although it may be possible to rework the assumptions of the trace strength conception and thus preserve the model, that may not represent the most prudent course. The modifications required are rather extensive and involve fundamental aspects of the model; little of the general orientation of the original model would survive. The development of a new model, which can account both for the findings that led to the trace strength conception and for more recent findings, is thus warranted. The tentative conception advanced in the following is designed to accomplish that goal. It is a highly eclectic model in which the ideas of others are borrowed freely, and just as freely modified and synthesized into a single theoretical viewpoint.

According to the model, presentation of a to-be-remembered event (i.e., sample stimulus, prestimulus, etc.) activates, rather than establishes a memorial representation. In this view STM consists of a subset of long-term memory

(LTM) that is the set of all currently active memories. Retention test performance in a STM preparation, then, is controlled by active memories that either remain active throughout the retention interval or become active through mechanisms of retrieval at testing. Memories are viewed as residing in one of two discrete states; memories active at testing are "remembered" while inactive memories are "forgotten." Although inactive memories never control behavior, an active memory may fail to control behavior in deference to a second active memory.

This view is not meant to imply, however, that new information cannot be added to a memorial representation at the time of activation. Contemporary information may be added to a long-term memorial representation at the time of activation through the process of "tagging." Tags are held to represent characteristics of a to-be-remembered event that are likely to change or vary from occasion to occasion. Temporal or time tags are one familiar example of a changing aspect of a to-be-remembered event that may be appended, temporarily, to a long-term memorial representation. Such tags are viewed as rather ephemeral characteristics or attributes of a memory that, because of their changing character, do not become strongly incorporated into the long-term memorial representation. The degree to which performance is controlled by such tags, therefore, is greatly reduced if performance is based on a currently active memory that had returned to an inactive state during the retention interval.

Although at present data obtained from the pigeon does not necessitate the assumption that the STM–LTM distinction derives from a more fundamental distinction between active and inactive memories, such a view does make contact with that espoused by others (Lewis, 1979; Spear, 1978). Such an assumption may also endow the present model with greater phylogenetic generality in that data from both rats (Feldman & Gordon, 1979; Grant, 1980, 1981a) and monkeys (Devine, Burke, & Rohack, 1979; Medin, 1976; Medin, Reynolds, & Parkinson, 1980) may be accounted for more readily within a model maintaining this type of STM–LTM distinction.

The memory (or memories) activated by presentation of a stimulus event in our type of tasks are held to be instructional. Such memories contain information about "what to do" rather than about "what happened." Instructional memories may or may not contain specific perceptual information, depending on task requirements. In the matching task, for example, memories do contain perceptual information (e.g., "peck green," "peck red," etc.) whereas in the advance key preparation they do not ("peck" or "no peck"). The probability that a stimulus will result in activation of its associated instructional representation is dependent on the discriminability of that stimulus, but is independent of the content of its associated representation.

An interesting question for future research concerns the issue of whether instructional coding is an inherent property of the pigeon's information-processing system, or whether the pigeon can retain an isomorphic representation of the sample under some conditions. Initial work on this question might employ a preparation that is essentially the converse of that developed by Maki et al.

(1977). That is, rather than associating several different samples with a single comparison, a single sample might be associated with several different correct choice stimuli. To the extent that encoding in the pigeon is sensitive to task demands (i.e., is a controlled process in Maki's sense, this volume), the pigeon might well learn to remember an isomorphic representation of the sample rather than coding the sample into multiple instructional memories.

The issue of whether the activation of an instructional memory is all-or-none or whether a memory can be activated to varying degrees (i.e., can vary in strength) deserves comment. Honig (1978) has suggested an all-or-none conception in the context of research using the advance key procedure and it is suggested here that the all-or-none character of memorial activation represents a general property of pigeon STM. Such an all-or-none view of memorial activation provides an account of repetition and spacing effects in delayed matching that is as plausible as that provided by an incremental view such as strength theory. The finding that delayed matching accuracy increases with increased sample exposure duration is not particularly problematic for an all-or-none view. The failure to obtain an interaction between exposure duration and retention interval suggests that the former variable does not influence rate of forgetting and, therefore, permits the argument that increased exposure to the sample simply increases the probability with which the instructional representation is activated.

The finding that initially spacing and subsequently massing sample repetitions within a trial leads to higher accuracy than the reverse ordering of temporal spacing (Roberts, 1972), may also be accommodated within an all-or-none conception. That is, massing repetitions in time immediately prior to the retention interval (space–massed condition) results in a high probability of memory activation at the onset of the retention interval. On the other hand, following initial massed repetitions by spacing intervals (massed–spaced condition) provides an opportunity for the activated representation to return to an inactive state by the time the retention interval onsets. Thus, better accuracy on spaced–massed trials would be anticipated.

Although data from repetition and spacing studies may be accounted for equally well by either an all-or-none or an incremental view of memorial activation, Roitblat obtained evidence that he interpreted as supporting an incremental view (1980, Exp. 2). Birds were trained to match to sample using three sample and comparison stimuli; red, green, and blue for three birds, and horizontal lines, vertical lines, and a triangle for the remaining two birds. On each trial presentation of a single sample stimulus was followed .5 sec later by presentation of all three stimuli as comparison stimuli. Roitblat argued that incremental and all-or-none models make different predictions regarding the expected pattern of first-choice errors (birds were allowed a second choice after an initial error, although this need not concern us here).

According to an incremental model, Roitblat argued, errors may occur even though the pigeon has partial information concerning the sample stimulus. If so, first-choice errors should be related systematically to the sample stimulus. On the other hand, an all-or-none model holds that errors may be traced to one of two sources. First, the pigeon may fail to encode the sample stimulus or second, the pigeon may respond to a comparison stimulus without regard to the sample memory (Roberts & Grant, 1978b suggested the operation of an "elicitation process" that would produce this latter type of error). Such an all-or-none model therefore anticipates that first-choice errors should be unrelated to the sample stimulus.

The data revealed that three of the five birds demonstrated a distribution of first-choice errors that differed significantly from a chance distribution. In other words, for three of the pigeons the pattern of first-choice errors was indeed related to the sample, a finding consistent with an incremental view. At least two factors, however, suggest caution in interpreting these results. First, only three of the birds behaved in accord with incremental assumptions, the other two behaved in accord with all-or-none assumptions. Second, as Roitblat notes, it is possible to suggest all-or-none models that are not contradicted by these data. In the context of the present viewpoint, for example, one might suggest that the long-term representation activated by a sample stimulus is composed of a number of components or attributes. If the activation of any particular attribute is at least in part independent of the activation of other attributes belonging to that memory, an all-or-none model of activation at the level of the attribute would permit the pigeon to respond on the basis of partial information concerning the sample. Alternatively, one might assume that the presentation of a sample stimulus occasionally activates a long-term representation associated with a different sample stimulus. It may be assumed further that the probability with which a sample will activate any particular erroneous representation is a direct function of the similarity between the erroneous representation and the representation associated with the sample stimulus. If so, a relation between sample and errors should be obtained.

The issue of whether encoding in the pigeon is better conceptualized as an incremental or all-or-none process awaits further research. At present there is little empirical basis for making such a decision. It may be noted, however, that an all-or-none conception is more in keeping with the general viewpoint being suggested here than is an incremental conception.

According to the present viewpoint the activation of an instructional representation may be maintained following offset of the event(s) giving rise to the activation by processes of maintenance rehearsal. In the absence of rehearsal, an active memorial representation returns to an inactive state over a finite time course. Maintenance rehearsal may be characterized loosely, then, as any activity or process, either internal or external, that tends to prolong the time period during which a memory remains active following termination of the event originally resulting in activation. Rehearsal is conceptualized as an imperfect process in the sense that a memory returns to an inactive state with some probability even though rehearsal may be occurring. This probability is reduced, however, as a direct function of the intensity and efficiency of rehearsal.

The present viewpoint permits maintenance rehearsal to occur in varying degrees. In agreement with Wagner (1978, 1979), surprising or unexpected events are held to engage more intense and/or prolonged rehearsal than expected events. Rehearsal is also viewed as a process subject to practice effects such that the intensity and/or efficiency of rehearsal may change over training. The efficiency of the rehearsal process is in part dependent on the complexity of the instructional content of the memory, but is independent of the nature of the event giving rise to activation of that memory. The greater the information load or complexity of the instruction, the less efficient is the rehearsal process in preventing the memory from returning to an inactive state. In this view, the more robust retention observed in the advance key procedure is a product, at least in large part, of the fact that the instructional content of memory is less complex than in the matching task. Processes of rehearsal are therefore more likely to maintain the memory in an active state in the former preparation. Finally, the termination of rehearsal may be brought under stimulus control by events such as trial termination and explicit forget cues. The efficiency of rehearsal termination, like the efficiency of the process itself, is related to memory content inversely; that is, rehearsal termination becomes less efficient as the complexity of the memory content increases.

As is clear, the model places the majority of explanatory burden on the process of maintenance rehearsal, and therefore may be characterized as a rehearsal model of pigeon STM. Space limitations do not permit a lengthy exposé concerning the manner in which the present rehearsal model would account for the known phenomena of pigeon STM. I do believe, however, that the model can provide a reasonable and coherent account of the facts. Such is not particularly surprising in light of the fact that the model was formulated after data collection and is sufficiently loose to permit considerable explanatory flexibility. There are, however, at least three reasons to justify serious consideration of the rehearsal model. First, to my knowledge it is the only model that can accommodate all the present findings on pigeon STM. Second, the model is likely to serve a heuristic function in suggesting fruitful avenues for additional research. Finally, the model has some promise of developing into a theory capable of integrating data collected from a number of species and tasks.

SUMMARY

Data from recent studies of pigeon short-term memory were considered in relation to two theoretical issues. The first concerned the question of whether short-term information processing in the pigeon is better characterized as an active or passive process. Research on retroactive interference, sample surprisingness, and stimulus control of forgetting provides considerable support for the hypothesis that pigeons actively process or rehearse information in contemporary short-term memory preparations.

A second issue concerned the nature of encoding in pigeon short-term memory. The specific question considered was whether memories correspond to an isomorphic representation of the sample or whether the pigeon remembers an instruction or disposition to respond. A considerable body of circumstantial evidence in favor of an instructional hypothesis has been generated by recent studies on retention and transfer in the advance key procedure and by studies on interference, sample repetition, and sample compounding in delayed matching. The most direct evidence in support of the idea that the pigeon remembers "what to do" rather than "what happened" comes from research in which the types of errors committed were analyzed. This work has shown that the majority of errors can be traced to confusions among similar choice stimuli rather than among similar sample stimuli.

To organize and account for these and other findings on pigeon short-term memory, a general theoretical viewpoint was offered. The model maintains a fundamental distinction between active and passive memories and places heavy emphasis on processes of rehearsal in maintaining memories in the active state. According to this view, a memory must be in an active state in order for that memory to exert control over behavior. To-be-remembered events are viewed as temporarily activating long-term instructional representations in an all-or-none fashion. The probability with which a stimulus event activates its associated long-term representation is dependent on the relative discriminability of that stimulus event. Processes of maintenance rehearsal serve to increase the temporal duration of memory activation following offset of the stimulus originally giving rise to the activation. Some of the salient properties of the rehearsal process include: (a) variable intensity, duration, and efficiency, all of which are subject to practice effects; (b) control of rehearsal termination by environmental events; and (c) a relation to memory content such that the efficiency with which rehearsal either occurs or is terminated is related inversely to the complexity of memorial content.

ACKNOWLEDGMENTS

Preparation of this chapter was supported by Grant A0443 from the Natural Sciences and Engineering Research Council of Canada. I would like to thank William A. Roberts and Willard N. Runquist, who read an earlier draft of this chapter and provided several valuable suggestions. Ralph R. Miller and Norman E. Spear provided a number of editorial comments and criticisms that greatly improved the quality of this contribution.

REFERENCES

Devine, J. V., Burke, M. W., & Rohack, J. J. Stimulus similarity and order as factors in visual short-term memory in nonhuman primates. *Journal of Experimental Psychology: Animal Behavior Processes,* 1979, *5,* 335-354.

Feldman, D. T., & Gordon, W. C. The alleviation of short-term retention decrements with reactivation. *Learning and Motivation,* 1979, *10,* 198-210.

Grant, D. S. Proactive interference in pigeon short-term memory. *Journal of Experimental Psychology: Animal Behavior Processes,* 1975, *1,* 207-220

Grant, D. S. Effect of sample presentation time on long-delay matching in the pigeon. *Learning and Motivation,* 1976, *7,* 580-590.

Grant, D. S. Delayed alternation in the rat: Effect of contextual stimuli on proactive interference. *Learning and Motivation,* 1980, *11,* 339-354.

Grant, D. S. Intertrial interference in rat short-term memory. *Journal of Experimental Psychology: Animal Behavior Processes*, 1981, *7,* 217-227. (a)

Grant, D. S. Stimulus control of information processing in pigeon short-term memory. *Learning and Motivation,* 1981, *12,* 19-39. (b)

Grant, D. S., & Roberts, W. A. Trace interaction in pigeon short-term memory. *Journal of Experimental Psychology,* 1973, *101,* 21-29.

Grant, D. S., & Roberts, W. A. Sources of retroactive inhibition in pigeon short-term memory. *Journal of Experimental Psychology: Animal Behavior Processes,* 1976, *2,* 1-16.

Honig, W. K. Studies of working memory in the pigeon. In S. H. Hulse, H. Fowler, & W. K. Honig (Eds.), *Cognitive processes in animal behavior.* Hillsdale, N.J.: Lawrence Erlbaum Associates, 1978.

Lewis, D. J. Psychobiology of active and inactive memory. *Psychological Bulletin,* 1979, *86,* 1054-1083.

Maki, W. S. Pigeon's short-term memories for surprising vs. expected reinforcement and nonreinforcement. *Animal Learning and Behavior,* 1979, *7,* 31-37.

Maki, W. S., & Leith, C. R. Shared attention in pigeons. *Journal of the Experimental Analysis of Behavior,* 1973, *19,* 345-349.

Maki, W. S., & Leuin, T. C. Information-processing by pigeons. *Science,* 1972, *176,* 535-536.

Maki, W. S., Moe, J. C., & Bierley, C. M. Short-term memory for stimuli, responses, and reinforcers. *Journal of Experimental Psychology: Animal Behavior Processes,* 1977, *3,* 156-177.

Maki, W. S., Riley, D. A., & Leith, C. R. The role of test stimuli in matching to compound samples by pigeons. *Animal Learning and Behavior,* 1976, *4,* 13-21.

Medin, D. L. Animal models and memory models. In D. L. Medin, W. A. Roberts, & R. T. Davis (Eds.), *Processes of animal memory.* Hillsdale, N.J.: Lawrence Erlbaum Associates, 1976.

Medin, D. L., Reynolds, T. J., & Parkinson, J. K. Stimulus stimilarity and retroactive interference and facilitation in monkey short-term memory. *Journal of Experimental Psychology: Animal Behavior Processes,* 1980, *6,* 112-125.

Riley, D. A., & Roitblat, H. L. Selective attention and related cognitive processes in pigeons. In S. H. Hulse, H. Fowler, & W. K. Honig (Eds.), *Cognitive processes in animal behavior.* Hillsdale, N.J.: Lawrence Erlbaum Associates, 1978.

Rilling, M., Kendrick, D. F., & Stonebraker, T. B. Stimulus control of forgetting: A behavioral analysis. In M. L. Commons, A. P. Wagner, & R. J. Herrnstein (Eds.), *Quantitative studies in operant behavior: Acquisition.* Cambridge: Mass.: Ballinger, 1981.

Roberts, W. A. Short-term memory in the pigeon: Effects of repetition and spacing. *Journal of Experimental Psychology,* 1972, *94,* 74-83.

Roberts, W. A. Distribution of trials and intertrial retention in delayed matching to sample with pigeons. *Journal of Experimental Psychology: Animal Behavior Processes,* 1980, *6,* 217-237.

Roberts, W. A., & Grant, D. S. Short-term memory in the pigeon with presentation time precisely controlled. *Learning and Motivation,* 1974, *5,* 393–408.

Roberts, W. A., & Grant, D. S. Studies in short-term memory in the pigeon using the delayed matching-to-sample procedure. In D. L. Medin, W. A. Roberts, & R. T. Davis (Eds.), *Processes of animal memory.* Hillsdale, N.J.: Lawrence Erlbaum Associates, 1976.

Roberts, W. A., & Grant, D. S. An analysis of light-induced retroactive inhibition in pigeon short-term memory. *Journal of Experimental Psychology: Animal Behavior Proccesses,* 1978, *4,* 219–236. (a)

Roberts, W. A., & Grant, D. S. Interaction of sample and comparison stimuli in delayed matching-to-sample with the pigeon. *Journal of Experimental Psychology: Animal Behavior Processes,* 1978, *4,* 68–82. (b)

Roitblat, H. L. Codes and coding processes in pigeon short-term memory. *Animal Learning and Behavior,* 1980, *8,* 341–351.

Spear, N. E. *The processing of memories: Forgetting and retention.* Hillsdale, N.J.: Lawrence Erlbaum Associates, 1978.

Tranberg, D. K., & Rilling, M. Delay-interval illumination changes interfere with pigeon short-term memory. *Journal of the Experimental Analysis of Behavior,* 1980, *33,* 33–49.

Wagner, A. R. Expectancies and the priming of STM. In S. H. Hulse, H. Fowler, & W. K. Honig (Eds.), *Cognitive processes in animal behavior.* Hillsdale, N.J.: Lawrence Erlbaum Associates, 1978.

Wagner, A. R. Habituation and memory. In A. Dickinson & R. A. Boakes (Eds.), *Mechanisms of learning and motivation: A memorial volume to Jerzy Konorski.* Hillsdale, N.J.: Lawrence Erlbaum Associates, 1979.

Wasserman, E. A. Successive matching-to-sample in the pigeon: Variations on a theme by Konorski. *Behavior Research Methods and Instrumentation,* 1976, *8,* 278–282.

Zentall, T. R. Memory in the pigeon: Retroactive inhibition in a delayed matching task. *Bulletin of the Psychonomic Society,* 1973, *1,* 126–128.

Zentall, T. R., & Hogan, D. E. Memory in the pigeon: Proactive inhibition in a delayed matching task. *Bulletin of the Psychonomic Society,* 1974, *4,* 109–112.

Zentall, T. R., & Hogan, D. E. Short-term proactive inhibition in the pigeon. *Learning and Motivation,* 1977, *8,* 367–386.

9

Studies of Long-Term
Memory in the Pigeon

David R. Thomas
University of Colorado

In a classic paper, McGeoch (1932) presented cogent arguments and evidence against the prevailing view, attributed to Thorndike (1913), that forgetting was primarily or entirely a consequence of decay of a memory "trace" with disuse. He reasoned that time elapsed subsequent to learning played no causative role but was normally required to permit the factors that produced forgetting to take effect. The two factors that McGeoch specified were: (1) interference by competing memories (most particularly retroactive interference); and (2) altered stimulating conditions (by which he meant internal and external contextual stimuli). The research reported in this chapter is concerned with these two factors and with the ways in which they interact. Thus it follows in a time-honored tradition of research on memory.

A unique contribution of our research program is a methodological one. Following the discovery that stimulus generalization gradients change lawfully with the passage of time subsequent to training (Thomas & Lopez, 1962), we have developed techniques to measure, via such changes in generalization, the effects of interference and of retrieval cue manipulations.

A conceptual contribution of our research is the distinction that it makes between different types of information that may be lost during forgetting. It will be shown that pigeons may forget the value of the stimulus to which they were trained to respond while remembering the response of key pecking per se. This distinction between response memory and stimulus–response association memory parallels that made by McGovern (1964) for human paired-associate learning. In our work we speak of a stimulus–response-reinforcer association on the assumption that the reinforcer is an integral part of the association formed by training. Evidence for this view was reported in a study by Peterson, Wheeler,

257

and Armstrong (1978) who showed that when hungry and thirsty pigeons learn a particular discrimination on the basis of food reward, that discrimination is lost if they are shifted to water reward.

Still another conceptual contribution is the proposal that an "attentional set" (Thomas, 1970) can be treated as a memory in its own right. We mean by attentional set the nonspecific effects of discrimination and nondifferential training, as reflected in sharp or flat generalization gradients, respectively, along dimensions orthogonal to those manipulated in such training. Our investigation of the retention of such sets reveals that interference between them operates in much the same way as it does in the case of specific stimulus–response-reinforcer associations.

After presenting an account of the general methodology of free operant generalization studies of memory, I first present several studies of "simple" forgetting, defined as a decrement in performance when the only *manipulated* source of that decrement is the passage of time since acquisition. These studies illustrate the various indices of forgetting that generalization gradients can provide. They do not signify an acceptance of the "decay theory" but only recognition of the fact that forgetting typically is defined operationally as a decrement in the performance of a learned behavior when retention testing is delayed subsequent to the conclusion of training. In all our work, forgetting is inferred from a decrement in performance after a delay, whether or not purported sources of forgetting, such as the presence of interfering memories, are also manipulated.

In the subsequent section I report several studies of forgetting in which interference with the target memory was produced via prior training of a conflicting stimulus–response-reinforcer association. In the largest section of the chapter I report on studies in which we investigated the role of "contextual" retrieval or reminder cues. Retrieval cues that facilitate the retention of a training experience may be categorized in several different ways. The internal versus external distinction was mentioned by McGeoch (1932). In addition we may distinguish between contemporary cues (e.g., the physical context that was present during training and can be reintroduced at the time of the retention test), and prior cues, which precede but do not accompany retention testing. One instance of a prior cue is a warm-up (i.e., a brief exposure to some or all of the conditions of training). Our research makes use of several different types of retrieval cues and seeks to determine the conditions under which such cues are or are not effective. Some of these experiments involve simple forgetting of either a response to a single stimulus or of a discrimination; others employ situations involving interference between conflicting memories.

In the final section of the chapter I present a new paradigm for investigating memorial effects, the conditional successive discrimination reversal paradigm, and I describe work just completed using this technique. In this work the conditional cue for reversal is the animal's memory of the prior training session and, with this paradigm as well as with several others, we may investigate the content of the animal's memory rather than just the extent of it.

GENERAL PROCEDURE

In virtually all the studies to be described, certain aspects of experimental procedure have been held constant. The subjects have been experimentally naive common pigeons obtained from local suppliers and maintained at approximately 80% of free-feeding weight. The birds have been trained in Skinner boxes with variable interval (VI) reinforcement for pecking at a key illuminated (in almost all cases) by a monochromatic light. Following substantial training, the birds have been tested for (wavelength) generalization in extinction with brief (e.g., 30-sec) exposures of various test stimuli arranged in as many as a dozen different randomized blocks. The basic procedure, as just described, was developed by Guttman and Kalish (1956) and has become standard in the investigation of dimensional stimulus control over operant responding.

The generalization test procedure is viewed by us as constituting a test of recognition memory in which responding maximally to a given stimulus value is thought to be analogous to a human adult subject making the verbal response "that stimulus is the one to which I was trained to respond." The generalization gradient provides several sensitive indices of animal memory (and forgetting). First of all, in the simple case where training has involved responding to a single stimulus, the fact that the generalization gradient peaks at that training stimulus value indicates that the subject remembers *what* that training value was. Many studies have indicated that generalization gradients flatten with the interpolation of a delay period between training and generalization testing, thus the slope of the generalization gradient provides an index of *how well* the target memory was retrieved. The slope of the gradient is thought to reflect the subject's confidence that its choice of stimulus to respond to is the correct one, and as forgetting takes place the degree of certainty is presumably reduced. It should be recognized that generalization slope can also be affected by a variety of nonmemorial factors. Inferences about forgetting are made only when such factors (e.g., drive level) are held constant. Relative generalization gradients (i.e., percent of total responses emitted to the different generalization test stimuli) are commonly used rather than absolute gradients in order to perform between-group (or between-subject) comparisons of stimulus–response association memory that are not confounded with differences in response strength per se. Response strength differences are often due to nonmemorial factors or to individual (i.e., between-subject) differences not under experimental control.

Another potential measure of the forgetting of a stimulus–response–reinforcer association is a change in the location of the peak of the generalization gradient (i.e., the value of the stimulus to which maximal responding occurs). Following intradimensional discrimination training between two closely spaced values on the continuum subsequently varied in testing, the resulting generalization gradient typically shows a peak displaced from S+ so as to be farther removed from S− (Hanson, 1959). Treatments designed to enhance or retard forgetting may reveal their effects in changes in the location of the (displaced) peak (the mode of the gradient) or in related measures (e.g., mean or median). One might wish to speculate on the basis for the change in the location of the gradient peak with the passage of time subsequent to training but as there is no strong agreement on the underlying basis for the peak shift (Newlin, Rodgers, & Thomas, 1979), such speculation is not likely to be fruitful at the present time. However, this does not diminish the usefulness of a peak shift measure of forgetting, as operationally defined. The generalization gradient is perhaps uniquely appropriate in investigating memorial processes in situations in which explicit sources of interference in memory are provided. In animal research this normally involves the training on one problem and then its reversal (e.g., passive followed by active-avoidance training, a right turn and then later a left turn in a T-maze, etc.). If the discrimination problem employed is, say, peck at green (S+) but not at red (S−), and then the reversal of this problem is trained, the two response tendencies can be (relatively independently) assessed. Evidence to be presented later indicates a strong recency effect (i.e., subjects in an immediate generalization test tend to respond in accordance with the contingencies most recently in effect). In the case in point, the immediate generalization test should thus reveal a peak at red. If the initial response tendency were strengthened during a delay interval this could result, during a delayed generalization test, in the obtaining of a gradient with a (second) peak at green. Note that no comparable analysis of the absolute strengths of the two competing memories can be made when they involve physically incompatible response tendencies (e.g., turn right versus turn left).

A unique situation exists when we wish to investigate retention of the nonspecific effects of discrimination and nondifferential training on stimulus control. As Thomas, Freeman, Svinicki, Burr, and Lyons (1970) and many others have shown, the effect of extradimensional discrimination training is to sharpen generalization gradients along dimensions orthogonal to the training dimension. This effect has been attributed by Thomas (1970) to the formation of an attentional set, called "general attention." On the other hand, nondifferential training is thought to create an inattentive set, reflected in flat generalization gradients. In this case, and only in this case, the production of a flat generalization gradient in a retention test would signify *good* retention of the inattentive set purportedly established by the nondifferential training procedure. Similarly, the production of a sharp generalization gradient following discrimination training would indicate *what* was being remembered, in that case an attentive set.

Summary.   The method of investigating dimensional stimulus control of operant behavior developed by Guttman and Kalish (1956) may be used to provide a variety of indices of long-term memory and forgetting in pigeons. In the case of specific stimulus–response-reinforcer associations due to single stimulus training, the location of the gradient peak indicates *what* is remembered, with relative generalization slope indicating *how well*. Where an intradimensional discrimination paradigm is used, amount of peak shift provides yet another index of retention loss. When retention of nonspecific effects of extradimensional discrimination and nondifferential training is investigated, gradient slope has an altered meaning. In this case it reflects what is remembered from prior training, rather than how well.

STUDIES OF SIMPLE FORGETTING

I first describe studies involving "simple" forgetting (i.e., those in which the source of forgetting *manipulated* is simply the time interval between training and retention testing). As will be seen, different experiments within this category made use of different measures of forgetting, all derived from stimulus generalization gradients.

Simple Forgetting Following Single Stimulus Training

In 1958, Perkins and Weyant reported a study in which generalization gradients based on the measure of running speed obtained with rats one week after training on a runway were shown to be reliably flatter than those obtained immediately after training. Four groups were used, one tested immediately with the training stimulus, one tested immediately with the novel stimulus (alley and goal box of different color), one group tested after a 1-week delay with the original alley, and one group tested after a 1-week delay with the novel alley.

Our first experiment in this area demonstrated that generalization gradients obtained in pigeons with the Guttman–Kalish methodology are sensitive to the manipulation of the passage of time between training and retention testing. Thomas and Lopez (1962) trained pigeons to peck a key illuminated by a monochromatic light of 550 nm. After 10 days of VI 1-min training, subjects were divided into three groups. One group was tested for generalization 1 min after the completion of training; a second group was tested 1 day later; the third group was tested 1 week later.

The mean generalization gradients of the three groups are presented in Fig. 9.1. The gradient of the immediate test group was reliably sharper than the gradients of the other groups that did not differ. The reduced slope of the delayed test gradients is taken to indicate forgetting of the training stimulus value, which is apparently largely complete after 24 hr. The finding of greatest forgetting in the period soon after learning is, of course, typical of forgetting curves since the time of Ebbinghaus (1913). In addition, there were no differences among the groups in the mean number of responses emitted during generalization testing.

The results were interpreted in terms of differential rates of forgetting for different types of learning. Apparently subjects forgot the exact value of the training stimulus more quickly than they forgot the motor response of pecking the key. This interpretation parallels that of Perkins and Weyant (1958), who suggested that: "forgetting the color of the runway occurs more rapidly than does the general tendency to run on elevated runways. Forgetting of the color would have the same effect as increasing the similarity of training and test stimuli [p. 599]."

Simple Forgetting Following Successive Discrimination Training

Thomas and Burr (1969) measured forgetting after a time interval but employed successive discrimination training between two wavelengths rather than single stimulus training with one wavelength. Their study is of interest from both a methodological and a theoretical standpoint. Theoretically, the use of discrimination training might lead to better learning about the training stimulus value(s), thereby making the memory more resistant to forgetting than in the case of single-stimulus training. Methodologically, because the intradimensional training procedure produces a postdiscrimination generalization gradient with a peak of responding displaced from S+ (the reinforced stimulus) in the direction opposite S− (the extinguished stimulus), the extent of this peak shift provides another index of forgetting.

The experiment by Thomas and Burr (1969) had three groups of subjects, only two of which will be described at this time. Both groups were trained to discriminate between 550 nm (S+, VI reinforced) and 570 nm S−, not reinforced). During discrimination training, positive and negative stimuli were randomly alternated, separated by brief blackouts.

Discrimination training was administered in daily 30 min sessions until a rigorous criterion was achieved. As the birds achieved this criterion, those in one group were immediately (i.e., after a 1-min blackout) tested for generalization; a second group was tested 24 hr later. The gradients of these groups are presented in Fig. 9.2.

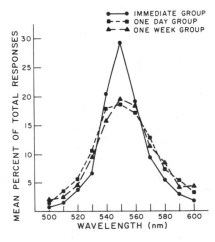

FIG. 9.1. Mean stimulus generalization gradients after three different training-test intervals (redrawn from Thomas & Lopez, 1962).

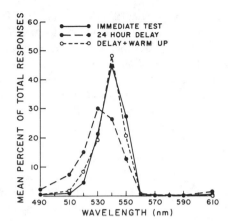

FIG. 9.2. Mean stimulus generalization gradients of subjects tested immediately or after a 24-hr delay (redrawn from Thomas & Burr, 1969).

For the present, ignore the gradient of the third group, identified as delay-warmup in the figure. Both the immediate and delayed test group gradients showed the expected peak shifts. The figure suggests, however, and statistical analysis confirmed that the peak shift was greater and the gradient was flatter in the delayed test group. Although no direct comparison of the amount of forgetting in the Thomas and Lopez (1962) and Thomas and Burr (1969) experiments can be made (because of several scaling problems), it is clear that memories established via discrimination training are subject to measurable forgetting. This opens the way for the use of the discrimination training paradigm for the investigation of forgetting in more complex situations.

Summary. The study by Thomas and Lopez (1962) found reliable flattening of the wavelength generalization gradient, following single-stimulus training, with a 24-hr delay between training and testing, and no further flattening with a 1-week delay. There was no difference in absolute response strength to the training stimulus, indicating that subjects had not forgotten to peck but only what to peck at.

Thomas and Burr (1969) replicated the finding of a flattened gradient with a 24-hr delay following intradimensional discrimination training, and found in addition a greater peak shift in the delayed test.

FORGETTING AS A CONSEQUENCE
OF CONFLICTING MEMORIES

Conflicting Memories in a Discrimination Reversal Task

The interference theory of forgetting (Keppel, 1968) has dominated research in human long-term memory for many years and it is not surprising that investigators of long-term memory in animals have followed in this tradition. Much of the research of Gleitman (1971) and Spear (1971) explores the role of conflicting memories in influencing retention performance in rats. We were interested in determining whether our measures of forgetting, derived from stimulus generalization gradients, would be sensitive to such manipulations. In studies of proactive or retroactive interference in humans, subjects are exposed in sequence to two different learning tasks (e.g., two lists of nonsense syllables) and then are instructed to recall one of them. If when instructed to recall Task 1, subjects perform more poorly than do others who never experienced Task 2, retroactive interference (RI) is demonstrated. Conversely, if when instructed to recall Task 2, subjects perform more poorly than do those who experienced only *this* task, proactive interference (PI) is revealed. The logical problem, then, is how to instruct animal subjects as to which of two memories is to be recalled at the time of a test. Honig (1974) solved this problem by having Task 1 and Task 2 differ in the stimulus dimensions involved. Thus, Task 1 involved line angles and Task 2 involved wavelengths. A retention test consisting of different line angles reflected memory of Task 1, whereas a test with different wavelengths reflected memory of Task 2. To the extent that subjects exposed to Task 2 showed altered line-angle gradients relative to untrained controls, RI was demonstrated in Honig's (1974) study.

One problem with Honig's procedure is that interference may be minimized by the dissimilarity of the stimuli used in Task 1 and Task 2. It would presumably be enhanced by the use of similar or the same stimuli in Task 1 and Task 2, but in that case how shall the subject be "instructed?" Fortunately, animal subjects typically respond in accordance with the last problem they learned, (i.e., they show recency). Indeed, in an immediate test there may be no indication that they had learned Task 1 at all. Thus it is as if subjects were operating under an implicit instruction to "recall Task 2." To the extent that a retention test after a delay shows degraded performance, in a group trained in both tasks, relative to a group that experienced only Task 2, PI is said to be demonstrated. The problem of how to instruct subjects to recall Task 1 when the same stimuli are used in both tasks is a difficult one and is treated later. (To anticipate that discussion here, we may admit that we know no way to accomplish this satisfactorily.)

It should be pointed out that the recency effect can be interpreted as a retrieval phenomenon (cf. Spear, 1978). It is assumed that internal and external contextual stimuli are elements of the target memory and that retrieval of that memory will be successful to the extent that these contextual stimuli are present at the time of the retention test. These (generally unspecified) contextual cues presumably change systematically with the passage of time; thus, at the time of a retention test they will be more similar to those present in the most recent training episode than they would be to those present during an earlier episode. Note that we use the recency effect as a tool that enables us to study PI in nonverbal organisms. For this purpose, the validity or invalidity of Spear's (1978) retrieval interpretation of the phenomenon is an irrelevant concern.

Interference theory postulates unlearning (extinction) of the first of two competing habits during learning of the second habit. Spontaneous recovery of the first habit over time is proposed as a major factor in PI (Underwood, 1948; Underwood & Postman, 1960).

In verbal learning, Keppel (1964) reported that spacing practice on a second task over several days reduced and perhaps eliminated PI, apparently through repeated extinction of the recovering prior habit. It is also possible that massed practice on the second task is conducive to the demonstration of PI because it leads to less effective learning of Task 2, rendering it more subject to interference.

A study by Burr and Thomas (1972) included the massing or spacing of training on Task 2 as an independent variable in addition to the presence or absence of (spaced) Task 1 learning, and immediate versus delayed generalization testing. It also employed two measures of retention or forgetting, the slope of the generalization gradient and the location of its peak. There were eight groups of subjects run in the experiment. The subjects assigned to the experimental (reversal) groups received discrimination training in which the initial positive stimulus was 570 nm and the negative stimulus was 550 nm. Subjects were trained on this problem until a predetermined criterion was achieved. They were then randomly assigned to one of the two conditions in Stage 2: massed practice (MP) or distributed practice (DP). Discrimination reversal training was begun 24 hr later. The MP subjects learned the reversal in a single continuous training session, whereas the DP subjects were trained 30 min daily as in Stage 1.

The remaining subjects served in control groups, receiving Stage 2 training only, under either the MP or DP condition. The same criterion of discrimination performance was required for all groups in the experiment. One group trained under each of the conditions described was tested for generalization immediately after the completion of Stage 2 training (after a brief blackout), whereas the other group was tested after a 24-hr delay.

As predicted, the group of subjects that received their reversal training under massed practice (and only this group) showed strong evidence of PI, and they showed it with both generalization measures. The immediate and delay gradients obtained under this condition are presented in Panel a of Fig. 9.3; Panel b presents the gradients for the corresponding nonreversal control groups. All four reversal groups in the experiment showed a strong recency effect (i.e., their gradients were more appropriate to the terminal discrimination than to the initial discrimination). Furthermore, forgetting was shown in all delayed testing groups in terms of a flatter gradient than obtained from the comparably trained immediate test group. The flattening was significantly greatest, however, in the reversal group with massed practice on the reversal problem. In agreement with the results of the earlier Thomas and Burr (1969) experiment, all groups also showed a greater peak shift after the delay, with the single exception of the MP reversal group for which the increased shift failed to materialize.

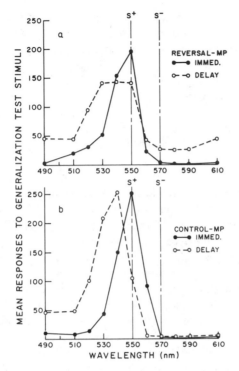

FIG. 9.3. Mean stimulus generalization gradients of massed practice groups tested either immediately or after a 24-hr delay. Panel a: reversal groups; Panel b: nonreversal (control) groups (redrawn from Burr & Thomas, 1972).

The fact that the reversal DP group performed comparably to its Stage 2 only control indicated that distributed practice led to more effective Task 2 learning or, at least, learning more resistant to PI. It is also the case that the DP groups took significantly longer to achieve criterion on Task 2 than did the MP groups. Our results are thus consistent with those of long-term memory research in rats by Spear, Gordon, and Chiszar (1972) as well as short-term memory studies in pigeons by Roberts and Grant (1976), which showed that PI is decreased as Task 2 training (or its equivalent in the delayed matching to sample task) is increased. In both of these cases the effect of amount of Task 2 training was slight, however, suggesting that the relevant factor in the Burr and Thomas study was the massing or spacing of Task 2 training trials rather than the number of trials required to achieve criterion.

Summary. Procedural problems hindering the investigation of proactive and retroactive interference were discussed in this section. In particular, when subjects have learned two competing habits, how may they be "instructed" as to which one to recall at the time of retention testing? Burr and Thomas (1972) used the strong recency effect in a discrimination reversal experiment to infer an implicit instruction to recall Task 2. They observed evidence for PI in a group that learned Task 2 under massed practice (and with less training) in comparison with controls who experienced only Task 2. Both generalization slope and peak shift measures reflected the effect of the prior learning.

FORGETTING OF "ATTENTIONAL SETS"

As will be seen, in our next study of proactive interference, the nature of the conflicting memories is somewhat more difficult to specify. In an experiment performed by Burr (1972) three groups of pigeons were eventually trained on an interdimensional discrimination problem with a 550 nm S+ (VI reinforced) and a black vertical line on a white surround S− (extinguished). The initial training conditions of the three groups differed however. These three conditions were: (1) pretrain on the stimulus that was to become the positive stimulus in the later discrimination paradigm (pretrain S+ group); (2) pretrain on the subsequent S− (pretrain S− group); and (3) pretrain on a stimulus that was orthogonal to the stimuli to be used in the later discrimination paradigm (pretrain S^n group). The "neutral" pretraining stimulus was a dim white light on the pecking key.

After eight days of VI 1-min single stimulus pretraining were completed, interdimensional discrimination training (as previously described) was begun. This training was continued until a discrimination criterion was reached, at which time each subject was assigned to either an immediate or a 24-hr delay test group.

As would be expected, the group pretrained on S− took much longer (actually four times as long) to achieve criterion as the group pretrained on S+, with the group pretrained on S^n intermediate between the two. The mean relative generalization gradients obtained in an immediate test are presented in Fig. 9.4a, those obtained after a delay are shown in Fig. 9.4b.

The immediate test gradients of the three groups are essentially identical. This is critical, because it indicates that despite the negative transfer observed in the pretrain S− group the eventual level of learning obtained was comparable to that of the other two groups. Retention, however, was clearly inferior in this group. The delayed test gradients shown in Fig. 9.4b reveal that the gradients of the pretrain S+ and pretrain S^n groups are still roughly comparable (though slightly flattened, relative to the immediate test condition); however, the gradient of the pretrain S− group is substantially (and highly reliably) flatter.

The obtained flattening of the gradient over time as a consequence of a previously established response tendency certainly meets the operational definition of PI. In this instance the finding is particularly intriguing because the effect is indirect. That is, the conflicting memories have to do with the tendency to respond or not to respond to the vertical line stimulus whereas the target memory (narrowly defined) concerns the association formed between the 550-nm key light and reinforced key pecking. The indirect nature of this interference effect suggests an interpretation in terms of Thomas' (1970) theory of "general attention." In this view, interdimensional discrimination training is thought to sharp-

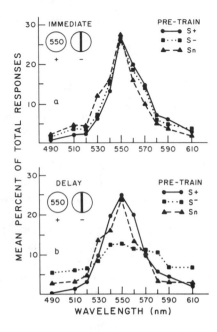

FIG. 9.4.   Mean stimulus generalization gradients of subjects given inter-dimensional discrimination training following three different pretraining conditions. Panel a: immediate tests; Panel b: delayed tests (from Burr, 1972).

en generalization gradients by instructing subjects to attend to stimuli (or to stimulus changes) because they signify events or contingencies of biological significance. This heightened attention presumably leads to sharpened generalization gradients. Alternatively, nondifferential training, in which both stimuli are reinforced, purportedly instructs subjects that stimuli are unimportant, thereby resulting in flattened generalization gradients.

In the pretrain S− group the recency effect (i.e., the strong tendency for most recent contingencies to control behavior) accounts for the sharp gradients in the immediate test. If after a delay period the subject remembers that the vertical line was previously reinforced, in addition to the 550-nm stimulus being reinforced, then what he remembers is functionally nondifferential training, and the flattened gradient is the straightforward consequence thereof.

In this conceptualization there are two memories that are *directly* in conflict, the memory of most recent (discrimination) training, which is predominant in an immediate test and leads to sharp generalization gradients, and the memory of all prior training, which is relatively stronger after a delay (when the recency effect is weakened), is functionally that of nondifferential training, and therefore results in a flattened generalization gradient.

Rather than pursuing the question of why PI in the retention of an attentional set was so striking in this one group in the Burr study, we decided that it would be more fruitful to investigate the retention of attentional sets in those training paradigms we have used to study the formation of attentional sets in the first place (i.e., extradimensional "true" discrimination (TD) and nondifferential

(ND) training). Although "general attention" was originally conceived of as a learning construct in the sense that it affects what is learned about subsequently experienced stimuli (Thomas, 1970), experiments reported by Turner and Mackintosh (1972) and by Honig (1974) demanded an extension of this conceptualization by showing that extradimensional discrimination and nondifferential training can influence (in the expected direction) the control exercised by a *previously experienced* stimulus. This finding is not inconsistent with the basic assertion that a TD or ND training experience will produce some effects that are nonspecific with regard to the training stimuli or the stimulus dimension involved in that training. Presumably the memory of a training experience will contain elements of both stimulus specific and nonspecific effects, both of which may be altered by the incorporation of subsequent information. In other words, in an extradimensional training paradigm the subject acquires knowledge of the value of the training stimulus on the test dimension and also acquires an attentive or inattentive set via orthogonal TD or ND training. The sequence of these two kinds of learning is unimportant. Knowledge of the value of the dimensional stimulus provides the vehicle through which the development and retention of the attentional set can be manifested. The opportunity to provide training on the dimensional stimulus first allows us strict control of the time between the establishment of an attentional set and the test for its retention.

A particularly intriguing test of the validity of these notions is possible for the case in which responding is first established via single-stimulus training with a wavelength value, then TD training is given with two line angles followed by brief ND training with the same line angles. An immediate wavelength generalization test should reveal a recency effect (i.e., a relatively flat gradient). In a delayed test, however, the relative strengthening of the memory of earlier TD training should result in a *sharper* gradient for this group. For a control group that never experienced TD line-angle training prior to their ND line-angle training, no such sharpening of the gradient with a delay is expected because there is no earlier conflicting memory to be strengthened. In this (control) group one might expect a slight flattening of the gradient to the extent that a 24-hr delay between training and testing leads to uncertainty about the appropriate response tendency and possibly some additional forgetting of the value of the original wavelength training stimulus. Such effects would occur in the experimental group as well, but in that group they would be opposed by PI from prior TD training.

Thomas and Vogt (1980) have recently completed an experiment like that just described. Initial single-stimulus training with a 555-nm stimulus was followed by two sessions of single-stimulus training with a 60° line in all subjects. Then members of the experimental group received six sessions of TD training with a 60° S+ and a 30° S− line, followed by one session of ND training with these two lines and then an immediate or delayed (24-hr) wavelength generalization test. After *their* initial wavelength training, the control group received two sessions of single-stimulus line-angle training and then were held without further training while the experimental subjects learned the line-angle discrimination. They then received one session of ND training with the line angles followed by either an immediate or a delayed wavelength generalization test.

The results of this experiment were entirely in accord with prediction. Note that in the control group, as in all studies reported in the literature, the effect of the 24-hr delay between training and testing was to flatten the generalization gradient. On the other hand, in the experimental group, for which extensive TD line-angle training had preceded the brief ND line-angle training, the opposite result was obtained (i.e., the gradient actually became sharper with the passage of time since training). This study attests to the fruitfulness of treating attentional sets as target memories in their own right as well as to the usefulness of generalization slope as a measure of what is remembered rather than how well.

Summary. Two experiments on proactive interference were reported in this section. The first, performed by Burr (1972) involved training pigeons on an interdimensional discrimination problem (green S+, vertical line S−) following initial training to peck at the green, the line, or a neutral white key. All three groups showed flattened wavelength gradients in a test delayed 24 hr but the group pretrained on the line showed greatest flattening (PI). It was hypothesized that at the time of the delayed test these subjects remembered that both the line and the green had previously been reinforced and the recollection of this "ND training" led to the production of an appropriate (i.e., flat) generalization gradient.

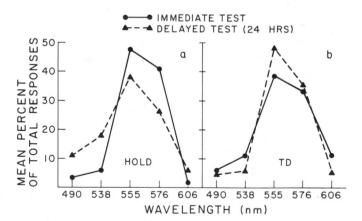

FIG. 9.5.   Mean stimulus generalization gradients in immediate and delayed testing for subjects given only ND line-angle training (Panel a) and for subjects given TD line-angle training prior to ND line-angle training (Panel b) (from Thomas & Vogt, 1980).

The experiment by Thomas and Vogt (1980) provided a test of these notions, utilizing an extradimensional design. After training to respond to a green light, experimental subjects received extensive line-angle TD training followed by brief ND line training and either an immediate or a delayed wavelength generalization test. It was predicted that in the delayed test the experimental subjects would show a *sharper* gradient, due to the relative strengthening of the effects of the earlier TD training. This prediction was confirmed, whereas a control group, without prior TD training, showed the expected flattening of the gradient during the delay interval.

THE ROLE OF CONTEXTUAL RETRIEVAL CUES IN RETENTION AND FOREGETTING

In the series of studies discussed next we test certain implications of the theoretical viewpoint proposed by Spear (1971, 1978). The crux of that position is as follows: We distinguish between storage (i.e., the establishing of an internal representation of an event or a relationship) and retrieval (i.e., the manifestation of that representation in overt behavior). We assume, with Spear, that the representation, once stored, is essentially permanent such that failure in a retention test can be attributed to a failure in the retrieval process. This conclusion would only be justified, of course, if the assumption of permanence of storage is correct and if it can be demonstrated that storage was successfully accomplished in the first place. The permanency notion is, admittedly, a matter of faith. It is generally a simple matter, however, to demonstrate the success of storage by obtaining good performance either at the end of training or on a retention test administered after a short delay.

We further assume, with Spear, that success at retrieval is a function of the extent to which the subject notices, during retention testing, ambient contextual stimuli that were present but inconsequential to the target learning task and were stored as attributes of the target memory. Thus this position emphasizes the predominant role played by the retrieval process in influencing long-term memory in animals. To investigate this role, we have performed a variety of experiments in which we manipulated various aspects of some of the potential retrieval cues available to subjects and have examined the influence of these manipulations on retention performance. The first retrieval cue manipulation we consider is that involved in providing a warm-up immediately prior to delayed generalization testing.

Retrieval Cues and the Warm-up Effect

In animal learning studies in which subjects are given daily training sessions, performance is generally poorer at the start of each session than it was at the end of the preceding session. This warm-up effect has been attributed by Spear (1978) to the reactivation of memory. With the reexposure to the stimuli (including reinforcing events) associated with prior training, it is assumed that the subject is more likely to notice an effective retrieval cue, which thereby increases the probability of retrieving the memory of that prior training.

Since the pioneering work of Guttman and Kalish (1956), studies of free-operant stimulus generalization in pigeons have often employed a reinforced warm-up (i.e., an abbreviated training session) immediately prior to the initiation of a generalization test in extinction. One purpose of the warm-up is to assure that the subject is attending to the pecking key at the time the test stimuli are presented. In addition, however, reinforcement (like shock in the case of Sidman avoidance) may reestablish the motivational condition necessary for good performance. It is very reasonable to consider the expectancy of reward, or its occasional physical presence, as an important attribute of the target memory of pecking at a key on which is displayed the former training stimulus. As such it may serve as an effective retrieval cue, along with various other aspects of the prior training environment that the subject notices during the warm-up.

In the experiment by Thomas and Burr (1969) reported earlier (see page 262), three groups of subjects were trained to peck at a light of 550 nm for VI reinforcement, with extinction in effect for pecking at 570 nm. Generalization testing was carried out immediately after the completion of training in one group and 24 hr later, without any warm-up, in another. This delay group yielded two indices of forgetting; its gradient was flatter than that of the immediate test group, and it showed enhanced peak (and area) shift. The third group, not previously described, was given a 3-min reinforced warm-up with the S+ immediately prior to their generalization test. Note that this was not a continuation of discrimination training, because the S− was not presented during the warm-up. Nevertheless, the warm-up treatment was fully effective in reestablishing the discrimination, as the gradient of this group was indistinguishable from that of the immediate test group. The results of this experiment are shown in Fig. 9.2.

It is difficult to characterize the reminder treatment in the Thomas and Burr experiment. It is not a "reinstatement" of the memory of training (i.e., a continuation of the same conditions that existed earlier). Neither is the S+ a contextual stimulus orthogonal to the target learning task, like the houselight or the white noise. The target memory is not that of responding to the S+ but rather that of discriminating between S+ and S−, which, indeed, results in a displacement of maximal responding away from S+.

However the reinforced warm-up with S+ is characterized, it is strong evidence, via the prior cuing technique, of the role of retrieval cues in reactivating the memory of prior training.

The Thomas and Burr (1969) experiment did not isolate which aspect(s) of the warm-up procedure were responsible for successful retrieval of the target memory. A subsequent experiment, recently performed by Moye and Thomas (1980)

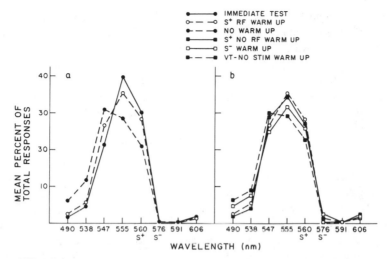

FIG. 9.6. Mean stimulus generalization gradients obtained either immediately or after a delay subsequent to wavelength discrimination training. Panel a: the effect of a reinforced warm-up on S+, a replication of the Thomas and Burr (1969) study; Panel b: a comparison of different warm-up treatments (from Moye & Thomas, 1980).

asked this question. Six groups of pigeons received wavelength discrimination training with 560 nm (S+) and 576 nm (S−) until a rigorous criterion was achieved. One group was tested for wavelength generalization 1 min after the completion of training; the other five groups were tested after a 24-hr delay. Four of the delay groups were given different types of warm-up treatments prior to generalization testing, and the fifth delay group was tested with no warm-up. The four warm-up treatments (each lasting for 5 min) consisted of: (1) S+ with VI reinforcement; (2) S+ with no reinforcement; (3) S− with no reinforcement; and (4) reinforcement on a variable time schedule with no stimulus presented on the key. The results of this experiment are presented in Fig. 9.6.

Note first the gradients of the groups that constitute a replication of the Thomas and Burr (1969) study (Panel a). The immediate test group's gradient peaks sharply at 555 nm, showing the expected peak shift. The delay group gradient (labeled "no warm-up") is flatter and shows greater shift, peaking at 547 nm. This replicates the finding with the comparable groups in the Thomas and Burr (1969) study despite many differences in procedure, specific stimulus values, etc. The S+ warm-up group gradient is sharper and shows less peak shift than the no warm-up group gradient and resembles that of the immediate test group; indeed, the gradients of these two groups do not differ significantly.

Consider next the gradients of the other warm-up groups (Panel b). The S+ warm-up without reinforcement was just as effective as the S+ warm-up with reinforcement, suggesting that reinforcement played no role in the reminder effect. This conclusion is confirmed by the VT reinforcement reminder group, which performed virtually identically to the delay no warm-up group. On the other hand the S− warm-up group showed a clear reminder effect; their gradient peaked unequivocally at 555 nm, and although it was not as sharp as that of the other groups, the slope difference did not achieve significance.

We conclude on the basis of this study that: (1) the warm-up must involve an element that is unique to the target discrimination; and (2) a reminder of the stimulus to which responding is appropriate *may be* more effective than a reminder of the stimulus to which responding is inappropriate. This study also illustrates the usefulness of having two measures of retention rather than one. The peak shift measure proved to be more responsive to our experimental manipulations than did the measure of gradient slope.

The Moye and Thomas experiment leaves some intriguing questions to be addressed by future research. Note, for example, that the warm-up treatments were effective to the extent that responding occurred in their presence. Would the S+ have been an effective reminder of the target discrimination if the subjects had been prevented from responding to it during the "warm-up" period?

Given that the "free" delivery of electric shock is a common reminder in aversive control situations, why didn't the free delivery of food have a comparable effect here? Our best guess is that feeding was ineffective because grain was not uniquely associated with the target memory; our pigeons receive supplementary grain in their home cages. This interpretation may be tested by the use of a distinctive food (e.g., Pigeon Chow) during the training of the discrimination, and such an experiment is planned.

The Role of Retrieval Cues in Forgetting Involving Conflicting Memories

In the research on the role of retrieval cues we present next, we have employed learning situations in which an explicit source of forgetting (i.e., the presence of conflicting memories) is incorporated. This paradigm is particularly informative because (theoretically, at least) it provides two alternative ways of modifying performance on a retention test. Retention may be facilitated by providing effective retrieval cues for the target learning task, or retention may be impaired by providing effective retrieval cues for a memory that conflicts with that of the target learning task. We have sought evidence for both of these effects.

In a study reported by Hickis, Robles, and Thomas (1977), 18 pigeons were given free-operant successive discrimination training in which, on alternative days, two different interdimensional problems were employed, 555 nm as S+ (VI reinforced) versus a 75° white line on a dark surround as S− (extinguished) on odd days and a 90° line as S+ versus 576 nm as S− on even days. Note that within a session the training problems are interdimensional ones. As Switalski, Lyons, and Thomas (1966) and many others have shown, interdimensional discrimination training sharpens the generalization gradient around the S+ value. Note, however, that if the subject disregards the training days (i.e., if the memories established on odd and even days are allowed to interact), then the problems can be construed as a pair of intradimensional ones, with 555 nm S+ versus 576 nm S− as the color problem and 90° S+ versus 75° S− as the line-angle problem. A consequence of (and thus, evidence for) this particular interaction of memories would be a peak shift in the obtained generalization gradients. If the memories established on odd and even days were stored and retrieved separately, as they might be with appropriately correlated contextual retrieval cues, then no peak shift would be obtained. To test this hypothesis, subjects in Group 1 ($n = 6$) were trained on the alternating discrimination problems in a single context (environment), houselight off with white noise, while Group 2 ($n = 6$) received the alternating problems with the context conditions being houselight off with white noise on odd days and houselight on with a tone on even days. For subjects in Group 3 ($n = 6$), the two contexts were *randomly* alternated on a daily basis (i.e., explicitly uncorrelated with the two discriminations).

Subjects were run with daily problem alternation until attainment of a discrimination criterion on two consecutive sessions on the same problem. Following attainment of criterion, subjects were tested for stimulus generalization as subsequently discussed.

Subjects were randomly assigned to testing conditions prior to their completion of discrimination training. Three subjects in each group were tested with stimuli from the wavelength dimension and three with line-angle stimuli. Those subjects to be tested with wavelengths were run with daily problem alternations until attainment of criterion on the 555 nm versus 75° line problem and then they were tested on the next day on which *that* problem was scheduled. Those subjects to be tested with line-angle stimuli were run with daily problem alternations until attainment of criterion on the 90° line versus 576-nm problem and then they were tested on the next day on which this problem was scheduled. Group 1 was tested in the same context used throughout training—houselight off and noise. Group 2 was tested in the same context in which the relevant discrimination problem was learned, that is, houselight off and noise for subjects tested with wavelengths, and houselight on and tone for those tested with line angles. In Group 3, because context conditions were randomly related to discrimination task conditions, it was arbitrarily decided to test for line-angle generalization in the houselight off and noise context and to test for wavelength generalization in the houselight on and tone context.

The results of this experiment were clearly in accord with prediction, as shown in Figure 9.7. Panel a presents the results of Group 1, which learned both problems in the same context. Five of the six birds showed peak shifts. Consistent with the finding of peak shifts in five of six subjects in Group 1 is the finding in all six cases of lower responding to the S− value than to a value still farther removed from S+. It is typical for generalization gradients following intradimensional discrimination training to show a trough in the vicinity of S− (Purtle, 1973).

Furthermore, no peak shifts were found in Group 2 (Panel b), for which the two alternative problems were trained, each in a different context. Note also that

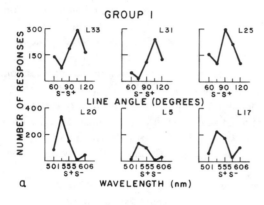

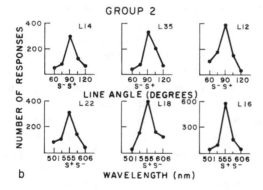

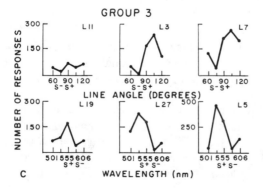

FIG. 9.7. Generalization gradients obtained under three different context conditions. Panel a: for Group 1 the same context was used for both problems; Panel b: for Group 2 a different context was used with each problem; Panel c: for Group 3 both contexts were used with each problem (redrawn from Hickis, Robles, & Thomas, 1977).

in no case was the minimum of responding of the "S−" value. This finding, along with the absence of peak shifts in this group, is compelling evidence indicating that, for these subjects, the functional S− was an orthogonal stimulus and not the value labeled as S− in the figure.

As shown in Panel c, most subjects in Group 3 showed peak shifts and all showed troughs in the gradient around S−. This indicates that the lack of peak shifts in Group 2 was not due to their exposure to two different contexts but rather to the consistent relationship between those contexts and the interdimensional discrimination problems with which they were associated. In other words, the different contexts in Group 2 were stored as attributes of the odd and even day memories and enabled subjects to maintain those memories separate and distinct from one another. They thus prevented the interaction of memories that otherwise would have occurred.

The procedure used in the Hickis et al. (1977) experiment resembles a conditional discrimination paradigm in certain respects. In that paradigm a superordinate stimulus (say, the presence or absence of a vertical line) signifies which of two stimuli will be reinforced. The most common type of conditional discrimination problem is the reversal (e.g., red may signal reinforcement when a vertical line is present whereas green may signal reinforcement when the line is absent). In the Hickis et al. study, the superordinate stimulus (the context) signaled the dimension of the stimulus (color or line angle) that was to be reinforced, but the same discriminative stimulus value never served as both S+ and S−. Our next experiment employed the more traditional conditional discrimination reversal problem. It differed from traditional usage, however, in several significant respects. Features of the experimental environment usually viewed as context constituted the superordinate stimulus. Furthermore, rather than repeated reversal of the discrimination problem our subjects experienced only one reversal, which took place between sessions. In a departure from our other work involving intradimensional discriminations, Thomas, McKelvie, Ranney, and Moye (1980) employed training stimuli that were widely spaced so that discrimination training would not be expected to produce a measurable peak shift (Hanson, 1959). As a consequence, the retrieval of the memory of a particular discrimination problem would result in a peak in the generalization gradient at the appropriate S+ value and the simultaneous retrieval of the memories of both problems could result in a gradient with peaks at both S+ values.

The logic of this experiment may be explained as follows: Burr and Thomas (1972) had trained their subjects on a discrimination problem and then its reversal. Immediate generalization testing had revealed a strong recency effect; indeed there was evidence of only the learning of the second problem. In a delayed test, however, although there was still a recency effect in that the gradient was most appropriate to the second problem, there was (particularly in the most appropriate, massed practice group) evidence of PI from the prior learning of the original problem. Many of the studies already described have demonstrated how retrieval cues can facilitate retention, and the Hickis et al. (1977) study revealed that contextual cues may serve as very effective reminders. We reasoned that it should be possible, therefore, to train the original problem and its reversal in different contexts and then, by testing in different contexts, to modulate the degree of PI obtained.

The strong recency effect observed following reversal learning indicates that subjects perform during generalization testing as if under the instruction "tell me what you learned last." Testing under the context in which the second problem was learned should further strengthen the already predominant memory of the second (reversal) task minimizing such interference as would otherwise occur. On the other hand, testing in the context in which the original problem was learned should retrieve (reactivate, strengthen, etc.) the memory of *that* problem, with the result being maximal interference during generalization testing.

There were three experimental groups in Experiment 1 of the Thomas et al. (1980) study. All these groups were given successive discrimination training with 538 nm S+ (VI reinforced) and 576 nm S− (extinguished) until they reached a discrimination criterion. Then the problem was reversed on the next day (i.e., 576 nm became S+ and 538 nm became S−), and the subjects were trained in a single extended session until they met the same criterion. They were tested for wavelength generalization 24 hr later. For two of the groups the context was changed between the original problem and the reversal. One of these was tested for generalization in the context (Context 1) in which Problem 1 (538 nm S+) had been learned. The other group was tested in the context (Context 2) in which Problem 2 (576 nm S+) had been learned. Two control groups were employed, one experiencing only Problem 1 and the other experiencing only Problem 2.

Two different contexts were used in this experiment, houselight and tone (HL T), and no houselight and noise (HL N). The experimental design permitted half the subjects in each group to be tested in each of these contexts.

The results of this experiment are presented in Fig. 9.8. The five rows correspond to the five groups and the two columns correspond to the two different contexts under which the subjects were tested. Consider first the gradients obtained in the control groups, pictured in the bottom two rows. All subjects in these groups yielded sharp gradients that peaked unequivocally at the appropriate S+ values. Consider next the gradients of the experimental group that experienced both problems in the same context. These subjects show a strong recency effect, with all gradients peaking at 576 nm, the S+ for Problem 2. Nevertheless, there is evidence to suggest PI from the prior problem; these gradients tend to be flatter than those of the Problem 2 control group and one of them shows a secondary peak at 538 nm, the Problem 1 S+.

The remaining question is whether the manipulation of the test context had the predicted effects of minimizing interference where the "reminder" was of Problem 2 and maximizing interference when the "reminder" was of Problem 1. A

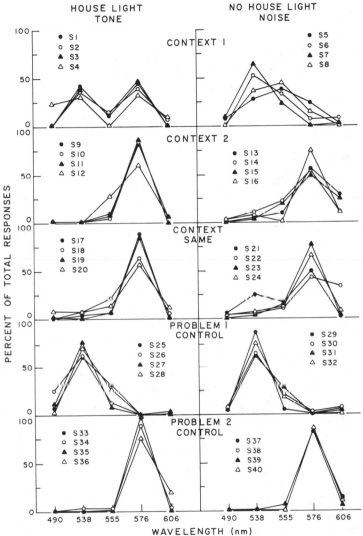

FIG. 9.8. Generalization gradients obtained following reversal or single-problem training, in one or two different contexts, with testing carried out in the original context (Context 1) or the reversal context (Context 2). See the text for group designations (from Thomas, McKelvie, Ranney, & Moye, 1980).

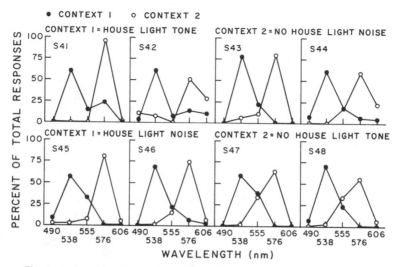

Fig. 9.9.   Generalization gradients obtained following original and reversal training in two different contexts, with the contexts alternated during the course of
generalization testing (from Thomas, McKelvie, Ranney, & Moye, 1980).

comparison of Row 2 and Row 3 in Fig. 9.8 suggests that the reminder of
Problem 2 (i.e., the use of Context 2 in testing) had no measurable effect; it did
not produce sharper gradients than those obtained in the Context Same group.
This might suggest that the subjects had not encoded the context as part of the
memory of the training experience, but the results of the Context 1 reminder
group indicate otherwise. In this group the specific stimuli that constituted Context 1 had a striking effect, but one thing was clear under both context conditions.
Not one subject in this group (as opposed to *all* subjects in all other groups)
yielded a gradient reflecting recency (i.e., peaking unequivocally at the most
recent S+). With the HL T reminder all four subjects yielded bimodal gradients
peaking at both S+'s. We have run some additional birds under this condition
and most (though not all) have yielded similar bimodal gradients. Under the HL N
reminder condition, two gradients peaked at 555 nm, a value never reinforced,
and two yielded gradients peaking clearly and sharply at 538 nm (i.e., their
gradients were entirely appropriate to the context present during testing). We
have run additional subjects under this condition and obtained both of these types
of gradient. In addition, we have run other subjects with different combinations
of contextual stimuli (i.e., HL N, HL T) as reminders of Problem 1. Again we have
obtained three types of gradient, bimodal, peaked at 555 nm, and peaked at 538,
the Problem 1 S+. Under no reminder condition we have tried do more than
about half of the subjects yield gradients appropriate to Problem 1. The only
consistency in the findings is that, when reminded of Problem 1 the subjects
never give gradients appropriate to Problem 2 (i.e., the recency effect is entirely

obliterated). Clearly Context 1 was associated with Problem 1 such that testing in that context strengthened the memory of that problem with the result being the predicted increase in PI. This makes it reasonable to assume that Context 2 was associated with Problem 2. Possibly it was ineffective as a reminder because the recency effect was so strong that the reminder cue was overshadowed and/or the strength of the recency effect left little room for improvement in performance (i.e., there was too little PI to be overcome).

An alternative way of viewing the data of the Context 1 reminder group questions the assumption that PI is involved at all. The distinction between PI and retroactive interference (RI) is based on which of two memories is being assessed. In human subjects, we need merely assume that subjects are following our explicit verbal instructions, and there is generally no reason to doubt this assumption. In animals the "intent" to retrieve a particular memory is more difficult to infer. The prevalence of the recency effect in most experiments makes the inference that the subject "intends" to remember the most recent problem a reasonable one. When a reminder cue of an earlier problem is presented, however, it might reasonably be argued that the subject "intends" to retrieve the memory of *that* problem. Two of the subjects in this experiment, S6 and S7, succeeded in doing so, with gradients quite similar to those in the Problem 1 control group. The other six subjects failed to retrieve the memory of Problem 1, showing substantial RI from Problem 2. It is clear that the performance of most of the subjects in the Context 1 reminder group reflects interference between the memories of two different problems, but the proper categorization of that interference (as PI or RI) remains equivocal and could conceivably be different in different subjects. A remaining question is whether the poor and inconsistent performance reflects only a retrieval problem or whether the encoding and/or storage processes were defective in some way.

The study reported earlier by Hickis et al. (1977) indicated that interaction between separate memories was prevented when each was established in a different context. Two factors might account for the successful retrieval of intact memories in *that* experiment in contrast to the failure in the present experiment. First of all, subjects had many opportunities to associate each context with the problem learned in its presence, and secondly the two memories were not directly opposed, as are those in a reversal situation. The suggestion that neither factor is critical, however, comes from a study by Spear, Smith, Bryan, Gordon, Timmons, and Chiszar (1980). In their Experiment 2, rats were given passive avoidance training in one room, followed by active avoidance training in a different room 3 min later. A retention test carried out 24 hr later showed excellent retention; rats behaved appropriately to the room in which they had been tested. Doubtlessly the success of this experiment was attributable to the close spacing of Task 1 and Task 2 training, which minimized the recency effect (cf. Gordon & Spear, 1973), thereby revealing the effectiveness of the context manipulation.

We hypothesized that the two memories in Experiment 1 had been encoded along with their contexts but that the implicit recency instruction made this difficult to demonstrate. We reasoned that we might accomplish this demonstration by increasing the saliency of the contextual cues during testing by allowing subjects the opportunity to compare the two contexts during the test session, an opportunity that was not available to them (within a session) during training. This was done in Experiment 2. Training was carried out as for the Context 1 reminder group of Experiment 1, except that for half of the subjects the contextual cues were HL T, HL N, whereas for the other half they were HL N, HL T. In generalization testing after each two blocks of the five test stimuli, the context present was switched to the alternate context. Half of the subjects started the test in Context 1, half in Context 2. This had no effect on test performance, and neither did the specific stimulus combinations used. As Fig. 9.9 reveals, test performance was remarkably consistent, and every subject yielded gradients that peaked unequivocally at the appropriate S+'s for each test context. This verifies the assertion that the interference in memory observed in Experiment 1 was entirely due to retrieval failure. Each problem doubtlessly was encoded and stored along with the context in which it was learned and, given appropriate testing conditions, the memory for each problem could have been retrieved with little or no loss.

The Thomas et al. (1980) study raises important theoretical and methodological issues about the investigation of interference between conflicting memories in nonverbal organisms. It makes sense to attribute memory loss to RI only when the subject's intent to recall Task 1 can reasonably be inferred. However, when the same stimulus dimension is employed for the two tasks this inference can only be made by viewing the context associated with Task 1 as an instructional cue. It can only serve this function if a different context is used with the two tasks. "Herein lies the rub," because training the two tasks in different contexts may provide the means whereby the two memories are separately encoded and stored such that they do not interact. We see here an application of the "Heisenberg Principle" (i.e., the procedure we employ to enable us to measure RI may well prevent its occurrence).

The situation with respect to the investigation of PI is little better. The recency effect in an immediate test permits a reasonable inference about the subject's intent to recall Task 2 *at that time*. In a delayed test the subject clearly performs less well but is it because it cannot remember which learning experience was most recent, or because the "recency instruction," is no longer operative? The upshot of this discussion is that in experimental paradigms employing the same stimulus dimension in Task 1 and Task 2, the unequivocal categorization of interference as RI versus PI may be a logical impossibility. When the manipulation of retrieval cues succeeds in modulating the amount of interference observed, it may be because it makes the implicit instructions to the subject at the time of testing more (or less) ambiguous. An extreme position, which is clearly untestable but might still be correct, is that interference observed in such cases is always attributable to retrieval failure.

Summary. Thomas and Burr (1969) had shown that a reinforced warm-up on the S+ value reinstated the memory of a discrimination between two wavelengths. Whereas the effect of delayed testing was to produce a flattened gradient with an increased peak shift, the warm-up produced a gradient indistinguishable from that of the immediate test group. A subsequent experiment by Moye and Thomas (1980) replicated these findings and determined that the presentation of either S+ or S− without reinforcement was also an effective reminder, but the presentation of food deliveries without any accompanying stimulus on the key was not.

Hickis et al. (1977) reported an experiment in which pigeons learned a different interdimensional discrimination problem on odd and even days (i.e., on odd days a wavelength was reinforced and a line angle extinguished; on even days a different line angle was reinforced and a different wavelength was extinguished). Interaction of the memories resulted in peak shifts on both dimensions; this did not occur when the two problems were learned in two correlated contexts.

In Experiment 1 of a study by Thomas et al. (1980) pigeons in each of five groups were tested for generalization 24 hr after the completion of training. Two groups learned only a single discrimination problem, either 538 nm S+ versus 576 nm S−, or the reverse. Three other groups learned both problems in sequence; in one of these the same context was present for each; for the other two, different contexts were used. For these latter two groups, one was tested in Context 1 and the other was tested in Context 2. The group that experienced both problems in the same context showed recency but it also showed some PI relative to the group that experienced only the 576 nm S+ problem. The reversal group tested in Context 2 showed no PI, but the reversal group tested in Context 1 showed massive PI. A second experiment revealed that this was due to a conflict between opposed (recency and contextual) instructions rather than between underlying memories. When tested alternately in both contexts, subjects showed sharp gradients that peaked at the appropriate S+ value in each context. This parallels findings by Spear et al. (1980) in the passive–active avoidance paradigm with rats.

MEMORIAL EFFECTS IN SUCCESSIVE REVERSAL PERFORMANCE

In this section I describe a series of studies that use a new procedure to investigate the role of memorial processes in successive conditional discrimination learning. The procedure used in this research, performed by McKelvie and Thomas (1980) borrows heavily from the procedures of the Hickis et al. (1977) and the Thomas et al. (1980) studies just described.

The general procedure may be described as follows: Pigeons were trained daily on a conditional discrimination reversal problem. On odd days, 555 nm was

S+ (VI reinforced) and 576 nm was S− (extinguished); the reverse was true on even days.

Our initial concern in these studies was with assessing the acquisition of control of behavior by the elements of a *compound* conditional cue. Thus on odd days, a vertical line was present on both colors; on even days a horizontal line was used (i.e., the compound conditional cues used were odd day–vertical line and even day–horizontal line). A control group was employed that received the same training but without the lines present. For these birds the day (odd or even) was the only conditional cue available.

The birds were trained on this paradigm for at least 40 days. During that time discrimination performance gradually improved with most birds reaching an asymptote on both problems of over 90% of total responses emitted to S+, except for the control subjects, who showed no evidence of learning the conditional discrimination reversal task.

A variety of generalization test procedures was employed in different experiments. For example, subjects tested for generalization 24 hr after a training session with appropriate conditional cues present (either odd–vertical or even–horizontal) yielded gradients with virtually all responding made to the appropriate S+, 555 nm if testing were on an odd day with vertical line present, and 576 nm if testing were on an even day with horizontal line present. Thus, the subjects had learned about the compound conditional cue (or some element thereof); that is, they did not need reinforcement as a cue to reverse their discrimination performance.

Of particular interest to us was the question of whether or not the birds had learned about the day element of the compound odd–vertical and even–horizontal conditional stimuli. To test this, four birds were given generalization tests on an odd day but with no line present. The same birds were then retrained with the normal procedure for 10 more days, followed by another generalization test without lines, this time on an even day. The results of this experiment are presented in Fig. 9.10.

The removal of the line from the key dramatically reduced the level of responding, as would be expected given the salience of this cue. One of the four birds (A6) gave essentially no responses during either test. Despite the low level of responding, Birds A7, A9, and A13 yielded gradients that clearly peaked at 555 nm, the appropriate S+, when tested on an odd day, and at 576 nm, the appropriate S+, when tested on an even day. This result has since been replicated in several other experiments performed in our laboratory. It provides unequivocal evidence that the day cue does gain control over reversal in the compound conditional training paradigm employed here, though it does not occur in subjects with only the day cue available (i.e., no lines present) during reversal training, as measured in acquisition or in generalization performance.

There is a remarkable parallel between these results and those obtained in a drug-conditional discrimination retention study recently reported by Spear,

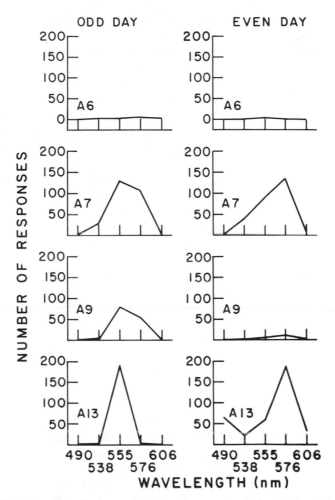

FIG. 9.10.   Generalization gradients of subjects tested on both odd and even days without lines present (from McKelvie & Thomas, 1980).

Smith, Sherr, and Bryan (1979). In that study, rats learned to turn in one direction in a T-maze to escape shock on odd days when injected with pentobarbital and to turn in the opposite direction on even days when injected with saline. A retention test was performed 24 hr after the completion of training under each of the drug-state conditions. The test revealed behavior generally appropriate to the drug state present during testing (i.e., state-dependent retrieval); however, performance was markedly poorer when the drug state used in test was the *same* as that used on the preceding day, rather than the alternative state, as was always the case in training. This finding implicates the memory of the previous day's training episode as a partial determinant of performance. In other words, part of what the subjects learned was to choose the arm of the maze opposite that which was correct on the previous day.

There is an interesting procedural difference in the way in which control by the "day" was revealed in the McKelvie and Thomas (1980) and the Spear et al. experiments. Spear et al. used a combined cue test; when day information was in conflict with drug-state information, retention performance was impaired. In the McKelvie and Thomas study a combined cues test was attempted but it was unsuccessful; the resulting gradients were entirely determined by the line angle present. The removal of the line-angle cue was necessary in order for the effect of day to emerge with their procedure.

The "day" cue may be characterized as temporal and/or sequential. That is, the birds have clearly learned something such that on a given day they respond to the stimulus different from the one to which they responded on the preceding day, approximately 24 hr earlier. Holloway and Wansley (1973) have demonstrated that circadian rhythms can provide retrieval cues following passive avoidance training in the rat; however, a simpler interpretation of the present study would be that the birds learned the sequential rule to respond to the stimulus different from the one responded to in the previous session. To test this interpretation, an experiment was run in which a group of subjects was subdivided and tested for wavelength generalization (without lines) 2 hr after training, half on an odd day and half on an even day. None of these subjects showed the reversal, all gradients peaking at the same value to which reinforced responding had occurred 2 hr earlier. Thus, reversal behavior is cued by something more than the animal's recollection of the stimulus reinforced in the previous session. Clearly the passage of a certain period of time and/or some event correlated with that passage of time is also necessary. The most obvious event that occurs between daily training sessions is the dark cycle in the colony room. In the next experiment, we tested the role of this cycle as a potential reversal cue. Two groups of pigeons were given the standard reversal training, with the compound line-plus-day conditional cues, except that one group was trained at 6:00 A.M. daily and one was trained at 6:00 P.M. The dark cycle in the colony room was from 8:00 P.M. to 4:00 A.M.

After asymptotic discrimination reversal performance was achieved, all subjects were tested for wavelength generalization (without lines) 12 hr after training. For the evening group the 12-hr interval between training and testing included a dark cycle; for the morning group, it did not. This difference turned out to be inconsequential, as the majority of birds under both conditions reversed their discrimination from the previous session. These results indicate that the birds had learned a temporal discrimination such that the passage of some period of time—in excess of 2 hr—was a cue leading to reversal behavior.

A question orthogonal to the temporal versus sequential nature of the reversal rule is that of identifying the functional cue for reversing. The cue might be prior behavior. That is, the subject's memory of what stimulus it responded to previously may determine the switch to the alternate stimulus on the subsequent occasion. On the other hand, the reversal cue might involve a representation of the entire stimulus–response-reinforcer relationship, such that the subject learns that the stimulus that signaled the availability of reinforcement for responding previously now signals extinction, and vice versa. The critical difference between these two interpretations is in the role of reinforcement information as a component of the memory trace. An experiment was performed to address this question. Upon reaching asymptotic reversal performance, six subjects were given a half session of discrimination training in which the appropriate wavelength was reinforced but no lines were present, and six received a half session with the normal line and color cues but without reinforcement. Both groups of subjects performed well on the discrimination during the half session. On the next day (i.e., 24 hrs later) all subjects were tested for wavelength generalization without the line. For those subjects who had received reinforcement but no lines, five showed *no* reversal and the other gave equal responding to both stimuli. For the group that had the line cue but no reinforcement, four subjects reversed and the other two gave equal responding to both of the training stimuli. Clearly then, the memory of reinforcement to a given wavelength does not control reversal behavior, but memory of an unreinforced conditional cue can.

This study is unique in the literature on long-term memory in animals because the index of retention is not how well the subject does what it did last, but how well it does the opposite (reverse) of what it did last. The McKelvie and Thomas study showed potentiation of learning about the ''day'' cue by the presence of the line, yet the birds never overcame their dependence on the line cue. They could only reverse their discrimination on a test day (without a line present) if the line had been present on the preceding day. Indeed subsequent research has revealed that if the line cue is removed and reversal training continues as before, performance quickly drops to a chance level. Like the expectancy of food reward in the Peterson et al. (1978) study referred to in the opening section, the line cue is a critical element of the target memory of the discrimination. Without the line present or in recent memory, good performance cannot be sustained. The discovery of this unexpected finding attests to the fruitfulness of using the conditional successive discrimination reversal procedure to analyze the contents of the pigeon's long-term memory, and future research is planned to take advantage of the many unique properties of this paradigm.

Summary. The successive conditional discrimination reversal procedure employed in a series of experiments by McKelvie and Thomas (1980) was described. In this procedure the day of training (odd or even) in compound with a vertical or horizontal line indicates which of two wavelengths is to be reinforced on that day. After 40 or more daily sessions of training the compound conditional cue controls responding in a wavelength generalization test in extinction. Furthermore, if the line is removed for testing, the day (odd or even) is sufficient to control reversal behavior. Similar evidence for the effectiveness of a day cue was reported by Spear et al. (1979) in a rat experiment in which day was compounded with drug state.

Further research by McKelvie and Thomas revealed that reversal was not merely sequentially controlled but required more than a 2-hr interval between one training session and the next. Furthermore, good reversal performance required that the subjects had been exposed to the line-angle cue on the previous day. The successive conditional discrimination reversal paradigm seems to provide a highly fruitful vehicle for the investigation of the contents of long-term memory in the pigeon.

GENERAL SUMMARY

The research reported in this chapter follows in the tradition established by McGeoch (1932) who maintained that there are two sources of forgetting: (1) interference from competing memories (most particularly retroactive interference); and (2) altered stimulating conditions (by which he meant internal and external contextual stimuli). Subsequent development of interference theory came to emphasize proactive rather than retroactive interference, and research on human long-term memory has emphasized the first of McGeoch's two factors, whereas animal research has tended to emphasize the second. In our research both factors receive approximately equal treatment and much of our work has been concerned with examining the interaction between the two.

Our approach has had several distinguishing characteristics. One is the fact that in addition to investigating the retention of simple stimulus–response–reinforcer associations we have examined retention of indirect nonstimulus-specific effects of discrimination and nondifferential training (which we call "attentional sets") and determined that their retention follows the same rules. We have also developed novel procedures for investigating the content of pigeons' long-term memory and not just the extent of it. Finally, we have demonstrated that properties of stimulus generalization gradients, including their slope and the location of their peak(s), may permit inferences about the various processes involved in long-term memory (and forgetting).

ACKNOWLEDGMENTS

I wish to take this opportunity to acknowledge the invaluable contributions of two individuals to my thinking about the issues addressed by this chapter and to my work in other areas as well. Charles C. Perkins, Jr. did the seminal research in two areas I have extensively pursued. He (and Weyant) first discovered that generalization gradients get flatter with the passage of time since the completion of training, and he (and Reinhold) demonstrated that discrimination training sharpens gradients along an orthogonal dimension. His encouragement and friendship, ever since the time we served together on the faculty of Kent State University, have been very much appreciated.

I owe a considerable debt to Norman E. Spear for his encouragement and for providing a theoretical framework that is most congenial to the memory research I have been doing for many years, much of it without the benefit of an organizing theme. Both his comments and those of his coeditor, Ralph Miller, have improved this chapter considerably, and I thank them for inviting me to participate in this conference.

I also wish to thank my students and collaborators for assisting me in various ways in the preparation of this manuscript. They include: Robert L. Newlin, James P. Rodgers, Thomas B. Moye, Alan R. McKelvie, and Mark Vogt. Last, but certainly not least, I am pleased to acknowledge grant support from NSF, NIH, and NICHD during various stages of this project. Support for the preparation of the manuscript was provided by NSF Grant BNS 81-02789.

REFERENCES

Burr, D. E. S. *The effects of prior experience and delayed testing upon postdiscrimination generalization gradients.* Unpublished PhD dissertation, University of Colorado, 1972.

Burr, D. E. S., & Thomas, D. R. Effect of proactive inhibition upon the postdiscrimination generalization gradient. *Journal of Comparative and Physiological Psychology,* 1972, *81,* 441–448.

Ebbinghaus, H. *Memory: A contribution to experimental psychology.* (Translated by H. A. Ruger & C. E. Bussanius. New York: Bureau of Publications, Teachers College, Columbia University, 1913.

Gleitman, H. Forgetting of long-term memories in animals. In W. K. Honig & P. H. R. James (Eds.), *Animal memory.* New York: Academic Press, 1971.

Gordon, W. C., & Spear, N. E. Effect of reactivation of a previously acquired memory on the interaction between memories in the rat. *Journal of Experimental Psychology,* 1973, *99,* 349–355.

Guttman, N., & Kalish, H. I. Discriminability and stimulus generalization. *Journal of Experimental Psychology,* 1956, *51,* 79–88.

Hanson, H. M. Effects of discrimination training on stimulus generalization. *Journal of Experimental Psychology,* 1959, *58,* 321–334.

Hickis, C. F., Robles, L., & Thomas, D. R. Contextual stimuli and memory retrieval in pigeons. *Animal Learning and Behavior,* 1977, *5,* 161–168.

Holloway, F. A., & Wansley, R. A. Multiple retention deficits at periodic intervals after passive avoidance learning. *Science,* 1973, *80,* 208–210.

Honig, W. K. Effects of extradimensional discrimination training upon previously acquired stimulus control. *Learning and Motivation,* 1974, *5,* 1–15.

Keppel, G. Facilitation in short- and long-term retention of paired associates following distributed practice in learning. *Journal of Verbal Learning and Verbal Behavior,* 1964, *3,* 91–111.

Keppel, G. Retroactive and proactive inhibition. In T. R. Dixon & O. L. Horton (Eds.), *Verbal behavior and general behavior theory.* Englewood Cliffs, N.J.: Prentice-Hall, 1968.

McGeoch, J. A. Forgetting and the law of disuse. *Psychological Review,* 1932, *39,* 352–370.

McGovern, J. B. Extinction of associations in forced transfer paradigm. *Psychological Monographs,* 1964, *78*(16, Whole # 953).

McKelvie, A., & Thomas, D. R. *The role of temporal–sequential cues in operant successive conditional discrimination reversal learning in the pigeon.* Manuscript in preparation, 1980.

Moye, T., & Thomas, D. R. *The warm-up effect as a reminder treatment in the pigeon.* Manuscript in preparation, 1980.

Newlin, R. J., Rodgers, J. P., & Thomas, D. R. Two determinants of the peak shift in human voluntary stimulus generalization. *Perception and Psychophysics,* 1979, *25,* 478–486.

Perkins, C. C., Jr., & Weyant, R. G. The interval between training and test trials as a determiner of the slope of generalization gradients. *Journal of Comparative and Physiological Psychology,* 1958, *51,* 596–600.

Peterson, G. B., Wheeler, R. L., & Armstrong, G. D. Expectancies as mediators in the differential conditional discrimination performance of pigeons. *Animal Learning and Behavior,* 1978, *6,* 279–285.

Purtle, R. Peak shift: A review. *Psychological Bulletin,* 1973, *80,* 408–421.

Roberts, W. A., & Grant, D. S. Studies of short-term memory in the pigeon using the delayed matching to sample procedure. In D. L. Medin, W. A. Roberts, & R. T. Davis (Eds.), *Processes of animal memory.* Hillsdale, N.J.: Lawrence Erlbaum Associates, 1976.

Spear, N. E. Forgetting as retrieval failure. In W. K. Honig & P. H. R. James (Eds.), *Animal memory.* New York: Academic Press, 1971.

Spear, N. E. *The processing of memories: Forgetting and retention.* Hillsdale, N.J.: Lawrence Erlbaum Associates, 1978.

Spear, N. E., Gordon, W. C., and Chiszar, D. A. Interaction between memories in the rat: Effect of degree of prior conflicting learning on forgetting after short intervals. *Journal of Comparative and Physiological Psychology,* 1972, *78,* 471–477.

Spear, N. E., Smith, G. J., Bryan, R. G., Gordon, W. C., Timmons, R., & Chiszar, D. A. Contextual influences on the interaction between conflicting memories in the rat. *Animal Learning and Behavior,* 1980, *8,* 273–281.

Spear, N. E., Smith, G. J., Sherr, A., and Bryan, R. G. Forgetting of a drug-conditional discrimination. *Physiology and Behavior,* 1979, *22,* 851–854.

Switalski, R. W., Lyons, J., & Thomas, D. R. The effects of interdimensional training on stimulus generalization. *Journal of Experimental Psychology,* 1966, *72,* 661–666.

Thomas, D. R. Stimulus selection, attention, and related matters. In J. H. Reynierse (Ed.), *Current issues in animal learning.* Lincoln, Nebr.: University of Nebraska Press, 1970.

Thomas, D. R., & Burr, D. E. S. Stimulus generalization and a function of the delay between training and testing procedures: A reevaluation. *Journal of the Experimental Analysis of Behavior,* 1969, *12,* 105–109.

Thomas, D. R., Freeman, F., Svinicki, J. G., Burr, D. E. S., & Lyons, J. The effects of extradimensional training on stimulus generalization. *Journal of Experimental Psychology,* 1970, *83* (Whole No. 1, Pt. 2, 1–21).

Thomas, D. R., & Lopez, L. J. The effect of delayed testing on generalization slope. *Journal of Comparative and physiological Psychology,* 1962, *44,* 541–544.

Thomas, D. R., McKelvie, A., Ranney, M., & Moye, T. B. *Elimination of interference in longterm memory of a reversal problem in pigeons by contextual retrieval cues.* Manuscript in preparation, 1980.

Thomas, D. R., & Vogt, M. *Proactive interference in the retention of an attentional set in the pigeon.* Manuscript in preparation, 1980.

Thorndike, E. L. *The psychology of learning.* New York: Teachers College, Columbia University Press, 1913.

Turner, C., & Mackintosh, N. J. Stimulus selection and irrelevant stimuli in discrimination learning by pigeons. *Journal of Comparative and Physiological Psychology,* 1972, *78,* 1–9.

Underwood, B. J. The effects of successive interpolations on retroactive and proactive inhibition. *Psychological Monographs,* 1945, *59* (3, Whole #273).

Underwood, B. J. "Spontaneous recovery" of verbal associations. *Journal of Experimental Psychology,* 1948, *38,* 429–439.

Underwood, B. J., & Postman, L. Extra-experimental sources of interference in forgetting. *Psychological Review,* 1960, *67,* 73–95.

10 Postacquisition Modifications of Memory

David C. Riccio
Debbie L. Ebner
Kent State University

The importance of retrieval deficits as a source of memory loss in a variety of paradigms has been increasingly recognized in recent years. While the development of retrieval oriented explanations of memory deficits represents an important alternative to models based on storage failure or decay, a number of questions about the nature of retrieval processes remain to be answered. In attempting to explore these questions, we have followed others in viewing retrieval as a general process that encompasses aspects of training as well as testing, rather than a mechanism simply activated during a retention test (Miller & Springer, 1973; Spear, 1973, 1978; Tulving, 1974). Retrieval then is intimately related to the conditions under which information was acquired. The incidental background stimuli, or contextual cues, that are present at training but not specifically related to the contingencies of the task constitute an important component of the acquisition conditions. Internal states as well as exteroceptive stimuli can be sources of contextual cues. Although contextual cues are not essential to original learning, they are considered to be potent modulators of retention. A frequent observation is that performance on a retention test is impaired by changes in contextual cues (Spear, 1978). The common interpretation of this effect is that changes in stimulus contexts between training and testing result in retrieval failure. Although this notion has permeated our own thinking about memory, we present later some considerations that appear troublesome to the general principle.

One approach to studying the nature of retrieval is to explore conditions that modulate access to memory or alter the characteristics of memory during retrieval. This chapter summarizes some of the recent efforts in this direction from our laboratory. Parenthetically, we might note that in the course of inquiring into matters of memory and retention, we have often found ourselves confronted by fundamental issues in conditioning and learning.

MALLEABILITY OF OLD AND NEW MEMORIES

That human memory is dynamic and undergoes changes involving more than just loss of original information was indicated by Bartlett's (1932) classic work. Processes of reconstruction and inference from a schema may result in actual distortion of the target material. Recently, this malleability of memory has been strikingly demonstrated in a series of studies by Loftus and her associates (Cole & Loftus, 1979; Loftus, 1979; Loftus & Zanni, 1975). These investigations have shown that established memories can be modified by introduction of information about the original event during the retention interval. For example, in the "leading question" effect, what a subject remembers about an event previously witnessed becomes distorted by the information in the question.

Does an analogous phenomenon of malleability exist at the level of animal memory? By a not totally unreasonable stretch of the imagination, inducing amnesia for an old memory might be considered to represent a type of malleability. That is, previous learning becomes transformed or reencoded in conjunction with the new stimulus context ("information") provided by the amnestic treatment.

But since around the turn of the century, when T. Ribot (1883) formulated his "law of regression" on the basis of clinical evidence from amnesic victims, it has been suspected that old memories are less vulnerable to amnesia than new information. Moreover, laboratory studies of experimentally induced retrograde amnesia (RA) in animals have confirmed the time-dependent nature of memory (McGaugh, 1966) and have demonstrated that the severity of memory loss diminishes as the interval between training and amnesic treatment lengthens (Gibbs & Mark, 1973; Glickman, 1961).

Although these findings would appear to preclude the possibility of RA for old memory, several reports have suggested that under certain conditions Ribot's principle can be violated (Misanin, Miller, & Lewis, 1968; Robbins & Meyer, 1970; Schneider & Sherman, 1968). Essentially, these studies indicate that if the cues or motivational conditions associated with original learning are experienced shortly prior to amnestic treatment, memory loss can be induced for episodes that occurred 24 hr (or more) earlier, an interval far exceeding the usual limits of the temporal gradient for retrograde amnesia. Because of the theoretical significance of such findings, and the fact that there were also reports indicating a failure to obtain this effect (Banker, Hunt, & Pagano, 1969; Dawson & McGaugh, 1969; Gold & King, 1972), Dr. Charles Mactutus, then a graduate student in our laboratory, began a project to examine amnesia for old memory.

Amnesia for Old (Reactivated) Memory

In the initial study (Mactutus, Riccio, & Ferek, 1979), rats received one trial step-through punishment training, followed 24 hr later by a brief reactivation episode. Reactivation consisted of a 30 sec extinction exposure to the compartment previously associated with shock. Half of these animals received no further treatment, while the other half were subjected to deep body cooling (21°C colonic temperature), an amnestic treatment that has received extensive examination in our laboratory (Hinderliter, Webster, & Riccio, 1975; Jensen & Riccio, 1970; Riccio, Hodges, & Randall, 1968). A third group was trained and received cooling 24 hr later without the reactivation episode, while a fourth received training only. When subjects were tested for passive avoidance of the shock compartment 48 hr after their initial training, the reactivation/hypothermia group displayed significantly shorter latencies than any of the comparison conditions. Thus, these data confirmed and extended previous observations of RA for old memory. Neither the reactivation per se, nor the hypothermia without prior cue exposure, were sufficient to substantially alter memory.

Was the memory loss attributable specifically to deep body cooling rather than to general stress effects? We believed so, as moderate reductions in body temperature, or immersion in normothermic temperatures, do not result in RA following new learning (Riccio et al., 1968). To verify this point, subjects in a second experiment were cooled until body temperatures reached either 30°C (mild) or 21°C (deep) after a reactivation exposure. The interesting but unexpected result was that the mild treatment also produced RA for reactivated information. To determine if the mild treatment was functionally more severe than intended, we carried out a third experiment in which the effects of the two levels of hypothermia treatment on new and old (reactivated) learning were compared directly. The results, shown in Fig. 10.1, confirmed the interaction of cooling condition with the age of memory. Reducing body temperature by only 7–8°C was as effective as more severe cooling in producing amnesia, but only for old reactivated memory. As Fig. 10.1 also illustrates, in the absence of reactivation there is no detectable impairment of memory with either level of hypothermia. Thus, once reactivated, a previously established memory may be more susceptible to disruption than new memory (Mactutus et al., 1979). This outcome seemed particularly intriguing because it implied that important differences, as well as similarities, might exist in the modifiability of memories of different ages and it stimulated us to compare old and new information with respect to several characteristic features of RA (cf. Gordon, 1977a).

An initial step in comparing amnesia for old and new learning was to measure persistence of the induced memory loss. Subjects that had already displayed amnesia were retested 3 or 5 days later. Repeated testing introduces the potential of confounding effects from the earlier test, but these effects should be present

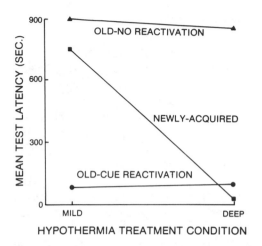

FIG. 10.1.   Mean cross-through latency in passive avoidance test for subjects receiving mild (30.0°C) or deep (21.0°) cooling after initial acquisition or reactivation treatment (from Mactutus, Riccio, & Ferek, 1979).

for all groups (Herz & Peeke, 1968; Riccio & Stikes, 1969). Thus, although the data cannot be taken as an absolute measure of "spontaneous" recovery, they can provide useful information. For the new learning groups, RA was stable over time, a finding consistent with several previous observations (Mactutus & Riccio, 1978; Riccio & Stikes, 1969). However, subjects in the reactivated memory condition showed a significant improvement in retention at retesting, and this recovery was independent of the severity of hypothermia (Mactutus et al., 1979). Although this outcome could reflect differences in severity of RA between new and old memories, the similarity in their performance on the initial test for RA makes this explanation less likely. The finding suggests a further distinction between the characteristics of RA for old and new information.

Time-Dependent Characteristics of Reactivated Memory

Once an old memory is reactivated, how long does it remain vulnerable to modification? Gordon has carried out an important series of studies examining several features of the temporal course of reactivated memories (Gordon, 1977a, 1977b; Gordon & Feldman, 1978; Gordon & Spear, 1973), but little information was available on the specific question of the temporal gradient of amnesia for old memory. Accordingly, as part of his dissertation, Mactutus (1979) varied the delay between either training or reactivation and the initiation of hypothermia treatment. (In this and subsequent studies, the condition with mild cooling after new learning was omitted, inasmuch as we had again shown that this treatment does not produce detectable RA.) All subjects were tested 24 hr after amnestic treatment. The major outcome is illustrated in Fig. 10.2. It is clear that there is a declining time course of sensitivity to amnestic insult in reactivated as well as new memories. Moreover, the time-dependent characteristic of reactivated memory was not radically different from that following original learning; save

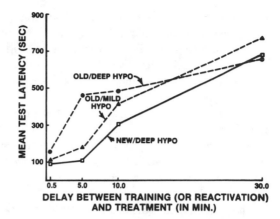

FIG. 10.2. Mean cross-through latency as a function of the delay between hypothermia treatment and either training (new memory) or reactivation (old memory).

for what may be an anomalous point in the old memory group subjected to deep hypothermia, the three gradients are quite comparable. In retrospect, more fine-grained sampling of the delay interval between .5 and 10.0 min would have been desirable. It is possible that the rather severe amnesia obtained in the old memory/mild hypo condition represents the anomalous point, but even if this were the case, the differences in temporal gradients would not be striking. Although the duration of vulnerability may differ with parameter values, the present results seem generally congruent with reactivation data from other memory paradigms in showing that differences in temporal gradients are slight.

Modifiability of memory of different ages might also be examined with respect to another characteristic of RA, the delayed onset of retention loss. A number of studies have shown that memory deficits do not occur immediately following amnestic treatment, but require a period of time to develop (Geller & Jarvik, 1968; Hinderliter, et al., 1975; McGaugh & Landfield, 1970; Miller & Springer, 1971). Although further parametric analysis is needed, we assessed the degree of memory loss in new and reactivated memories 4 hr after amnestic treatment. The reactivated groups, whether given mild or deep cooling, showed a significant memory impairment at this interval, whereas the new learning/deep hypo group did not. As a further point of reference, under relatively comparable conditions RA for new learning is not apparent until 12 to 16 hr after treatment (Mactutus & Riccio, 1978). Thus, the very rapid onset of amnesia for reactivated memory provides another instance where old information is in some ways more vulnerable to disruption.

Reversal of Amnesia for Old Memory

The fact that recovery from amnesia can be induced by procedures not involving retraining provides another characteristic on which new and old memories could be compared (Hinderliter, et al., 1975; Miller & Springer, 1972, 1973;

Thompson & Neely, 1970). It seemed possible to us that the memory failure for reactivated learning might reflect quite different processes than those involved in RA. If this were the case, then manipulations that lead to recovery from RA would be unlikely to have similar effects on the hypothermia-induced retention deficits of reactivated memory. To test this notion, we carried out an experiment using the general paradigm described earlier, except that one half of each group was reexposed to the amnestic treatment prior to testing. Previous work had demonstrated that hypothermia-induced RA can be reversed when subjects are recooled and tested at body temperatures around 30°C (Mactutus & Riccio, 1978). The increase in test latencies is not attributable to motor impairment but appears to be based on increased availability of cues for memory retrieval (Hinderliter, et al., 1975).

The present data indicated substantial reversal of the amnesia in all groups; moreover, no differences in recovery related to the age of the memory were obtained. These findings are in keeping with a retrieval-oriented explanation of the amnesia, which postulates that the hypothermia treatment serves as an encoding or contextual stimulus associated with posttrial processing of information (Hinderliter, et al., 1975; Riccio, Mactutus, Hinderliter, & McCutcheon, 1979). Reinstatement of cooling cues at testing would permit access to the target information linked to those cues. Furthermore, the reversal of amnesia for old memory indicates an important commonality with amnesia for new learning. Perhaps more interestingly, this outcome makes it highly unlikely that retroactive interference is the basis for "amnesia" for reactivated memory. The unexpected effectiveness of mild cooling in producing RA for old memory had raised our suspicions that reactivation simply might be making information unusually vulnerable to nonspecific types of interference. Cooling after reactivation could be tantamount to training on a second competing task, although retroactive interference effects, unlike amnesia, are not usually considered to be strongly influenced by the time between the original training and the subsequent interfering event (Newton & Wickens, 1956). In any event, the induced recovery of the original conditioning indicates that the memory decrement cannot easily be explained in terms of an interference model, since exposure to the interpolated event ("task B") prior to testing should not improve retention of the target episode ("task A").

These experiments are consistent with other reports demonstrating that amnesia can be obtained long after "consolidation" has presumably ceased. Also, they provide support for the proposition that the state of activity of memory, rather than age of the habit per se, is an important determinant of the susceptibility to amnesia (Howard, Glendenning, & Meyer, 1974; Lewis, 1979; Robbins & Meyer, 1970). (Although the necessary components of the cue exposure used to reactivate old memory remain to be determined, Wagner's (1976) concept of "retrieval generated priming" may be pertinent.)

With respect to malleability, the data suggest that in some respects old memories can be transformed more readily than new ones. We think this conclu-

sion is consistent with the intriguing Robbins–Meyer phenomenon: Electroconvulsive shock (ECS) after a third discrimination task suppresses memory for a
habit acquired earlier under the same motivational conditions while not impairing
retention of the task that immediately preceded ECS (Robbins & Meyer, 1970).
Furthermore, allowing the third habit to become "old reactivated memory" by
introducing a delay after training and presenting a warm-up trial prior to ECS
does produce amnesia for the final task (Howard et al., 1974). That amnesia for
old memory can be reversed leads us to believe that the "priming" results in
renewed processing that persists for a brief period and, like processing of new
learning, becomes associated with the internal context produced by the amnestic
agent. If this analysis is generally correct, then it is probably more accurate to
characterize the malleability involved in amnesia as related to alterations in
retrieval mechanisms, rather than to a modification in the nature or composition
of the target memory. A particularly compelling analog to studies of distortion of
human memory would be provided if the nature or characteristics of the target
episode could be altered. Currently, Mary Jamis, an NSF Undergraduate Research Participant working in our laboratory, is using a variant of a counterconditioning paradigm to investigate whether the emotional quality of an old memory
can be changed.

Future Directions

Among the aspects of amnesia for reactivated memories that deserve further
exploration, two areas are of particular interest to us. First, what components or
attributes are sufficient to activate old memory such that RA can be induced? We
are currently attempting to determine the influence of changes in explicit training
stimuli and the role of implicit contextual cues, both external and internal, as
reactivators of old memory. For example, Richardson and the authors have
begun to investigate the possibility that an exteroceptive background or contextual cue (e.g., tone) present at training would be adequate by itself to activate the
memory at a later time. In brief, we are asking if contextual stimuli in the
absence of the original conditioned stimuli can provide sufficient attributes to
arouse memory. The other side of the issue is whether the internal context
elicited during fear conditioning can reactivate target memory. Will administration of a stress-related hormone such as ACTH in a neutral environment prior to
hypothermia treatment permit induction of RA? Are internal cues per se capable
of priming the target memory?[1]

A second issue might be posed as follows: If old memory can be reactivated,
can a new memory be deactivated? A state of deactivation would imply that the

---

[1]Since this chapter was written, a report (Gold & Reigel, 1980) has appeared indicating that
injection of epinephrine shortly prior to an amnestic treatment extends the temporal gradient for RA
from minutes to days. We think this result is consistent with our notion that interoceptive cues can
reactivate memory.

memory is no longer vulnerable, so one approach is to introduce postacquisition manipulations that might halt processing and thereby reduce the duration of susceptibility to RA. Wagner, Rudy, and Whitlow (1973) have shown that Pavlovian conditioning is impaired when trials are followed by a surprising event, such as a CS+ which is no longer followed by a UCS. If this finding indicates a limited processing capacity, then it might be reasonable to expect other behaviorally surprising events to deactivate processing. Although the unexpected event itself might impair retention, it could also result in protection from amnesia for whatever learning is established. In an attempt to employ an undisputed and potent distractor event, we have exposed rats to a brief but realistically life threatening situation (LTS) after a punishment training trial. In the LTS the rat is forcibly submerged in water for about 45 sec, and while there are no apparent untoward long-term consequences of this treatment, we think the vigorous attempts to escape permit the inference that the rat is attending to its present predicament. Thus, it is of some interest that in three different experiments, Richardson and Riccio have failed to find any convincing evidence that the LTS after training either produces amnesia, or that it deactivates memory sufficiently to reduce hypothermia-induced amnesia.

HORMONAL REDINTEGRATION OF MEMORY

Recently, increased attention has been given to the role of hormones in influencing behavioral processes such as memory and learning. Stress-related hormones have been of special concern, particularly with respect to their UCS-like characteristics. For example, marked changes in the retention of a passive avoidance response have been produced by administration of epinephrine (Gold & Van Buskirk, 1975) or ACTH (Gold & Van Buskirk, 1976) following a single training trial. Administration of these hormones also has been demonstrated to induce recovery of memory in several paradigms. Klein (1972) has shown that the deficit in performance at intermediate retention intervals after active avoidance training can be eliminated by administration of ACTH. This attenuation of the "Kamin effect" appears to be based on improved retention rather than motivational changes. Presumably ACTH administration provides some of the contextual cues necessary for retrieval. A similar interpretation has been proposed to account for the finding that exogenous ACTH prior to testing can reverse the retrograde amnesia produced by a number of different agents (see Riccio & Concannon, in press).

A different but related issue is whether new learning can be formed on the basis of hormonal mediation alone. Can appropriate hormonal states reactivate a representation of prior trauma that would lead to new associative connections? That is, would induction of the internal context previously associated with aversive stimulation be sufficient to establish fear to neutral environmental cues? Our question is clearly influenced by James' view that the "feeling of bodily changes is the emotion" (James, 1890), although our study should not be construed as a "test" of his theory of emotion.

Indirect evidence that bodily changes modulate fear is suggested in an interesting experiment by Anderson, Crowell, Koehn, and Lupo (1976). Decreased activity in an open field test was found in rats that a week earlier had received footshocks in a very different apparatus. As stimulus generalization of fear between the two situations was highly unlikely, the authors proposed that the novelty of the open field elicited an emotional response and that, for previously shocked animals, this emotional response to novelty included internal cues associated with prior shock, resulting in an augmentation of the mild fear state.

Transfer of Learning Based on Hormonal Mediation

But could hormones mediate acquisition of new learning as well as amplify an elicited response? In collaboration with James Concannon, then a postdoctoral fellow, we initiated several studies to explore this topic (Concannon, Riccio & McKelvey, 1980). The basic experimental design consisted of three phases, each separated by 24 hours: (1) initial noncontingent footshock (NCFS) experience; (2) hormone injection in conjunction with exposure to distinctive environmental stimuli; and (3) a spatial avoidance test to assess fear acquired to the environmental stimuli present in Phase 2.

In the initial experiment, four groups of rats that had received three brief noncontingent footshocks on each of 2 days were given either saline or epinephrine (0.01, 0.05, or 0.10 mg/kg) 20 min prior to exposure to the black compartment of a black–white shuttle box. When tested the following day, subjects showed an elevation of cross-through latencies that increased with dose levels, as seen in Fig. 10.3. The finding could not be based simply on stimulus generalization from the NCFS treatments, as the saline group had the same sequence of shock and cue exposure.

FIG. 10.3. Mean latency to enter black compartment as a function of epinephrine dose. Animals had received noncontingent shocks and exposure to the black compartment in conjunction with the hormone injection. Controls for any inherent aversiveness of epinephrine (Place-Aversion) and for sensitization (Sens) effects are also represented (from Concannon, Riccio, & McKelvey, 1980).

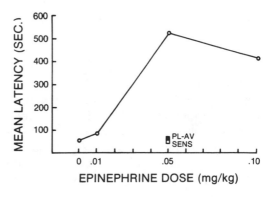

To determine whether epinephrine injection resulted in an aversive state even without prior shock (place aversion), or if the effect of NCFS and epinephrine was independent of exposure to the particular cues (sensitization), two additional control groups were run. Epinephrine and cue exposure were given to one group that lacked the NCFS treatment, while another received the NCFS but was exposed to an irrelevant pine box apparatus following epinephrine injection. Test latencies in both of these groups were very comparable to the saline controls. Thus, the aversiveness of the situational cues in the experimental condition seemed attributable to the specific experimental sequence. This outcome was consistent with the idea that a hormonally induced internal state can mediate an association between prior shock and contemporary cues. However, the animals in the initial experiment had served previously as subjects in an unrelated but stressful study. Although this experience was constant for all subjects and thus should not yield differential outcomes, a replication was undertaken using experimentally naive rats. Groups received NCFS and either epinephrine (0.05 mg/kg) or saline at the time of cue exposure. Two additional groups that did not receive NCFS were given epinephrine followed by exposure to the black compartment or exposure to an irrelevant apparatus. Again, rats with prior shock experience in the NCFS apparatus and later exposed to the situational cues after administration of epinephrine showed more avoidance (fear) than did the other three groups. It should be emphasized that in these experiments epinephrine injections were given only during the "pairing" phase, and not at testing.

A third experiment examined the possibility that elevated cross-through latencies in the experimental condition were based on impaired extinction rather than new learning. That is, if exogenous epinephrine hinders extinction of generalized fear during exposure to the black compartment, or if removal of the hormone reduces the transfer of such extinction, then these effects, rather than new learning, could account for avoidance of the test cues. Accordingly, this experiment included groups that, in lieu of exposure to the conditional stimuli after epinephrine injection, were placed in environments different from that used in testing. Inasmuch as the results indicated an aversion to the test cues only in the experimental animals, we concluded that neither sensitization nor differential extinction were responsible for the increased fear.

Memory Redintegration

Transfer of the noxious effects of prior aversive experience to new cues through administration of epinephrine may represent a type of "redintegration," to borrow a term from James (1890). By redintegration James meant that a portion of the original stimulus situation could activate a memory of the entire episode. In the present case, administration of the hormone may result in redintegration of an unpleasant episode, and subjects then "attribute" this noxious condition to stimuli in their environment. That stress-related hormones can reestablish a previously acquired fear response is suggested also by other types of experiments. For example, developmental retention loss ("infantile amnesia") can be attenuated by reinstatements in which Pavlovian fear cues are "re-paired" with epinephrine or ACTH during the retention interval (Haroutunian & Riccio, 1977, 1979; Riccio & Haroutunian, 1979). Retrograde amnesia can be reversed by administration of ACTH to subjects shortly prior to testing (Rigter & van Riezen, 1975) and the persistence of memory recovery, which usually lasts several hours after injection, can be extended to several days by combining the hormone administration with exposure to the conditioning cues (Mactutus, Smith, & Riccio, 1980).

The effect of epinephrine in this redintegration paradigm appears analogous in some respects to the recovery of memory produced by noncontingent footshock. Administration of noncontingent footshock prior to testing has been found to alleviate performance deficits based on such diverse sources as retrograde amnesia (Miller & Springer, 1972), maturation (Riccio & Haroutunian, 1979; Spear & Parsons, 1976), or extinction (Rescorla & Heth, 1975), presumably because this manipulation reinstates attributes of the target memory (Spear, 1978) or activates a representation of the original UCS (Rescorla & Heth, 1975). Similarly, administration of epinephrine results in an internal milieux previously produced by distress. We assume that this form of aversive "UCR," or the reactivation of a memorial representation of the UCS (in this case, noncontingent footshock), can then become linked with environmental cues. Conversely, hormone-induced changes without prior traumatic insult should be ineffective, as was the case. The sequence of events in redintegration also can be described in terms of the paradigm of Pavlovian higher-order conditioning. Endogenous hormones released during the initial noncontingent shock become an internal cue (CS_1) by virtue of their pairing with subsequent shock. Later exogenous administration of the hormone (CS_1) then elicits fear in the presence of new environmental cues, resulting in transfer of the response to these stimuli (CS_2). The unusual feature is that a hormonal condition provides the putative CS_1.

Several caveats about the redintegration effect should be noted, however. For example, the strength of the acquired aversion was weaker in the two experiments using naive rats, which suggests that a series of traumatic experiences may be more effective than a single episode of several noncontingent shocks. Also, the generality of the effect in terms of other learning situations clearly needs to be established. Perhaps the most fundamental issue is whether the redintegration of fear is indeed an associative process that is independent of exteroceptive (generalized) stimuli. Although we were able to show that the outcome is not a direct effect of stimulus generalization from features of the environment (e.g., grids, odors, etc.) where NCFS is given, it is difficult to rule out with certainty a contribution from exteroceptive cues. Reberg (1972) has shown that fear conditioned to contextual cues in an operant chamber may fail to suppress bar pressing but may be detected using a summation procedure. It remains possible that a modicum of generalized fear elicited during the transfer phase is a prerequisite for the action of epinephrine.

OVARIAN HORMONES AND MEMORY

Although research on the role of contextual cues in memory retrieval typically has focused on exteroceptive background stimuli, evidence of drug-induced state-dependent retention (Overton, 1964, 1978) demonstrates that some internal physiological conditions can also function as a retrieval context. However, in contrast with the burgeoning literature on drugs, relatively little attention has been paid to whether naturally occurring internal states also serve as contextual cues. An early report suggested that circadian rhythms influence memory (Stroebel, 1967); more extensive work by Holloway and Wansley (1973) has demonstrated waxing and waning of retention depending on the similarity of phases of circadian rhythms at training and testing. And in a recent study using human subjects, Bower, Monteiro, and Gilligan (1978) found that under certain conditions hypnotically induced mood states affected retention of verbal materials in a manner akin to state-dependent retention.

Endogenous Ovarian States and Memory

These findings raise the question of whether other types of endogenous stimuli can modulate retention. The hormonally related changes associated with various aspects of the female reproductive cycle represent one pervasive source of fluctuations in endogenous stimuli. These hormonal changes have been shown to affect several nonreproductive behaviors, including emotionality and mood (Anderson, 1940; Birke & Archer, 1975; Burke & Broadhurst, 1966; Paige, 1971). In addition, estrous cycles and pregnancy are often mentioned as naturally occurring sources of variation in internal contextual cues (Spear, 1978). We wondered if endogenous changes associated with these conditions might affect retention in a state-dependent manner (Ebner, Richardson, & Riccio, in press). For example, does information acquired during one stage of estrus become encoded with that internal context such that at another phase of the cycle it is more difficult to retrieve the memory?

The only directly pertinent prior research appears to be a study by Gray (1977). Although Gray found no evidence that estrous and diestrous phases influenced retention of one-way avoidance in a state-dependent manner, it remained possible that other conditions would prove more sensitive. Accordingly, proestrus and diestrus were selected as the phases of estrous cycle in an attempt to increase further the differences in hormonal states. In addition, Pavlovian conditioning was chosen as the behavioral measure, since Stroebel (1967) found a CER task to be influenced by circadian rhythms when active avoidance was unaffected.

In the first experiment, female rats received Pavlovian differential fear training in which a series of brief shocks were delivered at unpredictable intervals during exposures to the black side of a black-white compartment. During exposures to the white compartment no shocks were administered. Estrous stages were monitored through daily vaginal smears. One to two cycles after training, subjects were given a passive avoidance test while in either the same phase of the estrous cycle as at training, or in a different stage. The two same state groups were both trained and tested in either estrus or proestrus. Four mismatched conditions were established by training and testing in different stages of estrus (E), proestrus (P), or diestrus (D) (i.e., groups E-D, D-E, P-D, and D-P). The E-P and P-E groups were omitted in the design of this experiment because hormonal changes between these stages are relatively slight compared to the hormonal changes between the other phases of the cycle. The results indicated that there was substantial retention of fear; more importantly, retention scores were comparable in all groups. Consistent with Gray's (1977) study, then, there was no indication of a state-dependent effect on memory related to estrous cycle (Ebner, Estill, Page, & Riccio, 1980).

Despite the lack of evidence that estrous cycles serve as contextual cues, it seemed possible that the marked changes in ovarian levels and other internal stimuli during pregnancy in the rat might be more salient contextual cues. A second experiment used a state-dependent model to examine the effect of stage of gestation upon retention of Pavlovian fear conditioning. Two same-state groups received training and testing during days 14–19 of pregnancy, when hormonal levels are relatively constant (Yoshinaga, Hawkins, & Stocker, 1969). Two mismatched groups were also trained between days 14–19 but were tested either on day 21 prior to parturition, when there is a dramatic shift in hormone levels, or on day 22 following parturition, when there are gross morphological changes as well. Retention test scores indicated that spatial avoidance in one of the same-state groups was significantly greater than in either mismatched group. Although these data suggested that ovarian changes during pregnancy might influence retention, it was not clear from our design whether the effect was strictly upon memory. An inherent difficulty in the use of endogenous reproductive states as an independent variable in memory research is that these conditions also may produce differences in acquisition, or performance at testing, which could artifactually influence measurement of retention. One or the other of these confounds can be eliminated, but at the cost of introducing differences in the retention interval. Thus, we attempted to replicate the finding with the addition of controls for slight differences in retention interval and for possible changes in performance unrelated to memory effects. As it turned out, the added control conditions were unnecessary—the original finding disappeared. As the more elaborate study revealed no evidence that stages of gestation modulate retention, it appears that the previous enticing result reflected performance artifacts, sampling error, or the existence of an elusive and not very robust influence of endogenous internal context on memory (Ebner, et al., 1980).

Exogenous Hormones and Memory

At this point we opted for a new strategy. Temporarily abandoning our rationale for studying endogenous changes, we decided that the advantages of greater control over experimental conditions and hormone levels made exogenous drug administration appealing. Although exogenous dosages of a hormone do not mimic either the physiological levels or the multiplicity of hormonal variations occurring during natural changes, obtaining a pharmacological state-dependent effect would point to a sufficient condition for modulating memory. Because it has been reported that exogenous progesterone injection can provide the basis for drug-discrimination learning in a T-maze escape task (Stewart, Krebs, & Kaczender, 1967), this hormone seemed an appropriate choice for investigating state-dependent retention.

Accordingly, overiectomized rats received 25-mg/kg aqueous progesterone (i.p.) at training and either progesterone or saline at testing, for the matched and mismatched hormone conditions, respectively. Another group of ovariectomized animals received saline at training and testing. (Because our initial interest was in the role of progesterone as a contextual encoding cue, we omitted the mismatch condition involving hormone administration only at testing.) All subjects were tested after a 7-day retention interval. Again, the data provided no evidence of impaired retention in the hormonal mismatch condition. Under these conditions even exogenous progesterone did not modulate memory.

The major effect of these negative results was to sensitize us to an obvious but relatively neglected question about contextual cues and memory: What are the necessary and/or sufficient conditions that permit incidental stimuli to function as a context for retrieval? Consider several specific examples: Must contextual cues be noticed or attended to by the organism, or is "contiguity" sufficient (Spear, 1973)? Are contextual cues subject to overshadowing and, if so, under what conditions? Do principles of preparedness and biological relevance apply to the role of contextual cues as they seem to apply to associations between other stimuli and reinforcement (Garcia & Koelling, 1966)? Does extensive training on a task enhance or diminish the role of contextual cues? Does latent inhibition apply to background stimuli, that is, does preexposure to stimuli (e.g., endogenous states) degrade their capacity to become retrieval cues? In short, do the variables that influence Pavlovian conditioning or discriminative learning apply also to the establishment of contextual cues?

Several of these concerns tentatively might be rejected on the grounds that stimuli associated with circadian rhythms are capable of serving as contextual cues, but the issue hardly seems settled. Because subjects in our initial experiments may have failed to "notice" their hormonal state during fear conditioning, we then focused on the possible role of attentional variables. In an attempt to increase the salience of the internal stimuli, we turned to a paradigm from stimulus generalization research.

Can Discriminative Experience Increase Attention to Context?

Honig (1969) and Thomas and his associates (Thomas, Freeman, Svinicki, Burr, & Lyons, 1970) have shown that discrimination learning along one dimension can steepen the stimulus generalization gradient obtained following single-stimulus training on a different, orthogonal continuum. If this effect of extradimensional discrimination training represents enhanced "general attention" to stimuli, as we believe Thomas (1970) has persuasively argued, then a similar approach might be used to increase attention to background cues. Although our particular concern was with hormonal states as potential cues, the strategy may provide a useful way to modify the salience of more traditional exteroceptive contextual stimuli.

The basic paradigm consisted of three phases. In the first, progesterone was employed as a discriminative cue in an operant bar press task. In the second phase, the hormone was present as an irrelevant background stimulus during Pavlovian differential fear conditioning in which one distinctive compartment was paired with shock, and another area with a shock-free period. Finally, the effect of removal of the context (mismatched condition) at testing was compared with a group not receiving discrimination training, as well as with a group for which training and testing contexts were held constant. As it turned out, progesterone administration, although sufficient to produce transient changes in locomotor ability, did not provide an effective discriminative stimulus. After 35 days of training, with drug days as S+ and saline days as S− (or the reverse for other subjects), nonreinforced probe trials failed to indicate any evidence of the acquisition of the discrimination. Substantial differences were obtained in response rates between the S+ and S− sessions, but these rates were apparently controlled by feedback from periodic delivery of food on the variable interval schedule of reinforcement associated with S+ and the absence of food on the S− component rather than internal cues (cf. Jenkins, 1965). (Incidentally, this finding does indicate that the progesterone did not impair appetitive motivation or sensitivity to reinforcement contingencies).

Assuming that some learning may have occurred that was not reflected in performance, we proceeded with fear conditioning. The test interval was shortened from 1 week to 24 hr in hopes that a shorter retention interval might further enhance any contribution of stimulus change. Under this condition, regardless of their prior discriminative history, both groups receiving progesterone during fear training and saline at testing showed poorer performance than same-state controls, an outcome in line with our original hypothesis.

The possibility that a relatively short period between the training and testing might be more sensitive in detecting the effect of a shift in background cues led us to repeat our original exogenous progesterone study using a 1-day retention interval. (The attempt to establish discriminative responding to the hormone was omitted.) Subjects received fear conditioning with progesterone or saline; half of each group was tested 24 later in the same condition, and half in the other. The findings presented in Fig. 10.4, conform to a pattern of "asymmetrical state-dependent retention." Test performance was significantly impaired in the P–S group. The S–P condition showed a slight but not reliable decrement, whereas the two same-state groups were comparable. One interpretative problem in this type of design is that subjects might fail to learn under the hormone, but obtain good scores when tested with the hormone (P–P) due to performance artifacts. In that case, the deficit in the P–S condition would not reflect *memory* failure. To check on this possibility, another group of rats that was never trained received a "test" in the progesterone state. As their performance was unaltered by the hormone, it appears the asymmetrical outcome does reflect memory processes.

These experiments offer little support for our hypothesis that ovarian hormonal states might modulate retention of learned responses, and only limited evidence that exogenous progesterone can influence memory. It could be argued that it would be biologically unadaptive if fluctuations in hormonal states impaired retention in female animals. But for humans it would seem similarly disadvantageous if mood states or incidental features of the learning environment were determinants of memory, yet "mismatches" in these attributes can markedly degrade retention test performance (Bower et al., 1978; Smith, 1979; Smith, Glenberg, & Bjork, 1978). The state-dependent-like effect of circadian cycles on

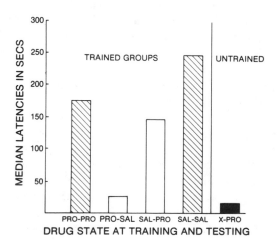

FIG. 10.4. Median passive avoidance scores using exogenous progesterone in a state-dependent retention paradigm. Testing was given 24 hr after training. The effect of the hormone per se on response latencies at testing is shown in the untrained group.

retention (Holloway & Wansley, 1973) in rats also cautions against presuming too easily how selection pressures must operate. A different, but not unrelated concern, is whether endogenous stimuli function as contextual cues in learning tasks more closely tied to biological or ecological demands. For example, would variations in endogenous ovarian states have a more clearly discernible effect on retention if learning were based on internal consequences, as in the case of conditioned taste aversion? Or would the endogenous context present be more likely to influence retention in a state-dependent manner when the learning involves primarily exposure to innocuous sensory stimuli, such as occurs with latent inhibition or sensory preconditioning paradigms? To date, these possibilities have not been tested. In conclusion, perhaps the major import of this series of experiments has been in helping to define and establish boundary conditions on the role of contextual cues.

CONTEXTUAL CUES, STIMULUS GENERALIZATION, AND THE RETENTION INTERVAL

As we have noted repeatedly, contextual cues, those stimuli present at training but irrelevant to the reinforcement contingencies, are considered to be critical sources of support for memory retrieval at testing. Perhaps this is not especially surprising in animal memory studies where context has been described as analogous to instructions for humans; without the appropriate context a nonverbal organism has no reason to perform in accordance with training. The importance of context is not limited to animals, however, as several recent studies have shown that changes in the physical features of the learning environment can markedly impair retention in humans (Smith, 1979; Smith et al., 1978).

But how well is context remembered? If the characteristics of a context are forgotten, do changes still impair retrieval? One approach to these issues is to determine whether changes in context at testing have an effect on memory that is invariant with the length of the retention interval, or whether there is differential impairment. Interestingly, in the Holloway and Wansley (1973) study on circadian rhythms, in which a number of intervals were sampled, mismatched conditions produced performance deficits except at the longest retention interval (66 hr), although this is only a single data point.

Forgetting of Stimulus Attributes

If contextual cues constitute some of the attributes of the target memory (Spear, 1978), then data on retention of characteristics of stimuli (attributes) are pertinent. Studies of this nature focus on whether responding is affected by changes in some aspect of the training situation after varying intervals. Forgetting is thus reflected rather differently than in studies of retention of a target response;

indeed, increased responding to a change in stimulus conditions is frequently the index of loss of memory about particular attributes. For example, information about memory of the UCS comes from experiments that have assessed the magnitude of contrast effects resulting from shifts in reward quality at various intervals after training. The fact that instrumental or consummatory responding is maintained following a retention interval, but that the degree of contrast declines, suggests that subjects forget the specific aspects of the reward used in training (Flaherty, Capobianco, & Hamilton, 1973; Gleitman & Steinman, 1964; Gonzalez, Fernhoff, & David, 1973; Gordon, Flaherty, & Riley, 1973).

Retention of features of the CS or discriminative stimuli has been assessed in stimulus generalization studies (See also Thomas, this volume). The basic empirical finding that generalization gradients tend to flatten with a delay between training and testing was first reported by Perkins and Weyant (1958). In their study, rats were trained to approach a food-baited goal box in a black (or white) runway. When subjects were tested immediately, a change in runway brightness produced a marked disruption in speed of running. However, the same change 1 week after acquisition had virtually no effect on responding (i.e., running speed was comparable to that obtained when tested immediately under the original training conditions [cf. Steinman, 1967]). The finding has been corroborated with pigeons in a free-operant, appetitively rewarded task (Thomas & Lopez, 1962). Moreover, Thomas has shown that the phenomenon is not limited to "single-stimulus training" situations; differential responding to test stimuli diminishes with delayed testing after discrimination learning (Thomas & Burr, 1969), although the flattening of the gradient is not obtained if components of the test procedure provide implicit reminder or reactivation treatments (Thomas, Ost, & Thomas, 1960). In a study employing human subjects, Bahrick, Clark, and Bahrick (1967) examined visual recognition performance when the target item (e.g., a picture of a cup) had to be selected from among alternatives graded in similarity. The tendency to pick (incorrectly) items increasingly different from the target strengthened as a function of the retention interval.

The finding that generalization gradients flatten over time can be interpreted as evidence of forgetting of specific attributes of the stimuli (Perkins & Weyant, 1958). Thus, the original response continues to be maintained, but more "false positives" are generated. Stimuli that are initially discriminable, as indexed by immediate test performance, become more equivalent in controlling responding. Moreover, this type of change may not be limited to studies of long-term retention. Estes (1980), addressing issues of short-term memory in humans, has pointed out the loss of "precision" about information that characterizes responding as the retention interval lengthens. Despite the vast differences in paradigms, we suspect the gradients of uncertainty presented by Estes are not unrelated to the phenomena being considered here.

Recently, we have used a slightly different technique to determine if stimulus attributes might be forgotten even when no apparent memory loss of the CR occurs (Thomas & Riccio, 1979). In that experiment, Dr. David A. Thomas took advantage of the Kamin "Blocking Effect" in which conditioning to one stimulus reduces or prevents learning to a second stimulus presented in compound with the first (Kamin, 1968). He reasoned that if some aspect of the original CS were changed during compound conditioning, blocking would not occur, as both elements would now be relatively novel. However, if forgetting of the CS attributes occurred, the same manipulation should still result in blocking of learning to the added cue. As in many blocking studies, the CER paradigm was used. This had the added advantage for our purposes of providing a conditioned response that has the reputation of being extremely resistant to forgetting (Gleitman & Holmes, 1967; Hoffman, Selekman, & Jensen, 1966). Adult rats received tone-shock pairings followed 1 or 21 days later by compound training to a tone and light. For some subjects, tone was unchanged during compound conditioning; for others a novel tone was used. All subjects were tested to the light alone to assess learning to the added element. Fig. 10.5 shows the suppression ratios on the initial test trial. As can be seen, at the short delay little fear was acquired by the light when compounded with the original CS (3000 Hz); however, this blocking did not occur when the value of the CS was altered. In contrast, the lack of suppression in all three conditions at the 21-day interval indicates that blocking to the added element now occurred to the novel as well as the original tone frequencies. This suggests that attributes of the tone (but not the CER itself) were forgotten, as in failing to acquire fear to the added element after a long delay subjects behaved as if an altered CS (novel tone) were the original CS (Thomas & Riccio, 1979).

Does a similar change in the discriminability of cues also occur with respect to contextual stimuli? The answer clearly seems to be yes. A study by McAllister and McAllister (1963) provides a particularly instructive example. Rats that had received pairings of a CS (light) with shock were tested after delays of 3 min or

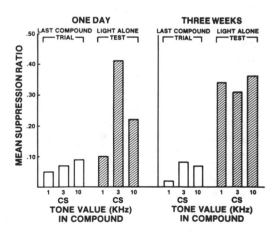

FIG. 10.5.   Mean suppression ratios for separate groups during testing to the light (added element) as a function of the CS value in the compound (shaded bars). Training to compound stimulus was given 1 or 21 days after original acquisition to the tone (3 kHz). Unshaded bars indicate suppression to the compound stimulus prior to testing.

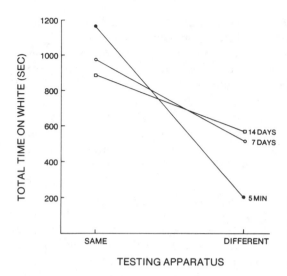

FIG. 10.6. Mean cumulative time on safe (white) side for groups tested in either the original or a different but highly similar apparatus after various retention intervals.

24 hr in either the original training apparatus or a different, but highly similar, test compartment. Although only the contextual cues were varied, this change impaired performance on the "escape from fear" test. However, the impairment occurred only at the short retention intervals; with long delays, performance was equivalent in both test situations. As has been noted, this finding indicates that "incubation" of fear could be an artifact of flattening of generalization gradients (Gabriel & Vogt, 1972; McAllister & McAllister, 1967).

This flattening of the contextual gradient, or forgetting of the differentiating features of the situations, has been found in several other studies, including a recent one conducted in our laboratory (Desiderato, Butler, & Meyer, 1966; Gabriel & Vogt, 1972; Pesselman & Riccio, 1980). In Pesselman's study, weanling rats were given differential Pavlovian fear conditioning to the dark compartment of a black–white chamber. Either 5 min, 7 days, or 14 days later, testing for fear of the black compartment was administered in either the same (original) apparatus, or a similar black–white apparatus in a different room. Fig. 10.6 illustrates the interaction of contextual stimuli (original or similar apparatus) with retention interval. Fear of black in the original apparatus was retained at a high level regardless of the test delay. Subjects tested in the similar apparatus showed much less avoidance of the black side at the immediate test than did those tested in the original chamber, an outcome that replicates an earlier finding in our lab (Rohrbaugh & Riccio, 1968). With longer delays, however, avoidance behavior became comparable to groups tested in the original box.[2] Thus, discriminably

---

[2]Ancillary data from this study (Pesselman and Riccio, 1980) indicated an interesting type of memory reactivation. Following a long delay interval, the administration of noncontingent footshock appears to steepen the contextual generalization gradient, producing performance more like that obtained shortly after training.

different contexts became more "interchangeable" over time. With respect to the retention of properties of stimuli then, an old French proverb that states "The more things change, the more they stay the same" may be quite apt.

Stimulus Change as a Source of Forgetting: A Paradox

As the aforementioned studies have indicated, one consequence of the loss of memory for stimulus attributes is that performance increases—responding comes under the control of a greater array of stimuli. The intriguing dilemma arising from these considerations of the retention of the features of stimuli probably is apparent by now. On the one hand, failure to retrieve a target memory often is attributed to subtle and implicit changes in stimulus contexts. Along with interference, alterations in stimulating conditions between training and testing were recognized by McGeoch (1942) as a major source of forgetting. McGeoch and Irion (1952) noted that although a retention test necessarily involved the same formal stimuli as acquisition, slight changes in these or incidental (contextual) background conditions were inevitable. In more recent years, the dependence of memory on correspondence between the encoding environment and retrieval conditions has been persuasively articulated by Spear (1973, 1978) and Tulving (1974), in particular.

On the other hand, research on stimulus generalization shows less disruption of responding when experimentally manipulated changes in stimuli are introduced after a delay. With increased time, different stimuli become more equivalent in controlling responding. If this is the case, how can loss of a response be attributed to small, implicit changes in context? If explicit changes in stimuli are not "recognized" after a delay, why would we expect subtle alterations in background conditions to lead to retrieval failure? Indeed, if different contexts become perceived as more similar after a period of time, retention of the target response might be expected to improve. Because forgetting is far more robust a phenomenon than reminiscence, this "prediction" is not borne out. We recognize that a flatter gradient would increase the opportunity for extinction to generalized stimuli to impair retention (cf. Berk, Vigorito, & Miller, 1979), but this retroactive interference model is quite different from the view that memory loss occurs because the retrieval environment fails to coincide with encoding conditions.

As we trust this chapter has indicated, our own research has been guided by a committment to the important role of contextual cues in retrieval. It is obvious that in a general sense the same stimulus conditions, or instructions, must be present at training and at testing. But within some broad boundary conditions, do changes in context really impair retention? Because we cannot yet offer a resolution to our paradox, we simply indicate our concern that appealing to changes in contextual stimuli as the basis for memory deficits may be unwarranted.

Perhaps there are some flaws in this analysis that have escaped our notice. At the risk of appearing defensive, we are reminded of a line from David Mamet's

(1978) fine contemporary play, *Duck Variations*. Two old men are engaging each other in a sometimes argumentative series of nonconversations, and one, after stating his case, heads off a rebuttal by declaring: "I don't want to hear it. If it's false, don't waste my time and if it's true, I don't want to know."

SUMMARY AND CONCLUSIONS

Whereas a substantial body of evidence now exists implicating retrieval deficits as sources of memory loss (Spear, 1978), a number of questions about the nature of retrieval processes deserves attention. In this chapter we have reviewed findings from four distinctive but not unrelated areas of research. These areas are linked by the broad goal of exploring variables that modulate memory. It is our belief that investigation of manipulations yielding postacquisition modifications of memory will increase understanding of the mechanisms of memory retrieval.

In the first set of studies, retrograde amnesia was employed to examine one type of malleability of memory. Evidence was presented that old learning, when reactivated by cue exposure, can become susceptible to hypothermia-induced amnestic treatment. Furthermore, differences as well as similarities in the modifiability of old (reactivated) and newly acquired information were observed. In our view, these findings support the general proposition that the state of activity of memory is a more critical determinant of vulnerability to amnesia than the age of the learned event.

Experiments on "redintegration" illustrate another approach to investigating aspects of memory retrieval. The basic question is: Can activation of the memory of a prior traumatic episode in the presence of neutral cues result in those stimuli acquiring fear-eliciting properties? Our approach assumed that epinephrine-elicited changes would provide attributes capable of activating the memory of prior traumatic experience. Rats that received noncontingent footshocks were later administered epinephrine and exposed to a novel stimulus situation (CS). Relative to a variety of control conditions, this redintegration group showed enhanced aversion to the CS on a subsequent test. The transfer of fear obtained suggests that the hormone injection produced a representation of the earlier state of distress, which then became linked with contemporary cues.

A third set of experiments explored the possibility that endogenous stimuli associated with estrous cycles or pregnancy might serve as a source of internal contextual cues for memory retrieval in a Pavlovian fear-conditioning task. However, the empirical data provided no support for our notion, an outcome consistent with several earlier reports. Some evidence that exogenous progesterone could influence retention in a state-dependent manner was obtained. These generally negative findings help to establish certain boundary conditions on the stimuli that can function as contextual cues, although it remains possible that endogenous ovarian states could influence retrieval of other types of learning.

A final section reviewed evidence on the retention of stimulus attributes. With respect to UCS or reinforcer characteristics, contrast effects produced by shifts in reward magnitude have been found to decline after a retention interval. With respect to contextual or discriminative stimuli, generalization gradients have been shown to flatten over time. These outcomes suggest that specific features of stimuli present at training are forgotten. A similar interpretation was applied to the demonstration that in the Kamin blocking paradigm the interval between Pavlovian conditioning to the element and to the compound markedly influences learning about the added stimulus. But the evidence that stimuli become more functionally equivalent in controlling responding after a retention interval also seems to pose a paradox for stimulus-change models of forgetting of a response. Disparities between encoding and retrieval context are widely acknowledged to be an important source of retention loss. However, if organisms are less able to recognize explicit changes in stimuli following a lapse of time, then how do subtle shifts in context result in retrieval failure? Like the King of Siam, we are led to conclude: "Is a puzzlement."

ACKNOWLEDGMENTS

Preparation of this chapter was supported by NIMH Grant MH30223 to the first author. The authors thank Rick Richardson for his many insightful comments and suggestions and Michelle Iannetta for her labors in translating D.C.R.'s hieroglyphics into a typed manuscript.

REFERENCES

Anderson, E. E. The sex hormones and emotional behavior. I. The effect of sexual receptivity upon timidity in the female rat. *Journal of Genetics and Psychology,* 1940, *56,* 149-158.

Anderson, D. C., Crowell, C., Koehn, D., & Lupo, J. V. Different intensities of unsignalled inescapable shock treatments as determinants of non-shock-motivated open field behavior: A resolution of disparate results. *Physiology and Behavior,* 1976, *17,* 391-394.

Bahrick, H. P., Clark, S., & Bahrick, P. Generalization gradients as indicants of learning and retention of a recognition task. *Journal of Experimental Psychology,* 1967, *75,* 464-471.

Banker, G., Hunt, E., & Pagano, R. Evidence supporting the memory disruption hypothesis of electroconvulsive shock action. *Physiology and Behavior,* 1969, *4,* 895-899.

Bartlett, S. C. *Remembering: a study in experimental and social psychology.* Cambridge, Eng.: Cambridge University Press, 1932.

Berk, A. M., Vigorito, M., & Miller, R. R. Retroactive stimulus interference with conditioned emotional response retention in infant and adult rats: Implications for infantile amnesia. *Journal of Experimental Psychology: Animal Behavior Processes,* 1979, *5,* 284-299.

Birke, L. I. A., & Archer, J. Open-field behavior of oestrous and dioestrous rats: Evidence against an "emotionality" interpretation. *Animal Behavior,* 1975, *23,* 509-512.

Bower, G. H., Monteiro, K. P., & Gilligan, S. G. Emotional mood as a context for learning and recall. *Journal of Verbal Learning and Verbal Behavior,* 1978, *17,* 573-585.

Burke, A. W., & Broadhurst, P. L. Behavioural correlates of the oestrous cycle in the rat. *Nature* (London), 1966, *209*, 223-224.

Cole, W. G., & Loftus, E. F. Incorporating new information into memory. *American Journal of Psychology*, 1979, *92*, 413-425.

Concannon, J. T., Riccio, D. C., & McKelvey, J. Pavlovian conditioning of fear based upon hormonal mediation of prior aversive experience. *Animal Learning and Behavior*, 1980, *8*, 75-80.

Dawson, R. G., & McGaugh, J. L. Electroconvulsive shock effects on a reactivated memory trace: Further examination. *Science*, 1969, *166*, 525-527.

Desiderato, O., Butler, B., & Meyer, C. Changes in fear generalization gradients as a function of delayed testing. *Journal of Experimental Psychology*, 1966, *72*, 678-682.

Ebner, D., Estill, R., Page, N., & Riccio, D. C. *Lack of evidence for endogenous ovarian hormones as contextual memory cues.* Paper presented at Eastern Psychological Association Meeting, Hartford, April 1980.

Ebner, D. L., Richardson, R., & Riccio, D. C. Ovarian hormones and retention of learned fear in rats. *Behavioral and Neural Biology*, in press.

Estes, W. K. Is human memory obsolete? *American Scientist*, 1980, *68*, 62-69.

Flaherty, C. F., Capobianco, S., & Hamilton, L. W. Effects of septal lesions on retention of negative contrast. *Physiology and Behavior*, 1973, *11*, 625-631.

Gabriel, M., & Vogt, J. Incubation of avoidance CR's in the rabbit produced by increase over time in stimulus generalization to apparatus. *Behavioral Biology*, 1972, *7*, 113-125.

Garcia, J., & Koelling, R. A. Relation of cue to consequence in avoidance learning. *Psychonomic Science*, 1966, *4*, 123-124.

Geller, A., & Jarvik, M. E. The time relations of ECS-induced amnesia. *Psychonomic Science*, 1968, *12*, 169-170.

Gibbs, M. E., & Mark, R. F. *Inhibition of memory formation.* New York: Plenum, 1973.

Gleitman, H., & Holmes, P. Retention of incompletely learned CER in Rats, *Psychonomic Science*, 1967, *7*, 19-20.

Gleitman, H., & Steinman, F. Depression effect as a function of retention interval before and after shift in reward magnitude. *Journal of Comparative and Physiological Psychology*, 1964, *57*, 158-160.

Glickman, S. E. Perseverative neural processes and consolidation of the memory trace. *Psychological Bulletin*, 1961, *58*, 218-233.

Gold, P. E., & King, R. A. Amnesia: Tests of the effect of delayed footshock-electroconvulsive shock pairings. *Physiology and Behavior*, 1972, *8*, 797-800.

Gold, P. E., & Reigel, J. A. Extended retrograde amnesia gradients: Peripheral epinephrine and frontal cortex stimulation. *Physiology and Behavior*, 1980, *24*, 1101-1106.

Gold, P. E., & Van Buskirk, R. B. Facilitation of time-dependent memory processes with post-trial epinephrine injections. *Behavioral Biology*, 1975, *13*, 145-153.

Gold, P. E., & Van Buskirk, R. B. Effects of post-trial hormone injections on memory processes. *Hormones and Behavior*, 1976, *7*, 509-517.

Gonzales, R. C., Fernhoff, D., & David, F. G. Contrast, resistance to extinction, and forgetting in rats. *Journal of Comparative and Physiological Psychology*, 1973, *84*, 562-571.

Gordon, W. C. Similarities of recently acquired and reactivated memories in interference. *American Journal of Psychology*, 1977, *90*, 242. (a)

Gordon, W. C. Susceptibility of a reactivated memory to the effects of strychnine: A time-dependent phenomenon. *Physiology and Behavior*, 1977, *18*, 95-99. (b)

Gordon, W. C., & Feldman, D. T. Reactivation-induced interference in a short-term retention paradigm. *Learning and Motivation*, 1978, *9*, 164-178.

Gordon, W. C., Flaherty, C. F., & Riley, E. P. Negative contrast as a function of the interval between preshift and postshift training. *Bulletin of the Psychonomic Society*, 1973, *1*, 25-27.

Gordon, W. C., & Spear, N. E. Effect of reactivation of a previously acquired memory on the interaction between memories in the rat. *Journal of Experimental Psychology*, 1973, *99*, 349–355.

Gray, P. Effect of the estrous cycle on conditioned avoidance in mice. *Hormones and Behavior*, 1977, *8*, 235–241.

Haroutunian, V., & Riccio, D. C. Effect of arousal conditions during reinstatement treatment upon learned fear in young rats. *Developmental Psychobiology*, 1977, *10*, 25–32.

Haroutunian, V., & Riccio, D. C. Drug-induced "arousal" and the effectiveness of CS exposure in the reinstatement of memory. *Behavioral and Neural Biology*, 1979, *26*, 115–120.

Herz, M. J., & Peeke, H. V. S. ECS-produced retrograde amnesia: Permanence vs. recovery over repeated testing. *Physiology and Behavior*, 1968, *3*, 517–521.

Hinderliter, C. F., Webster, T., & Riccio, D. C. Amnesia induced by hypothermia as a function of treatment-test interval and recooling in rats. *Animal Learning & Behavior*, 1975, *3*, 257–263.

Hoffman, H. S., Selekman, W., & Jensen, P. Stimulus aspects of aversive controls: Long-term effects of conditioned suppression procedures. *Journal of the Experimental Analysis of Behavior*, 1966, *9*, 659–662.

Holloway, F. A., & Wansley, R. A. Multiple retention deficits at periodic intervals after passive avoidance learning. *Science*, 1973, *80*, 208–210.

Honig, W. K. Attentional factors governing the slope of the generalization gradient. In R. M. Gilbert & N. S. Sutherland (Eds.), *Animal discrimination learning*. London: Academic Press, 1969.

Howard, R. L., Glendenning, R. L., & Meyer, D. R. Motivational control of retrograde amnesia: Further explorations and effects. *Journal of Comparative and Physiological Psychology*, 1974, *86*, 187–192.

James, W. *The principles of psychology*. New York: Holt, 1890.

Jenkins, H. M. Measurement of stimulus control during discriminative operant conditioning. *Psychological Bulletin*, 1965, *64*, 365–376.

Jensen, R. A., & Riccio, D. C. Effects of prior experience upon retrograde amnesia produced by hypothermia. *Physiology & Behavior*, 1970, *5*, 1291–1294.

Kamin, L. J. "Attention-like" processes in classical conditioning. In M. R. Jones (Ed.), *Miami Symposium on the Prediction of Behavior: Aversive stimulation*. Miami: University of Miami Press, 1968.

Klein, S. B. Adrenal-pituitary influence in reactivation of avoidance-learning memory in the rat after intermediate intervals. *Journal of Comparative and Physiological Psychology*, 1972, *79*, 341–359.

Lewis, D. J. Psychobiology of active and inactive memory. *Psychological Bulletin*, 1979, *86*, 1054–1083.

Loftus, E. F. The malleability of human memory. *American Scientist*, 1979, *67*, 312–320.

Loftus, E. F., & Zanni, G. Eyewitness testimony: The influence of the wording of a question. *Bulletin of the Psychonomic Society*, 1975, *5*, 86–88.

Mactutus, C. F. *Retrograde amnesia for old (reactivated) memories: An examination of some anomalous characteristics*. Unpublished doctoral dissertation, Kent State University, 1979.

Mactutus, C. F., & Riccio, D. C. Hypothermia-induced retrograde amnesia: Role of body temperature in memory retrieval. *Physiological Psychology*, 1978, *6*, 18–22.

Mactutus, C. F., Riccio, D. C., & Ferek, J. M. Retrograde amnesia for old (reactivated) memory: Some anomalous characteristics. *Science*, 1979, *204*, 1319–1320.

Mactutus, C. F., Smith, R. L., & Riccio, D. C. Extending the duration of ACTH-induced memory reactivation in an amnestic paradigm. *Physiology and Behavior*, 1980, *24*, 541–546.

Mamet, D. *Sexual perversity in Chicago and the duck variations*. New York: Grove Press, 1978.

McAllister, W. R., & McAllister, D. E. Increase over time in the stimulus generalization of acquired fear. *Journal of Experimental Psychology*, 1963, *65*, 576–582.

McAllister, D. E., & McAllister, W. R. Incubation of fear: An examination of the concept. *Journal of Experimental Research in Personality*, 1967, *2*, 180-190.

McGaugh, J. L. Time-dependent processes in memory storage. *Science*, 1966, *153*, 1351-1358.

McGaugh, J. L., & Landfield, P. W. Delayed development of amnesia following electroconvulsive shock. *Physiology and Behavior*, 1970, *5*, 1109-1113.

McGeoch, J. A. *The psychology of human learning: An introduction*. New York: Longmans, Green & Company, 1942.

McGeoch, J. A., & Irion, A. L. *The psychology of human learning*. New York: Longmans, Green & Company, 1952.

Miller, R. R., & Springer, A. D. Temporal course of amnesia in rats after electroconvulsive shock. *Physiology and Behavior*, 1971, *6*, 229-233.

Miller, R. R., & Springer, A. D. Induced recovery of memory in rats following electroconvulsive shock. *Physiology and Behavior*, 1972, *8*, 645-651.

Miller, R. R., & Springer, A. D. Amnesia, consolidation and retrieval. *Psychological Review*, 1973, *80*, 69-79.

Misanin, J. R., Miller, R. R., & Lewis, D. J. Retrograde amnesia produced by electroconvulsive shock after reactivation of a consolidated memory trace. *Science*, 1968, *160*, 554-555.

Newton, J. M., & Wickens, D. D. Retroactive inhibition as a function of the temporal position of interpolated learning. *Journal of Experimental Psychology*, 1956, *51*, 149-154.

Overton, D. State-dependent or "dissociated" learning produced with pentobarbital. *Journal of Comparative and Physiological Psychology*, 1964, *57*, 3-12.

Overton, D. A. Major theories of state-dependent learning. In B. Ho, D. Chute, & D. Richards (Eds.), *Drug discrimination and state-dependent learning*. New York: Academic Press, 1978.

Paige, K. E. Effects of oral contraceptives on affective fluctuations associated with the menstrual cycle. *Psychosomatic Medicine*, 1971, *33*, 515-537.

Perkins, C. C., Jr., & Weyant, R. G. The interval between training and test trials as determiner of the slope of generalization gradients. *Journal of Comparative Physiological Psychology*, 1958, *51*, 596-600.

Pesselman, M. L., & Riccio, D. C. *Forgetting of stimulus attributes of a fear stimulus*. Paper presented at Eastern Psychological Association Meeting, Hartford, April, 1980.

Reberg, D. Compound tests for excitation in early acquisition and after prolonged extinction of conditioned suppression. *Learning and Motivation*, 1972, *3*, 246-258.

Rescorla, R. A., & Heth, C. D. Reinstatement of fear to an extinguished conditioned stimulus. *Journal of Experimental Psychology: Animal Behavior Processes*, 1975, *104*, 88-96.

Ribot, T. A. *The diseases of memory* (J. Fitzgerald, trans.), New York: Humboldt Library, No. 46, 1883.

Riccio, D. C., & Concannon, J. T. ACTH and the reminder phenomena. In J. Martinez, R. A. Jensen, R. B. Messing, H. Rigter, & J. L. McGaugh (Eds.), *Endogenous peptides and learning and memory processes*. Academic Press, in press.

Riccio, D. C., & Haroutunian, V. Some approaches to the alleviation of ontogenetic memory loss. In B. A. Campbell & N. E. Spear (Eds.), *Ontogeny of learning and memory*. Hillsdale, N.J.: Lawrence Erlbaum Associates, 1979.

Riccio, D. C., Hodges, L. A., & Randall, P. K. Retrograde amnesia produced by hypothermia in rats. *Journal of Comparative and Physiological Psychology*, 1968, *66*, 618-622.

Riccio, D. C., Mactutus, C. F., Hinderliter, C. F., & McCutcheon, K. Severity of amnesia and the effectiveness of reactivation treatment: Evidence for a retrieval process. *Physiological Psychology*, 1979, *7*, 59-63.

Riccio, D. C., & Stikes, E. R. Persistent but modifiable retrograde amnesia produced by hypothermia. *Physiology and Behavior*, 1969, *4*, 649-652.

Rigter, H., & Van Riezen, H. Anti-amnesic effect of $ACTH_{4-10}$: Its independence of the nature of the amnesic agent and the behavioral test. *Physiology and Behavior*, 1975, *14*, 563-566.

Robbins, M. J., & Meyer, D. R. Motivational control of retrograde amnesia. *Journal of Experimental Psychology*, 1970, *84*, 220-225.

Rohrbaugh, M., & Riccio, D. C. Stimulus generalization of learned fear in infant and adult rats. *Journal of Comparative and Physiological Psychology*, 1968, *66*, 530-533.

Schneider, A. M., & Sherman, W. Amnesia: A function of the temporal relation of footshock to electroconvulsive shock. *Science*, 1968, *159*, 219-221.

Smith, S. M. Remembering in and out of context. *Journal of Experimental Psychology: Human Learning and Memory*, 1979, *5*, 460-471.

Smith, S. M., Glenberg, A., & Bjork, R. A. Environmental context & human memory. *Memory & Cognition*, 1978, *6*, 342-353.

Spear, N. E. Retrieval of memory in animals. *Psychological Review*, 1973, *80*, 163-194.

Spear, N. E. *The processing of memories: Forgetting and retention.* Hillsdale, N.J.: Lawrence Erlbaum Associates, 1978.

Spear, N. E., & Parsons, P. Analysis of a reactivation treatment: Ontogeny and alleviated forgetting. In D. Medin, R. Davis, & W. Roberts (Eds.), *Coding processes in animal memory.* Hillsdale, N.J.: Lawrence Erlbaum Associates, 1976.

Steinman, F. Retention of alley brightness in the rat. *Journal of Comparative and Physiological Psychology*, 1967, *64*, 105-109.

Stewart, J., Krebs, W. H., & Kaczender, E. State-dependent learning produced with steroids. *Nature*, 1967, *216*, 1223-1224.

Stroebel, C. F. Behavioral aspects of circadian rhythms. In J. Zubin and H. F. Hunt (Eds.), *Comparative psychopathology,* New York: Grune & Stratton, 1967.

Thomas, D. A., & Riccio, D. C. Forgetting of a CS attribute in a conditioned suppression paradigm. *Animal Learning and Behavior*, 1979, *7*, 191-195.

Thomas, D. R. Stimulus selection, attention and related matters. In J. H. Reynierse (Ed.), *Current issues in animal learning.* Lincoln: University of Nebraska Press, 1970.

Thomas, D. R., & Burr, D. E. S. Stimulus generalization as a function of the delay between training and testing procedures: A reevaluation. *Journal of the Experimental Analysis of Behavior*, 1969, *12*, 105-109.

Thomas, D. R., Freeman, F., Svinicki, J. G., Burr, D. E. S., & Lyons, J. The effects of extra-dimensional training on stimulus generalization. *Journal of Experimental Psychology*, 1970, *83*, 1-21.

Thomas, D. R., & Lopez, L. J. The effects of delayed testing on generalization slope. *Journal of Comparative and Physiological Psychology*, 1962, *55*, 541-544.

Thomas, D. R., Ost, J., & Thomas, D. Stimulus generalization as a function of the time between training and testing procedures. *Journal of the Experimental Analysis of Behavior*, 1960, *3*, 4-14.

Thompson, C. I., & Neely, J. E. Dissociated learning in rats produced by electroconvulsive shock. *Physiology and Behavior*, 1970, *5*, 783-786.

Tulving, E. Cue-dependent forgetting. *American Scientist*, 1974, *62*, 74-82.

Wagner, A. R. Priming in STM: An information-processing mechanism for self-generated or retrieval-generated depression in performance. In T. J. Tighe & R. N. Leaton (Eds.), *Habituation: Perspectives from child development, animal behavior and neurophysiology.* Hillsdale, N.J.: Lawrence Erlbaum Associates, 1976.

Wagner, A. R., Rudy, J. W., & Whitlow, J. W., Jr. Rehearsal in animal conditioning. *Journal of Experimental Psychology Monograph*, 1973, *97*, 407-426.

Yoshinaga, K., Hawkins, R. A., & Stocker, J. F. Estrogen secretion by the rat ovary in vivo during the estrus cycle and pregnancy. *Endocrinology*, 1969, *85*, 103.

11 Mechanisms of Cue-Induced Retention Enhancement

William C. Gordon
University of New Mexico

For some time now, we have been interested in treatments that modulate retention performance in animals. In essence it has been our view that if we can determine the mechanisms by which such treatments either increase or decrease performance, we will better understand the conditions necessary for the successful retrieval of information and, conversely, the conditions that promote forgetting. The present chapter concerns an analysis of one such treatment, pretest cuing, that often improves retention performance dramatically. The data and discussion focus on the question of what mechanisms mediate cue-induced retention enhancement.

THE CUING PHENOMENON

In recent years it has become well established that a variety of retention deficits in animals can be alleviated by pretest cuing treatments (Lewis, 1979; Spear, 1978). Such cuing treatments normally have involved exposing animals to a portion of the stimulus complex that was present at the time of learning, without allowing the animals to experience a complete relearning trial. Animals that have been exposed to some source of forgetting, but that have received such treatments prior to testing, often have exhibited substantially better retention performance than their nontreated counterparts.

The wide range of experimental situations in which cuing procedures have been used attests to the robustness of the cuing effect. For example, cuing treatments have been used to restore retention performance that has declined over long retention intervals (Gordon, Smith, & Katz, 1979; Spear & Parsons, 1976).

Likewise, pretest cuing has been used to alleviate amnesia resulting from such postlearning treatments as electroconvulsive shock (ECS) (Miller & Springer, 1973) and cycloheximide (Quartermain, McEwen, & Azmitia, 1970). In a similar fashion, retention deficits due to the acquisition of competing memories and the extreme deficits often exhibited by preweanling animals both appear to be amenable to reduction via pretest cues (Campbell & Jaynes, 1966; Spear, Gordon, & Martin, 1973). Finally, recent evidence suggests that even short-term retention performance can be improved significantly with cuing procedures (Feldman & Gordon, 1979; Gordon & Feldman, 1978).

Although the evidence that has accrued in recent years leaves little doubt that cuing treatments can facilitate retention performance, there has been relatively little work directed toward determining how this improved performance is produced. It is possible, of course, that the mechanisms underlying the cuing effect may be different depending on what the source of forgetting is in a given situation. It is also possible that different types of cuing treatments might produce improved retention via different mechanisms. However, until at least some of the mechanisms underlying the cuing effect have been isolated, the question of generality remains moot. For this reason our own work concerning cuing mechanisms has not, as yet, dealt with the question of generality. Instead, we have attempted to concentrate on whether certain explanations for the cuing phenomenon are applicable in a few specific situations.

CUING HYPOTHESES

To this point at least three separate hypotheses have been proposed to explain the effects of pretest cues on retention performance. The first of these hypotheses proposes that pretest cuing may produce motivational changes that proactively facilitate performance. The second explanation is based on the notion that forgetting normally reflects a loss of information from storage. This view suggests that cuing may allow an organism an opportunity for additional learning that can replace the information that has been lost. The final hypothesis emphasizes the role of retrieval failures in forgetting. According to this view, cuing induces processing that renders a previously inaccessible memory more accessible on a subsequent test. In the remainder of this chapter, these three hypotheses are discussed and evaluated in greater detail. Special emphasis is given to the notion that cues may improve the accessibility of stored information, a notion that has drawn increasing support in recent years (Lewis, 1979).

The Motivational Hypothesis

The idea that cues enhance retention performance by increasing an animal's motivation is the simplest and probably the least compelling of the three cuing hypotheses. This hypothesis has been invoked primarily in those situations in which original learning has involved some aversive event and that aversive event or a similar one is used as the pretest cue. The idea has been that after a long retention interval or some other source of forgetting, an animal's motivation for performing drops to a low level relative to what that level was during acquisition. The cue, especially if it is an aversive event such as a footshock, restores the high motivational level, better preparing the animal to perform on later test trials.

Almost certainly there are some cases of improved retention performance that can be explained in this manner. However, as a general explanation for cue-induced retention enhancement, the motivational hypothesis is not tenable. First, most studies in which aversive stimuli have been used as cues have included control animals that received no training prior to retention testing. If the cuing procedures used in these experiments had produced enhanced motivation, one might expect differences in test performance depending on whether even these untrained animals were cued or not prior to testing. By and large, such studies have reported no differences between nontrained, cued, and nontrained, non-cued animals in terms of retention test performance (Miller & Springer, 1972).

Second, if cuing procedures act simply by increasing an animal's motivation level then the effects of these cues on performance should be relatively temporary. This does not appear to be the case. In many studies, cuing has been found to enhance retention performance even when cuing precedes testing by 24 hr or more (Gordon et al, 1979). Such findings make it unlikely that cues affect retention performance solely by inducing a temporary change in motivation.

A third group of experiments that argues against this interpretation are those in which seemingly "low arousal" cuing treatments have been used. A notable example is the study by Miller, Ott, Berk, and Springer (1974) in which apparatus exposure was used as a cue to alleviate the forgetting of a food location in the apparatus. Such findings are difficult to explain as a case of increased motivation unless one argues that the apparatus cues have become secondary reinforcers and are somehow producing increased incentive motivation.

Finally, several studies have directly assessed motivational changes induced by cuing (Gordon, McCracken, Dess-Beech, & Mowrer, in press; Spear & Parsons, 1976) and have found cue-induced retention enhancement in the absence of apparent changes in motivation. Taken together, these lines of evidence argue convincingly that cuing effects cannot be explained solely on the basis of temporary motivational changes.

The New Learning Hypothesis

The new learning explanation of cuing effects has been stated most explicitly by Cherkin (1972) and by Gold and King (1974). It should be noted that these researchers proposed this hypothesis to deal specifically with what is termed the "reminder effect" (i.e., the use of cuing to alleviate retrograde amnesia). However, this hypothesis is clearly applicable to any situation in which pretest cues are employed, regardless of the specific source of forgetting.

According to this view, forgetting is often the result of a partial loss of information from storage. By a "partial loss" it is meant that a residual memory of training may remain in storage even though an animal exhibits substantial forgetting. Cuing, it is suggested, represents an opportunity for an animal to acquire new information. And, because pretest cues are the same as training stimuli, the information acquired during cuing is often "compatible" with the information acquired at the time of learning. In this context "compatible information" is presumably information that would transfer positively to a retention test for prior learning. Gold and King (1974) argue that although the information acquired at the time of cuing may not itself be enough to affect later performance, the combination of the residual training memory with the new compatible information often is enough to result in the improved performance exhibited by cued animals.

As with the motivational hypothesis, there is little question that in some instances cuing does provide new information that might affect later performance (Gold, Haycock, Macri, & McGaugh, 1973). However, the critical questions are whether new learning, relevant to the retention test, *usually* occurs as the function of cuing and, if so, whether the new learning is *necessary* for the enhancement of retention. Several facts argue against such an interpretation of most cuing effects.

First, the vast majority of cuing treatments used do not qualify technically as learning trials. This does not mean, of course, that animals exposed to a training apparatus, a CS, or a US might not acquire new information as the result of the exposure. However, one would not expect such exposures to provide an optimal opportunity for relevant new learning, and yet the effects of such exposures on performance are often substantial. Furthermore, in many cases in which CS or US exposures have been used successfully for cuing, these exposures have taken place outside the original training apparatus (Miller & Springer, 1972). Thus, the new learning hypothesis would require that information acquired under nonoptimal conditions would have to generalize to the training situation to be effective. Certainly, these factors strain the plausibility of this interpretation.

A second type of argument is even more damaging to the new learning hypothesis. In several successful cuing studies, the cuing treatments used met at least the procedural requirements of extinction trials. These studies have shown that exposing animals either to the training CS or to the portion of the training apparatus in which the reinforcer earlier had occurred, can function effectively as a cuing procedure, even though such exposures occur in the absence of any reinforcing event (Gordon & Spear, 1973a; Rohrbaugh & Riccio, 1970; Wickens, 1973). Such data raise problems for the new learning hypothesis inasmuch as one would assume that the information acquired by an animal on an extinction trial would be *incompatible* with the information acquired during learning. That

is, extinction information should transfer negatively, not positively, to the retention test situation. Yet such trials often act to enhance rather than decrease
subsequent performance, suggesting that the enhanced performance is due to
something other than the extinction information contained in the cuing procedure.

Extinction Trials as Cuing Treatments.   Recent evidence from our own laboratory strengthens the foregoing conclusion by showing that it is possible to
separate empirically the cuing- or performance-enhancing function of an extinction trial from the effects of new information acquired on such a trial. We began
this series of experiments with the assumption that any cuing procedure has the
potential to affect subsequent performance in two ways. First, such procedures
should result in the activation or retrieval of the stored training memory, and this
activation, in and of itself, might alter subsequent performance relevant to that
memory. Second, such procedures should contain information that could be
acquired at the time of cuing and combined with the recently activated training
memory. This latter function of the cuing procedure, is, of course, the function
emphasized by Cherkin (1972) and Gold and King (1974). We further
hypothesized that the two functions of a cuing procedure should occur sequentially. In other words, we suggested that the activation of the training memory
would precede the addition of any new information to that memory.

Following these assumptions, we felt that it should be possible to determine
the effects of cue-induced activation of a training memory in isolation from any
effects of new information acquired at the time of cuing by using an extinction
trial as the cuing procedure. In our first experiment (Gordon et al, 1979, Exp. 1)
we decided to vary the duration of the extinction trial that was used as the cuing
treatment. The rationale was that if a short duration extinction trial were used,
this should allow enough time for activation of the training memory to occur, but
should preclude any substantial acquisition or addition of the new extinction
contingency. On the other hand, a long exposure to such a trial should allow time
both for activation and new learning to occur. We predicted in the first case that
subsequent performance would be enhanced because of activation of the training
memory and in the latter case, decreased because the acquisition of an incompatible contingency would ultimately overpower the former effect.

In this experiment, rats either were trained to perform a one-way active-
avoidance response or were given noncontingent footshocks and handling.
Avoidance training took place in an avoidance apparatus consisting of a white,
translucent start chamber that was separated by a door from a black goal
chamber. The training involved placing an animal in the white chamber of the
apparatus and opening the door leading to the black chamber. Opening the door
initiated a flashing light located behind the white chamber. An animal was
required to cross over into the black chamber within 5 sec after the light was
initiated or a footshock was administered through the grid floor of the white

chamber. This shock remained on until an animal escaped to the black chamber. Following either an escape response or a successful avoidance, an animal was removed from the apparatus and placed in a holding cage for a 30-sec intertrial interval (ITI). To attain criterion, each animal was required to perform five consecutive avoidance responses. Each animal given noncontingent footshocks was yoked to one of the trained animals in terms of the number and sequence of shocks, the amount of apparatus exposure, and the amount of handling. Footshocks were administered in a large chamber dissimilar from the training apparatus.

Seventy-two hours after either training or noncontingent footshocks, each animal was returned to the training room for cuing. Cuing consisted of a single response-blocking trial in which animals were confined in the start chamber of the apparatus with the flashing light activated. No shocks were administered on this trial. One group of animals was brought to the room but given no exposure to the start chamber (0-sec condition). Two other groups were confined in the chamber for either 15 or 75 sec. Twenty-four hours after cuing, each animal was returned to the training room for a single retention test trial in which the latency to cross into the black chamber was assessed. This trial was identical to a training trial except that no shocks were administered.

Fig. 11.1 represents the median test latencies for animals in each of the treatment conditions. On this test, animals that took longer than 10 sec to move to the black chamber were assigned a score of 10 sec. This relatively low cutoff criterion was used because we found in pilot work that virtually all animals that remained in the white chamber for 10 sec remained in that chamber for several minutes.

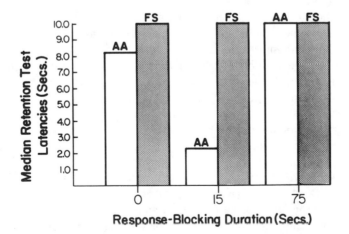

FIG. 11.1.   Median retention test latency as a function of type of training and duration of the extinction trial. (AA = active avoidance training; FS = yoked footshocks).

Analyses of the data revealed the expected pattern of results. The different cuing treatments had no differential effects on the noncontingent footshock animals. However, among the animals given active avoidance training, those given the 15-sec exposure exhibited significantly *shorter* latencies than the noncued animals (0-sec condition), whereas the 75-sec condition animals had significantly *longer* latencies than the noncued animals. These findings are consistent with the notion that a short exposure to an extinction trial facilitates performance by activating the training memory, whereas the longer exposure allows for acquisition of the extinction contingency, thereby decreasing performance.

A second study relevant to this problem (Gordon et al., 1979, Exp. 3) involved varying the placement of a constant duration extinction trial within a retention interval. The rationale for this manipulation was that an extinction trial of a given duration should have different effects depending on how accessible the memory of training is at the time of the extinction treatment (cuing). Specifically, we proposed that shortly after learning, the training memory should be easily accessible and that cue-induced activation of the memory should occur quickly. Long after learning, however, the memory should be less accessible and it should require a longer cuing exposure for activation to occur. Based on these notions, we predicted that a short duration extinction trial might give an animal adequate exposure time to acquire the extinction contingency if given just after learning. However, long after learning, the same trial might constitute only enough exposure to activate the training memory.

The procedures for initial training and for testing were the same as in the first experiment. As to cuing, some animals received no response-blocking cue trial (NB), whereas the others received a 15-sec response-blocking cue trial either 15 min or 72 hr after training. All animals were tested 96 hr after training. Fig. 11.2 represents the results of this experiment. Analyses of these data showed again that the various cuing manipulations had no significant effect on animals that had received only prior footshocks. Among animals given active-avoidance training, however, exposure to the blocking trial 15 min after training decreased perfor-

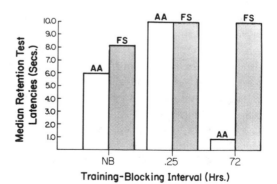

FIG. 11.2. Median retention test latency as a function of training and the training–extinction trial interval. (AA = active avoidance training; FS = yoked footshocks; NB = no response-blocking extinction trial).

mance relative to the noncued (NB) animals. Conversely, exposure to the same blocking trial 72 hr after training enhanced performance relative to the noncued condition. Again we interpreted these findings as showing that long after learning the memory activation function of the response-blocking trial predominated, whereas shortly after learning the acquisition of the extinction contingency took precedence.

A final study concerning the use of extinction trials as cues (Gordon & Mowrer, 1980) followed the same rationale as the previous experiment (i.e., that the effects of a given extinction trial should depend on the accessibility of the training memory at the time the extinction trial occurs). In this case, however, we manipulated the accessibility of the training memory with an amnesic treatment (ECS) rather than with an extension of the training–cuing interval. The basic design of this experiment was a 2 by 2 by 2 factorial in which animals were given either active-avoidance training or yoked footshocks, ECS or a sham treatment, and an extinction trial (E) or no extinction trial (NE) prior to testing. In this study the training procedures were identical to those described earlier except that noncontingent footshocks were administered in a white chamber similar to that in the avoidance apparatus. ECS was a 50-ma shock delivered through ear clips immediately after training, and the extinction trial consisted of a 60-sec response-blocking trial 15 min prior to testing. The total retention interval was 72 hr and the retention test consisted of five nonshock test trials in which animals could remain in the white start chamber for a maximum of 60 sec. In addition to the eight basic treatment conditions, one additional condition was included (baseline condition) in which animals received noncontingent footshocks in a chamber dissimilar to the apparatus and then were simply tested 72 hr later.

The results of this experiment can be seen in Fig. 11.3, which presents the mean log latency scores for the treatment groups averaged over the five retention trials. These latency scores were converted to logs because of extreme differences in individual group variances. An analysis of variance performed on these data revealed a three-way interaction of the three treatment variables. In essence, the different ECS-Extinction trial combinations did not differentially affect the performance of the noncontingent footshock animals. Also, animals in these conditions did not differ from the baseline group performance. Among the animals given active avoidance training and no ECS, the extinction trial decreased performance (sham-E versus sham-NE). The sham-E animals did not differ from baseline performance, whereas the sham-NE animals performed significantly better than baseline. For those animals that received ECS after training, the extinction trial improved performance (ECS-E versus ECS-NE). In these conditions the ECS-NE performed more poorly than the baseline animals whereas the ECS-E animals performed significantly better. These data again are consistent with the notion that, when the training memory is relatively inaccessible (e.g., following ECS), an extinction trial is likely to improve performance,

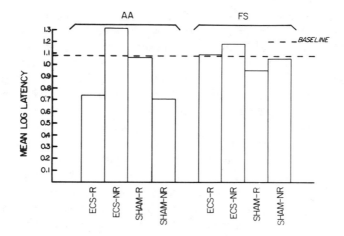

FIG. 11.3.   Mean of the average log latencies (over the five test trials) as a function of training and treatment conditions.

whereas the same trial is more likely to decrease performance as a result of extinction when the memory is more easily accessible.

All three of these experiments were undertaken to determine if a cuing treatment can affect subsequent performance in some way other than by providing a new learning opportunity. Because in these studies an extinction trial was used as the cuing treatment, we reasoned that the new information contained in the treatment should decrease subsequent performance if it were acquired. Evidence for such a decremental effect was obtained in all three studies. However, it also was demonstrated that under certain parametric conditions, these same extinction trials could enhance rather than decrease performance. It is difficult to explain this enhancement as resulting from the acquisition of new information inasmuch as the information contained in such a trial should presumably decrease performance. Thus, this enhancement suggests that an extinction trial affects performance not only by providing new information, but also by serving some other function. It will be argued subsequently that this enhancement is a result of activation of the training memory. In any event, it seems clear from these and other experiments that the retention enhancement produced by pretest cuing may be contributed to, but does not arise solely from, the acquisition of new information at the time of cuing.

The Retrieval Hypothesis

The basic premise underlying the retrieval hypothesis is that poor retention performance often can be traced to an animal's inability to retrieve information that is available in storage (Spear, 1971, 1973, 1978). In general then, this view holds that a pretest cuing procedure increases the accessibility or retrievability of stored information, thereby improving subsequent performance relevant to that information. Although there have been several statements of this hypothesis (see, for example, Feldman & Gordon, 1979; Miller & Springer, 1973; Sara, David-Remacle, & Lefevre, 1975; Spear, 1973), probably the most explicit treatment of this view appears in a recent paper by Lewis (1979).

Lewis proposes that permanent information storage occurs almost instantaneously with the input of that information. However, once this storage occurs, the memory of training still can be in either an active or inactive memory state. For example, at the time of learning, the memory of training automatically enters the active state and remains in this state for some period of time after a learning experience has ended. An active memory (AM) is one that is being elaborated, organized, or coded for later retrieval or that is being prepared for immediate use. Normally, after this organizational processing is complete, a training memory enters the inactive state. An inactive memory (IM) can be defined as a permanently stored memory that provides the potential for subsequent performance, but that is not presently being processed or used. Actual performance at any given time depends on memories that are in the AM state.

According to this view, stimuli that are noticed by an animal at the time of acquisition become represented as part of the memory for training. Thus, when animals are reexposed to stimuli noticed at the time of learning, the inactive training memory containing representations of these stimuli is returned to the AM state to help control contemporary performance. One by-product of activating the previously stored training memory is that the memory undergoes further processing when it reenters the active state. In other terms, the training memory, by virtue of being activated, is elaborated or additionally organized in much the same way a newly acquired memory undergoes such processing. Apparently, this additional processing renders the training memory more accessible on a subsequent test. Thus, in Lewis' view, forgetting presumably occurs because of inadequate processing of a new memory or because the particular processing that does occur results in a memorial organization that is inappropriate for retrieval on a particular retention test. Pretest cuing alleviates such forgetting by activating the training memory and allowing it to be processed either more adequately or more appropriately for later retrieval.

This theoretical framework is appealing for at least two reasons. The first is that it has much in common with recent theoretical proposals in the human retention area (see, for example, Atkinson & Shiffrin, 1971; Baddeley & Hitch, 1974; Craik & Lockhart, 1972). The second reason for the appeal of this line of reasoning is that the alternative hypotheses used to explain the cuing phenomenon appear to be inadequate. Still, unless the retrieval hypothesis is to remain only an appealing alternative, there must be evidence generated to support the basic tenets of the hypothesis. Two lines of evidence would seem to be particularly crucial if the retrieval hypothesis is to gain acceptance. First, it is necessary to demonstrate the plausibility of the idea that cuing activates an inactive training memory. Evidence supporting this point has grown in recent years and is reviewed in the following section. Second, it is necessary to demonstrate that cuing results in some change or modification in the organization or structure of a training memory that might be expected to facilitate later retrieval. Although evidence concerning this point is scant, recent findings from our own laboratory will be discussed as support for this idea.

Does Duing Activate a Training Memory?   According to the retrieval hypothesis, cuing returns a training memory to a state similar to that the memory was in shortly after learning. If this is the case, then one must predict that recently acquired and recently cued memories should share many of the same characteristics. A great deal of recent evidence supports this hypothesis.

The first line of evidence suggesting that newly acquired and recently cued memories are similar comes from studies that look at retention curves following acquisition and cuing. It is well known that in most situations retention performance by animals is excellent shortly after a learning experience, but that such performance decreases steadily as the retention interval is extended (Gleitman, 1971). Recently, it has been shown that an almost identical retention function results if one measures retention at various intervals after cuing (Feldman & Gordon, 1979). In such studies, cuing treatments usually are given long after retention performance has begun to decline. However, usually the cuing treatments restore retention to a high level, and then the retention performance tends to decline steadily as the cuing–test interval is extended. Thus, the accessibility of newly acquired and recently cued memories is similar and this accessibility declines similarly with time.

A second set of experiments attesting to this similarity concerns the susceptibility of memories to disrupting and enhancing treatments. It has long been known that retention of a training memory can be disrupted by treatments such as ECS and hypothermia if these treatments are administered shortly after acquisition (McGaugh & Dawson, 1971; Riccio, Hodges & Randall, 1968). Likewise, the retention of a training memory may be enhanced by the immediate postlearning administration of treatments such as CNS stimulants (Calhoun, 1971) and electrical stimulation of the mesencephalic reticular formation (McGaugh & Herz, 1972). Both disrupting and facilitating treatments, however, lose effectiveness when the acquisition–treatment interval is extended (Calhoun, 1971; McGaugh & Dawson, 1971). These retrograde amnesia and facilitation gradients normally are interpreted as evidence that a memory is susceptible to modification only shortly after learning, while processing is occurring.

The first indication that recently cued memories might also be susceptible to the effects of such treatments came from an experiment by Misanin, Miller, and Lewis (1968). This experiment showed that although a training memory is not normally susceptible to the effects of ECS 24 hr after acquisition, amnesia for that memory can be produced under these conditions if ECS administration is shortly preceded by exposure to a training cue. This finding subsequently has been replicated numerous times using a variety of parameters, cuing treatments, and amnesic agents (cf. Lewis, 1979; Spear, 1978). Importantly, it also has been demonstrated that as the interval between cuing and the amnesic treatment is extended, the effects of the amnesic treatment decline steadily (DeVietti & Kirkpartrick, 1976).

As to treatments that enhance retention performance, similar findings have been reported. For example, Gordon and Spear (1973b) showed that, although strychnine sulphate normally has little effect on a training memory when administered 72 hr after training, such an effect can be obtained by reexposing animals to the training apparatus just prior to the drug treatment. Similar effects have been found using other enhancing treatments such as pentylenetetrazol (Gordon, unpublished findings) and electrical stimulation of the mesencephalic reticular formation (DeVietti, Conger, & Kirkpatrick, 1977). As with the amnesic treatments, the effects of these enhancing treatments seem to decline steadily as the cuing-treatment interval is extended (Gordon, 1977b).

These data must be tempered by the fact that some researchers have reported subtle differences between the amnesias or enhancements produced by giving treatments after learning and after cuing (see for example, Riccio & Ebner, this volume). However, it is unclear whether such differences imply qualitative differences in recently acquired and recently cued memories, or whether such differences are parametric anomalies (see Lewis, 1979). What is striking is the degree to which a new training memory and a cued training memory share the susceptibility to amnesic and facilitory treatments.

A final group of studies suggesting similarities in new and recently cued memories deals with interference effects in animals. If animals are trained to perform conflicting responses sequentially in the same apparatus, acquisition of the first response will interfere with retention of the more recently acquired response (Spear, 1971). This interference effect has been shown to depend critically on the interval separating the acquisition of the two tasks. In essence, interference occurs only to the extent that the second task is acquired shortly after the first. The longer the intertask interval the less interference results (Gordon & Spear, 1973a). This finding was interpreted as showing that the second task must be acquired while the memory of the first task is still active and being processed in order for interference to occur. It has been demonstrated, however, that interference can be induced even when a long intertask interval is used, as long as an animal is given a cue for Task 1 just prior to learning Task 2 (Gordon & Feldman, 1978; Gordon & Spear, 1973a). Also, it has been shown that the interference produced by the cuing treatment decreases as the cuing–Task 2 acquisition interval is increased (Gordon, 1977a). Furthermore, it is now clear that interference due to Task 1 acquisition and cuing both increase as the retention interval following Task 2 acquisition is increased (Gordon, Frankl, & Hamberg, 1979). These findings suggest not only that both new and cued memories are capable of producing interference but also that the interference produced by a cued memory is similar to that caused by a recently acquired memory.

In summary, all the data reported earlier suggest strong similarities between newly acquired and recently cued memories. These findings do not, in and of themselves, demonstrate that cuing returns a training memory to an active state similar to that the memory was in shortly after learning. However, these data clearly are consistent with this tenet of the retrieval hypothesis.

Is Memory Structure or Organization Modified by Cuing?   The retrieval hypothesis proposes not only that cuing activates a training memory, but also that the training memory can be modified at the time of activation to improve its later accessibility. Recently, we have gathered data in our own laboratory to support this contention. These studies were carried out to test a specific hypothesis proposed in some of our earlier papers (Feldman & Gordon, 1979; Gordon & Feldman, 1978; Gordon & Mowrer, 1980). This hypothesis suggests that cuing always occurs in a context that is at least slightly different from the training context, because a context never can be exactly reproduced. We proposed that a representation of the contextual stimuli present at the time of cuing might become an integral part of the training memory, and that this incorporation of contextual stimulus representations might be expected to facilitate later retention.

The idea that the incorporation of a cuing context into a training memory should facilitate subsequent retention is a logical extension of the view of memory retrieval proposed by Spear (1973). According to this conception, the probability of retrieving a training memory depends on the similarity of stimuli noticed at the time of testing and those stimuli that are represented as part of the training memory. In effect, the greater similarity of these stimuli, the greater the probability that the training memory will be retrieved. To explain why forgetting occurs over extended retention intervals, Spear suggests that both an animal's internal and external context changes over time. Thus, the longer the time between training and retention testing, the greater should be the difference between an animal's test context and the stimuli represented in the training memory. This increasing mismatch between training and test stimuli could be expected to lower progressively the probability of successful retrieval on the retention test.

Based on this view we reasoned that one mechanism for enhancing retention performance would be to increase the similarity between the contextual stimuli represented in a training memory and those stimuli present during testing. Because pretest cuing normally occurs relatively close in time to retention testing, the cuing and test contexts should be more similar than the training and test contexts are. Thus, one would predict enhanced retention performance if the cuing context were incorporated into the training memory at the time of cuing.

We planned a series of experiments to test the notion that a cuing context becomes represented as part of the memory being cued. These studies (Gordon et al., in press) were designed to demonstrate that if animals receive cuing in a context other than that in which they were trained, the cuing context would begin to function as if it were the training context. The different contexts employed in these experiments were actually different rooms that varied in terms of such characteristics as lighting, ambient noise level, and odor stimuli. The particular characteristics of the rooms employed are shown in Table 11.1.

The purpose of the first experiment was simply to demonstrate empirically that two of these contexts (rooms A and B) were perceived as different by the animals being used. Each of these rooms contained an avoidance apparatus constructed identically to the one described earlier. Animals were trained on an active-avoidance task either in Room A or Room B. Then, 24 hours later, half the animals were tested in the same room in which training had occurred while the other half were tested in the alternate room. In this and the remaining experiments, active-avoidance training was identical to that described earlier, whereas retention testing consisted of five nonshock test trials.

Figure 11.4 represents the mean latencies on Test Trial 1 as a function of the training–testing sequence. These data also are shown as a function of whether or not animals changed rooms between training and testing. An analysis of the data revealed that changing contexts between training and testing produced significant deficits in avoidance performance relative to the performance of animals that experienced no change. This effect was most pronounced in those animals trained in Room A and tested in Room B. These animals exhibited significantly longer latencies than animals in both of the nonchanged conditions. The pattern

TABLE 11.1
Characteristics of Treatment Rooms

Room	A	B	C
Dimension (ft.)	16.0 x 7.5	16.0 x 11.0	13.5 x 7.5
Lighting	Dark	Bright	Dim
Odor	Lemon	Rose	None
Noise	Fan	None	None
Gloves	Rough	Smooth	Textured
Holding Cage	Wire Mesh	Wooden	Breeding Cage

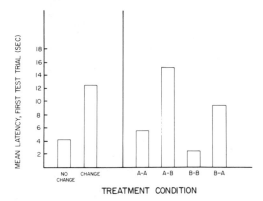

FIG. 11.4.   Mean Trial 1 latency as a function of treatment condition. (No charge = combined A-A and B-B scores; change = combined A-B and B-A scores).

of results was identical when each animal's retention score was the average latency over the five test trials. These data demonstrate clearly that the particular contexts employed in this experiment were not viewed as the same by animals trained and tested in them.

The purpose of the second experiment was to determine if this performance decrement due to context change could be alleviated by cuing in the test context prior to testing. If such a reduction in the performance decrement could be shown, this would provide preliminary evidence suggesting that a cuing context begins to function in the same manner as the training context. In this experiment, animals were assigned to one of five conditions. In the A-B condition, animals were trained to avoid in Room A and tested in Room B. In the B-B condition, both training and testing occurred in Room B. These conditions served to replicate conditions used in the first study. A third condition A-B-B involved training animals in Room A and testing in Room B. However, animals in this condition were given a 15-sec cuing treatment in Room B, 3.5 min prior to testing. The cuing treatment involved placing an animal in a white chamber (constructed identically to the start chamber in the avoidance apparatus) that contained a grid floor and then confining animals in a holding cage in Room B for the 3.5-min cuing-test interval. A fourth condition, A-C-B was identical to the A-B-B condition except that cuing and confinement occurred in Room C (Table 11.1). In the final condition (A-conf.), animals were trained in Room A and tested in Room B but were confined in a holding cage in Room B for 3.75 min just before testing. For animals in all five conditions, the total retention interval was 24 hr.

Figure 11.5 reflects the latency data for Test Trial 1 as a function of the treatment conditions. As this figure suggests, animals trained in Room A and tested in B perform significantly worse than animals trained and tested in Room B. However, this deficit due to a change in context is eliminated completely if animals are cued in Room B prior to testing there (cf. condition A-B-B versus A-B). Cuing in a context other than the test context (A-C-B) or simply confin-

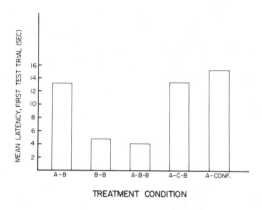

FIG. 11.5. Mean Trial 1 latency as a function of treatment condition.

ing animals in the test room before testing (A-conf.) did not alleviate the poor performance caused by the context change. As in the first experiment, virtually identical results were obtained when all five test trials were considered.

These results provide a strong indication that when a training memory is cued in a novel context, that context begins to function as if it has been present at the time of training. However, the data from the second experiment are open to alternate interpretations. First, it is possible that the particular treatment conditions used in that experiment might produce an identical pattern of test results even if no prior acquisition were given. Second, animals in the A-B-B condition were the only animals that received both a cuing treatment as well as confinement in Room B prior to testing. It is possible that the cuing treatment itself need not occur in Room B in order for test performance to be enhanced. It may only be necessary that a cuing treatment be given in any context and that confinement occur in Room B prior to testing. The third experiment tested these alternative interpretations.

In this experiment, animals were assigned to one of six treatment conditions. Two of these conditions (A-B and A-B-B) were identical to the corresponding conditions in the previous study. A third condition (A-X) involved training animals to avoid in Room A and then testing the animals 24 hr later in Room B. Prior to testing, however, animals in the A-X condition first received 3.5 min of confinement in Room B followed by the 15-sec cuing treatment given in Room C. The 3.5-min cuing-test interval was spent in a holding cage in Room C. Each of the remaining three conditions (NC-B, NC-B-B and NC-X) was identical to one of the conditions already described except that animals in these conditions received yoked, noncontingent footshocks in Room A rather than active-avoidance training. The footshock treatments were the same as those described earlier in this chapter.

The results of this experiment for the first test trial are depicted in Fig. 11.6.

In this experiment, the test latencies were converted to logs because of extreme differences in the individual group variances. Analyses of these findings showed that the poor performance by animals in the A–B condition was eliminated by cuing animals in Room B prior to testing. Animals given confinement in Room B, but cuing in Room C, showed no significant improvement over the performance of the A–B animals. Finally, the various treatment conditions produced no significant differences among animals given only footshocks rather than active-avoidance training. These results also hold for the averaged data from all five test trials. Taken together, these results indicate: (1) that cuing must occur in the test context to effectively eliminate the performance decrement; and (2) that the cuing treatment is effective only if a training memory is present to be activated.

To strengthen these conclusions we conducted a fourth experiment in which the alternate cuing context was different from the Room C context used in the previous experiments. This study was done to determine if the specific context in Room C had in some way simply depressed or inhibited the effects of cuing in the prior studies. The alternate context used in this study (Room D) measured 13 by 19 ft, was well lit, and had no specific odor or noise stimuli introduced. The treatment conditions in this experiment included an A–B and A–B–B condition identical to those described previously. A third condition A–D–B was the same as A–B–B except that the pretest cuing and confinement occurred in Room D. First test trial latencies (in sec) for these three conditions were as follows: A–B, 10.45; A–B–B, 4.56; A–D–B, 13.35. As in the previous studies, analyses showed that the deficit produced by context change (A–B) was significantly reduced only when cuing occurred in the test context (A–B–B).

These findings make it clear that cuing in a test context can reduce the performance deficit that normally occurs when a training and test context differ.

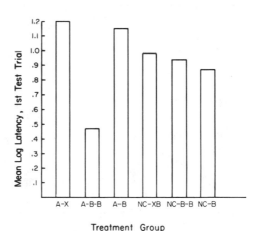

FIG. 11.6.   Mean Trial 1 log latency as a function of treatment condition.

However, it seemed to us that at least two interpretations still could be applied to these data. The first, which we favor, is that cuing activates the memory of active avoidance training and that the cuing context becomes represented as part of the training memory. The second related interpretation is that cuing simply arouses a fear response in previously trained animals and that the cuing context becomes associated with this fear response. Thus, when animals are tested later in the same context in which they had been cued, they exhibit shorter latencies simply because of greater fear.

This latter interpretation is difficult to test conclusively. However, we reasoned that if this were the case, it should be possible to assess differential fear in the B context, for animals previously cued in Room B and C. In previous studies, we had found that animals would reliably suppress exploration in an open field in the presence of a feared stimulus but not in the presence of a neutral stimulus. Thus, in a final experiment, two groups of animals were trained to avoid in Room A and then one group was cued in Room B and the other in Room C. Following cuing, both groups were placed in an open field apparatus in Room B and the number of squares crossed in the open field was measured for 2 min. During min 1, animals cued in Room B crossed a mean of 37.4 squares, while animals cued in Room C crossed a mean of 33.1 squares. The comparable figures for the second min were 27.5 and 22.9, respectively. Statistical analyses revealed no significant differences between the groups in terms of square crossings in either the first or second min. These data suggest that the cuing procedures used in the previous studies do not result in substantial differences in exploratory activity when animals are exposed to the test stimulus context. Such findings appear contrary to the notion that the A-B-B animals are simply more fearful than the A-C-B animals when placed back into the B context for testing.

The data from these five experiments show that a change of context between the time of training and testing normally results in a decrement in test performance. However, this decrement can be reduced significantly by cuing in the test context prior to testing. Animals given such cuing perform as if they had been trained in the cuing (or test) context. We interpret these results as indicating that cuing activates a training memory and that at the time of activation the cuing context becomes associated with, or represented as part of, the training memory. Certainly, these data are consistent with such an interpretation.

Thus, we believe these findings indicate that pretest cuing can result in a modification of the structure of a training memory. Furthermore, this modification (i.e., the addition of contextual representations) is one that might be expected to enhance retention performance related to that memory. We do not suggest, of course, that this is the *only* mechanism by which cuing alters retention performance. We do offer, however, that the present data represent a beginning in the process of identifying mechanisms underlying cue-induced retention enhancement, and that such data supports the retrieval hypothesis explanation of cuing effects.

SUMMARY

In the present chapter we reviewed and evaluated three hypotheses that have been used to explain pretest, cue-induced retention enhancement. Two of these explanations—the motivational and new learning hypotheses—were found to be capable of explaining a portion of, but not all the cuing data. In contrast, we not only found that the retrieval hypothesis is consistent with most of the cuing data, but also we were able to summarize evidence that supports the basic tenets of this hypothesis. First, we reviewed research suggesting that recently acquired memories and cued memories share similar characteristics. These data are clearly consistent with the notion that a cuing procedure returns a training memory to the same active state the memory was in shortly after learning. Second, we described recent evidence from our own laboratory suggesting that cuing produces at least one modification of a training memory that might be expected to enhance later performance relevant to that memory. Specifically, these data suggest that one of the mechanisms underlying cue-induced retention enhancement is the incorporation of a cuing context into a training memory.

The implications of such an analysis of the cuing phenomenon go beyond simply increasing our understanding of the phenomenon itself. This type of analysis suggests that it may be productive to begin to look at the structure or organization of stored information in order to better understand fluctuations in retention performance. In such an endeavor, the pretest cuing procedure should prove to be an invaluable tool.

ACKNOWLEDGMENTS

The research reported in this chapter, as well as the preparation of the chapter itself was supported by a grant from the National Science Foundation to the author. I am especially indebted to Robert R. Mowrer for his contributions to the research in this chapter as well as for his helpful reading of the manuscript. I also am indebted to the following students for their contributions to the research cited in this chapter: Nancy Dess-Beech, Diane Feldman, David Katz, Kathryn McCracken, Gregory Smith, and Margaret Wittrup.

REFERENCES

Atkinson, R. C., & Shiffrin, R. M. The control of short-term memory. *Scientific American*, 1971, *225*, 82–90.

Baddeley, A. D., & Hitch, G. Working memory. In G. H. Bower (Ed.), *The psychology of learning and motivation* (Vol. 8). New York: Academic Press, 1974.

Calhoun, W. H. Central nervous system stimulants. In E. Furchtgott (Ed.), *Pharmacological and biophysical agents and behavior*. New York: Academic Press, 1971.

Campbell, B. A., & Jaynes, J. Reinstatement. *Psychological Review*, 1966, *73*, 478–480.

Cherkin, A. Retrograde amnesia in the chick: Resistance to the reminder effect. *Physiology and Behavior,* 1972, *8,* 949–955.

Craik, F. I. M., & Lockhart, R. S. Levels of processing: A framework for memory research. *Journal of Verbal Learning and Verbal Behavior,* 1972, *11,* 671–684.

DeVietti, T. L., Conger, G. L., & Kirkpatrick, B. R. Comparison of the enhancement gradients of retention obtained with stimulation of the mesencephalic reticular formation after training or memory reactivation. *Physiology and Behavior,* 1977, *19,* 549–554.

DeVietti, T. L., & Kirkpatrick, B. R. The amnesia gradient: Inadequate as evidence for a memory consolidation process. *Science,* 1976, *198,* 438–440.

Feldman, D. T., & Gordon, W. C. The alleviation of short-term retention decrements with reactivation. *Learning and Motivation,* 1979, *10,* 198–210.

Gleitman, H. Forgetting of long-term memories in animals. In W. K. Honig and P. H. R. James (Eds.), *Animal memory,* New York: Academic Press, 1971.

Gold, P. E., Haycock, J. W., Macri, J., & McGaugh, J. L. An explanation of the reminder effect: A case for retrograde amnesia. *Science,* 1973, *180,* 1199–1201.

Gold, P. E., & King, R. P. Retrograde amnesia: Storage failure versus retrieval failure. *Psychological Review,* 1974, *81,* 465–469.

Gordon, W. C. Similarities between short-term and reactivated memories in producing interference in the rat. *American Journal of Psychology,* 1977, *90,* 231–242. (a)

Gordon, W. C. Susceptibility of a reactivated memory to the effects of strychnine: a time-dependent phenomenon. *Physiology and Behavior,* 1977, *18,* 95–99. (b)

Gordon, W. C. *Effects of pentylenetetrazol on newly acquired and reactivated memories.* Unpublished manuscript.

Gordon, W. C., & Feldman, D. T. Reactivation induced interference in a short-term retention paradigm. *Learning and Motivation,* 1978, *9,* 164–178.

Gordon, W. C., Frankl, S. E., & Hamberg, J. M. Reactivation-induced proactive interference in rats. *American Journal of Psychology,* 1979, *92,* 693–702.

Gordon, W. C., McCracken, K. M., Dess-Beech, N., & Mowrer, R. R. Mechanisms for the cueing phenomenon: The addition of the cueing context to the training memory. *Learning and Motivation,* in press.

Gordon, W. C., & Mowrer, R. R. The use of an extinction trial as a reminder treatment following ECS. *Animal Learning and Behavior,* 1980, *8*(3), 363–367.

Gordon, W. C., Smith, G. J., & Katz, D. S. Dual effects of response blocking following avoidance learning. *Behavior Research and Therapy,* 1979, *17,* 479–487.

Gordon, W. C., & Spear, N. E. The effect of reactivation of a previously acquired memory on the interaction between memories in the rat. *Journal of Experimental Psychology,* 1973, *99,* 349–355. (a)

Gordon, W. C., & Spear, N. E. The effects of strychnine on recently acquired and reactivated passive avoidance memories. *Physiology and Behavior,* 1973, *10,* 1071–1075. (b)

Lewis, D. J. Psychobiology of active and inactive memory. *Psychological Bulletin,* 1979, *86,* 1054–1083.

McGaugh, J. L., & Dawson, R. G. Modification of memory storage processes. In W. K. Honig and P. H. R. James (Eds.), *Animal memory.* New York: Academic Press, 1971.

McGaugh, J. L., & Herz, M. J. *Memory Consolidation.* San Francisco: Albion Publishing Company, 1972.

Miller, R. R., Ott, C. A., Berk, A. M., & Springer, A. D. Appetitive memory restoration after electroconvulsive shock in the rat. *Journal of Comparative and Physiological Psychology,* 1974, *87,* 717–723.

Miller, R. R., & Springer, A. D. Induced recovery of memory in rats following electroconvulsive shock. *Physiology and Behavior,* 1972, *8,* 645–651.

Miller, R. R., & Springer, A. D. Amnesia, consolidation and retrieval. *Psychology Review*, 1973, *80*, 69–79.

Misanin, J. R., Miller, R. R., & Lewis, D. J. Retrograde amnesia produced by ECS after reactivation of a consolidated memory trace. *Science*, 1968, *160*, 554–555.

Quartermain, D., McEwen, B. S., & Azmitia, E. C., Jr. Amnesia produced by ECS or Cycloheximide: Conditions for recovery. *Science* 1970, *169*, 683–686.

Riccio, D. C., Hodges, L. A., & Randall, P. K. Retrograde amnesia produced by hypothermia in rats. *Journal of Comparative and Physiological Psychology*, 1968, *66*, 618–622.

Rohrbaugh, M., & Riccio, D. C. Paradoxical enhancement of learned fear. *Journal of Abnormal Psychology*, 1970, *75*, 210–216.

Sara, S. J., David-Remacle, M., & Lefevre, D. Passive avoidance behavior in rats after electroconvulsive shock: Facilitative effect of response retardation. *Journal of Comparative and Physiological Psychology*, 1975, *89*, 489–497.

Spear, N. E. Forgetting as retrieval failure. In W. K. Honig and P. H. R. James (Eds.), *Animal memory*, New York: Academic Press, 1971.

Spear, N. E. Retrieval of memory in animals. *Psychological Review*, 1973, *80*, 163–194.

Spear, N. E. *The processing of memories: Forgetting and retention*. Hillsdale, N.J.: Lawrence Erlbaum Associates, 1978.

Spear, N. E., Gordon, W. C., & Martin, P. A. Warm-up decrement as failure in memory retrieval in the rat. *Journal of Comparative and Phsyiological Psychology*, 1973, *85*, 601–614.

Spear, N. E., & Parsons, P. J. Analysis of a reactivation treatment: Ontogenetic determinants of alleviated forgetting. In D. L. Medin, W. A. Roberts, & R. T. Davis (Eds.), *Processes of animal memory*, New York: Wiley, 1976.

Wickens, D. D. Classical condition as it contributes to basic psychological processes. In J. McGuigen (Ed), *Current problems in learning and conditioning*. New York: Winston and Sons, 1973.

12 Extending the Domain Of Memory Retrieval

Norman E. Spear
State University of New York, Binghamton

This chapter is concerned with remembering. The specific topic is not so much when remembering is most likely to occur or when it is not, but rather, how it proceeds. I suggest that one clue toward determining how remembering proceeds is found in its consequences. Throughout the history of the science of learning and retention, the basic consequence of remembering that has been of singular concern is the concurrent, or immediately subsequent, overt behavior measured to infer remembering. In this chapter, I focus instead on how characteristics of the animal's representation of a previous episode (i.e., the memory), change when that episode is remembered. I argue that the processes engaged when an animal initially represents an episode as a memory ("memory storage") are much the same as those operating when a stored memory is made active ("memory retrieval"). This leads to the prediction that variables introduced at the time of memory retrieval will have the same effect on later retention as when these variables are introduced at the time of memory storage. Finally, I suggest that phenomena of conditioning and learning currently explained in terms of mechanisms operating at the time of memory storage (e.g., latent inhibition, blocking) may in fact be due to mechanisms that act on memory retrieval.

At the experimental level, there have emerged analyses of a phenomenon common to most of us—that remembering certain things in a new context can both change our view of those "things" or of associated events and alter our chances of remembering them at a later time. For instance, the memory of a superb meal at a new restaurant can be altered, the meal later remembered differently, if your dining partner should say: "Remember that meal? I became ill afterwards, due probably to their dirty kitchen and rancid meat." And, having remembered that meal, with or without negative remarks, remembering it again at a later time becomes more likely. Experimental documentation and analysis of such effects have begun to emerge (Cooper & Monk, 1976; Gordon, this volume; Loftus, 1979). Remembering, therefore, can alter the nature and accessibility of a particular memory.

Remembering is different from learning, both conceptually and analytically. For experimental purposes we usually refer to the more operationally based term, *retention,* rather than *remembering.* It is patent that learning and retention are not the same. Learning is necessary but not sufficient for retention. A variety of events before or after learning can alter retention (by which I mean, simply, the measured residue of learning) and forgetting (meaning, the measured decrement in retention). Many of the factors that alter rate of learning have no effect on forgetting, and vice versa, and some variables have opposite effects on learning and forgetting (Spear, 1978). Forgetting is not merely an index of the strength of original learning. If it were, if we could always predict retention knowing only the strength of original learning, forgetting would be simpler to understand, but dull. The point that makes forgetting interesting is that there are other factors, beyond how well learning was accomplished originally, that determine forgetting. For analytical purposes we must keep these factors separate in our experiments.

Yet my focus in this chapter is on the *similarities* of learning and retention. I conclude that the processes operating during learning and retention, what the organism does in each of these cases, are to some degree the same. Hence, the consequences in each case—whether or not the memory is changed and, if so, how—will be similar subsequent either to learning or to remembering an event. I suggest further that this commonality has important implications for our theories of learning as well as our theories of forgetting.

Theories of Forgetting.   My interest in a theory of forgetting is in how forgetting occurs, whether its basis is the same regardless of the specific "source" of forgetting, and when forgetting can be expected to this or that degree. This chapter does not present such a theory. It seems to me, in spite of my optimistic nature, that it is premature to promote such a theory that is specific enough to test and yet general enough to be significant.

Why is it premature? Certainly not because of a lack of ideas on this topic. One could argue that 2500 years of thinking and writing on this topic have produced all plausible ideas about forgetting; the argument could be the familiar one predicting production of the Encyclopedia Britannica given enough monkeys with typewriters pecking at random over a sufficiently long period. Everyone, including every scholar who has written down his or her thoughts on the topic, has had extensive experience in forgetting and usually some scheme for understanding it.

The reason a theory of forgetting is premature is simply because we do not yet know enough about what makes a difference in forgetting. Suppose, for instance, that except for strength of original learning and for retroactive and proactive interference, nothing makes a difference in forgetting, not what is learned, not how learning or subsequent practice takes place, and not even differences between one member of a species and another. At one point in the analysis of human forgetting this actually seemed to best summarize the facts (Underwood, 1972). Whether this would make the spinning of forgetting theories easier or just less interesting is a matter that need not be considered. It now appears that the puzzle cannot be so readily simplified on a general basis, at least until we make a great deal more progress toward reducing empirical differences in forgetting to a relatively few intervening variables (Spear, 1978).

It is from such a functionalistic orientation that this chapter approaches the study of forgetting, in a manner quite different from the increasingly theoretical orientation of studies of basic conditioning (Wagner, this volume) or retention over very short intervals (Grant, this volume; Honig, this volume; Maki, this volume; Roberts, 1979; Roberts & Grant, 1976). Both of these topics have a more systematic data base than the topic of forgetting in the general sense. It seems to me that, as an alternative, a healthy dose of functionalism might be of greatest benefit now to our general understanding of forgetting. Perhaps this would complement the developing theories of conditioning and of short-term retention of individual events. Also, this approach could ultimately provide the systematic relationship needed for a general theory of forgetting.

The phenomena of greatest interest for a theory of forgetting seem likely to be derived from broad questions such as these: (1) What factors beyond its original storage promote or permit the retrieval and expression of an acquired memory? (2) Are some episodes forgotten more rapidly than others? (the issue of "memory content"); and (3) Could and would the animal itself engage in activities that promote remembering (the issue of "mnemonic preparation")? These issues emerge constantly throughout the memory literature, in one form or another. They emerge in deciding among alternative theories of memory and with regard to a wide variety of sources of forgetting, from simple lengthening of a retention interval to brain insult (Spear, 1978, Chapter 8). Although it was in terms of human memory processing that these issues initially received most attention, in recent years they also have become considered in depth, and with significance, in studies of animal memory.

But beyond their pervasiveness, these three questions also serve to bring into focus an important pretheoretical distinction in the study of forgetting—between initial storage of the memory and later retrieval of the memory. Whereas the first of the first questions listed in the foregoing clearly is concerned with retrieval, those of memory content and mnemonic preparation may seem just as clearly to be concerned with initial storage of the memory. These impressions are derived, I believe, from the temporal correlation between when the variables are introduced by the experimenter and when the processes of storage and retrieval are thought to occur. To answer the first question, manipulations are introduced just prior to, or during, the retention test; to answer the latter two, manipulations are either in what is to be stored or in the environmental circumstances during, or just after storage. I suggest later that this temporal correlation may mislead us into underestimating the importance of memory retrieval as a determinant of many phenomena of basic conditioning and retention. But first, some consideration of the constructs of memory retrieval and memory storage is in order.

THE RELATIONSHIP BETWEEN MEMORY
STORAGE AND MEMORY RETRIEVAL

Memory storage and memory retrieval are hypothetical constructs representing processes believed to promote, after termination of a significant episode, the manifestation of behavior associated with that particular episode. It is assumed that an internal representation of the episode (the memory) is the fundamental unit of this promotion. Memory storage is the process that establishes the episode as a memory and represents it for further reference. The retrieval process acts on the stored representation of the episode (the memory) at some later time to distinguish it from others and, perhaps simultaneously, to manifest it in terms of behavior (Spear, 1976). Although theoretically distinct, the processes of storage and retrieval are bound intrinsically through their action on a common hypothetical construct—the memory that represents an episode—and probably also by the dependence of retrieval on the degree of similarity between environmental circumstances during memory storage and those when retrieval is required. The "principle of encoding specificity" applies here (Tulving, 1972; Tulving & Thomson, 1973). Those test events that also were represented during memory storage as part of the original episode will determine what is remembered. The simplicity of such a principle should not be taken for lack of power; its application in the field of human memory has touched on some of the most basic issues and controversies (Tulving & Watkins, 1975). Its present reference is to indicate one sense in which memory storage and retrieval are related.

Historically it has seemed useful to delineate storage and retrieval in terms of the locus at which manipulations are introduced to influence remembering. Variables introduced prior to, or simultaneously with, the episode to be remembered are commonly said to have some influence on memory storage; those introduced just prior to the retention test or coincident with it are said to influence memory retrieval. These relationships are no more than a convenience. More importantly, they may be misleading. This can be seen in the following historical account of an important issue in the psychobiological study of animal memory.

A Point of History

When it was established experimentally that later retention could be disrupted or enhanced by electrical or chemical interventions administered to the brain shortly after a conditioning episode, the temporal relationships suggested an influence on memory storage. This was an entirely reasonable judgment. It seemed that the memory otherwise resulting from the conditioning episode was, due to the electrical or chemical disruption, no longer represented and hence unavailable (McGaugh, 1966; McGaugh & Dawson, 1971). It was later determined, however, that the memory in fact remained available in spite of such drastic intervention and could be accessed contingent upon certain cuing events that preceded the retention test and hence were thought to operate on memory retrieval (Lewis, 1969, 1976; Miller & Springer, 1973, 1974). It was determined also that other sources of forgetting as well, such as a long retention interval or the consequences of hormonal duress, could similarly be modified in their effect through such prior cuing manipulations and so viewed as acting on memory retrieval rather than storage (Klein & Spear, 1970; Riccio & Ebner, this volume; Spear, 1971, 1973; Spear, Klein, & Riley, 1971; Spear & Parsons, 1976).

This point of history is to remind us that close temporal contiguity between experimental manipulations of variables and the presumed object of memory storage (the episode to be remembered) does not mean that the effect of these variables on later remembering is due to their action on memory storage. Accordingly, this is an appropriate occasion to acknowledge that a stage analysis treating separately memory storage and memory retrieval is not ideal. A logical difficulty inherent in this sort of analysis is that it precludes decisions about disruption in memory storage. The basic impediment, simple but irrevocable, is that one can assess storage of a memory only in terms of its retrieval, never independently. One can never be certain that a specific bit of information has been eliminated from memory storage, or even that it has been weakened, altered, or strengthened at that stage of processing, because any result indicating these effects might be due to influences at the retrieval stage. Strong conclusions about memory storage, therefore, are pretty much restricted to when one has perfect faith, usually based on a theory or model, that it is indeed memory storage being affected. Given our present state of knowledge, I find this an unsatisfactory basis for conclusions about memory storage.

Inferences about Memory Retrieval

Are we in any better position to draw conclusions about memory retrieval? If one cannot be certain that a manipulation coincident with memory storage in fact influences memory storage, how then can one conclude that a manipulation coincident with memory retrieval, such as prior cuing, influences retrieval but not storage? The fact is that one cannot do so categorically and this is in a sense an indictment against the conceptual framework that distinguishes storage and retrieval as the chief processes in remembering. Some of the difficulties in such a framework have been stated nicely by Watkins (1978), but with the conclusion that for the present there is no better framework through which to work; in this, I agree completely with Watkins. Yet there remains—the disadvantages of stage analysis notwithstanding—the possibility for independent assessment of retrieval effects. An elementary observation is that the events at retrieval cannot work backward in time to affect initial memory storage, not in any simple manner. What we can therefore conclude is that experimental manipulations at the time of memory retrieval cannot *readily* be conceived as affecting memory storage,[1] without a complex array of unlikely assumptions to accommodate the retrograde action, whereas manipulation at the time of memory storage could, with relative ease, be conceived as acting on memory retrieval. By such exclusion, therefore, inferences about memory retrieval are often reasonable.

It is through this sort of reasoning that experimentally derived inferences about memory retrieval have been achieved. The basic experimental strategy has been to determine, following forgetting, whether events presented either prior to testing or during testing would alleviate the forgetting. A number of experiments have confirmed this possibility for a wide variety of sources of forgetting and ways of alleviating it (for a review, see Spear, 1976, 1978). Although a number of excellent experiments have tested these phenomena further since those reviews (Gordon, this volume; Riccio & Ebner, this volume; Rilling, Kendrick, & Stonebraker, in press; Thomas, this volume), it is not my intention to review them here. Comment is needed, however, on two points that immediately arise in consideration of treatments that alleviate forgetting.

The first is how such treatments are defined. What are the necessary and sufficient conditions for alleviating forgetting? There are unfortunately few systematic research programs that have addressed this problem (one is that of Riccio, this volume). Perhaps the best available idea here continues to be the very general one mentioned earlier, "encoding specificity." This principle states, in essence, that the effectiveness of treatments for alleviating forgetting depends not solely on the absolute properties of these treatments, but that an equally important determinant is their relationship with how the target events were encoded and stored originally (Fisher & Craik, 1977; Tulving & Thomson, 1973).

More pertinent to the present chapter is the second point to be considered about these treatments: What are the full consequences of treatments that alleviate forgetting? This question contains several parts. For instance; What are the physiological mechanisms that mediate these effects? (we do not know); or; Is the alleviated forgetting only apparent and the enhanced performance merely an artifact induced by the treatment? (no, at least not in most cases; see Miller & Springer, 1974; Spear, 1973, 1976). The component of this question most relevant here, however, is whether or not the characteristics of the memory change as a consequence of this treatment. That the answer clearly can be affirmative is shown, for example, by Gordon (this volume). It is this factor, I suggest, that has

---

[1]Note that reference to "memory storage" throughout this chapter is only to the initial process through which a memory is stored.

special significance for understanding the relationship between memory storage and memory retrieval.

For proper perspective, however, it is well to remember that a memory made more accessible through such a treatment can be shown to influence the animal's behavior dramatically in circumstances not previously encountered and yet scarcely be altered in many characteristics when reaccessed at a later time. The example I have in mind concerns forgetting induced by retroactive interference from a conflicting memory. Suppose that an animal first acquires memory A and then conflicting memory B, the expression of which is incompatible with that of A. In this case, B weakens or eliminates the immediate tendency to express A. Is this because the animal's representation of A is permanently lost or distorted in storage? That the answer is "no" is shown not only by experiments with pigeons (Thomas, this volume) but also in the following experiments with rats.

Maintained Integrity of a Memory Subjected to Retroactive Interference after It Is Retrieved

We trained rats on two consecutive avoidance tasks in a simple, two-compartment (one black, one white) apparatus. The tasks had a great deal in common. For instance, trials began exactly the same way, with the animal placed in the white compartment followed by the opening of the door to the black compartment. But the response requirements for the first task were exactly contrary to those of the second. To learn the first task the animal had to perform a "passive avoidance" and remain in the white side; if it stepped into the black compartment, a footshock was delivered. The second task, an "active avoidance," required that the animal move from the white to the black compartment within five seconds to avoid a footshock in the white compartment (no shock was delivered in the black compartment). Except for the response–shock contingencies, treatment was the same during the two learning tasks and the retention test. The retention test began with the animal placed in a white compartment in exactly the same manner as in each of the avoidance tasks, but with no shock delivered anywhere. We have worked with this task for a number of years (Spear, 1971) and have a pretty good understanding of its controlling parameters. We know that the following phenomena can be expected with the training parameters we applied in the present experiments: (1) a good deal of negative transfer (slowed escape speeds) occurs on the first active avoidance trial following passive avoidance learning, indicating an active memory for passive avoidance through its maintenance or retrieval, but is nonexistant thereafter and has no influence on rate of learning active avoidance; (2) immediately after active avoidance training the animal behaves little differently than if it had learned only active avoidance; (3) twenty-four hours later (or even an hour or so later) the animal is about as likely to exhibit passive-avoidance behavior as active-avoidance behavior on any particular trial; this presumably indicates a conflict between the two acquired memories.

The question of importance here is whether the characteristics of the passive-avoidance memory were altered because it was active during at least the initial active-avoidance contingencies (inferred from the initial negative transfer). More generally, does the apparent conflict in the later expression of the two memories actually reflect a fundamental change in the memories themselves, such that the initial representation of the passive-avoidance episode, and perhaps also that of the active-avoidance episode, no longer exists? Alternatively, the memories for these two episodes might remain completely intact but with their equally proba-ble expression determined by a random process. Or, perhaps more likely, expres-sion is determined by fluctuations in aspects of the exteroceptive and interocep-tive contexts of testing, on one occasion being more similar to the context that had accompanied passive avoidance and on another more similar to that of the active-avoidance episode. From the last hypothesis, we should be able to pair distinctive contexts with each avoidance contingency and later present one or the other of these contexts to promote expression of the appropriate behavior, with the expectation that the behavior would not be much different than if only that behavior had been learned.

We (Spear, Smith, Bryan, Gordon, Timmons & Chiszar, 1980) conducted two experiments to test this. In the first, a distinctive interoceptive context was associated with each of the alternative episodes. For some animals, passive avoidance was learned following their injection with 15 mg/kg of the barbiturate pentobarbital, whereas active-avoidance learning occurred under the "normal" state (following injection of only the vehicle, saline); for the remaining animals the pairing of drug state and task was reversed. The results, shown in Fig. 12.1, indicate a maintained integrity for each of the conflicting memories. When the animals were tested under the drug state present during passive-avoidance train-ing, mean latency to step from the white to the black (previously shocked, for this task) was a little over 47 sec (maximum possible was 60 sec); in contrast, mean latency to leave the white compartment when tested under the active-avoidance drug state was a little over 10 sec. When tested under the drug state present during passive-avoidance learning, about eight times as many animals exhibited mainly passive-avoidance behavior as exhibited mainly active-avoidance behavior, and when tested under the drug state previously paired with active-avoidance learning, this ratio was almost exactly reversed, with eight times as many animals exhibiting active avoidance as exhibited passive avoidance behavior.

We replicated this pattern of results when distinctive exteroceptive contexts differentiated the occasion of the passive-avoidance and active-avoidance con-tingencies (see Fig. 12.2). The integrity of each behavior was not maintained quite as sharply as when the contextual stimuli were drug states, but we believe this can be attributed to our particular choice of exteroceptive context. The animals learned the two tasks in two different rooms that held different (though

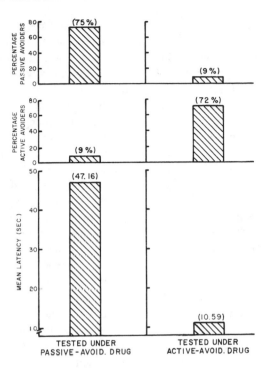

FIG. 12.1.   The results of the retention test are shown separately for animals tested under the drug state associated with passive-avoidance learning (saline or pentobarbital) and those tested under that present during active-avoidance learning. The bottom panel shows mean latency over all five test trials. The top and middle panels indicate the percentage of animals in each condition that behaved in accord with the criterion for passive avoidance and active avoidance, respectively, on more than half of the test trials (adapted from Spear, Smith, Bryan, Gordon, Chiszar, & Timmons, 1980).

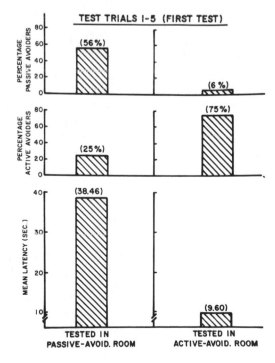

FIG. 12.2.   The results of the retention test (Trials 1–5) are shown separately for animals tested in the room used for passive-avoidance learning and those tested in the room used for active-avoidance learning. The bottom panel shows mean latency over all five test trials. The top and middle panels indicate the percentage of animals in each condition that behaved in accord with the criterion for passive avoidance and active avoidance, respectively, on more than half of the test trials.

nominally identical) apparatuses, and we made no attempt to ensure distinctly different ambient stimulation otherwise. We now believe, based on more recent data I mention in a later section, that exteroceptive control closer to that of the drug could have been obtained by placing distinct odors in the two rooms.

These experiments provide a simple illustration of the power of the contemporary context manipulation. But they also show that under at least some circumstances, a memory can remain surprisingly intact even though active during acquisition of a clearly conflicting memory (by an "intact memory," I mean that the behavior observed reflects quite faithfully the effects of the particular training episode known to produce that behavior). This is of interest in light of evidence that this is not always so. To the contrary, there are indications that a memory becomes susceptible to modification of two kinds whenever it enters an active state. In the next section I consider the experimental paradigms that have provided evidence for such modification of a memory. After a discussion of issues that bear on the interpretation of tests with these paradigms, I suggest that evidence for modification of memories in their active state implies a special commonality in the processes of memory storage and memory retrieval. This leads to the prediction that the effect on later retention of variables introduced at the time of memory storage would be duplicated if these same variables were introduced whenever the memory is made active. A related suggestion is that the effects of a variety of variables introduced at the time of memory storage may in fact be due to influences on memory retrieval.

STUDYING MEMORY RETRIEVAL THROUGH MANIPULATIONS OF CONTEMPORARY CONTEXT

It is well established empirically that retention depends on the context at the time of testing (contemporary context) in relation to that when the episode to be remembered occurred originally. It is also established that such retention can depend on events that precede the test but do not coincide with it (prior cuing), insofar as these events are like those that constituted the episode to be remembered (for further discussion of both phenomena, see Spear, 1976, 1978). This section is concerned with principles that might explain these effects. First, however, there is a need to dispose of what I believe to be an inappropriate, although common explanation for these effects.

"Generalization Decrement" is not a Sufficient Explanation for Contemporary Context Effects

There is an unfortunate tendency to explain retention deficits that accompany a contextual change as "due to simple generalization decrement." The concept "generalization decrement" has been sorely misused in considerations of retention and forgetting. This concept alone could only rarely provide an adequate explanation of alterations in retention caused by contextual changes between learning and testing. The reasons why such an explanation is not appropriate are elementary and require no new empirical evidence.

The term *generalization decrement* originated in reference to the difference between response strength to the conditioned or discriminative stimulus and that to a different stimulus on the same dimension. It arose empirically with respect to psychologically unitized stimuli that had clearly quantifiable physical referents, such as color (wavelength) or tone (frequency). Given certain theoretical assumptions concerning the nature of the discrimination under question and whether generalization is a fundamental property of response strength to a unitized stimulus or is instead derived from a discrimination process, it is perfectly reasonable to use "generalization decrement" to refer to the lesser response strength to such a similar but untrained stimulus. But it is not so reasonable when the nominal test stimulus (the CS or S^D) is identical to the training stimulus and is known to be detected as such by the subject, whereas presumably redundant features of the context, having dimensions different from those that define the target stimulus, are altered between training and testing. This latter case best represents the paradigm of forgetting induced by contextual change in spite of the subject's maintained perception of the more predictive stimuli (CS, S^D) or in other words, an "effect of contemporary context."

My view is that there are at least two sources of decrement in responding when contextual stimuli are changed between training and testing but perception of the CS or S^D is held constant: (1) due to the absence of certain stimuli or because of the equivalent of generalization decrement for the contextual stimuli themselves, there is inadequate contextual support for retrieval of the memory that represents the training episode; and (2) regardless of the support for retrieval of the target memory, the new stimuli introduced upon a change in context may serve to elicit competing memories that interfere with retention of the target. The point is that one never merely removes stimulus elements; what happens is that the context changes, whether by the addition of newly attended stimuli or by a change in the configuration originally presented (Winograd & Rivers-Bulkeley, 1977). Any new configuration or new elements are likely to elicit new responses or, more generally, new memories to compete for expression with that being measured by the experimenter. A third source that has been considered separately, but might be subsumed under the first two sources, is a perceived change in "instructions" as to which response is appropriate (Zentall, 1970). In short, generalization decrement does not help to identify the specific changes in context that are relevant and detrimental.

Generally speaking, to refer to the myriad causes of the forgetting induced by contextual change as, collectively, a simple instance of generalization decrement is to assume a very special (to me, untenable) theory of generalization and stimulus control. Certainly, the theory thereby assumed would be an inappropriately simplistic one having little contact with the classical use of the concept. It is notable that in a related instance, Capaldi (1971) has argued in detail the differences between his elegant theory of how sequential effects determine extinction rates and that of a generalization-decrement theory of extinction. My assumption is that a similarly detailed argument is now unnecessary to dismiss generalization decrement as a self-contained explanation of contextual influences on retention and forgetting.

Principles of Contemporary Context Effects

The development of principles that govern the influence of contemporary context on retention has been impaired in general because of the great diffuseness of the problem, and in particular because manipulations of contemporary context most often combine the deletion of previously present stimuli with replacement by new ones. Analysis of the effects of prior cuing is made simple, by comparison. The prior cuing treatment includes only an additional event not found for the control condition—some sort of cue prior to testing—and the context of testing is held constant.

Another difficulty is simply that the state of the experimental analysis of contextual influences is rather primitive. For instance, if from gross contextual manipulations we are to derive statements as to the required proportion or number of originally acquired memory attributes necessary at testing for the promotion of memory retrieval, we must determine what is and what is not noticed by the subject. An exhaustive assessment of what is noticed at any time by an animal is beyond our present techniques.

But even with these problems of analysis, a step toward developing principles in this area could begin by examining the relationship between different kinds of contextual stimuli. For any two classes of contextual events, for example, is there always equal weighting in terms of the probability of the animal's attention, or will the weighting always differ in accord with, say, an event's biological significance? Or, is each event's relative weighting conditional upon some second or third set of factors? The situation may be still more complicated. Different classes of contextual stimuli might influence the animal's behavior through quite different processes. For instance, one class of stimuli might function exclusively in the promotion of memory retrieval, whereas another acts exclusively on, say, arousal.

I take as a working hypothesis the simple view that all events noticed by the subject, whether endogenous or not and regardless of sensory channeling, can and do influence memory retrieval through the same mechanisms. To test such a homogeneity view, one could, for example, compare the degree of contextual control exerted over expressed memories by exogenously induced drugs and that exerted by exteroceptive stimuli. Reference here is to state-dependent retention and a special case of conditional discrimination. The former is when a memory acquired under drug state A is more likely expressed if the animal is again under drug state A than if in a neutral or different drug state. Overton (1974) has suggested that a better paradigm for testing such drug control in retention is in terms of a conditional discrimination task in which the animal learns that a particular response X is appropriate under drug A but response Y is appropriate in a neutral or different drug state. The present discussion focuses on evidence produced by this latter paradigm.

It has been difficult to deny the argument that contextual control in terms of such a drug-conditional discrimination is of a different kind than that exerted by exteroceptive stimuli. For instance, control over retention simply has seemed so much more rapidly acquired by a variety of drugs than with exteroceptive contextual stimuli as to suggest the operation of different processes in these two cases (for reviews, see Overton, 1966, 1972, 1978; Spear, 1978). My purpose in this section is to note some apparently contrary evidence suggesting instead that drugs and exteroceptive contextual stimuli control memory retrieval through a common mechanism. First, I want to illustrate one aspect of the problem through a long-term research project in my laboratory that, in essence, failed.

Stimulus Control by Drugs and Exteroceptive Stimuli.   Our preliminary intention was simple enough. We planned to compare forgetting of the stimulus control exerted over a conditional discrimination by a drug, with that exerted by an exteroceptive stimulus.

The learning task was the conditional discrimination described previously. The rat was required to learn a spatial discrimination for the efficient escape of a mild footshock; for one drug state or one set of exteroceptive stimuli, the correct spatial location was on the right side of the T-maze, and for the alternative drug state or set of exteroceptive stimuli, the left side was correct. The test for stimulus control by either of these "contextual" events was whether, in the absence of the original reinforcement contingencies defined by location of escape from footshock, the animal would respond correctly in accord with the contemporary contextual event. Such a test can be accomplished either in terms of the first trial of each day (10 trials were given per day, with one value of the contextual stimuli given on odd-numbered days and the other on even-numbered days), by equating the escape contingencies at each alternative spatial location (e.g., by making escape contingent upon entry into either location) or by providing a reversal test (Spear, Smith, Sherr, & Bryan, 1979).

The comparison of forgetting rates was to be accomplished in two simple steps: (1) train the animals until an equivalent level of control is acquired by the drugs and exteroceptive stimuli; and (2) administer a retention test to independent groups of these animals after retention intervals varying between 1 and 60 days. We never got beyond Step 1. The exteroceptive stimuli we used never acquired control comparable to that exerted by the drug. More precisely, the control by any of several sets of exteroceptive stimuli was not acquired at a rate sufficiently comparable to that of the drugs to permit a clean comparison unconfounded by either terminal level of learning or drastic differences in the amount of training needed to achieve that learning. Within 6 to 8 days of training, essentially all animals for whom the drug predicted the discrimination had achieved unerring accuracy in responding on the first trial of a day. In comparison, it was rare with any of several combinations of exteroceptive stimuli to see such control developed within 30 or 40 days of training.

Our persistence in this was remarkable, although not necessarily intelligent. After each replication that told us only that we had an ineffective set of exteroceptive stimuli, we developed new intuition or "insights" from the literature as to which exteroceptive stimuli would surely be effective. We tried room lights on versus off, tones and buzzers and white noise on or off, experimenters wearing or not wearing gloves in handling the animals, Experimenter A versus Experimenter B (i.e., different experimenters that presumably handled the animals slightly differently), and even, at the risk of compromising the term "exteroceptive," training at one time of day versus training at another. None of these, either alone or in combination, had effectiveness comparable to that of the drug (15 mg/kg pentobarbital versus saline).

We did extract some useful information as to the forgetting of only those animals that had acquired their discrimination conditional upon the drug state. We found that over a 60-day period, there was remarkably little forgetting. That adult rats can have excellent retention over very long intervals is hardly newsworthy (cf. Gleitman, 1971; Spear, 1971), but we knew that over the same period, there is substantial forgetting of the simple discrimination (right versus left) imbedded within this conditional discrimination (Smith & Spear, 1981). It seemed reasonable that the conditional version of this discrimination would show no less forgetting. We also found that for those animals tested under the influence of the drug, significantly less forgetting occurred than for those animals tested in a normal state. This suggests the possibility of special protection from "normal" sources of forgetting for memories both acquired and retrieved under a relatively unusual drug state (for a similar possibility, see Concannon, Smith, Spear, & Scobie, 1979).

Control by Exteroceptive Stimuli Through Interaction with Drug Stimuli.   In spite of our failure to solve the original problem, there was still another "spinoff" return from the project. This matter involves the comparability of contextual control by drugs and by exteroceptive stimuli in another way—in terms of how these two classes of stimuli interact. Suppose that we form a stimulus compound of drug state and exteroceptive stimuli. The general question is whether there are interactions between these two kinds of stimuli such that they function in pretty much the same way as two compounded exteroceptive stimuli of differing salience, and so are processed according to the same principles of stimulus selection (e.g., overshadowing or blocking).

Some indication of such a "conventional" interaction between interoceptive (drug) and exteroceptive stimuli was obtained from a small experiment conducted in our laboratory at Rutgers University in collaboration with Professor Leonard Hamilton. We did this when rather desperately seeking a technique through which exteroceptive contextual stimuli would acquire a degree of control comparable to that induced by the drug (a barbiturate) we were using as a standard. The Overton technique described earlier (the conditional discrimination) was used.

We trained rats with alternative compound contextual stimuli consisting of a distinctive drug state plus a distinctive set of exteroceptive stimuli. For instance, when the correct alternative was on the left side of the T-maze, a given rat was exposed to an injection of 15 mg/kg of pentobarbitol plus lights on, white noise on, and gloves when handled; the corresponding exposure when the right side was correct included an injection of saline, lights off, white noise off, and no gloves used during handling. Under these conditions, the animals began within 6 days or so to respond in accord with the contextual events on the first trial of each day (and, of course, on subsequent trials as well). From the bitter experience described earlier, we were aware that it was the drug state that was exerting the control, not the exteroceptive stimuli. After a few days of testing under these conditions to assure us of the contextual control we had expected, the drug stimulus was "faded out" by reducing the dosage in discrete steps. First the 15 mg/kg was reduced to 10 mg/kg, then to 5, and then to 0, so that only the vehicle was injected in the same manner as on the days when the alternative goal box was correct. What we found was that the animals continued to behave as if the drug difference were still compounded with the differences in the exteroceptive stimuli, even when only the vehicle was injected. In other words, the animals continued to respond correctly on the first trial of each day (and thereafter), and this could only have been in accord with the exteroceptive stimuli because there were no longer any differences in drug states. Because we knew from our previous experiments that the exteroceptive stimuli would not have begun to acquire comparable control by this time, it appeared that the exteroceptive stimuli had absorbed the control from the drug stimuli. That the "fading" technique is commonly used to transfer stimulus control from an easy exteroceptive discrimination to a more difficult one suggests that the same processes operating for exteroceptive stimuli were responsible for the present case of transfer of drug control.

I want to emphasize that this was simply an initial experiment. We did not include several control conditions needed to conclude decisively about this trade-off of control between drug and exteroceptive stimuli. The result is interesting nevertheless because of the analytical possibilities it presents. The remaining question is whether the "fading" technique served to transfer control from the drug state to the exteroceptive stimuli in the same manner as is found conventionally in transferring control from easily discriminated exteroceptive stimuli to a second, more difficult discrimination of this same kind (Miller & Balaz, this volume). An affirmative answer would support our working hypothesis, the homogeneity view.

Two other experimental results also suggest that the behavioral consequences of a drug-based manipulation of contemporary context (i.e., state-dependent retention) may be governed by the same principles that determine effects of contemporary context manipulations with only exteroceptive stimuli. First and most compelling is the recent discovery by Overton (1979) that rats can learn to discriminate their normal state from that of surprisingly low drug doses if they are trained first to discriminate between higher drug doses and their normal state. With exteroceptive stimuli the relative ease of transfer from easy to hard discriminations is a well-known principle applied to permit learning of otherwise unsolvable discrimination problems. Overton's observation provides therefore another functional similarity between drugs and exteroceptive stimuli. From his data Overton (1979) concludes: "the results support sensory interpretations of SDL (state dependent learning) and of DDs (drug discrimination) [Page 721]." The second result, from a recent experiment by Sheila Corrigan in our laboratory, is that by including alternative novel odors among the exteroceptive stimuli in the Overton paradigm, the rate of acquisition of the conditional discrimination approaches that found with alternative drug states. This not only provides for the experimental comparisons we had sought earlier but also confirms our suspicion that the extraordinary stimulus control exerted by drug states might be matched with the proper selection of exteroceptive stimuli.

PRIOR CUING: IMPLICATIONS FOR THE RELATIONSHIP BETWEEN MEMORY STORAGE AND MEMORY RETRIEVAL

Prior cuing is a paradigmatic technique for alleviating forgetting. It includes presentation, prior to the retention test, of an event associated with the target memory. These items or events are likely to be some aspect of the context of original learning, but prior cuing is distinct, temporally, from contemporary context. For prior cuing the relationship between the contextual circumstances of training and testing are held constant, and variation is only in the stimulation conditions *prior* to the test; the corresponding variation of contemporary context is concurrent with the test. For purposes of analysis it is important to keep these two paradigms separate, and when the manipulations of prior cuing lead to systemic effects in the animal that might continue into the time of the retention test, these effects must be accounted for very carefully (for elaboration, see Spear, 1976).

Application of the prior-cuing paradigm is one area of memory research in which analytical tests with animals have preceded, and far exceeded, those with human subjects (for review, see Spear, 1976, 1978). This imbalance has continued since the last review of this work (for exceptions, see Macht & O'Brien, 1980; Macht & Spear, 1977; and several papers by Rovee-Collier and her associates, e.g., Rovee-Collier, 1980). The most extensive use of this paradigm has been to decide whether the storage-failure hypothesis for particular instances of forgetting can be rejected (Lewis, 1969). The paradigm itself has also been studied to determine its characteristics and boundary conditions and hence, presumably, those of memory retrieval (Riccio & Ebner, this volume). A third application of this paradigm has been for comparing the characteristics of recently acquired memories and those previously acquired but only recently retrieved (Gordon, 1977; Spear, 1976). Fourth, this paradigm can be applied toward understanding exactly how (or if) memories change as they "age" (i.e., the longer the time since their acquisition [Spear, Hamberg, & Bryan, 1980]). And it can be used to resolve a variety of other issues in forgetting, such as infantile amnesia (Spear & Parsons, 1976).

The application of greatest interest for the present chapter, however, is to understand the full set of consequences of bringing a memory to an active state. One such consequence may be illustrated in the following experiment.

Possible Strengthening Effects of Reactivation

With rats as subjects, we conditioned an aversion to a compound stimulus consisting of a particular location and a flashing light, and then tested the strength of this aversion after 3 min, 1, 3, or 7 days (Spear et al., 1980). The intention was to compare rate of forgetting by these rats with that of another set of animals given the same kind of conditioning but then returned to their home cages for 4 weeks. We knew the latter animals would exhibit extensive forgetting after this period (Spear & Parsons, 1976). After this 4-week interval, these rats were exposed to a prior-cuing treatment (the unconditioned stimulus—a single footshock—in an apparatus quite different from the one in which they were conditioned). We knew that this treatment would alleviate the forgetting and yield retention about equal to that found after original conditioning (Spear & Parsons, 1976). The sequence, to this point in the experiment, was: learn, forget, prior-cuing treatment. The question was, how would the subsequent decline in retention over a 7-day interval compare with that following only original learning?

The answer to this question was totally unexpected. What we found was less rapid forgetting following prior cuing than following original conditioning. Three or 7 days after prior cuing, retention was markedly superior to that found 3 or 7 days following original conditioning (Fig. 12.3). It is notable that for those animals tested 3 or 7 days following prior cuing, it had been over a month since they were given conditioning. The control conditions we tested in this series of experiments excluded relatively trivial factors such as systemic effects of the prior-cuing treatment or direct transfer between the contingencies of the prior-

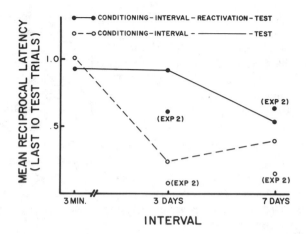

FIG. 12.3.   The decline in retention is shown as a function of length of the interval since the memory was last made active. For those subjects represented by the solid circles, the memory was last made active by a reactivation treatment that had followed original conditioning by 28 days and so the test followed conditioning by 28, 31, or 35 days; for subjects represented by the open circles, the last time the memory previously had been active was during original conditioning and so the test followed conditioning by 3 min, 3 days, or 7 days. The index of retention in this figure is reciprocal latency to escape stimuli previously paired with an aversive footshock; for this task, the higher the reciprocal latency, the better the retention.

cuing treatment and the testing situation (by the latter, I refer to the possibility of "new learning," an issue that may be resolved empirically in a number of ways; e.g., Gordon, this volume).

Three potential interpretations of these data are concerned with age of the memory at the time of prior cuing, accessibility of the memory at prior cuing, and activation-induced changes in the memory. As to the former two, it is possible that simply as a consequence either of having been a part of one's repertoire of memories for a long period (Jost, 1897; Ribot, 1896) or of having reached the low level of accessibility that usually accompanies such "aging" of a memory, the memory's later activation by prior cuing would induce a "strengthening" that could include increased resistance to subsequent forgetting. The alternative of present interest, however, is the third one. One case of a change in the *quality* of a memory upon its reactivation has been analyzed by Gordon (this volume); I consider next the type of change suggested by Fig. 12.3—that in the probability of later accessibility—due to reactivation of a memory.

The Effect of Test Trials on Later Retention by Humans

In relation to a second retention test, an initial retention test is, by operational definition, a special case of a prior-cuing treatment. Conventional tests of retention have, therefore, a potential for promoting memory retrieval. Whether a particular test does in fact do so probably depends on the commonality of events at the test trial and those of the original learning episode, and perhaps also, on the particular activities of mnemonic preparation the subject engages in when tested (Spear, 1971, 1976, 1978). Experiments on human learning in particular indicate a facilitating influence of test effects on later retention. A fine review of this literature has been published by Cooper and Monk (1976). My intention here is to illustrate the scope of the effects and something of their interpretations and implications, with selected evidence not covered by Cooper and Monk.

The phenomenon of fundamental interest is this: When humans are tested for retention of learned sets of words, with or without feedback as to accuracy, one consequence is to enhance retention for these words at a later time in comparison with subjects not given the initial test. For instance, Engle and Mobley (1976) presented subjects with 20 lists of 12 high-frequency words each. Some subjects were presented the words projected on a screen and others heard them spoken through headphones. Free recall was tested immediately after presentation for a randomly determined half of these lists, but not for the remainder. Subjects were not told whether a list would be tested until after it was presented. After all 20 lists had been presented, the subjects were asked, without prior warning, to recall as many of the words as they could from all lists. Whether presentation of the words had been auditory or visual, more than twice as many words were recalled from previously tested lists as from those lists not previously tested.

It is this facilitating effect of prior testing that is of interest here. But we must keep in mind that this is not the only effect possible. Under certain circumstances an opposing consequence of a recall test is to *impair* retention of items from the same episode that have not yet been expressed by the subject (Roediger, 1974; Tulving & Arbuckle, 1966). Moreover, some tests of recognition also may include sources of interference that impair later retention, and the basic effect is not limited to verbal materials (Postman, 1975; see Jones & Holding, 1975 for a general disrupting effect of testing in terms of the McCollough effect). Facilitation in retention of some attributes of a memory by prior retrieval of other attributes of that memory is therefore only one of two opposing consequences of prior cuing; the other consequence can be impairment in retention. Both must be considered carefully when evaluating memory retrieval phenomena. At this point, however, the focus is on the *beneficial* consequences of testing on later retention, and on the processes responsible for this benefit. For instance, evidence suggests that later retention benefits more from testing, the longer the interval between initial acquisition and the first test (prior cuing) (Cooper & Monk, 1976, p. 136; for an analogous conclusion from the effects of prior cuing in animals, see Spear, Hamberg, & Bryan, 1980, Exp. 4). What processes underlie this effect?

What Determines How Much a Test Helps Subsequent Retention?   Retention seems to benefit from prior testing in direct relation to the subject's difficulty in remembering during the initial test. It is as if active processing by the subject during testing is important for the promotion of later retrieval. For instance, Whitten and Bjork (1977) established that initial testing aided later recall more the longer the interval between original presentation and the initial test. Retrieval at the initial test was more difficult the longer the interval since the items were presented, as evidenced by the poorer initial recall. This effect on recall was quite similar to that of spacing of an actual repetition (the interval between one presentation of an item and the next). This suggests that similar processes might contribute to the retention effects of testing and those of another powerful determinant of retention, distribution of practice (Spear, 1978, 1979).

That later retention benefits especially from active attempts to recall—the sort promoted when recall is difficult—is suggested by other data of Whitten and Bjork. They found that asking the subject merely to rehearse the item in place of the actual test did not aid later recall as much as when subjects were required actually to retrieve and produce the items.

Another illustration of the role of initial retrieval difficulty in later retention is in a study by Whitten and Leonard (1980). They examined the effects of a recognition test on later recall. Generally speaking, recognition performance can be impaired by increasing either the number of distracters or the semantic similarity between the distracters and the target items. In this experiment, recall on a later test benefited from initial recognition testing more, the greater the number of distracter items and the greater the similarity between the distracters and targets.

The Bjork–Geiselman Experiments.   A final illustration of this point is provided by Bjork and Geiselman (1978). These authors report three experiments applicable to the question of whether the requirements of a retention test affect retention on a later test. They focused on whether difficulty in initial memory retrieval determines later retention. The design of these experiments took advantage of a characteristic of "directed forgetting" (for a consideration of this phenomenon in animals, see chapters by Grant, Honig, and Maki, this volume). For the prototypic test of directed forgetting with humans, subjects are presented verbal units, usually words. Each work is followed by a signal to either remember it or forget it. The characteristic exploited by Bjork and Geiselman is that subjects conduct additional mnemonic operations on words they are signaled to remember. These operations apparently differ from those when the signal is to forget, because the product differs. For instance, recall of the remember words is greater than that of the forget words.

The experimental variable of central interest in these experiments was duration of the delay between presentation of a word and the signal to forget or remember it. By occupying the subject during this delay, the probability of recalling the word for processing upon receiving a remember signal could be expected to decrease, and retrieval presumably made more difficult, as the delay lengthened. The question was, would this greater difficulty in initial retrieval increase the probability of recalling these items later? Ultimately the answer was yes, but for points of further interest, a few details must be described.

The subjects were instructed that after the appearance of each pair of words (simple, four-letter nouns) a signal would tell them whether to remember or forget that pair. Between each pair and the signal, the subjects were occupied with simple arithmetic problems for either 3, 6, 9, or 12 sec. After 16 pairs had been presented in this manner, each subject worked on another of these problem-solving tasks for 90 sec. At this point some of the subjects were asked to recall the pairs from that list while the others merely continued with the problems. A second list of 16 noun pairs was then presented in the same manner as the first. Ninety seconds later, subjects that had recalled the first list simply continued with their problem-solving activities while the others recalled list 2. Finally, at the end of the experiment, all subjects were asked to recall all the words they could from both lists, only half of which they had attempted to recall earlier. In summary, the important variation was in length of the interval between exposure to an item and the signal to remember or forget it, and in whether or not a particular list had previously been tested for recall.

There were two major results. First, as hinted earlier, recall of a word pair on the later tests was better the longer the delay between initial presentation of the word and the signal that it was to be remembered. This was so whether the recall test was given immediately after the entire list had been presented or at the end of the experiment (for the latter test there was, in addition, significantly better recall for items that had been tested earlier). Because a similar effect did not occur for words followed by a forget signal, we can infer that this relationship was due to the specific mnemonic operations performed by the subject on words signaled to be remembered. We can infer also that these operations included those that ordinarily accompany memory retrieval after short intervals. Finally, because processing of items between the time of their presentation and the signal to remember was minimized or prevented by the distracter activity, we can infer that the primary influence of increasing the duration of this interval was to make their initial retrieval more difficult.

Further experiments by Bjork and Geiselman determined that these effects were not magical consequences of the instruction "remember" in contrast to "forget." They arranged for promotion of the retrieval of each word pair regardless of the signal that followed. They did this by asking the subject to check, when the forget-remember signal was presented, whether they did or did not remember the left or right member of the pair, regardless of how they were signaled (the signal, they were told, applied only for later testing). The result was better recall on the later test for *all* words the longer the interval between their presentation and the signal (and hence, presumably, the poorer the initial recall). When the subjects had to check whether they did or did not remember an item, thus simulating a retention test, it did not matter whether the signal had been to remember or to forget.

To summarize, Bjork and Geiselman found, first, that later recall of words was facilitated when subjects previously had applied retrieval operations to these same words. This result had good generalizability in that it occurred for three kinds of retrieval operations: (1) explicit attempts to retrieve the items on an actual test; (2) implicit retrieval of the words induced by a signal to remember them (as opposed to forget); and (3) implicit retrieval induced by having the subjects respond to all items in such a way as to require indirectly that they remember something about all words, whether accompanied by the forget or remember signal. Second, they found that the more difficult the initial retrieval (i.e., the less the initial recall expected due to longer delays between presentation of the words and the cue to forget or remember) the greater the advantage of this retrieval for later recall.

What Test Effects Might Tell Us about the Relationship between Memory Storage and Memory Retrieval

That subsequent recall of a set of verbal units is increased by a test of their retention is central to the point of this chapter. This is a substantial effect. Is it of interest beyond the effects of mere physical repetition that can be provided by some tests of human memory? I believe so, but the issues and evidence require too great a diversion to be discussed here (for further consideration, see Spear & Mueller, in preparation). Generally it seems safe to assume that these test effects are not attributable to relatively uninteresting factors such as extra recall time, a factor known to account for other cases of facilitated retention (Roediger & Thorpe, 1978).

Equally important to the present theme is the evidence indicating an extra benefit for later recall when memory retrieval is relatively difficult during the earlier test. This benefit from "difficult" processing during memory retrieval seems to occur also when the processing is for initial memory storage. Discussion of this correspondence requires a brief diversion.

Current theories of memory processing in humans emphasize an active organizational or quasi-organizational processing in which individuals purposefully engage, upon presentation of verbal materials to be remembered. These analyses include principles for distinguishing purposeful or "voluntary" (or "control") processing from processing that seems relatively automatic (Hasher & Zacks, 1979; Shiffrin & Schneider, 1977). For some theorists, the nature or extent of such voluntary processing is believed to determine later accessibility of the target material. Attempts have been made to dimensionalize "nature" or "extent" with constructs such as "levels," "distinctiveness," or "effort" (Cermak & Craik, 1979; Tyler, Hertel, McCallum, & Ellis, 1979). Although controversy remains as how best to conceptualize the dimension, there is agreement empirically that those episodes accompanied by "deeper," more "distinctive," or more "difficult" processing upon their initial occurrence are remembered better. This general phenomenon has important similarity to the testing effect reviewed earlier—namely, that when retrieval is difficult and so presumably extra process-ing is required during an initial test, retention is better at a later test. The similarity of this effect during original learning and during a retention test is notable. It is one of the factors that suggests the action of common processes in memory storage and memory retrieval, in accord with our earlier discussion.

The general proposition that common processes are used for initial storage and later retrieval of a memory has slowly been emerging in a variety of settings. The idea is by no means new. Semon (1923) included it as an important part of his theory, as elaborated by Schacter, Eich and Tulving (1978). But more recently, from the vantage point of better evidence, this idea seems increasingly useful. For instance, Jacoby and Craik (1979) suggest the following: "First, if the original encoding is difficult to accomplish, later memory of the event will usually be good.... As initial encoding becomes easier (with practice, say), there is a concommitant increase in the level of recognition....The effects of difficulty of *retrieval* on subsequent retention of the event can also be described in this way [Page 6]." These authors state further: "Thus retrieval operations vary in their extensiveness.... It is assumed that retrieval processes mirror initial encoding processes and may thus also be described as varying in depth, elaboration, and distinctiveness [Page 8]." And finally: "Retrieval is regarded as being quite analogous to a second encoding; just as study processing is under the control of task demands, so is retrieval processing [Page 18]."

I share this view. It seems to me wholly plausible that during initial memory storage, some previously acquired information must be accessed for proper "understanding" of the to-be-stored episode—call it categorizing, cataloging, application of schema, or whatever. Something in the spirit of Piaget's assimilation–accommodation sequence seems unlikely to be very wrong albeit unwieldy in such general form. During memory retrieval this same process of accessing previously acquired information would seem to proceed on a more focused level. And, just as previously stored information may be changed (e.g., recategorized) to accommodate storage of a new memory, modification of a previously acquired memory may also occur at the time it is retrieved, in accord with contemporary events (Gordon, this volume; Loftus, 1979). For this latter case, as with initial memory storage, we might expect that the extent of the modification will depend on how unusual these events are in the context of those represented by the retrieved memory (possibly consistent with the system pro-posed by Wagner, this volume).

It is dangerous to skip from an empirical base derived from verbal memory processing by humans to the more general level I seek. With animal subjects there is no direct counterpart to the empirical analysis of test effects in humans. Animals cannot be merely instructed to recall, and so their "tests" must include (not unlike the case with human subjects) at least some of the events intrinsic to original learning. For a properly conservative examination of this effect with animals, therefore, the initial "test" would need to be structured so as to preclude new learning that might transfer to the previously acquired memory. This is exactly analogous to the problem addressed by Gordon (this volume) in evaluating reactivation treatments, of which test trials are a special case. And, the solution is the same—the most conservative approach is to use extinction procedures as the initial "test." Extinction procedures ensure that subsequent enhancement of retention cannot be due to new learning about the original contingencies of reinforcement; the new learning during extinction is diametrically opposed to the net facilitation produced by the reactivation treatment.

Are there any indications that extinction trials improve later retention scores for animal subjects in the way that tests of recall do for humans? No systematic series of studies with animals has directly addressed this particular problem. A fair assessment of the enhancement effect would in any case require that the counterconditioning or inhibitory effects of extensive extinction treatment be subtracted somehow from the overall effect. But even with such an analysis, reasonably analogous examples within the study of basic conditioning indicate that extinction test trials can enhance later test performance, beyond transient systemic effects such as frustration. This topic has ordinarily been raised, however, in terms of whether some particular class of response-contingent event is necessary to establish learning (see, for example, Guthrie, 1935; Spence, 1956).

What is needed for illustration purposes is a study of the effect of test trials on later retention unconfounded by positive effects of particular reinforcer contingencies on that test trial, or in other words, tests that involve extinction operations. In the absence of a previously stimulus- or response-contingent reinforcer, enhanced retention by such test trials would be especially impressive because it must override the negative effects of these extinction operations. A reasonably applicable example with simple instrumental learning is found in a series of experiments by Jensen and Cotton about 20 years ago. These studies indicated that in the context of instrumental responding for food reward, the effect of an interpolated series of extinction trials was strikingly similar to that of further conditioning trials, in terms of the subsequent elevation of performance when the contingency between the response and the food were reinstated. With rats as subjects, this effect was found for speed of running in a straight alley runway (Jensen & Cotton, 1960), for discrimination behavior in a T-maze (Cotton & Jensen, 1963), and to some extent for free-operant lever pressing (Jensen, 1961). The related fact in studies intended to investigate memory retrieval—that modified extinction "test" trials can enhance retention performance in the role of a prior-cuing treatment—has of course been established frequently (Gordon, this volume; Gordon & Spear, 1973b; Spear, 1971).

Perhaps, however, the retention enhancement derived from test trials with human subjects has no connection with the strengthening of conditioned responding by animals after extinction trials or prior-cuing treatments. I do not believe this for a minute, but the argument could be made in plausible fashion. An important basis for this argument could be the special facility often assumed in humans for dealing symbolically with the sorts of verbal materials used to study the test-trial effects. It might be suggested, for instance, that the human has a singular facility during test trials to repeat and reorganize the verbal materials to be remembered later. But although it is hard to deny that in some circumstances the process or reorganization of materials unique to humans might be important for this effect, it is equally difficult to accept this as the sole mechanism (see review by Cooper & Monk, 1976).

Are there any cases in which a treatment similar to prior cuing with animals (i.e., re-presentation of some fraction of a conditioning trial) has benefited later retention performance for human subjects when verbal materials are not used, organization not particularly beneficial, and verbal mediation of any kind relatively unlikely? At least one such result has been reported, by Kimble, Mann, and Dufort (1955, Exp. IV) in terms of aversive conditioning of the eyelid response in humans. This sort of evidence suggests (though of course does not demand) that a common feature of memory processing is being tapped in this whole array of experiments.

I propose the following inference from prior-cuing experiments and the effects of prior test trials: The information processing in which an animal engages when tested is much the same as that during training. To say this in another way: Whenever retrieval of a memory is required, the processing of information— whether of events physically present or of stored representation of events—is like that that occurs during original storage of the memory. It seems likely, moreover, that a memory acquired to represent a particular episode is continually subject to modification through the processing that occurs whenever it is retrieved, becoming integrated with contemporary information. The test-trial effect of increased retention on later tests suggests that a frequent consequence of such a process is more ready access to the memory at a later time. One might speculate that a contemporary-context relationship is in part responsible for this test-trial effect: perhaps the enhanced access is controlled by circumstances ''at a later time'' (second test) that are similar to the (previously) ''contemporary information'' provided by the first test and incorporated within the attributes of the originally stored target memory.

This sort of reasoning, especially as verified in experiments like those of Gordon (this volume) and Miller (1981), helps us to understand the retrieval process. I suggest that we carry this line of reasoning still further, to help us understand what happens during initial storage of a memory. In the next section, I propose that we apply concepts needed to explain prior-cuing treatments and the characteristics of memory retrieval to help us understand the basic learning process, because the processes of initial memory storage may be revealed more readily through analysis of common processes in memory retrieval.

What Prior-Cuing Effects Might Tell Us about Original Conditioning and Learning

Forgetting due to many sources can be alleviated by a prior-cuing treatment (also termed *reactivation treatment,* or *reminder*) that includes, fundamentally, re-presentation of some isolated aspect of the episode to be remembered. From this effect we can infer that the treatment serves to transform the target memory from an inactive to an active state, thus increasing the later accessibility of the target's behavioral attributes for retrieval and promotion of the memory's manifestation in behavior.

This inference has led to this question: What is the relationship between a recently acquired memory and one recently reactivated by a prior-cuing treatment? It is understood that in the latter case, the memory was acquired earlier and made relatively inactive by a source of forgetting, and that the prior-cuing treatment itself is insufficient to yield the behavior that indexes the target memory. The following are the major functional similarities that have been determined so far: (1) both are susceptible to the disruptive effects of electroconvulsive shock (DeVietti & Holliday, 1972; Lewis, Bregman, & Mahan, 1972; Misanin, Miller, & Lewis, 1968); (2) both are susceptible to the facilitative effects of strychnine (Gordon, 1977; Gordon & Spear, 1973b); (3) both can interfere proactively with retention of later learning (Gordon, Frankl, & Hamberg, 1979; Gordon & Spear, 1973a); and (4) both are susceptible to increased forgetting as the interval lengthens between acquisition or prior cuing and the retention test (Gordon & Feldman, 1979; Rovee-Collier et al., 1980; Spear, Hamberg, & Bryan, 1980).

In the experimental study of these effects, it has been common to ask this slightly more precise question: How similar are these particular effects on recently acquired and recently reactivated memories? For Items 1 and 2 in the previous paragraph, studies have compared the shapes of the retrograde amnesic or hypermnesic gradients relating degree of amnesia or hypermnesia to length of the interval between activation of the memory (by original learning or prior cuing) and introduction of the amnestic or hypermnestic treatment. For Item 3, the effect of the intertask interval on proactive interference was compared when the "Task 1" memory was either acquired for the first time or merely reactivated. For Item 4, experiments have compared the functions relating retention and length of the interval between original acquisition or prior cuing and the retention test. Except for Item 4, where conclusions have been mixed, no significant differences were found in these characteristics of recently reactivated and recently acquired memories. A similar conclusion was reached with respect to Item 4 for two of the studies (Gordon & Feldman, 1979; Rovee-Collier et al., 1980), whereas in the other study in this category, rate of subsequent forgetting was less rapid following prior cuing than after simple acquisition of a memory (Spear et al., 1980).

The point of this review is to consider an inference from these sorts of studies:

the aforementioned similarities between the characteristics of recently acquired and recently activated memories suggest similarities in the processes active in these two circumstances. Stated simply, it appears that there are significant similarities in the way an animal processes the information in a memory when it is initially acquired and when it is retrieved. The suggestion I wish to advance is that the processes of memory storage and of memory retrieval may be more than just similar—certain subprocesses may in fact be common to both storage and retrieval. What are these common subprocesses? A likely candidate is the series of operations needed for release of the stored information that provides a schema for interpreting (perceiving) the contemporary events of an episode to be learned; a further common step would be the integration of this previously acquired and newly acquired information. It seems likely, in view of how contextual similarity can control memory retrieval, that some aspect of the animal's set of previously acquired, stored information will be retrieved when a "relevant" new episode is encountered. "Relevant" indicates the existence of contemporary events sufficiently similar to some of those represented in a previously acquired memory so as to promote its arousal into an active state. This treatment of thoroughly integrated, previously acquired information is in the sense of Tulving's (1972) "semantic" memory, Bergson's (1911) "pure" memory, or D. Locke's "factual" memory (see Hintzman, 1978, p. 367). Probably it need not be added that this "previously acquired" information that provides the interpretive schema is meant to incorporate species-specific dispositions for which only nonspecific experience, or a minimum of specific experience, might be required.

That previously acquired memories become integrated with contemporary events accompanying their retrieval is shown by Gordon (this volume). To a certain extent, this same process is shown during many cases of transfer of learning, to the extent that the "fate" of the alternative memories is assessed thereafter (Barnes & Underwood, 1959; Spear, 1978). It is important, however, to be cautious about overstating the extent to which contemporary events become integrated with retrieved memories and thereby influence the form of their subsequent expression. An extreme case of this sort of overstatement is this paraphrasing of Bartlett (1932): ". . . that remembering can in no sense be regarded as the mere retrieval of earlier experience; it is a process of active reconstruction, much of it based on factors of general impression and attitude, together with the reinstatement of a small amount of critical detail . . . recall is far more decisively an affair of construction than one of mere reproduction." (Zangwill, 1972, p. 126; in the case of animals, one might feel more comfortable in reading "acquired dispositions" for "general impression and attitude"). Although such "cognitive" activity might seem rather remote to the rat's dispositions or capacities, it might be noted that as a determinant of retention, this sort of factor may have in any case been exaggerated by Bartlett (see Zangwill, 1972). Yet, the evidence has begun to converge on the conclusion that previously acquired memories are made active upon the occurrence of sufficiently similar contemporary events. Common processes are engaged whether the contemporary events include contingencies to be learned for the first time (memory storage) or a subset of those events to which the animal must respond after a source of forgetting has been introduced (memory retrieval).

Can any of this be tested? Is there any more to this than speculation? I submit again that the sort of paradigm introduced by Gordon (this volume) can be applied to this set of ideas, as can the paradigm for comparison of recently acquired and recently reactivated memories (Spear, 1976). Following a brief summary, I consider specific predictions arising from this discussion and how these predictions might be tested.

SUMMARY, PRINCIPLES, PREDICTIONS AND TESTS

My intention has been to emphasize three points about memory retrieval. Each of these is concerned with the relationship between this process and that of initial memory storage. The first point is that special temporal contiguity between original learning and any particular condition that influences later retention is not a sufficient basis for inferring that this condition affected initial storage. In spite of close temporal contiguity, the conditions of storage might ultimately have their effect through modification of memory retrieval, by altering either the retrieval process itself or the effectiveness of this process (Spear, 1976). The second point is that there is extensive overlap among the subprocesses that make up memory storage and those that constitute memory retrieval. Because of this—and this is the third point—we should be able to predict how certain conditions will affect the consequences of prior cuing (when retrieval is inferred), from how these same conditions are known to affect the initial storage of a memory. If this constitutes a model, it is one of the simplest imaginable. It is in fact merely an empirical generalization within the functionalist tradition, that happens to yield interesting predictions.

The predictions fall into two classes. One has to do with principles for predicting the effects of prior-cuing treatments. The other is concerned with localization of the mechanisms responsible for effects on conditioning and learning produced by variables introduced concurrent with (or prior to) the episode to be remembered.

A Principle of Prior Cuing

I suggest a principle of prior cuing that is quite simple: Whatever influences original learning will act during prior cuing to have a similar effect on later retention. Said another way, variables that have a particular effect on original learning when introduced at the time of the episode to be remembered will have the same effect on later retention if introduced at the time of the prior-cuing treatment. It is understood that content of the memory—i.e., components of the particular episode to be remembered—is held constant for original conditioning and the prior-cuing treatment. Reference here, therefore, is primarily to environmental variables and secondarily to subject variables (individual differences).

Experiments to test this principle would be quite straightforward. Consider, for instance, the effects of variation in how an episode is presented. A common example (for some episodes) is distribution of practice—the more distributed the practice, the better the retention. We could then expect that following forgetting, a distributed series of prior-cuing treatments would have greater benefit for subsequent retention than would a massed series (provided that the prior-cuing treatment does not have extinction consequences that might themselves be facilitated by distributed practice). As another illustration, we know that conditioning with certain episodes is more effective at one point in the animal's circadian cycle than at another; an example is conditioned flavor aversion, which is more effective for adults when conditioning is given during their light cycle (Infurna, Steinert, Freda, & Spear, 1979). We would expect that prior-cuing treatments effective in alleviating forgetting of conditioned flavor aversion would be more beneficial to later retention if administered during the light phase of the cycle, compared to during the dark phase. A corollary prediction concerns subject variables: Because the optimal time of day for conditioning of flavor aversion seems to vary slightly for animals of different ages, we would expect that the effectiveness of a reactivation treatment at a particular time of day would vary for infants and adults in parallel with the corresponding variation in conditioning effectiveness (Caza, Steinert, & Spear, 1980; Infurna, 1980).

In a more general sense, we could expect that any of the class of "mnemonic preparation" variables having a particular effect on original learning would, when initiated instead at the time of prior cuing, have the same effect on later retention. "Mnemonic preparation" refers to any of a variety of activities in which organisms may engage to alter their retention or forgetting. Even though an animal in nature could not control the circumstances of memory retrieval or the intrinsic nature of the episode that is to be remembered, it could nevertheless vary such things as the amount of exposure to a particular episode, the distribution of that exposure, characteristics of its attention to that episode, and potentially, at least, mnemonic activities that constitute posttrial processing (evidence for the latter is described in the chapters by Wagner, by Maki, and by Grant, this volume; for a review of specific cases of mnemonic preparation, see Spear, 1978).

Conditioning Variables that Affect Memory Retrieval

I alluded earlier to instances in which treatments administered concurrent with the operations of original conditioning or shortly thereafter have been shown to affect memory retrieval. We can acknowledge that such variables—amnestic treatments, for instance—may also have influenced the efficacy of initial storage of the memory. Storage processes such as consolidation or rehearsal could in relatively easy fashion account for, say, retrograde *gradients* of amnesia, whereas it is admittedly less than obvious how a retrieval process could do so. Yet it must equally be acknowledged that even here, certain mechanisms that might be responsible for retrieval could provide plausible explanations (Miller & Marlin, 1979). This point, in combination with the fundamental impossibility of concluding about initial memory storage independently of memory retrieval, has seemed to indicate that at least for now, there is a certain analytical advantage in focusing on understanding the latter.

A similar skepticism seems warranted with regard to a memory-storage in-terpretation of more innocuous circumstances that alter learning when they are introduced coincident with the episode to be remembered. Among the fundamen-tal phenomena of conditioning, conventional examples might include the effects of CS and US characteristics as well as the characteristics of their contingency. Given experimental variation in the intensity or quality of the CS or US, the ecological importance of a particular combination of CS and US or the temporal relationships between them during conditioning, can we be certain that the fun-damental effects on later expression of this learning are through action on initial memory storage rather than a memory's later retrieval? The same question can be raised about variables conventionally believed to affect the "strength" of in-strumental learning through action on initial memory storage; that effects of reinforcement schedules, for instance, can be understood only in terms of re-trieval and storage interaction has been shown nicely by Capaldi (1971).

Consider at another level the effects of latent inhibition, overshadowing or blocking, phenomena that have provided a focal center for alternative theories emphasizing either attentional or reinforcement processes. Is it necessary that for latent inhibition—when an animal's expression of its conditioning to stimulus A is weakened due to prior exposure to A in the same context—the impediment must be traceable to what is stored originally? Is it not possible that this reflects a retrieval deficit? Is there a strong a priori demand that for blocking—when prior conditioning of A to a particular US impairs that of B to the US when a com-pound of B and A is paired with the same US—memory storage of the relation-ship between B and the US is inadequate? Can we be certain that this phenome-non does not reflect instead a perturbation of the effectiveness or the process of memory retrieval?

At still another level are the effects of classes of variables like those in the categories of memory content or mnemonic preparation (Spear, 1978). The latter was discussed earlier. As to examples of effects of memory content: The rat, for instance, seems to show better short-term retention for auditory than visual events (Wallace, Steinert, Scobie, & Spear, 1980), is more likely to remember what it did in response to the duration of a particular interval than the duration itself (Church, 1980), and is more effective in remembering conditioned excitation than conditioned inhibition (Henderson, 1978; Thomas, 1979). Pigeons differ in how well they remember lines compared to colors (Farthing, Wagner, Gilmour, & Waxman, 1979; Roberts & Grant, 1978), monkeys show a different propensity for remembering order information than item information (Devine, Burke, & Rohack, 1979), and both pigeons and monkeys show better short-term retention for events presented with longer duration (e.g., Grant, this volume, 1977; Herzog, Grant, & Roberts, 1977; Nelson & Wasserman, 1978; Shimp & Moffitt), with the effect for pigeons more apparent with colors than with particular line tilts (Farthing et al., 1977).

These examples and numerous others found in several chapters in the present book indicate that we know of many variations in memory content and menemonic preparation that, when presented at the time of the episode to be remembered, determine in very clear and predictable ways the probability that learning about that episode will be expressed later. Are these cases, too, interpretable only in terms of how these variables affect how, or in what form, the memory is stored originally? I suggest that we do not know until we determine how much, if any, of the variance in these effects can be altered by manipulating experimentally the circumstances of memory retrieval. The point of history mentioned earlier and the indications that some of the same processes occur during both storage and retrieval of a memory seem to me to support this suggestion.

Tests and Implications

How do we determine whether effects such as these, any or all of them, are due to influences on memory retrieval? We do so by applying the *Principle of differential retrieval effects*. This principle states that differential effects of prior cuing or contemporary context are sufficient to infer an effect on retrieval. In other words, if for any effects such as those listed in the foregoing—those of CS or US characteristics, latent inhibition, blocking or overshadowing, memory content or mnemonic preparation—when their magnitudes are increased, decreased, or eliminated by experimental manipulations of prior cuing or contemporary context, then we can attribute those differences in size of effect to memory retrieval. And we could do so in spite of the fact that the independent variables responsible for these differences happen to have been introduced at the time of initial memory storage.

Are there theories, mechanisms, or phenomena to aid in explaining how variation at the time of memory storage could exert its effect at the time of memory retrieval? The most obvious is the general view of encoding specificity (Tulving & Thomson, 1973). Variables during initial storage might alter the animal's encoding in such a way as to make what is actually stored as the memory more or less congruent with the circumstances of memory retrieval, thus sensitizing retention to alterations in the latter. A second mechanism that might apply to retrieval explanations of "storage" phenomena is a cataloging device

(Miller & Springer, 1973), a hypothetical process contemporaneous with memory storage viewed as ultimately related to later retrieval.

A third possibility, one that need not exclude the others and that I find particularly appealing, rests on an empirical extension from a phenomenon of memory retrieval in humans. The phenomenon can be described generally as impairment in retention of some portion of a learned episode due to the successful retrieval of another portion of that episode; the effect is termed "output interference" (Roediger, 1974; Roediger & Schmidt, 1980; Tulving & Arbuckle, 1966). Output interference has good generality as well as special pertinence to interpreting effects of experimental manipulations of prior cuing or contemporary context (Spear, 1976, 1978), but there is no need at this point to elaborate it or its potential explanations.

It seems to me that such "output interference" is likely when a single context has the potential for activating either of two sets of memory attributes. This could apply potentially to other mechanisms of interference as well, such as response competition. A general example is when a common context has been the occasion for contingencies between different consequences (USs) and a common CS, as in the case of latent inhibition. An equally likely case for output interference is when within a common context, a single US has been contingent upon either or both of two CSs, as in blocking or overshadowing. That context may acquire an eliciting or enabling capacity for specific contingencies has been suggested earlier (Spear, 1973, 1976) and confirmed in an elegant set of experiments by Balaz, Capra, Hartl, and Miller (1981). The concept of output interference would apply something like this: When the context at the retention test elicits one of two CSs or CS–US contingencies with a relatively high probability—analogous to when a human is instructed to recall, say, the first half of a list of words—the alternative CS or contingency will be less likely to be activated and this "weaker" memory therefore less likely to be manifested in behavior than if only this single CS or CS–US contingency had occurred in the first place. This is not to imply a direct analogy between the empirical cases of output interference and basic conditioning but only that the form of the data base underlying the concepts of "output interference" and even "cue overload" (Watkins, 1979), together with the concepts themselves, may lead us to a conceptual framework suitable for understanding retrieval effects of "conditioning" variables (see Roediger & Tulving, 1979, for a view of output interference incorporating the attribute model of a memory).

In the case of blocking, to take a particular example, we know that the novel (nonpretrained) CS acquires some associative strength with the US on the first compound-stimulus trial but maybe little or none thereafter as the novel CS simultaneously tends to be habituated in that context (Mackintosh, 1975; Mackintosh, Dickinson, & Cotton, 1980; Sharpe, James, & Wagner, 1980). It is of course unclear what this means for the relative strength of the previously novel and previously conditioned CSs in memory storage. This can be determined only with a test of retention when, I suggest, equally stored memories might be

subject to differential influences in retrieval. For an effect such as output interference, at the time of retrieval the greater tendency for the context to activate
representations of the pretrained stimulus would lessen the probability of accessing the contingency between the blocked stimulus and the US. From this view,
one might expect such "output interference" to be most apparent when the
context of the original conditioning with the CS is most similar to that of the
retention test, although even with an "off baseline" procedure such an effect
might still occur depending on how "context" is defined by the animal.

Whether this particular explanation is appropriate is problematic. What is
perhaps more significant is that this obscure suggestion that an effect such as
blocking might be a retrieval effect—derived from a simple, functionalistic,
empirical extension—has recently received some empirical support. Balaz, Gutsin, Cacheiro, and Miller (manuscript submitted) have reported the alleviation of
blocking by a prior-cuing treatment. Furthermore, consistent with the "output
interference" explanation, Mackintosh (personal communication, 1980) has
shown that blocking of the previously novel stimulus can later be alleviated if the
previously conditioned stimulus is extinguished in a context like that in which the
blocking procedure had been applied, and Bolles and Kaufman (1980) have
reported similar release from an overshadowing effect by extinction of the previously "more salient" stimulus that had been responsible for the overshadowing. Whereas the Balaz et al. study presents direct support of the present retrieval
interpretation, the results of Mackintosh and of Bolles and Kaufman are equally
confirmative in showing that the consequences of conditioning the blocked
(Mackintosh) or overshadowed (Bolles) stimulus may indeed enter memory storage to await the proper circumstances of memory retrieval for their expression.

GENERAL SUMMARY

I have suggested that what is known and supposed about memory retrieval has
vital importance for our understanding of basic conditioning and learning. In its
strongest form, the view of memory retrieval I find most appealing suggests that
even though introduced at the time of initial training, common variables conventionally believed to determine strength of conditioning do not in fact do so in any
absolute sense. From this perspective, all effects of such variables on "learning"
depend on their particular interaction with how the learning is expressed, or in
other words, the circumstances of memory retrieval.

Toward developing this point, it was noted that the temporal relationship
between when variables are introduced and when the process of initial memory
storage occurs has not been sufficient, historically, to permit the inference that
their effect on retention is through action on memory storage. From considerations of currently available tests and the relationship between memory storage
and memory retrieval, an analytical advantage was asserted for theoretical focus

on retrieval rather than storage. On the whole, however, the conventional storage-retrieval distinction is not entirely satisfactory. The need for their joint consideration is dominant. Of particular importance are functional similarities between storage and retrieval that may be inferred from, for instance, common consequences of conditioning and testing. Such evidence implies that the processes of storage and retrieval—what the subject actually does during these two stages—may have a good deal in common. Process similarity between storage and retrieval has important implications for theories of learning and memory.

Within this framework, consideration of certain characteristics and consequences of memory retrieval, assessed empirically by applying either the "contemporary context" or "prior cuing" paradigms, generated two predictions. One prediction was that similar effects on later retention would be observed whether a particular variable is introduced at the time of initial memory storage or in conjunction with a prior cuing treatment; data in support of this possibility have been reported, but the prediction has not yet been fully tested. The second prediction was that standard "conditioning and learning" variables (e.g., specific characteristics of the CS and US, conditions of reinforcement, or more generally, variation in memory content or mnemonic preparation) and related phenomena (e.g., blocking or overshadowing) exert their principle effects on memory retrieval, not initial memory storage as is usually presumed; some empirical confirmation of this has emerged.

ACKNOWLEDGMENTS

Preparation of this chapter was supported by grants from the National Science Foundation (BNS 78–02360) and from the National Institute of Mental Health (1 RO1 MH35219-01). I am grateful for the excellent secretarial assistance of Teri Tanenhaus and Sharon Eisenberg, the technical assistance of Norman G. Richter with regard to the data reported in this chapter, and the editorial suggestions of my colleague Christian Mueller.

REFERENCES

Balaz, M. A., Capra, S., Hartl, P. & Miller, R. R. *Non-associative contextual control of acquired behavior*. Submitted for publication.

Balaz, M. A., Gutsin, P., Cacheiro, H., & Miller, R. R. *Alleviation of blocking by a reminder treatment*. Submitted for publication.

Barnes, J. M., & Underwood, B. J. Fate "Fate" of first-list associations in transfer theory. *Journal of Experimental Psychology*, 1959, *58*, 97–105.

Bartlett, S. C. *Remembering: A study in experimental and social psychology*. Cambridge: Cambridge University Press, 1932.

Bergson, H. [*Matter and memory*.] (trans. by N. M. Paul & W. S. Palmer.) New York: MacMillan, 1911.

Bjork, R. A., & Geiselman, R. E. Constituent processes in the differentiation of items in memory. *Journal of Experimental Psychology: Human Learning and Memory*, 1978, *4*, 347–361.

Bolles, R. C., & Kaufman, M. A. *A reconstructive memory model of overshadowing*. Paper presented at meetings of the Psychonomic Society, St. Louis, 1980.

Capaldi, E. J. Memory and learning: A sequential viewpoint. In W. K. Honig & P. H. R. James (Eds.), *Animal memory*. New York: Academic Press, 1971.

Caza, P. A., Steinert, P. A., & Spear, N. E. Comparison of circadian susceptibility to LiCl induced taste aversion learning between preweanling and adult rats. *Physiology and Behavior*, 1980, *25*, 389–396.

Cermak, L. S., & Craik, F. I. M. (Eds.). *Levels of processing in human memory*. Hillsdale, N.J.: Lawrence Erlbaum Associates, 1979.

Church, R. M. Short-term memory for time intervals. *Learning and Motivation*, 1980, *11*, 208–219.

Concannon, J. T., Smith, G. J., Spear, N. E., & Scobie, J. A. Drug cues, drug states and infantile amnesia. In F. C. Colapert & J. A. Rosencranz (Eds.), *First International Symposium on Drugs as Discriminative Stimuli*. Amsterdam, Elsevier/North Holland Medical Press, 1979.

Cooper, A. J. R., & Monk, A. Learning for recall and learning for recognition. In J. Brown (Ed.), *Recall and recognition*. New York: Wiley and Sons, 1976.

Cotton, J. W., & Jensen, G. D. Successive acquisitions and extinctions in a T-maze. *Journal of Experimental Psychology*, 1963, *65*, 546–551.

DeVietti, T. L., & Holliday, J. H. Retrograde amnesia produced by electroconvulsive shock after reactivation of a consolidated memory trace: A replication. *Psychonomics Science*, 1972, *29*, 137–138.

Devine, J. V., Burke, M. W., & Rohack, J. J. Stimulus similarity and order as factors in visual short-term memory in nonhuman primates. *Journal of Experimental Psychology: Animal Behavior Processes*, 1979, *5*, 335–354.

Engle, R. W., & Mobley, L. A. The modality effect: What happens in long-term memory? *Journal of Verbal Learning and Verbal Behavior*, 1976, *15*, 519–527.

Farthing, G. W., Wagner, J. M., Gilmour, S., & Waxman, H. M. Short-term memory and information processing in pigeons. *Learning and Motivation*, 1977, *8*, 520 532.

Fisher, R. P., & Craik, F. I. M. Interaction between encoding and retrieval operations in cued recall. *Journal of Experimental Psychology: Human Learning and Memory*, 1977, *3*, 701–711.

Gleitman, H. Forgetting of long-term memories in animals. In W. K. Honig & P. H. R. James (Eds.), *Animal memory*. New York: Academic Press, 1971.

Gordon, W. C. Susceptibility of a reactivated memory to the effects of strychnine: A time-dependent phenomenon. *Physiology and Behavior*, 1977, *3*, 95–99.

Gordon, W. C., Frankl, S. E., & Hamberg, J. M. Reactivation-induced proactive interference in rats. *American Journal of Psychology*, 1979, *92*, 693–702.

Gordon, W. C., & Feldman, D. T. The alleviation of short-term retention decrements with reactivation. *Learning and Motivation*, 1979, *10*, 198–210.

Gordon, W. C., & Spear, N. E. The effect of reactivation of a previously acquired memory on the interaction between memories in the rat. *Journal of Experimental Psychology*, 1973, *99*, 349–355. (a)

Gordon, W. C., & Spear, N. E. The effects of strychnine on recently acquired and reactivated passive avoidance memories. *Physiology and Behavior*, 1973, *10*, 1071–1075. (b)

Guthrie, E. R. *The psychology of learning*. New York: Harper, 1935.

Hasher, L., & Zacks, R. T. Automatic and effortful processes in memory. *Journal of Experimental Psychology*, 1979, *108*, 356–388.

Henderson, R. W. Forgetting of conditioned fear inhibition. *Learning and Motivation*, 1978, *9*, 16–30.

Herzog, H. L., Grant, D. S., & Roberts, W. A. Effects of sample duration and spaced repetition upon delay matching-to-sample in monkeys (*Macaca arctoides* & *Saimiri sciureus*). *Animal Learning & Behavior*, 1977, *5*, 347–354.

Hintzman, D. L. *The psychology of learning and memory*. San Francisco: W. H. Freeman & Company, 1978.

Infurna, R. N. *The influence of daily biological rhythmicity on the homing-behavior, psychophar-macological responsiveness, learning and retention of suckling rats.* Unpublished doctoral dissertation, State University of New York at Binghamton, 1980.

Infurna, R. N., Steinert, P. A., Freda, J. S., & Spear, N. E. Sucrose preference and LiCl illness-induced averaion as a function of drug dose and phase of the illumination cycle. *Physiology and Behavior,* 1979, *22,* 955–961.

Jacoby, L. L., & Craik, F. I. M. Effects of elaboration of processing at encoding and retrieval: Traced distinctiveness in recovery of initial context. In L. S. Cermak & F. I. M. Craik (Eds.), *Levels of processing in human memory.* Hillsdale, N.J.: Lawrence Erlbaum Associates, 1979.

Jensen, G. D. Partial reinforcement effects (PREs) and inverse PREs determined by position of a non-reward block of responses. *Journal of Experimental Psychology,* 1961, *62,* 461–467.

Jensen, G. D., & Cotton, J. W. Successive acquisitions and extinctions as related to percentage reinforcement. *Journal of Experimental Psychology,* 1960, *60,* 41–49.

Jones, P. D., & Holding, D. H. Extremely long-term persistence of the McCollough Effect. *Journal of Experimental Psychology: Human Perception and Performance,* 1975, *1,* 323–327.

Jost, A. Die Assoziationsfestigkeit in ihrer Abhangigkeit der Verteilung der Wiederholungen. *Zeitschrift Psychology,* 1897, *14,* 436–472.

Kimble, G. A., Mann, L. A., & Dufort, R. H. Classical and instrumental eyelid conditioning. *Journal of Experimental Psychology,* 1955, *49,* 407–417.

Klein, S. B., & Spear, N. E. Reactivation of avoidance-learning memory in the rat after intermediate retention intervals. *Journal of Comparative and Physiological Psychology,* 1970, *72,* 498–504.

Lewis, D. J. Sources of experimental amnesia. *Psychological Review,* 1969, *76,* 461–472.

Lewis, D. J. A cognitive approach to experimental amnesia. *American Journal of Psychology,* 1976, *89,* 51–80.

Lewis, D. J., Bregman, N. J., & Mahan, J. J. Cue-dependent amnesia in rats. *Journal of Comparative and Physiological Psychology,* 1972, *81,* 243–247.

Loftus, E. F. The malleability of human memory. *American Scientist,* 1979, *67,* 312–320.

Macht, M. L., & O'Brien, E. G. Familiarity-based responding in item recognition: Evidence for the role of spreading activation. *Journal of Experimental Psychology: Human Learning and Memory,* 1980, *6,* 301–318.

Macht, M. L., & Spear, N. E. Priming effects in episodic memory. *Journal of Experimental Psychology: Human Learning and Memory,* 1977, *3,* 333–341.

Mackintosh, N. J. A theory of attention: Variations in the associability of stimuli with reinforcement. *Psychological Review,* 1975, *82,* 276–298.

Mackintosh, N. J. Personal communication, 1980.

Mackintosh, N. J., Dickinson, A., & Cotton, M. M. Surprise and blocking: Effects of the number of compound trials. *Animal Learning & Behavior,* 1980, *8,* 387–391.

McGaugh, J. L. Time-dependent processes in memory storage. *Science,* 1966, *153,* 1351–1358.

McGaugh, J. L., & Dawson, R. G. Modification of memory storage processes. In W. K. Honig & P. H. R. James (Eds.), *Animal memory.* New York: Academic Press, 1971.

Miller, R. R. The contribution of retrievability to "acquisition" curves. *Journal of Experimental Psychology: Animal Behavior Processes,* 1981, in press.

Miller, R. R., & Marlin, N. A. Amnesia following electroconvulsive shock. In J. F. Kihlstrom & F. J. Evans (Eds.), *Functional disorders of memory.* Hillsdale, N.J.: Lawrence Erlbaum Associates, 1979.

Miller, R. R., & Springer, A. D. Amnesia, consolidation and retrieval. *Psychological Review,* 1973, *80,* 69–79.

Miller, R. R., & Springer, A. D. Implications of recovery from experimental amnesia. *Psychological Review,* 1974, *81,* 470–473.

Misanin, J. R., Miller, R. R., & Lewis, D. J. Retrograde amnesia produced by electroconvulsive shock after reactivation of a consolidated memory trace. *Science,* 1968, *160,* 554–555.

Nelson, K. R., & Wasserman, E. A. Temporal factors influencing the pigeon's successive matching-to-sample performance: Sample duration, intertrial interval, and retention interval. *Journal of the Experimental Analysis of Behavior,* 1978, *30,* 153–162.

Overton, D. A. State-dependent learning produced by depressant and atropine-like drugs. *Psychopharmacologia,* 1966, *10,* 6–31.

Overton, D. A. State-dependent learning produced by alcohol and its relevance to alcoholism, in B. Kissin & H. Begleiter (Eds.), *The biology of alcoholism, Vol. II, physiology and behavior.* New York: Plenum Press, 1972.

Overton, D. A. Experimental methods for the study of state-dependent learning. *Federation Proceedings,* 1974, *33,* 1800–1813.

Overton, D. A. Major theories of state-dependent learning. In B. T. Ho, D. W. Richards, & D. L. Chute (Eds.), *Drug discrimination and state-dependent learning.* New York: Academic Press, 1978.

Overton, D. A. Drug discrimination training with progressively lower doses. *Science,* 1979, *205,* 720–721.

Postman, L. Tests of the generality of the principle of encoding specificity. *Memory & Cognition,* 1975, *3,* 663–672.

Ribot, T. A. *Diseases of memory: An essay in positive psychology.* New York: Appleton, 1896.

Rilling, M., Kendrick, D. F., & Stonebraker, T. B. Stimulus control of forgetting: A behavioral analysis. In M. L. Commons, A. R. Wagner, & R. J. Herrnstein (Eds.), *Quantitative studies in operant behavior: Acquisition.* Cambridge, Mass.: Ballinger, in press.

Roberts, W. A. Spatial memory in the rat on a hierarchical maze. *Learning and Motivation,* 1979, *10,* 117–140.

Roberts, W. A., & Grant, D. S. Studies of short-term memory in the pigeon using the delayed matching-to-sample procedure. In D. L. Medin, W. A. Roberts, & R. T. Davis (Eds.), *Processes of animal memory.* Hillsdale, N.J.: Lawrence Erlbaum Associates, 1976.

Roediger, H. L., III. Inhibiting effects of recall. *Memory & Cognition,* 1974, *2,* 261–269.

Roediger, H. L., III, & Schmidt, S. R. Output interference in the recall of categorized and paired associate lists. *Journal of Experimental Psychology: Human Learning and Memory,* 1980, *6,* 91–105.

Roediger, H. L., III, & Thorpe, L. A. The role of recall time in producing hypermnesia. *Memory & Cognition,* 1978, *6,* 296–305.

Roediger, H. L., III, & Tulving, E. Exclusion of learned material from recall as a postretrieval operation. *Journal of Verbal Learning and Verbal Behavior,* 1979, *18,* 601–616.

Rovee-Collier, C. K., Sullivan, M. W., Enrite, M., Lucas, D., & Fagin, J. W. Reactivation of infant memory. *Science,* 1980, *208,* 1159–1161.

Schacter, D. L., Eich, J. E., & Tulving, E. Richard Semon's theory of memory. *Journal of Verbal Learning and Verbal Behavior,* 1978, *17,* 721–743.

Semon, R. The mneme. London: George Allen & Unwin, 1921.

Sharpe, P. E., James, J. H., & Wagner, A. R. Habituation of a "blocked" stimulus during Pavlovian conditioning. *Bulletin of the Psychonomic Society,* 1980, *15,* 139–142.

Shiffrin, R. M., & Schneider, W. Controlled and automatic human information processing: II. Perceptual learning, automatic attending, and a general theory. *Psychological Review,* 1977, *84,* 127–190.

Shimp, C. P., & Moffit, M. Short-term memory in the pigeon: Delayed-pair-comparison procedures and some results. *Journal of the Experimental Analysis of Behavior,* 1977, *28,* 13–25.

Smith, G. J., & Spear, N. E. Role of proactive interference in infantile forgetting. *Animal Learning & Behavior,* in press.

Spear, N. E. Forgetting as retrieval failure. In W. K. Honig & P. H. R. James (Eds.), *Animal memory.* New York: Academic Press, 1971.

Spear, N. E. Retrieval of memory in animals. *Psychological Review,* 1973, *80,* 163–175.

Spear, N. E. Retrieval of memories. In W. K. Estes (Ed.), *Handbook of learning and cognitive processes, Vol. IV, attention and memory.* Hillsdale, N.J.: Lawrence Erlbaum Associates, 1976.

Spear, N. E. *Processing of memories: Forgetting and retention*. Hillsdale, N.J.: Lawrence Erlbaum Associates, 1978.

Spear, N. E. Memory storage factors in infantile amnesia. In G. Bower (Ed.), *The psychology of learning and motivation*. (Vol. 13). New York: Academic Press, 1979.

Spear, N. E., Hamberg, J. M., & Bryan, R. G. Effect of retention interval on recently acquired or recently reactivated memories. *Learning and Motivation*, 1980, in press.

Spear, N. E., Klein, S. B., & Riley, E. P. The Kamin Effect as "state dependent learning": Memory retrieval in the rat. *Journal of Comparative and Physiological Psychology*, 1971, *74*, 416–425.

Spear, N. E., & Mueller, C. On the meaning of consolidation during memory storage and memory retrieval. In H. Weingarter & E. S. Parker (Eds.), *Memory Consolidation: Towards a Psychobiology of Cognition*. Hillsdale, New Jersey: Lawrence Erlbaum Associates, 1982, in preparation.

Spear, N. E., & Parsons, P. Alleviation of forgetting by reactivation treatment: A preliminary analysis of the ontogeny of memory processing. In D. Medin, W. Roberts, & R. Davis (Eds.), *Processes in animal memory*. Hillsdale, N.J.: Lawrence Erlbaum Associates, 1976.

Spear, N. E., Smith, G. J., Bryan, R., Gordon, W., Timmons, R., Chiszar, D. Contextual influences on the interaction between conflicting memories in the rat. *Animal Learning & Behavior*, 1980, *8*, 273–281.

Spear, N. E., Smith, G. J., Sherr, A., & Bryan, R. G. Forgetting of a drug-conditional discrimination. *Physiology and Behavior*, 1979, *22*, 851–854.

Spence, K. W. *Behavior theory and conditioning*. New Haven: Yale University Press, 1956.

Thomas, D. A. Retention of conditioned inhibition in a bar-press suppression paradigm. *Learning and motivation*, 1979, *10*, 161–177.

Tulving, E. Episodic and somatic memory. In E. Tulving & W. Donaldson (Eds.), *Organization of memory*. New York: Academic Press, 1972.

Tulving, E., & Arbuckle, T. Y. Input and output interference in short-term associative memory. *Journal of Experimental Psychology*, 1966, *72*, 145–150.

Tulving, E., & Thomson, D. M. Encoding specificity in retrieval processes in episodic memory. *Psychological Review*, 1973, *80*, 352–357.

Tulving, E., & Watkins, M. J. Structure of memory traces. *Psychological Review*, 1975, *82*, 261–275.

Tyler, S. W., Hertel, P. T., McCallum, M. C., & Ellis, H. C. Cognitive effort in memory. *Journal of Experimental Psychology: Human Learning and Memory*, 1979, *5*, 607–617.

Underwood, B. J. Are we overloading memory? In A. W. Nelson & E. Martin (Eds.), *Coding Processes in Human Memory*. Washington, D.C.: Winston, 1972.

Wallace, J., Steinert, P. A., Scobie, S. R., & Spear, N. E. Stimulus modality and short-term memory in the rat. *Animal Learning and Behavior*, 1980, *8*, 10–16.

Watkins, M. J. Engrams as cue-grams and forgetting as cue overload: A cuing approach to the structure of memory. In C. R. Puff (Ed.), *Memory organization and structure*. New York: Academic Press, 1979.

Whitten, W. B., II, & Bjork, R. A. Learning from tests: Effects of spacing. *Journal of Verbal Learning and Verbal Behavior*, 1977, *16*, 465–478.

Whitten, W. B., II, & Leonard, J. M. Learning from tests: Facilitation of delayed recall by initial recognition alternatives. *Journal of Experimental Psychology: Human Learning and Memory*, 1980, *6*, 127–134.

Winograd, E., & Rivers-Bulkeley, N. T. Effects of changing context on remembering facts. *Journal of Experimental Psychology: Human Learning and Memory*, 1977, *3*, 397–405.

Zangwill, O. L. Remembering revisited. *Quarterly Journal of Experimental Psychology*, 1972, *24*, 123–138.

Zentall, T. R. Effects of context change on forgetting in rats. *Journal of Experimental Psychology*, 1970, *86*, 440–448.

Author Index

Italics denote pages with bibliographic information.

Subject Index

387